Programming the Absolute

Programming the Absolute

NINETEENTH-CENTURY GERMAN MUSIC

AND THE HERMENEUTICS OF THE MOMENT

Berthold Hoeckner

PRINCETON UNIVERSITY PRESS

PRINCETON AND OXFORD

PUBLISHED BY PRINCETON UNIVERSITY PRESS, 41 WILLIAM STREET,
PRINCETON, NEW JERSEY 08540
IN THE UNITED KINGDOM: PRINCETON UNIVERSITY PRESS,
3 MARKET PLACE, WOODSTOCK, OXFORDSHIRE 0X20 ISY

LIBRARY OF CONGRESS CATALOGING-IN-PUBLICATION DATA

HOECKNER, BERTHOLD.

PROGRAMMING THE ABSOLUTE:

NINETEENTH-CENTURY GERMAN MUSIC AND THE

HERMENEUTICS OF THE MOMENT / BERTHOLD HOECKNER.

P   CM.

INCLUDES BIBLIOGRAPHICAL REFERENCES AND INDEX.

ISBN: 0-691-00149-9 (ALK. PAPER)

ABSOLUTE MUSIC—19TH CENTURY. 2. MUSIC—GERMANY—

19TH CENTURY—PHILOSOPHY AND AESTHETICS. I. TITLE

ML3854 .H64 2002

780'.943'09034—DC21

2001058002

BRITISH LIBRARY CATALOGING-IN-PUBLICATION DATA IS AVAILABLE

THE BOOK HAS BEEN COMPOSED IN SABON WITH COCHIN DISPLAY

PRINTED ON ACID-FREE PAPER. ∞

WWW.PUPRESS.PRINCETON.EDU

PRINTED IN THE UNITED STATES OF AMERICA

1 3 5 7 9 10 8 6 4 2

To Eva, Julia, and Markus
for their trust, inspiration, and love

Contents

List of Figures and Tables   i x

List of Examples   x i

Preface   x v

Introduction
Musical Moments and the
Moment of German Music   1

Chapter One
Beethoven's Star   12

Chapter Two
Schumann's Distance   51

Chapter Three
Elsa's Scream   115

Chapter Four
Liszt's Prayer   155

Chapter Five
Schoenberg's Gaze   189

Chapter Six
Echo's Eyes   224

Notes   266

Bibliography   317

Index   339

Figures and Tables

Figures

Figure 1   Leonore's "Tödt erst sein Weib" in Beethoven's   44
            autograph of *Leonore*

Figure 2   Franz Liszt, *Ce qu'on entend sur la montagne,*
            inserted "Andante Religioso"
            a. D-WRgs A1a, p. 17   182
            b. D-WRgs A1a, p. 17a   183
            c. D-WRgs A1a, p. 17b   184

Figure 3   Schoenberg's Gazes and the Enucleated Eye
            a. *Self-Portrait,* 1910   192
            b. *Blue Self-Portrait,* 1910   192
            c. *Green Self-Portrait,* 1910   192
            d. *Self-Portrait,* 1910   192
            e. *Self-Portrait,* 1910   193
            f. *Red Gaze (Face),* 1910   193
            g. *Gaze,* 1910   193
            h. *Red Gaze (Eyes),* 1910   193

Figure 4   a. Arnold Schoenberg, *Hands*   194
            b. Arnold Schoenberg, *Vision*   195
            c. Arnold Schoenberg, *Tears*   195

Figure 5   Fly leaf of the Arietta theme in Adorno's hand   230
            with annotations for Thomas Mann

Tables

Table 1   Leonore's B and B♭   45

Table 2   Alternative Sonata Forms in Liszt's *Ce qu'on*   171
            entend sur la montagne

Table 3   Synopsis of Correspondences in the Different   180
            Conceptions of the Mountain Symphony

Examples

Example 1.1 *Fidelio* No. 9 Recitative and Aria mm. 1–55   3 0

Example 1.2 *Fidelio* No. 14 Quartet mm. 77–86:   3 7
Leonore's scream

Example 1.3 *Fidelio* No. 14 Quartet mm. 39–49:   3 9
Pizzaro's "rhythm of rage"

Example 1.4 *Fidelio* No. 14 Quartet mm. 84–85:   4 0
Leonore's "rhythm of rescue" 1805 and 1814

Example 1.5 *Fidelio* No. 14 Quartet mm. 127–29:   4 0
Trumpet call 1805 and 1814

Example 1.6 Leonore's scream in *Leonore*   4 2

Example 2.1 a. *Papillons,* op. 2, no. 1 mm. 1–4   6 0
b. no. 12, "Finale" mm. 47–91   6 1

Example 2.2 Franz Schubert, Symphony in C Major,   6 9
D. 944, "Andante con moto" mm. 144–62

Example 2.3 Carl Gottlieb Reissiger, "Heimweh,"   7 3
op. 50, no. 1

Example 2.4 Robert Schumann, "An Anna" vs.   7 5
Piano Sonata in F# Minor, op. 11, "Aria"

Example 2.5 Robert Schumann, *Davidsbündlertänze*, op. 6,   8 3
Book 2, no. 8, "Wie aus der Ferne" mm. 1–58

Example 2.6 a. Clara Wieck, *Valse Romantiques,* op. 4   8 9
b. Robert Schumann, *Carnaval,* op. 9
("Valse allemande")
c. Robert Schumann, *Davidsbündlertänze*, op. 6
("Etwas hahnbüchen")
d. Schumann, *Davidsbündlertänze*
("Mit gutem Humor")
e. Schumann, *Davidsbündlertänze*
("Wie aus der Ferne")

Example 2.7   Clara Wieck, *Valse Romantiques,* op. 4   9 0
               mm. 1–32

Example 2.8   Robert Schumann, *Fantasie,* op. 17,   9 5
               first movement mm. 295–309

Example 2.9   Schumann, *Fantasie,* op. 17, second theme vs. 1 0 0
               Beethoven, *An die Ferne Geliebte,* op. 98

Example 2.10   a.–c. Clara Wieck, *Romance variée,* op. 3   1 0 5
               d.–e. Robert Schumann, *Fantasie,* op. 17
               ("Im Legendenton")

Example 2.11   Robert Schumann, *Fantasie,* op. 17,   1 0 7
               first movement mm. 154–60

Example 2.12   The voice exchange between "S"/E♭ and C   1 0 9

Example 2.13   a. Clara Wieck, *Soirées musicales,* op. 6   1 1 0
               ("Notturno")
               b.–d. Robert Schumann, *Novelletten,*
               op. 21, no. 8

Example 3.1   First harmonic progression from *Lohengrin*   1 1 9
               as it appears in Wagner's article

Example 3.2   Second harmonic progression from *Lohengrin* 1 1 9
               as it appears in Wagner's article

Example 3.3   *Lohengrin,* act 1, scene 2, Elsa enters   1 2 1

Example 3.4   *Lohengrin,* act 1, scene 2, Elsa's dream   1 2 7
               narration (beginning of second half)

Example 3.5   *Lohengrin,* act 1, scene 2, Elsa's dream   1 2 9
               narration (end)

Example 3.6   *Lohengrin,* act 1, scene 2, Elsa prays   1 3 4

Example 3.7   *Lohengrin,* act 1, scene 3, Elsa surrenders 1 4 1

Example 3.8   *Lohengrin,* act 1, scene 3, the forbidden   1 4 2
               question

Example 3.9   *Lohengrin,* act 3, scene 2, Elsa recalls her 1 4 7
               first encounter with Lohengrin

Example 3.10   *Lohengrin,* act 3, scene 3, Elsa's resignation 1 5 2
               and Lohengrin's arrival

Examples

Example 4.1   *Ce qu'on entend sur la montagne:*   157
              "Andante religioso" (first section)

Example 4.2   *Ce qu'on entend sur la montagne:*   164
              Themes of Nature and Humanity

Example 4.3   *Ce qu'on entend sur la montagne:*   174
              Climactic Chorale

Example 5.1   Georg Benda, *Ariadne auf Naxos,*   201
              Ariadne's memory with genre quotation

Example 5.2   Musico–textural counterpoint in *Erwartung*
              a. "Am Wegrand" mm. 3–4   207
              b. "Am Wegrand" mm. 22–24   207
              c. *Erwartung* mm. 411–12   207

Example 5.3   *Die Jakobsleiter,* conclusion of libretto   212

Example 5.4   *Die Jakobsleiter* mm. 602–607 with   221
              opening motif from *Tristan*

Example 6.1   Beethoven op. 111, Arietta Variations   232
              mm. 100–130

Example 6.2   a. Mahler's allusion to *Kindertotenlieder*   253
              in the "Adagissimo" from the last movement
              of the Ninth Symphony
              b. The "Adagissimo" concluding   254
              Mahler's Ninth

Example 6.3   *Kindertotenlieder* no. 2 mm. 10–14   257
              ("O Augen")

Example 6.4   Background Graph of *Kindertotenlieder*   258
              no. 2 by Kofi Agawu

Example 6.5   *Kindertotenlieder* no. 2 mm. 38–47   259

Preface

Some layers of this book go back to the late 1980s, when I left the Conservatory and University of Cologne to study musicology at King's College London and later at Cornell University. Although I had studied music in Germany, my academic training as a musicologist took place almost exclusively in English-speaking academia. This twofold background became foundational for my work, which not only sought to traverse the gap between the language of music and the language about music, but also had to consider German music from a foreign perspective.

My education took place at the time when Joseph Kerman's *Musicology* was on everyone's mind and Carl Dahlhaus's *Foundations of Music History* and *Nineteeth-Century Music* had appeared in translation. It was the time of paradigmatic changes in Anglo-American musicology, driven to a good measure by provocative studies in the journal *Nineteenth-Century Music*. The lively reception of Dahlhaus's history of genres, ideas, and institutions in the early 1990s coincided with the attempt of a younger generation of musicologists to free themselves from the "old musicology," that is, from the history centered around great composers and masterworks practiced by the generation of their teachers, many of whom were (or were influenced by) German musicologists who had fled the Nazis during the Third Reich and who had been instrumental in establishing American musicology as a university discipline in the 1930s and 1940s. Paradoxically, as the 1990s progressed, the *Musikwissenschaft* of the Dahlhaus school was often seen (and sometimes lumped) together with the old musicology, particularly in their characterization as Eurocentric.

This book is in part a response to that development. It was born out of the impulse to relativize the aesthetic aspirations of German music and the scientific ambitions of German musicology, which emerged as two sides of the same cultural project in the nineteenth century and held sway well into the twentieth. But I will also take this impulse as an opportunity to reevaluate these aspirations and ambitions and to reassess their historical merits and liabilities, now that the nineteenth century has receded from its position as the foremost forum of change in the field. Indeed, in the context of a growing pluralism that characterizes musicology and the humanities today, it seems prudent not to throw out the baby with the bathwater. This will be evident from the central role Theodor W. Adorno plays in my book, not only because his philosophy of music is a philosophy of German music, but also because Adorno's critical reception (which waxed in England and America as it waned in Germany) can serve as a sign of the successful changes in a discipline willing to combine musical criticism with philosophical critique and thus willing to distinguish between what is still valid, and what is not. That Adorno's own focus on German music is thereby unmasked as a fixation may be a measure of such success. Adorno should not have wanted it any other way.

Needless to say, this book itself, in dealing with German music and with Adorno, is inevitably caught up in the dialectic of critique and affirmation. When I presented an impassioned account of my Beethoven chapter during a colloquium at the University of California at Berkeley, a couple of brilliant graduate students pressed me on the relevance of my subject and its implications for the kind of musicology that they would want to practice. Taking the opportunity to formulate an answer in print, I would say to them (and my readers) that today, more than ever before, we are allowed to acknowledge how the impetus of our work grows out of, and is necessarily slanted and limited by, particular conjunctions of personal history and collective history; and that my agenda, therefore, need not be theirs, but is theirs to understand.

Many individuals have made contributions—large or small, but all valuable—to this book. Since it seems impossible to rank my heartfelt appreciation by singling anyone out, I hope they will quickly find themselves in this alphabetical list: Kofi Agawu, Joseph Auner, Daniel Barolsky, Karol Berger, Reinhold Brinkmann, Scott Burnham, Thomas Christensen, Daniel Chua, David Clampitt, Richard Cohn, Martha Feldman, John Daverio, James Deaville, Arthur Groos, Monika Hennemann, James Hepokoski, Paula Higgins, Stephen Hinton, Leander Hotaki, Brian Hyer, Christian Kaden, Elizabeth Keathley, Friedhelm Krummacher, Henri Lonitz (Adorno Archiv Frankfurt), Helga Lühning (Beethoven Haus Bonn), Yonathan Malin, Ryan Minor, Rena Mueller, Therese Muxeneder (Arnold Schönberg Center Vienna), Gerd Nauhaus (Robert Schumann Haus Zwickau), Severine Neff, Roger Parker, Tobias Plebuch, Don Randel, Bruce Redford, Anne Robertson, Linda Correll Roesner, Charles Rosen, Robert Snarrenberg, Sem Sutter, Matthias Tilke, Gary Tomlinson, James Webster, Philip Weller, Matthias Wendt (Schumann Forschungsstelle Düsseldorf), and the staff of the Music Library in the Joseph Regenstein Library at the University of Chicago.

I am also thankful for the important inspiration by the students who attended my research seminars on Beethoven, musical hermeneutics, absolute music, and the second Viennese School. They provided an invaluable forum for testing ideas and arriving at new ones. In addition, I have greatly benefitted from feedback at lectures and colloquia given at various instituions in North America and Europe. I would also like to express my gratitude to the Gesellschaft der Musikfreunde Wien, the Handschriftenabteilung der Universitätsbibliothek Bonn, the Eda Kuhn Loeb Music Library at Harvard University, the Deutsche Staatsbibliothek, the Thomas Mann Archiv Zürich, the Newberry Library in Chicago, and the Goethe and Schiller Archiv Weimar. Chapter 2, slightly revised, has been reprinted with permission of the University of Chicago Press and chapter 3, also slightly revised, has been reprinted with the permission of Cambridge University Press.

Work on this book was immensely helped by two free quarters at the Humanities Institute (now Franke Institute for the Humanities) at the University of Chicago in 1996 and 1997, as well as two Junior Faculty Summer Fellowships by the Humanities Division at the University of Chicago in 1997 and 1998. I was fortunate to see the book through the final stages of the publication process during a sabbatical leave as a Research Fellow of the Alexander von Humbolt Foundation at the University of Cologne in 2001–02. This book would not have been possible without the vision and encouragement of the editors, past and present, of Princeton University Press, Malcolm Litchfield and Frederick Appel, the logistical management of Sara Lerner, the advice on layout and appearance by Don Giller, as well as the meticulous attention to detail by the copyeditor, Laura Nash.

Immeasurable support and inspiration, finally, have come from friends and family, above all from my wife, Eva, and my children, Julia and Markus. Their joy and optimism proved, again and again, to be a healthy counterweight to the sometimes severe subject and melancholic mood of this book.

There is one name I have not mentioned. When I moved to Hyde Park in the fall of 1994 to begin teaching at the University of Chicago the phone rang minutes after the connection had been hooked up. On the other end of the line was Hans Lenneberg, who had just retired from his long-time position at the University not only as music bibliographer, but also from a teaching appointment in the music department. Before he and his family fled from the Nazi Regime in the 1930s, Hans had grown up fifty miles east of Cologne in the same small town where I grew up, had gone to the same *Gymnasium,* and had known some of the same teachers. With a sense of urgency, Hans, who was terminally ill with cancer, asked me over to his house and so we sat down, talking about his past and about the coincidence of life bringing us together in the present. During the 1970s, I had passed the house in which he had lived as a child every day on my way to school. But I did not know then, for we had been taught the history of the Third Reich as a history that happened somewhere else, not as a history that had happened here, where teachers had participated in rounding up the Lennebergs and vandalizing their home during the *Reichskristallnacht*.

During our conversation, I shared not only Hans' just anger about such hypocrisy, but also experienced the warmth of his friendship, which had made him a mentor of many graduates and colleagues in the Chicago Music Department. I know that Hans, who passed away just a few weeks later, would have been such a mentor for me, not only as someone who had arrived in the same place, but also as someone sharing the same roots. But I am grateful that I was granted at least a glimpse of his friendship, even if it was to be only once, like the amicable exchange of glances in a revolving door.

However brief, this moment of reconciliation between the émigré by coercion and the immigrant of choice has given my work a sense of continuity and belonging. I fancy, moreover, that the deeper meaning of that moment might emerge from what I call in this book a hermeneutics of the moment, which is nothing less than a hermeneutics of hope.

Programming the Absolute

MUSICAL MOMENTS AND THE MOMENT
OF GERMAN MUSIC

Language of Music. Music speaks a universal language, through which
the spirit is freely, indefinitely animated; this makes the spirit feel so well,
so familiar, so fatherlandish; in these short moments it is at [its Indian]
home. All the love and goodness, future and past stir in it, hope and
longing. [Attempt to speak *definitely* through music.] Our language was
originally more musical; it has only gradually become prosaic [so *toneless*]. It has become now more a reverberation [*Schall*], if one wants to
debase this beautiful word: It needs to become song again. Consonants
transform tone into *Schall*.[1]

I n an early issue of his *Neue Zeitschrift für Musik*, Robert Schumann
had printed the above fragment, which derived from Novalis's *Das
allgemeine Brouillon* (1798–99), a poetic encyclopedia of more than a
thousand entries of notes, responses to readings, and sketches. It was
perhaps the most ambitious, if unfinished, project of early German
Romanticism associated with the brothers August Wilhelm and Friedrich
Schlegel, Ludwig Tieck, and Friedrich von Hardenberg, alias Novalis.
But the grand effort to poeticize the world was thwarted not only by
Novalis's early death in 1801, but also—like Friedrich Schlegel's notion
of a *progressive Universalpoesie*—by its utopian universality. If they had
sought to capture the universe in the form of the literary fragment, a
masterful miniature of pithy prose, Novalis's unedited notes are elliptical and cryptic by comparison. Yet like the shards and splinters in
Hölderlin's drafts, they ofen reveal more poignantly the greater philosophical ideas and poetic vision behind them. In this entry on "Music,"
Novalis contemplates music's relationship both to language and to the
moment. While music is a universal language that animates the spirit
indefinitely, there is the "attempt to speak *definitely* through music."
And while music grants us short moments in which we feel at home,
these moments may encompass "*all* the love and goodness": our past
and future, as well as our maternal "Indian home" and our paternal

Vaterland. Even if Novalis did not mean moments *in* music, but moments *of* music, both those musical moments matter: not only were they made (and taken) to *speak* for the whole, but they were also made (and taken) to speak for *the whole.*

Novalis's fragment formulates the link between the two principal concerns of this book as encapsulated in its title. "Programming the Absolute" and "Hermeneutics of the Moment" refer to the interpretive practice of seizing on moments in music that seem ineffable, and nevertheless of putting their meaning in words.[2] This meaning may range from a fleeting emotion to a broad historical category; from a private and personal memory to what I will call "the moment of German music." The latter requires some explanation. Framed by Viennese Classicism and the Second Viennese School, the moment of German music, as a primarily cultural category, is an extension of what David Blackbourn has called the "long nineteenth century" in German political history: "the period between the 'double revolutions' of the late eighteenth century (the French Revolution of 1789, the Industrial Revolution in Britain) and the First World War"; or between the fall of the Holy Roman Empire and the fall of the *Kaiserreich.*[3] The moment of German music thus does not reach back as far as Schütz and Bach (though it includes them through their romantic reception), but expands Blackbourn's period until the fall of the Third Reich (thereby treating the Weimar Republic as an overlapping segment belonging to the twentieth century). This is to emphazise the continuity of an important strand of post-Enlightenment bourgeois culture, framed by Beethoven's coming of age and Schoenberg's death, or by Goethe's *Faust* and Thomas Mann's *Doctor Faustus.* It begins with the conception of the lyric moment as the beginning of modern, romantic, subjectivity that David Wellbery has located in the poetry of the young Goethe; and it ends that subjectivity in the condensed lyricism of Webern's last works.[4]

The present book articulates this historical frame in the first and last chapters, which offer two different hearings of Beethoven from the perspective of 1945. The four middle chapters are more loosely connected to this framework, exploring different analytical and historical aspects of the hermeneutics of the moment. In chapter 2, it is Schumann's struggle to define the historical significance of "new music" in his public appreciation of Schubert and to communicate private thoughts through the programmatic use of Beethoven's music. In chapter 3, it is Wagner's claim to establish himself as Beethoven's heir by trying to reenact, in *Lohengrin,* the ultimate moment of programming the absolute—the word *Freude* in the last movement of the Ninth—as the momentuous birth of music drama. In chapter 4, it is Liszt's project of the symphonic poem, combining the Beethovenian symphonic tradition with the heritage of

European literature, in order to reconcile the aspirations of art religion (*Kunstreligion*) with those of religious art. And in chapter 5, it is Schoenberg's attempt to secure the hegemony of German music through the revolutionary creation of a new method of composition and a conservative recovery of music's spiritual message. More chapters, to be sure, could be added: on Mendelssohn, on Brahms, on Bruckner, on Strauss, on Mahler, each of whom has blurred the line between absolute and program music; and all have a more or less problematic place in German culture.

The central values associated with absolute music—the identity of the bourgeois subject, the aesthetic autonomy of art, and the intrinsic worth of high culture—have been widely criticized for their mandarin conservatism, nationalist ideology, and neglect of social and political concerns. Today, however, the idea (and ideology) of absolute music has finally lost its privileged position in Western art music and it is no longer a dominating paradigm in the scholarly study thereof. Absolute music has become relative. The point may be blunt, but it expounds the critical impulse behind the conjunction of absolute music and hermeneutics in this book. On the one hand, absolute music has been central in advancing the idea that German music could transcend its Germanness and become universal (which was then, of course, taken to be a prime virtue of its Germanness). On the other hand, the "moment of German music" is nevertheless no more than a moment in the history of music, in the way Adorno quoted Eduard Steuermann as saying that "the concept of great music, which has today been passed on to radical music, belongs itself only to a moment in history."[5] Indeed, the twofold legacy of German music has been that the ecumenical claims of both great and radical works became associated both with the catastrophe of a fascist dystopia and the promise of a communist utopia. While Wagner took the C♯ in measure seven of the Eroica to be the note that "represents *all* modern music" (also meaning, of course, *German* music), the C♯ in the final statement of the Arietta theme in the last movement of op. 111 became, for Mann, the last modern note. And while the *Eroica*'s C♯ established, as Scott Burnham has shown so well, the program of musical heroism, the Arietta's C♯, as I will show, was "programmed" by Adorno to pre-echo the end of such heroism.[6]

Thus this book is not a history of the relationship between absolute and program music, but rather an essay on musical and historical hermeneutics.[7] Since the question of musical meaning has remained the crux of modern musicology (which came into being during the nineteenth century), "programming the absolute" is no less than a trope for our field, expressing that the link between music and *logos* is the lifeline of musicology. Although the standard historical narrative states that music emancipated itself to become a language in its own right during Romanticism, this new musical language remained, nevertheless, inseparable from the language *about* music.[8] Romantic musical aesthetics and modern musicology are predicated not only on the difference between language and music, but also on the mediation of that difference. Around 1800, the indefinite nature of the musical language was, as Mark Evan Bonds incisively put it, no longer considered a "liability" but an "asset."[9] Music cannot be considered apart from its interpretation, the work apart from its listener, autonomy aesthetics apart from reception aesthetics. The absoluteness of absolute music has never been an obstacle, but is the very condition of its meaning.

Moment, in German, means both instant (*Augenblick*) and part (*Bestandteil*). The former is a temporal category, the latter a material one. The former refers to a point in time, the latter to a particular detail. The paradox of the musical moment is its place at the intersection between part and whole in the material realm, and between instant and process in the temporal realm. However short the instant, it may touch eternity; and however minute the detail, it may encompass all. As such, therefore, moment is also used in this book as a conceptual category. In the theory and practice of interpretation, it operates not only on the level of musical history and culture, but also touches on broader concerns in the phenomenology and philosophy of music.

When Hermann Kretzschmar set out to develop a systematic musical hermeneutics in the early twentieth century, he sought to reconcile what Ian Bent (following Carl Dahlhaus) identified as the "two opposing principles of music analysis" in the nineteenth century.[10] Whereas the scientific principle was driven by the impulse to *describe* musical phenomena, the hermeneutic principle was concerned with the impulse to *interpret* musical content. Though Bent has treated the descriptive and the interpretive modes as an intrinsic part of music analysis, the rift between analysis and hermeneutics, as distinctly separate genres in the writings about music, had become more pronounced in the nineteenth century. Even if analytical and hermeneutic modes of speaking about music are both essentially metaphorical, the difference between technical and nontechnical language still has had wide-ranging social and institutional implications. Despite Kretzschmar's hope to close the gap between *Kenner* and *Liebhaber,* there continues to be a distinction between those who read music and those who do not. The professional terminology of close reading remains remote from the jargon used to bring music close to a nonprofessional audience. The dubious reputation of musical hermeneutics stems not only from its penchant for purple prose and its predilection for individual passages, but also from the

4

combination of the two. If Wackenroder's art-loving friar exclaimed that "certain passages in music appeared to him so clearly and vividly that the tones appeared like *words*," then the most common critique of hermeneutic criticism has been that those words, as Dahlhaus put it, were "abused as a vehicle for reaching a state, in which the sentiment itself—and not the music—becomes the object of attention and pleasure."[11] To avoid the critical mode that Friedrich Schlegel diagnosed as the "declaiming enthusiasm about individual passages," Hans-Georg Nägeli stipulated that the future critic of the *Allgemeine musikalische Zeitung* "must never utter more rapture than in the moments of immediate consumption of art. In such moments, one does not review. He may never break out into exclamations. That suits him badly. Judgement counts for more than enthusiasm."[12]

Thus the isolated particular became a potential problem precisely when the whole came into view. While Schlegel, in the early era of German literary criticism, observed that there was a tendency "toward beautiful moments and single images," he noted that "[i]t was *Herder*, who first knew to grasp a whole with an emphatic imagination and to express this feeling in words."[13] In music criticism, understanding the relationship between part and whole was also a measure of musical education and social status. Consider Jean Paul's striking observation that "[t]he folk, like cattle, only hear the present, but not the two poles of time; only musical syllables, no syntax."[14] Quite apart from the phenomenological problem of whether we hear moments as part of a local chain of events or as part of a larger whole, the social implications of a listener's musical competence persists through Adorno's sociological analysis of regressive, or "atomistic," listening as the mere consumption of culinary moments: "No longer do the partial moments serve as a critique of that whole; instead, they suspend the critique which the successful esthetic totality exerts against the flawed one of society."[15] Where Jean Paul identified a "good hearer" as the one who "memorizes the antecedent of a musical period, in order to grasp beautifully the consequent," Adorno's "structural listener" retains the ability to discern, in aesthetic synthesis, the promise of a social order in which the individual is reconciled with the whole. Still, Adorno was more ambivalent, asserting in his radio broadcast "Beautiful Passages" (*"Schöne Stellen"*) that "musical *Bildung* in a humanly dignified sense" not only meant the ability to perceive music as "a meaningful whole," but also that "[t]he light of beauty from particulars, once perceived, cancels the illusion with which *Bildung* suffuses music," namely, "that it would already be the happy whole that humanity denies itself until today." The image of that whole would be captured "rather by a scattered measure than by a victorious totality."[16]

Adorno's paradoxical use of the whole as a foil for the fragment has its roots in the romantic reception of idealist philosophy where "particular" and "whole" enter into a dialetical relationship (chapter 1 will treat this in greater detail). "Even the greatest system," Friedrich Schlegel noted succinctly, "is still only a fragment."[17] Yet inasmuch as the idea of the absolute can be reduced to a fragment, the fragment may in turn aspire, again, toward the absolute. Thus Schlegel also defined that "[a] fragment, like a small work of art, has to be entirely isolated from the surrounding world and be complete in itself like a hedgehog." Hence Philippe Lacoue-Labarthe has pointed out that just as "absolute" means "detached" or "set free," "the detachment or isolation of fragmentation is understood to correspond exactly to completion and totality."[18] If all "critical reading . . . is cyclical," argued Schlegel, such "cyclization is like a totalization from below."[19] Because the initial conception of the whole is provisionary, the particular offers the most concrete and tangible entry into the hermeneutic circle, which binds the word into a sentence, the sentence into a work, the work into an oeuvre, the oeuvre into an epoch, and the epoch into all of history. The inherent contradiction in what Hölderlin called "the *apriority* of the individual over the whole" is nowhere, perhaps, more pronounced than in one of Novalis's definitions of the Romantic: "Absolutization—universalization—*classification* of the individual moment, the individual situation etc. is the true essence of romanticizing."[20] From this perspective, the critical intent behind the notion of a moment of German music also runs the risk of detaching that moment and making it absolute once more.

Since romantic hermeneutics brought the particular into consideration together with the totality *and* vice versa, the issue was not only where interpretation should begin, but also where it should end. Thus, Wilhelm Dilthey noted that "all understanding remains only relative and can never be completed. *Individuum est ineffabile.*"[21] Dilthey used Goethe's famous dictum to capture the premise of modern hermeneutics as established by Friedrich Schleiermacher: the inexhaustible meaning of an artwork makes interpretation an infinite process. It was Kant's notion of the aesthetic idea that "no language can express it completely and allow us to grasp it."[22] Schleiermacher's two hermeneutic axioms— that "understanding is an unending task" and that it is possible to "understand the author better than he understood himself"—stand in the liberal tradition of moral individualism.[23] In music criticism, this shift from rule-bound textual hermeneutics to what might be called an emancipated hermeneutics occurred when (according to Mary Sue Morrow) the "importance of being correct" ceded to the "reign of genius."[24] Because obscure passages were no longer wrong, but enigmatic, they stimulated a quest for multiple, and potentially conflicting, interpretations. What Peter Szondi identified as the "displacement of the hermeneutics of the individual passage" with the notion of "*spiritual understanding*" meant a reevaluation of the particular.[25] The old hermeneutics of the individual passage became, as the new hermeneutics of the moment, the very passage to the individual.

> Every artwork is a moment; every successful artwork is an instant, a momentary suspension of its process, as that process reveals itself to the persistent eye.[26]

> Intentional language wants to mediate the absolute, and the absolute escapes language. . . . Music finds the absolute immediately, but at the same moment it becomes obscured, just as too powerful a light blinds the eye which can no longer see what is completely visible.[27]

In combination, these two passages by Adorno create a variant of the fragment by Novalis quoted at the outset. They assert not only the totalization of the moment (*every* artwork is a moment); but also music's superior grasp of the absolute in comparsion to language. Like Novalis, Adorno treated the two claims as two sides of the same coin: the musical absolute appears in the moment. Adorno's aesthetics of the moment is rooted in romantic idealism not only because of Romanticism, but also because of its modernity. The experience of suddenness and the sudden experience, especially, are central to modern aesthetic consciousness: the infinite irony in Schlegel, the diagnostic astonishment in Kleist, the demonic appearance in Kierkegaard, the abrupt aphorism in Nietzsche, the aesthetic ecstasy in Pater, the involuntary memory in Proust, the pure instant in Woolf, the experiential epiphany in Joyce, the "other state" in Musil, the constellation in Benjamin, and, of course, the celestial apparition in Adorno.[28] If modernist aesthetics crystallizes in Adorno's aesthetics of the (musical) moment, it calls for a hermeneutics of the (musical) moment. Thus Adorno claimed not only that "as in music what is beautiful flashes up in nature only to disappear in the instant one tries to grasp it," but also that "appearing nature wants silence at the same time that anyone capable of its experience feels compelled to speak in order to find a momentary liberation from monadological confinement."[29] What Schopenhauer called the "short hour of celebration" where art succeeds in "freeing us momentarily from the service of the will" pertains to the art of interpretation as well.[30] Yet the paradox of all music, for Adorno, is that it is a "sphinx" that "mocks the one who contemplates it, in that it relentlessly promises meanings, and even intermittently offers them, while all the time such promised meanings are actually, in the truest sense, contributing to the death of meaning, and hence it will never be exhausted in these meanings."[31]

This paradox is also reflected in the influential distinction between symbol and allegory, which Paul de Man associated with two different modes of temporality that are fundamental to modern consciousness. "Whereas the symbol postulates the possibility of an identity or identification," wrote de Man, "allegory designates primarily a distance in relation to its own origin, and, renouncing the nostalgia and the desire to coincide, it establishes a language in the void of its temporal difference. In so doing, it prevents the self from an illusory identification with the non-self, which is now fully, though painfully, recognized as a non-self. It is this painful knowledge that we perceive at the moments when early romantic literature finds its true voice."[32] Clearly, the éminence grise behind de Man's essay was Benjamin, who had claimed, in The Origin of German Tragic Drama, that time was the decisive category romantic thinkers had brought to the distinction between symbol and allegory. Benjamin referred to Friedrich Creuzer's seminal Symbolik und Mythologie der alten Völker (1819) which held that "[i]n the symbol an idea appears momentarily and entirely, and seizes all our spiritual powers. It is a ray that reaches our eye in a straight line from the dark bottom of being and thinking, and it passes through our whole essence. Allegory entices us to glance up and pursue the path the idea takes, hidden in the image. In the former there is momentary totality; in the latter progress occurs in a series of moments."[33]

Symbolic experience, then, is simultaneous; allegory works in succession. While in the symbol "the transfigured face of nature is fleetingly revealed in the light of redemption," allegory exposes the "historicality" of the particular that is doomed to die.[34] And while the symbol mystifies meaning, allegory uncovers its conventional constructedness.[35] Yet for Benjamin, romantic symbol and baroque allegory converge in the mode of sudden appearance: one to show unity, the other to show difference. The "mystical now" of symbolic experience is not unlike the allegorical clash between "cold and ready-made technique" and "eruptive expression."[36] While Creuzer had compared symbolic recognition with a "ray that reaches our eye in a straight line from the dark bottom of being and thinking" (see above), Benjamin saw the sententia in the baroque tragedy—like the light effect in baroque painting—"flash from the darkness of allegorical entanglement" and thus produce "the intermittent rhythm of constant arrest, jerky reversal, and renewed petrification."[37] The rhythm of modern reading pulsates between the symbol's systolic contraction into the mystical moment of the whole, and allegory's diastolic dissipation into a series of momentary particulars—in other words, between the identical and the nonidentical. Its inherent hermeneutic, as Rolf Tiedemann put it, is marked by its modern morality: "The interpretive immersion in inherited texts, which Adorno supported and practiced, is nuance nonetheless aiming at the whole; naturally, postmodernism wants to know nothing of this, and so knows nothing. Still other concepts essential to Adorno's philosophy are also missing in postmodernism. The whole merely one of them, history yet another, utopia together with its theological archetype of reconciliation a third. Not inappropriately, postmodernism has been defined as a modernism that has taken its leave of history and emerged without utopia."[38]

It is tempting to defend Adorno (as he defended Bach) against one of his devotees—not because of Tiedemann's unflagging support of Adorno's modernism, but because of his acrimonous critique of postmodernism. Recalling that Jürgen Habermas had noted in 1960 the "minimal exchange value of utopia" upon the occasion of the appearance of Ernst Bloch's *The Principle of Hope*, Tiedemann bemoaned bitterly that today utopia is "traded on the stock markets of neither science nor society."[39] Such diagnosis seems overly grim. If the postmodern residues of modernist utopia are apocryphal at worst, it is precisely their minimal exchange value that might keep them from being sold out as a commodity. Adorno would have wanted it no other way. In light of the routine charge against his elitism we should keep in mind that the opposition between high and low art is an essential aspect of his dialectics between integral whole and nonidentical particular. Otherwise he would not have claimed in his monograph on Mahler that "the power of the name is often better protected in kitsch and vulgar music than in high music that even before the age of radical construction had sacrificed all that to the principle of stylization." Where Mahler "picks up the broken glass by the roadside and holds it up to the sun so that all the colors are refracted," the total spectrum reflected in the part stands for the lost whole that only art might recuperate—if only momentarily.[40] This is why, for Adorno, the "moment" of the traditional artwork was constituted by "the sudden fusion of its particular moments into a totality"; and this is why "[a]s an expression of that totality art lays claim to the dignity of the absolute."[41] Modern art, by contrast, had to shrink that totality into a fragment, a shard, a relic, or a splinter. At the moment of crisis, the modern subject reconstitutes itself through moments of intense experience that may be triggered by the trivial. Thus for Hofmannthal's Lord Chandos a "watering can, a harrow left standing in a field, a dog in the sun, a run-down churchyard, a cripple, a small farmhouse, any of these can become the vessel for my revelation. Each of them, or for that matter any of a thousand others like them that the eye glides over with understandable indifference can all at once, at some altogether unpredictable instant, assume for me an aspect so sublime and moving that it beggars all words."[42]

Adorno had learned from Benjamin that this physiognomic gaze at the detail might turn up the absolute: that "the eternal is in any case rather a frill on a dress than an idea."[43] Writing about the horn calls at the end of the first movement of the *Les Adieux* Sonata, he noted that here "the eternal attaches itself precisely to this most transient moment."[44] At the very end of *Negative Dialectics*, the whole of philosophy depends on detail: "The smallest traits of this world would be of relevance to the absolute, for the micrological view cracks the shells of what, measured by the subsuming cover concept, is helplessly isolated and explodes its identity, the delusion that it is but a specimen. Such thinking shows solidarity with metaphysics at the moment of its fall."[45] In light of such philosophical pathos the critique Adorno leveled at Benjamin's *Arcarde Project* must, at least partially, be applied to himself. "If one wanted to put it rather drastically," he wrote to Benjamin, "one could say that your study is located at the crossroads of magic and positivism. This spot is bewitched. Only theory could break this spell—your own resolute and salutarily speculative theory. It is simply the claim of this theory that I bring against you here."[46]

It is a claim that we also may well bring against Adorno. His unfinished *Aesthetic Theory* is nothing less than the attempt to reconcile the physiognomic gaze with a theoretical gaze, and to mediate between the process of materialist history and the sudden advent of messianic time. The result is an aesthetization of theory, or musicalization of philosophy. As a "song without notes" (to adopt a trenchant phrase by Christine Eichel), Adorno's aesthetics followed, like the music it championed, the double impulse toward the total and the particular.[47] What Ernst Bloch valued in music as the "coincidence of expressive truth and constructional truth" has its equivalent in Adorno's aesthetics in the coincidence of what Hans Heinrich Eggebrecht called the "logic of imagination" and "logic of construction."[48] Adorno's voice is caught between both the objective claims of philosophy and the subjective expression of the artist. While Andreas Huyssen has noted that today "the discourse of subjectivity has been cut loose from its moorings in bourgeois individualism," the narrative or mimetic impulse of Adorno's subjective voice—however parallel with the postmodern—could never be cut loose from its moorings in the modernist utopia of a reconciled whole.[49] Despite Adorno's postmodern "repudiation of system and the commitment to the fragmentary and the occasional, to a freedom in the instant that eshewed the traditional Germanic longing for the *Hauptwerk* and the architectonic truth" (Fredric Jameson), a sense of the whole is nevertheless preserved in his ongoing commitment to truth.[50] Lambert Zuidervaart has highlighted this commitment as the primary motivation of *Negative Dialectics*: "the need to lend a voice to suffering is a condition of all truth."[51] Hence Adorno's claim that music which is "compressed into a moment . . . is true as a reflex of negative experience. It pertains to real suffering."[52] The ideal of such a voice of suffering emerges in the Webernesque fusion of utmost rationality and pure sound. That is the only music we hear when Adrian Leverkühn himself performs the *Lamentations of Doctor Faustus*: a dissonant chord that represents the twelve-tone system and "at the same time" an expressive wail that represents the sound of nature. And that is the particular moment of German music that could transcend the moment of German music as a whole.[53]

This tortured dialectic of the moment, I will argue in the last chapter of the book, is a symptom of modern melancholia. What Max Pensky has identified as Benjamin's "melancholy dialectics" affected not only writers such as Mann and philosophers such as Adorno, whose condition was endemic to the generation that lived through the German catastrophe and the Jewish Holocaust; it also affected, as Eric Santner has shown, the *Nachkriegsgeneration*.[54] The melancholic condition of Mann, Adorno, and Benjamin has proven to be an ineluctable cultural and intellectual legacy. As a reflex of such melancholic dialectics, the totalizing and particularizing impulses in the present book, its calculated constructions and expressive gestures, are in plain sight. This is also the dilemma of an essayistic musicology, stranded in the no-man's-land between scholarship and criticism. The tensions between rational logic and emotional whim accord with Freud's diagnosis of the melancholic individual, who, instead of suffering from "a loss in regard to an object" projects "a loss in regard to his ego," so that "one part of the ego sets itself over against the other, judges it critically, and, as it were, takes it as its object."[55] Despite the narcissistic identification with, and critical disdain for, my substitute object of absolute music, however, I would agree with Dominique LaCapra that melancholy has traditionally been not only an obstacle to, but also a condition for, true mourning.[56] Freud's prognosis that "when the work of mourning is completed the ego becomes free and uninhibited again" is nothing less than a clinical vision of utopia.[57] Coupled with hope, however, melancholy is part of the human condition. Although Adorno's agenda is not mine, but mine to understand, one may well understand my book as a reaction to the ending of his *Negative Dialectics*: as a gesture of solidarity with the metaphysics of German music at the moment of its fall.

BEETHOVEN'S STAR

"O Freunde, nicht diese Töne!"

No, I will not speak here of the Ninth, except for that moment near the beginning of the last movement when the baritone breaks through the *Schreckensfanfare* to call for more pleasant (*angenehmere*) and more joyful (*freudenvollere*) tones. What Stephen Hinton has called the hermeneutic crux of Beethoven's last symphony resonates with the crux of another hermeneutic: how to hear such pleasant and joyful tones in light of a line with which I will end this chapter: "In life there are no tones like these."[1] For such denial takes the Ninth back. It goes beyond the distancing irony that Beethoven may have injected into his most affirmative music, seeking to prevent the abuse of affirmation. For history has not merely made the gap between terror and joy in Beethoven's music appear more glaring; it even reversed them by associating joy with oppression and terror with protest. That reversal will concern me here because of a hidden, but profound, bond between Beethoven's sublime irony and Walter Benjamin's paradoxical hermeneutics of hope: "Only for the sake of the hopeless have we been given hope." However hermetic, that bond also illuminates how deeply Adorno's philosophy of Beethoven was inspired by Benjamin, namely in the image of the falling star flashing in the dark sky. The hermeneutics of hope is the hermeneutics of that moment. And the hermeneutics of that moment in *Fidelio* will be my first example of a hermeneutics of the moment.

This chapter has three parts. The first introduces Adorno's aesthetics of the particular as the negation of Hegel's aesthetics of the whole. The second illuminates how Benjamin's image of the falling star becomes a central trope of transcendence in Adorno's philosophy of Beethoven. And the third invites us to listen anew to Leonore's vision of the star of hope. I will begin and end with two poems. One is about a torso of Apollo; the other about Beethoven's *Fidelio*. One is about a fragment, asserting its fullness; the other about a whole, asserting its lack. One culminates in a star that shines in beautiful illusion; the other sees that illusion extinguished in sublime despair. To assert that the concluding poem nevertheless carries a message of hope would seem to be an impossible project. The paradox that hovers over the critical project in this chapter, however, is that only this impossibility can make the poem carry that message of hope.

The Dialectics of *Augenblick* and Argus-Eyedness

Archaischer Torso Apollos

Rainer Maria Rilke

Wir kannten nicht sein unerhörtes Haupt,
darin die Augenäpfel reiften. Aber
sein Torso glüht noch wie ein Kandelaber,
in dem sein Schauen, nur zurückgeschraubt,

sich hält und glänzt. Sonst könnte nicht der Bug
der Brust dich blenden, und im leisen Drehen
der Lenden könnte nicht ein Lächeln gehen
zu jener Mitte, die die Zeugung trug.

Sonst stünde dieser Stein entstellt und kurz
unter der Schultern durchsichtigem Sturz
und flimmerte nicht so wie Raubtierfelle;

und bräche nicht aus allen seinen Rändern
aus wie ein Stern: denn da ist keine Stelle,
die dich nicht sieht. Du mußt dein Leben ändern.

Apollo's Archaic Torso

We did not know his unheard-of head,
in which the eyeballs ripened. But
his torso still glows like a candelabra,
in which his gaze, only reduced,

remains and shines. Or else the breast's bow
could not blind you, nor in the soft turn
of the loins could run a smile
toward that center which bore creation.

Or else this stone would stand disfigured and just
below the shoulders' transparent lintel,
nor shimmer like predators' skin;

nor break through all its boundaries
like a star: for there is no place
that does not see you. You must change your life.[2]

Rilke's sonnet can be read as a variant of Johann Joachim Winckelmann's 1759 essay on the Belvedere Torso, emulating its blend of objective observation and subjective commentary.[3] The premise of Winckelmann's essay, a landmark in the history of German literature and art criticism, was a paradox that turned the torso into a paradigm of perfection, where "in every part of this body"—even in those that are lacking— "the whole hero [is] revealed."[4] Rilke, too, works through this paradox by beginning with the absent eyes in the missing head, but concluding with the total gaze of the fragmented body. The tight sequence of two sentences beginning with "Sonst" (lines 5 and 9) sutures the sonnet's division between octave and sestet, so that the seamless rhetorical curve can culminate in the penultimate verse: "for there is no place that does not see you." But ending halfway through the last line, the poem threatens to reinstate the lack from which it sprang and thereby undercut its affirmation of plenitude. Displacing the caesura from the center to the periphery replicates the liminal state of the torso, which "breaks through all its boundaries like a star." It is only after the beholder has scanned the entire surface of the sculpture that it is seen to look back, as if the visual palpation of the "persistent eye" had itself planted the eyes on the object to return its gaze. And so the final sentence—"You must change your life"—appears to break forth with great force, not from the speaker's self-admonishment (as one would normally read it), but as if issued from the mouthless torso itself. Let us note that Rilke speaks of this breakthrough as a "star."

Rilke's poem is also a comment of sorts on Hegel's notion of beauty. Beauty, as Hegel defined it, is "truth unfolding into external reality," while "every part of this unfolding makes this soul, this totality, appear in each part." "But if we ask," he continued,

> . . . in which particular organ the whole soul appears as soul, we will at once name the eye. . . . Now as the pulsating heart shows itself all over the surface of the human . . . body, so in the same sense it is to be asserted of art that it has to convert every shape in all points of its visible surface into an eye, which . . . brings the spirit into appearance. —Or, as Plato cries out to the star in his familiar distich: "When thou lookest on the stars, my star, oh! would I were the heavens and could see thee with a thousand eyes," so, conversely, art makes every one of its productions into a thousand-eyed Argus, whereby the inner soul and spirit is seen at every point. And it is not only the bodily form, facial expression, the gesture and posture, but also actions and events, speech and tones, and the series of their course through all conditions of appearance that art has everywhere to make into an eye, in which the free soul is revealed in its inner infinity.[5]

Argus Panoptes was a figure in Greek legend whose surname refers to the hundred eyes in his head or all over his body; *panoptes* means "all seeing." Total vision, the complete regime of the eye, constitutes beauty as synonymous with truth. The ideal of Hegel's aesthetics is what I will call the *aesthetics of Argus-eyedness*. Let us note that the distich which Hegel appropriated from Plato speaks of the eyes as "stars."

"The true is the whole," said Hegel. "The whole is the untrue," rebutted Adorno.[6] The antithesis of Hegel's dialectics is Adorno's negative dialectics. The clash of two philosophies correlates with a clash of two aesthetics. Hence the premise of Adorno's *Aesthetic Theory*:

> Every artwork is a moment; every successful artwork is an instant, a momentary suspension of its process, as this process reveals itself to the persistent eye.[7]

There is more here than meets the eye, because Adorno did not choose the word *Moment* (moment), but rather the more idiomatic *Augenblick*— literally "an eye's glance." As a bodily gesture, the *Augenblick* fuses objecthood and personhood: "What nature strives for in vain, artworks fulfill: They open their eyes."[8] What is more: Adorno's monadic aphorism speaks about itself. It is itself a moment, a brief epiphany that suspends his philosophy, suddenly looking at us, like the poetic quotation inserted in Hegel's prose; and like the distich itself, divided by the *exclamatio* of the "oh"—which says it all. There is an inner affinity between Hegel's aesthetics of Argus-eyedness and what must be called Adorno's aesthetics of the *Augenblick*. Adorno's advocacy of the particular partakes, paradoxically, of a totalizing logic; his negation of Hegel aims at completeness: "*Every* artwork is a moment." The reversal of idealist aesthetics becomes a new aesthetic ideal. Its generic paradigm is the essay which shares with romantic poetry its fragmentary construction—what Karl-Heinz Bohrer called the "appearance of the sudden in prose."[9] For Adorno, the essay "rebels" against the notion that the "ephemeral is unworthy of philosophy," but it also causes "totality to be illuminated in a partial feature . . . without asserting the presence of the totality."[10] Sudden illumination makes the whole momentarily appear and disappear. This is the paradoxical mode of essayistic philosophy.

That Adorno's conception of the particular remains dependent on the idea of the whole is hardly news. It is the locus of the (post-)modernist dilemma—the difficulty of dissolving binary oppositions instead of merely inverting them. It is part of a process that continues to revolve around the idea of the absolute rather than to reject or replace it. (This distinguishes Adorno from Nietzsche.) If any critique of Adorno's critical theory has to ask, as Peter Uwe Hohendahl proposed, "whether negative dialectic can retreat from the presupposition of an absolute as the Archimedean point of the dialectic process," any defense of that theory must take into account what Hohendahl identifies as the "crucial aspect of Adorno's thought: namely, the idea of redemption (*Versöhnung*)."[11] The fundamental aporia in Adorno's philosophy is that the idea of redemption is inextricably linked to this absolute Archimedean point. Both are anchored in his notion of truth, figured as the moment of simultaneous appearance *and* disappearance, of presence *and* absence, part *and* whole. The logic of contradiction upon which he built his negative dialectics cannot exist without invoking what is contradicted. This paradox is Adorno's trope of truth.

Rilke's sonnet is a site of such a paradox, caught between Argus-eyedness and *Augenblick*. Adorno reported that Benjamin held the line "for there is no place that does not see you" in high esteem, because it "codified the nonsignificative language of artworks in an incomparable fashion: Expression is the gaze of artworks."[12] Since the "true language of art is mute," "its muteness takes priority over poetry's significative element, which is not altogether lacking in music."[13] This runs directly counter to Hegel's content-based aesthetic, where the "*unutterable—feeling sensation*—far from being the highest truth, is the most unimportant and untrue."[14] Thus Rilke's sonnet negotiates a position between a classicist and modernist aesthetic: it affirms the classical concept of beauty through the torso's Argus-eyedness, yet makes it into a mouthpiece that utters the unsayable in a single moment, rupturing the total vision. "The strict immanence of the spirit of artworks," noted Adorno in the *Aesthetic Theory*, is contradicted "by a countertendency that is no less immanent: the tendency of artworks to wrest themselves free of the internal unity of their own construction, to introduce within themselves caesuras that no longer permit the totality of the appearance . . . this breakthrough is the moment of *apparition*."[15] Adorno's aesthetics of the *Augenblick* is an aesthetics of apparition: "The artwork as appearance approaches most closely the *apparition,* the celestial vision."[16]

The aesthetics of the *Augenblick* calls for a hermeneutics of the moment. Although the significance of the moment for Adorno's aesthetics has not gone unnoticed, Günter Figal has claimed that the *Aesthetic Theory* lacks "a hermeneutic of the instantaneous and hence a hermeneutic of absolute modernity."[17] This lack, according to Figal, is the missing link in Adorno's reception of Benjamin's idiosyncratic notion of a "dialectics at a standstill" (*Dialektik im Stillstand*). The concept has an aesthetic dimension, which is Figal's primary interest and which will concern us first; and a historical one, which we will consider later on.[18]

"If *apparition* illuminates and touches," Adorno wrote in the *Aesthetic Theory,* "the image is the paradoxical effort to transfix the most evanescent instant. In artworks something momentary transcends; objectification makes the artwork into an instant. Pertinent here is Benjamin's formulation of a dialectic at a standstill, which he developed in the context of his conception of a dialectical image. If, as images, artworks are the persistence of the transient, they are concentrated in appearances as something momentary. To experience art means to become conscious of its immanent process as an instant at a standstill. This may perhaps have nourished the central concept of Gotthold Ephraim Lessing's aesthetics, that of the 'pregnant moment'."[19] In his controversial 1766 treatise, *Laocoön: An Essay on the Limits of Painting and Poetry*, Lessing had posited, rather rigidly, that painting captured best the essence of an ongoing action in a single instant, whereas the temporal art of poetry (music included) depicted such action in succession. Lessing's boundaries are Adorno's bonds: "The arts converge only where each pursues its immanent principle in a pure way."[20] What intrigued Adorno was Benjamin's objectification of the historical process in the image. In it, "what has been coalesces in lightning like fashion with the Now. In other words, the image is the dialectic at a standstill. For while the relationship of the present to the past is a purely temporal one, the relationship of what has been to the Now is dialectical: of a pictorial rather than a temporal character. . . . The interpreted image, that is to say, the image in the Now in which it is recognized, bears, to the highest degree, the stamp of the critical, dangerous moment, which is the basis of all reading."[21]

According to Figal, the central idea Benjamin developed in the *Arcade Project* is not only "that the instantaneous is the readable," but that reading is also instantaneous.[22] This "absolute modernity" dwells in the moment that is literally "set free" (absolved) from the constraints of decline or progress.[23] Hence, for Figal, absolute modernity requires a hermeneutics that is based on the simultaneity of the readable and its reading—a hermeneutics of the moment. Dialectics at a standstill is a suspension of the historical dialectic, so that one can recognize the moment, divested from the historical continuum, as an emphatic *Jetzt*. This very "now of recognizability" is the foundation of Benjamin's epistemology, doubly opposed to positivist historicism (which fetishizes the past) and idealist philosophy (which usurps the future).[24]

Benjamin's thinking influenced Adorno more deeply than Figal is willing to acknowledge. In his 1931 inaugural lecture, whose publication he intended to dedicate to Benjamin, Adorno wrote that "[t]rue philosophical interpretation does not aim at a fixed meaning that lies readily behind the question, but illuminates it suddenly and momentarily, while consuming it at the same time." Philosophical inquiry operates through "changing constellations" where "the particular and scattered elements of the question are arranged differently until they fuse into the figure from which the solution jumps out while the question disappears."[25] Adorno's aesthetics of *apparition* and Benjamin's hermeneutics of *constellation* are two sides of the same coin: both invoke celestial phenomena. Their conjunction figures the deep affinity between Adorno's idea of the *Augenblick* and Benjamin's notion of *Aura* in the gaze, the moment, and the star. For Benjamin, "to experience the aura of an appearance" meant not only "to invest it with the ability to look at us in return," but also to bind it to the "here and now" of the present moment that is lost in the process of mechanical reproduction.[26] And in a sketch for his essay "On the Mimetic Faculty," he asked:

> Are there earthly beings as well as things that return their gaze from the stars? That open their eyes only in the skies? Are the stars with their glance from afar the original phenomenon of aura?[27]

Of course, the notion that material objects look at us borders on magical thinking: idolatry, totemism, and animism, whose modern equivalents turn objects into sites of consciousness, subjectivity, and desire.[28] This might prompt a Marxian critique of commodity fetishism, which results from objects being treated "as persons whose will resides in those objects"; or a Lacanian analysis which holds that seeing such objects is inextricably bound to being seen by them.[29] But my interest in Benjamin's speculative mix of epistemology and astrology is hermeneutic: "Ideas relate to things like constellations relate to the stars."[30] Hermeneutic cognition is instantaneous: "the perception of similarity is in any case bound to a flash of light. . . . It is presented to the eye as fleetingly and transiently as a constellation of stars."[31] Moreover, if *Augenblick* and *Aura* coalesce in the sudden gaze of the stars, both Benjamin and Adorno saw the mysterium of hope appear only through a particular kind of star—the one falling from the sky.

The Falling Star

Here is a beautiful passage from Adorno's *Aesthetic Theory* about beautiful passages:

> Whoever lacks an appreciation for beautiful passages— in painting, too, as with Proust's Bergotte, who, seconds before his death, is captivated by a small section of a yellow wall in a Vermeer painting—is as alien to the artwork as one who is incapable of experiencing unity. All the same, those details receive their luminous power only by virtue of the whole. Some measures in Beethoven sound like the sentence in *Elective Affinities*: "Like a star, hope shot down from the sky"; thus in the slow movement of the Sonata in D minor op. 31, no. 2. One only has to play the passage in the

context of the whole movement and then alone in order to hear how much it owes its incommensurability, its radiance beyond the structure, to that structure. The passage becomes tremendous because its expression transcends what precedes it through the concentration of a cantabile, humanized melody. It is rendered individual in relation to, and by way of the totality; it is its product as well as its suspension. Even totality, the gapless structure of artworks, is no closed category. As an indispensable antidote against regressive–atomistic perception, it is relativized, because it proves its power only in relation to the particular into which it radiates.[32]

"Hope shot across the sky above their heads like a falling star." Quoting Goethe, Adorno also quoted Benjamin's essay on *Elective Affinities,* where that sentence (here the original) becomes the novel's caesura.[33] Benjamin appropriated the term from the theory of tragedy by Hölderlin, where it refers to the appearance of the "pure word, the counterrhythmic rupture."[34] Here, "along with harmony, every expression simultaneously comes to a standstill, in order to give free reign to an expressionless power inside all artistic media": this is the moment where "something beyond the poet interrupts the language of the poetry."[35] The caesura is Benjamin's example of what he calls "the expressionless" (*das Ausdruckslose*), in which "the sublime violence of the true appears," and which "shatters whatever still survives as the legacy of chaos in all beautiful semblance: the false, errant totality—the absolute totality."[36] In Goethe's novel, the beautiful—the ideal of classical aesthetics—is incarnate in Ottilie, object of Eduard's adulterous desire. The very moment Ottilie and Eduard declare their illicit love, "Hope shot across the sky above their heads like a falling star." Moments later, the confused Ottilie accidentally drowns Eduard's child, which he had sired with his wife, Charlotte, while fantasizing of Ottilie. And from here the story spirals downward, ineluctably, to its end: the death of the lovers.

But whereas Goethe figured the falling star as hope lost for the lovers, Benjamin, in a typically esoteric twist, turned this loss into the "hope of redemption, which we nourish for all the dead."[37] Since spatial distance is imagined as temporal distance by different peoples, "the shooting star, which plunges into the infinite distance of space, has become the symbol of a fulfilled wish."[38] A star shines brightest at the moment of its fall. At the moment of its fall it holds the greatest promise. "Like a star falling out of the sky, hope flashed over their heads." That sentence lit up for Benjamin a novel notorious for the clinical coldness of its narrative technique and the allegorical chill of its poetry. The caesura is the symbolic moment where language reaches beyond itself to represent what words cannot express: the "mysterium of hope." "This," Benjamin explained in another esoteric association, "is etched on the plate that [Stefan] George put up on Beethoven's birthplace":

Eh ihr zum kampf erstarkt auf eurem sterne
Sing ich euch streit und sieg von oberen sternen.
Eh ihr den leib ergreift auf diesem sterne
Erfind ich euch den traum bei ewigen sternen.

Before you wage the battle of your star
I sing of strife and victory on higher stars.
Before you seize the body on this star
I shape you dreams among eternal stars.[39]

The phrase "Before you seize the body," Benjamin remarked, "appears destined for a sublime irony. Those lovers never seize the body. What does it matter if they never gathered strength for battle?" "Only for the sake of the hopeless," he concluded his essay, "have we been given hope." A similar gesture of irony has often been heard in the note of hope by which Goethe concluded the novel with the image of the tomb that Charlotte had endowed for Eduard and Ottilie: "what a friendly moment it will be when they will once awaken again, together." A remark that Adorno jotted down on a journey a few years before his death comes to mind: "In the night before the departure I dreamt this: that I could not let go of metaphysical hope was not at all because I cling so much to life, but because I want to awaken with Gretel."[40]

Benjamin's whimsical conjunction of Goethe's star and George's star struck Adorno profoundly. It left a trace in his musical writings, where star and hope appear together with particular passages of Beethoven's music, such as in the slow movements of the *Tempest* Sonata and the first Razumovsky Quartet; in Leonore's aria from *Fidelio;* in the Arietta Variations op. 111. In his edition of Adorno's Beethoven monograph, Rolf Tiedemann arranged many of these fragments together, suggesting that they would have formed the center of a projected chapter, for which Adorno chose as a possible motto, a line from Goethe's sketches for *Faust:* "And joy hovers like the sounds of stars/ before us only in a dream."[41] Here Beethoven's stars fuse into a figure that bears the face of hope and humanity; and the light they shed on the idea of redemption reflects back on Adorno. They preserve the critical impulse of his philosophy precisely by suspending its relentless dialectic. They give a glimpse on Adorno's aesthetics of hope.

To appreciate this tension, it will be worth recalling Adorno's fragment "Zur Theorie Beethovens" (Towards a Theory of Beethoven), the argument of which can be understood as a proposition, a thesis, an antithesis, and a failed synthesis—nothing less than an attempt to understand and overturn Hegel's philosophy through a philosophy of Beethoven.[42]

> Proposition. "In the totality of its form," Adorno claimed, "Beethoven's music represents the social process. In doing so it shows how each individual moment . . . is made comprehensible only in terms of its function within the reproduction of society as a whole. . . . Beethoven's music is, in a sense, a means for putting to the test the idea that the whole is the truth."
> Thesis. Adorno's parallel between the "systems of Beethoven and Hegel" was based on the notion of a unified whole. Beethoven's form is an "integral whole, in which each individual moment is determined by its function within that whole only to the extent that these individual moments contradict and cancel each other, yet are preserved on a higher level in the whole."
> Antithesis. "Beethoven's music is Hegelian philosophy: but at the same time it is truer than that philosophy. . . . Logical identity as immanent to form . . . is both constituted and criticized by Beethoven. Its seal of truth in Beethoven's music lies in its suspension: through transcending it, form takes on its true meaning. This formal transcendence in Beethoven's music is a representation—not an expression—of hope."
> Failed synthesis as critique. "The key to the very late Beethoven probably lies in the fact that in this music the idea of totality as something already achieved had become unbearable to his critical genius. . . . In a sense, the dissociation found in the last works is a consequence of the moments of transcendence in the 'classical' works of the middle period." Beethoven's "discovery of the inadequacy of mediation" is the "truly critical aspect" of the last works.

Of course, the total organization of divergent parts is the *locus classicus* of the Beethoven myth, whose progressive dialectic the Hegelian Franz Brendel recognized in the composer's ability "to develop an overriding perspective that controls these parts and forges them into a unity. Beethoven created the most richly structured totality; he was led in this direction by historical necessity."[43] Because Beethoven "put together his material in the presence of the listener," Edward Dannreuther noted in 1876, "the whole course of growth, from a simple germ to its final glory, is visible at one glance."[44] Adorno's distinction between atomistic and structural listening rides on such an "overriding perspective": "Structural listening is . . . when one hears the first measure of a classical symphony only when hearing the last, which redeems it. The illusion of frozen time—that movements like the first of the Fifth and Seventh Symphonies or even the very extended *Eroica* do not last in proper rendition seven or fifteen minutes, but only one moment—is produced by the structure like the feeling of a coercion that does not leave out the listener." This "symphonic authority" is exercised through its "immanent meaning" so that the listener is "being surrounded by the symphony," which is "the ritualistic reception of the particular in a developing whole."[45] Citing Riemann's claim that the "classical" mode of composition "always has the *overall development,* the broad outline, in view," Adorno held that "highly organized music" had to be listened to "multidimensionally, both forwards and backwards at the same time. . . . One must know a whole movement, be retrospectively aware at each moment of what has gone before."[46] The underlying epistemology turns successive apprehension into simultaneous comprehension: the *Augenblick* of the traditional artwork is "the fusion of its particular moments into a whole."[47] For Adorno, therefore, "the truly Hegelian quality of Beethoven is, perhaps, that in his work, too, mediation is never merely something *between* the moments, but is immanent in the moment itself."[48] The works from the heroic period share with Goethe's organicism and Hegel's philosophy of identity that "[t]he smallest detail can become the whole because it is already the whole."[49] Hence the momentariness of Beethoven's symphonic movements, "whose virtual effect is as if they lasted only a second."[50] This music not only *has* moments—it *is* a moment.

And yet the identity between all moments and single moment is "both constituted and criticized" by Beethoven's music, whose "seal of truth" lay in the "suspension" of that identity by driving a wedge between the moment as part and the moment as whole. This begins in the middle period works with moments of transcendence that cut through the aesthetic appearance (*Schein*) of unity and expose it as false. It leads to the trend towards dissociation that has become the *locus classicus* of the late style, succinctly formulated again by Brendel: "With the stepping out of that objective life of the mind, with the assertion of a particular subjectivity, all those forms are being left behind and being broken, and only fragments are taken along, only subjective caprice and arbitrariness being applied."[51] On this traditional reception of Beethoven's late style Adorno put his Benjaminian spin: "the force of subjectivity in late artworks" is "the flaring-up gesture with which it departs from them. This gesture explodes them, not to express itself, but to shed—expressionless—art's appearance. This gesture leaves behind only fragments of the works and communicates, like ciphers, only through the holes through which it breaks out. Touched by death, the masterly hand releases the material which it formed before; the fissures and cracks in this material—testimony to the finite impotence of the self in the face of being—are its last deed."[52] In his ostensibly bleak conclusion, Adorno projected what Rose Rosengard Subotnik described so well as "the early symptom of a fatal condition"[53]—the split between object and subject: "The fragmented landscape is objective, while the light in which alone it glows is subjective. [Beethoven] does not bring about their harmonious synthesis. As a dissociative force he tears them apart in time, perhaps in order to preserve them for the eternal. In the history of art, late works are the catastrophes."[54]

However bleak this vision, Adorno did not give up on the absolute. The apocalyptic outlook of the last sentence is tempered by the one that precedes it. The invocation of the eternal echoes George's line: "I shape you dreams among eternal stars." And the flaring-up gesture with which subjectivity departs from the artwork mimics the hope that "flashed over their heads like a star falling out of the sky." Its light is like the one that subjectivity casts on the desolate landscape. If *Spätstil Beethovens* strikes a precarious balance between the rise of the particular and the demise of the whole, Adorno ended, thirty-two years later, his *Negative Dialectics* with a reprise of sorts: "The smallest traits of this world would be of relevance to the absolute, for the physiognomic view cracks the shells of what, measured by the subsuming cover concept, is help-lessly isolated and explodes its identity, the delusion that it is but a specimen. Such thinking shows solidarity with metaphysics at the mo-ment of its fall."[55]

Only at the moment of its fall does a star shine the brightest. Only then does it becomes a source of hope. In catching metaphysics at the moment of its fall, negative dialectics affords solidarity with that which it negates. The philosophy of the particular must help the helplessly isolated point toward the absolute. Paradoxically, the more minute the detail (and the more micrological the view required to perceive it), the greater that solidarity will be. Thus Adorno wrote in the last paragraph of the early introduction to his *Aesthetic Theory*, "When, just before the close of the first movement of Beethoven's *Les Adieux* sonata, an evanescently fleeting association summons up in the course of three measures the sound of trotting horse hooves, the swiftly vanishing pas-sage, the sound of disappearance, which confounds any effort to pin it down anywhere in the context of the phrase, says more of the hope of return than would any general reflection on the essence of the fleetingly enduring sound. Only a philosophy that could grasp such micrological figures in its innermost construction of the aesthetic whole would make good on what it promises."[56]

Adorno's claim, elsewhere, that this "clatter of horse hooves moving away into the distance carries a greater guarantee of hope than the four Gospels"; and "that the eternal attaches itself precisely to this most transient moment,"[57] radically raises the stakes for the critical and ana-lytical project that sustains it. The shorter a moment, the larger its promise. That was meant by Benjamin's dictum that "the eternal is in any case rather a frill on a dress than an idea."[58] Hence the modulation to C♭ major in measure 8 of the first movement of the *Les Adieux* sonata can be for Adorno "one of the most magnificent allegories of hope in Beethoven, comparable only to *Fidelio*." Because hope is "always *secret*, because it is not 'there'—it is the basic category of mysticism and the highest category of Beethoven's metaphysics."[59] With such utopian aspiration being the measure of interpretive pressure, it seems impossible to imagine a musical detail more overdetermined. And yet the hermeneutics of hope hinges on that being "not 'there'."

Leonore's Impossible Tone

"Come, hope, do not dim the last star of the weary." Leonore's line from her act 1 aria in *Fidelio* inevitably resonates with Benjamin's essay on *Elective Affinities*. Of course, *Fidelio* is a far cry from Goethe's novel: a celebration of conjugal love, in which Leonore rescues and embraces her husband, Florestan. They will "seize the body on this star." *Fidelio* embodies what Ernst Bloch called the "Principle of Hope" whose paradigm is "the fulfilled moment" when Leonore releases Florestan from his chains, singing "O Gott, welch ein Augenblick":

> . . . and at these words, which Beethoven has raised to metaphysical heights, there arises a song, a veritable tarrying moreover, which would deserve to go on arriving for ever. First the sudden switch to a distant key, then an oboe melody expressing fulfillment; the Sostenuto assai of time standing still and absorbed in the moment. Every future storming of the Bastille is implicitly expressed in *Fidelio*, and an incipient substance of human identity fills up the space in the Sostenuto assai. The Presto of the final chords just adds the reflected glory, the rejoicing around Leonore-*Maria militans*. Beethoven's music is chiliastic, and the form of the "rescue opera," which was not uncommon at the time, only furnished the superficial material for this music's moral contents. Does not the character of Pizarro bear all the features of a Pharaoh, of Herod, Gessler, the demon of winter and indeed that same gnostic Satan who put Man into the dungeon of the world and keeps him prisoner there? Here and nowhere else music becomes a rosy dawn, militant–religious, the dawning of a new day so audible that it seems more than simply a hope. It shines forth as the pure work of Man, as one which had not yet appeared in the world surrounding Beethoven, a world that existed irrespective of men. Thus music as a whole stands at the farther limits of humanity, but at those limits where humanity, with new language and *haloed by the call to achieved intensity, to the attained world of "we,"* is first taking shape. And this ordering in

our musical expression means a house, indeed a crystal, but one derived from our future freedom; a star, but one that will be a new Earth.[60]

For Bloch, *Fidelio* promises and delivers fulfillment—the utopian image of a *new* star, not one that expires. Whereas Bloch looked ahead to the future, Benjamin defined progress in his stark image of the *Angelus Novus*, the angel of history, whose "face is turned toward the past"; who "sees one single catastrophe which keeps piling wreckage upon wreckage and hurls it in front of his feet"; who would like "to make whole what has been smashed"; and who is caught in the storm "blowing from Paradise" that "irresistibly propels him into the future to which his back is turned, while the pile of debris before him grows skyward."[61] The antithetical historical visions of Bloch and Benjamin, who were friends, are the starting point of Hans Mayer's essay on *Fidelio*: "Beethoven and the Principle of Hope."[62] Predictably, Bloch wins out by having recognized the singular historical moment of the opera; and Beethoven for having realized the utopian bliss of the high couple (*das hohe Paar*)—despite the colportage, despite the Jacobean terror, despite the fact that Pizarro lives on. That was the last wish of the blind ninety-two-year-old philosopher, on the night before his death: to hear the third *Leonore* Overture with the trumpet signal. "Ernst Bloch cried at that last evening, when he heard the trumpet signal once again" reported Mayer and concluded movingly, "One has always reason to cry, when encountering them again: Beethoven, the high couple Leonore and Florestan, the principle of hope."[63] Tears of joy, we may assume.[64]

Benjamin did not die blessed by the fullness of age, but committed suicide in September 1940 with no hope of escaping from the Gestapo on his flight through the Pyrenees. Hence a reading that might remember his death and do justice to his historical vision would not hold up *Fidelio* as a moment of utopian *Vorschein*, but would explode that illusion from within. The tension between such Benjaminian and Blochian tendencies reflects the inner aporia of Adorno's philosophy of music, caught between critique and affirmation, demythologization and remythologization, ongoing Enlightenment and resuscitation of nature, Marxist materialism and messianic mysticism. Like Bloch and Benjamin, Adorno found utopia in traces—the "unassuming, irrelevant, and apocryphal" particular. And yet, as Rolf Tiedemann put it, "the philosopher of *Negative Dialectics* could not concede that hope is a *principle*."[65] If *Fidelio* signals a Blochian hope for a new star, that star makes a Benjaminian fall from the sky—for the sake of hope. Hearing the opera this way bears, in Benjamin's words, "the stamp of the critical, dangerous moment, which is the basis of all reading." It is a risk worth taking.

"Come hope, do not dim the last star of the weary." These words had not been part of the "Air" which Beethoven's librettist, Joseph Sonnleitner, adapted from Jean Nicholas Bouilly and Pierre Gaveaux's 1798 *Léonore ou l'amour conjugal* for their 1805 *Leonore, or The Triumph of Married Love*. Even after the libretto had been printed, Beethoven requested an extra quatrain of text, and composed it as a slow movement which he inserted after the first four lines of the "Air" (set as recitative) and the remainder of the text (set as a fast aria).[66] It is a beautiful moment, made to make a musical star shine—the star, Bloch asserted, "being Leonore herself."[67] But its brightness must be seen in light of another brilliant moment of the opera when Leonore cries out to make happen that for which she hoped. And the rift between the two, I will argue, is the very source of that hope.

Beethoven's heroine, of course, is both anxious to see her husband (prisoner of the tyrannical Pizarro) and afraid to be detected by the daughter of the prison's warden, Rocco, whose service she had entered in disguise. The double dilemma proved symptomatic for the opera itself. With Leonore playing the trouser role of Fidelio, *Fidelio* was in multiple dangers of being caught between *comédie larmoayante* and *tragédie bourgeoise*, between *Singspiel* and *opera seria*, between idyll and utopia, between colportage and high art, between the domestic and the public sphere, in short: between Revolution and Restoration.[68] Given such tensions, there has been no shortage of efforts to tilt the opera to the left and to salvage what Bloch called the music's "moral content."[69] Leonore's courage might even afford an opportunity to temper the much criticized image of Beethoven's heroic imagination as masculine, since her heroic deed coincides with the very moment she reveals herself as a woman. And yet, it seems impossible to resolve the opera's deep contradictions, ranging from its origin in Bouilly's Thermidorean libretto to Schiller's line in the final chorus (anticipating the finale of the Ninth), which celebrates the heroine along with the husband who once "conquered" her: "Wer ein holdes Weib *errungen*, stimm in unseren Jubel ein." If such rejoicing rings false today, *Fidelio* cannot be rescued. But Leonore might.

"Come hope, do not dim the last star of the weary." That this generates some of Beethoven's most glorious music matters, for opinions were varied as to whether his instrumental approach in *Fidelio* constituted an asset or a obstacle to the opera's dramatic vision. "How irrevocable it may be that *Beethoven's* music . . . awakens that infinite longing, which is the essence of Romanticism,—still, it is no less true that these powers may be attributed primarily to his instrumental music, and that he therefore does not succeed in vocal music precisely, perhaps, since it does not, because of the added words, allow for the character of indefinite yearning."[70] Alluding to E.T.A. Hoffmann's article on the Fifth, the

1823 reviewer of *Fidelio* for the Berlin *Zeitung für Theater und Musik* surely knew what was at stake when raising doubts about Beethoven's fitness for opera. Since "all the glamor" had fallen to the orchestra, he bemoaned "that [such] beautiful and excellent voices had to labor so hard as to become languid and weary in their struggle against any variety of string and wind instruments, without even in a single instant appearing independent and prevalent."[71]

In one of the fragments for the Beethoven book, Adorno reported that his wife had asked him "why composers, almost without exception, cling to vocal composition despite the spiritualization of music"; and that he had "tried to answer: because the transition from the vocal to the instrumental, the true spiritualization ('subjectification') of music through its reification, was infinitely difficult for humanity, so that composers have repeatedly and tentatively reversed this form of Enlightenment."[72] But then Adorno continued: "this is not a pure regression, for the vocal is inalienably *preserved* in all instrumental music. . . . The imagination of *all* music, and especially of instrumental music, is vocal. . . . Only angels could make music freely." For Adorno, this was not just "one of the innermost dialectical moments in Beethoven," but also "the *Ur*–phenomenon of all musical dialectics"—clearly a musical dialectics of Enlightenment. Implicit in it is the problem of language: "Music is name in the state of absolute impotence; it is also the remoteness of name to meaning, and both are the same thing."[73]

The notion of the Name is, of course, Benjamin's. The Name does for the ear what the constellation does for the eye: it recovers a magical connection to the material world.[74] In the name of the Name, Benjamin had refuted, on mystical grounds, both Plato's dualism and Edmund Husserl's doctrine of intentionality. Adam is the "father of philosophy" because his "action of naming things is so far removed from play or arbitrariness that it actually confirms the state of paradise as a state in which there is as yet no need to struggle with the communicative significance of words."[75] Hence philosophy must reclaim the word's "name-giving rights" and recover how "[i]deas are displayed, *without intention,* in the act of naming."[76] While Husserl had distinguished between "empirical" objects (which actually exist) and "intentional" objects (which exist in thought), Benjamin held that "truth is the death of intention"; that "[t]ruth is not an intent which realizes itself in empirical reality," but "the power which determines the *essence* of this empirical reality." Hence the "state of being, beyond all phenomenality, to which alone this power belongs, is that of the name."[77]

Music, for Adorno, tapped that power, despite being powerless. Music is both "name in the state of absolute impotence" and "the remoteness of name to meaning," because meaning already bears the alienating mark of mediation. This is how Adorno echoes Benjamin in a much-quoted passage from his fragment on music and words:

> The language of music is quite different from the language of intentionality. It contains a theological dimension. What it has to say is simultaneously revealed and concealed. Its idea is the divine Name which has been given shape. It is demythologized prayer, rid of efficacious magic. It is the human attempt, doomed as ever, to name the Name, not to communicate meanings.[78]

Here negative dialectics reveals its other side: negative theology. Adorno's music cuts across the messianic and materialist eschatologies: "[T]he holiness of music is its purity from dominance over nature; but its history is the inevitable development of that dominance as it became master of itself; its instrumentalization cannot be separated from its assumption of meaning."[79] And again Adorno appropriates his intellectual mentor with a characteristic twist: "Benjamin speaks of song, which may possibly rescue the language of birds as visual art rescues that of things. But this seems to me the achievement of *instruments* much rather than of song; for instruments are far more like the voices of birds than are human voices. The instrument *is* animation."[80] Animated, instruments can undo their instrumentalization, become voice, and close the gap between art and nature. This is why, for Adorno, the reconciliation of vocal nature and instrumental reason is the raison d'être of Leonore's Adagio as an instance of the "connection of the ethical to natural beauty."[81] Given that nature is both good and remote, Adorno noted that the "decisive dialectical category which is relevant here is that of *hope*, the key to the image of humanity."[82]

Hence, in *Fidelio,* the rescue of Florestan is synonymous with the rescue of natural beauty. Its alignment with *ethos* in Adorno's *Aesthetic Theory,* overturns a fundamental premise in Hegel's *Aesthetics,* where "the beauty of art is *higher* than nature."[83] For Adorno, however, "natural beauty vanished from aesthetics as a result of the burgeoning domination of the concept of freedom and human dignity."[84] According to the logic of the *Dialectic of Enlightenment,* the truth of such "freedom for the subject" is that it becomes "unfreedom for the other."[85] *Fidelio* figures that unfreedom doubly: through the abuse of public power and through domination in the domestic sphere. The arranged marriage with Marzelline threatens to lock Leonore into the suffocating idyll of the coming Biedermeier, whose calcified moral code is not only composed into the canon of the "Mir is so wunderbar" quartet ("How weak is the glimmer of hope" sings Leonore), but also in the pretty praises of matrimony in the Leonore/Marzelline duet, which had preceded Leonore's aria in 1805.[86] Cutting this duet clearly pushed the opera toward the heroic. Now Leonore's aria became a direct reaction to Pizarro's plans. Beethoven further tightened the dramatic progression in the 1814 version by composing a new recitative and by eliminating the spoken text that had preceded it.[87] Now the *Allegro con brio* of the Pizarro–Rocco duet is inflicted upon Leonore with great physical immediacy. The A major of the duet becomes the dominant of the recitative's dominant, whose violent thrust propels the harmonic progression along the circle of fifths deep into the recitative, where it does not come to rest until Leonore's outrage over Pizarro's barbaric oblivion toward "the voice of humanity" settles on a pleading B♭ major (ex. 1.1, m. 12). As if that energy had not run aground, her second outburst picks up A major again, initially following the same harmonic path, but the D-major sixth suddenly shifts to a C-major sixth together with a change in register, orchestration, and dynamics (tremolo strings in *forte* to sustained woodwinds in *piano*): "so leuchtet mir ein Farbenbogen, der hell auf dunkeln Wolken ruht."

Though it had been missing in Treitschke's draft, this evocative line creates the most significant dramatic transformation in the first act.[88] The rainbow, a sign of natural plentitude and of God's covenant with his people, gives rise to hope, as its "peaceful gaze mirrors" the golden times of the past ("der blickt so still, so friedlich nieder, der spiegelt alte Zeiten wieder"). *Alte Zeiten*, to be sure, figures doubly. Paradise lost. The white light of the sustained C-major chord, which harks back to the iridescent shimmer at the beginning of the E-major Overture (mm. 23–24), now envelops Leonore's melodic glance that looks up for help to heaven, just as Elsa will in *Lohengrin*. And heaven looks back with a brief melody in C major (*Adagio* and *poco sostenuto*), which slips away to the E-minor $\frac{6}{4}$ that initiates the modulation to the E major of the prayer. Thus the flat submediant appears in retrospect, as Susan McClary has noted in another context, to be "Arcadian."[89] Seen in this light, the C-major *Lichtblick* in the woodwinds foretells, like a celestial apparition, the opera's concluding "ode of matrimony" in the same key. Recollections of the beauty of nature nourish the promise of future happiness, just as Schiller's progressive path of history "leads to *Elyseum* the human being who now can no longer return to *Arcadia*."[90]

That is the definition of modern historical consciousness, where the imagination of utopia is a remembrance of paradise, quite in the way Benjamin defined the "dialectics of happiness" to unfold between "a hymnic and an elegiac form of happiness. The one: the unheard-of, the never-was, the summit of beatitude. The other: the eternal once-again, the eternal restoration of the originary, first happiness."[91] And so, without being "compromised by the Rousseauian *retournons*," for Adorno, "[a]uthentic artworks, which hold fast to the idea of reconciliation with

Example 1.1. Fidelio No. 9 Recitative and Aria mm. 1–55

nature by making themselves completely a second nature, have consistently felt the urge, as if in need of a breath of fresh air, to step outside of themselves. . . . Thus the last act of *Figaro* is played outdoors; and in *Freischütz,* Agathe, standing on the balcony, suddenly becomes aware of the starry night."[92] Hence the horns that open, so touchingly, Leonore's Adagio and Allegro (echoing the overture's introduction and exposition)

Example 1.1. (cont.)

Example 1.1. (cont.)

Example 1.1. (cont.)

Example 1.1. (cont.)

lend their voices to this stepping out into the open. And the E-major invocation of the star does bring to mind Beethoven's comment to Czerny about the E-major Adagio of the second Razumovsky Quartet, which "occurred to him while looking at the stars and thinking of the harmony of the spheres."[93]

By Beethoven's time, to be sure, obbligato instruments in opera already had a long tradition, as did charges of their excess preventing natural expression and intelligibility (think of the virtuosity in *opera seria* or the complexities of Mozart's *buffa* style). If the "pretty, if at the same time somewhat overloaded accompaniment" of the horns in Leonore's prayer was registered by reviewers,[94] such complaints were common enough to prompt the early nineteenth-century critic Amadeus Wendt to come to Beethoven's defense. Not *every* word needed to be heard in opera, because "the most characteristic music makes up for the missing word; vocal melody, instrumentation, and text mutually explain each other."[95] For instance: "We are lacking the words to describe Leonore's heavenly scene. . . . The *inner feeling [Innigkeit]* of the melody in the voice; the magnificent harmonic flow, the original accompaniment of the obbligato horns, which pervades all the nerves with a sweet shudder, and furthermore the fitting, richly felt key (E major)—all this has the combined effect of portraying exuberantly and inimitably hope's sweet solace, deepest longing, blissful remembrance of past days, and the uninhibited courage of the faithful wife."[96] And yet Wendt had no ear for the subtleties of the 1814 revisions: neither did he like the new recitative, for it "appeared to modulate insecurely"; nor the cut of the long coloratura in the Adagio, "which appeared to destroy beautiful passages in the melody"; nor the "small alteration" in the Allegro, where Beethoven cut almost a third, including its bravura cadence.[97]

But even if these changes were partly motivated by external circumstances (Anna Milder's refusal to perform "the unbeautiful, unsingable passages, unsuited to her voice"[98]), they served Beethoven by throwing into relief the one extended melisma that he kept and revised to great effect in the middle of the Adagio, when Leonore asks the star of hope to light up the "goal, however distant," so that "love will reach it." Here the vocal line detaches itself from the squarely constructed melody and its verbal component. The symbolism is apparent. This is the romantic trope of reaching out for the distant beloved with wordless voice, which becomes the extension of instrumental imagination. Beethoven gradually approaches the melodic climax in three phases, initiated, as it were, from the new measure 35 that concludes with a sixteenth-note ascent in the first horn (G♯-A-B-C♯). As if the star began to shine brighter and hope would gradually grow, the ascent is picked up in the first full measure of the melody, which hits $c\sharp^2$ twice on "Stern." While the top notes of phrases two and three move up to $e^2/d\sharp^2$ and $f\sharp^2/e^2$, it is not until the vocal melisma takes on the momentum of the ascending horn figure (now in thirty-second notes) that the melody reaches, in a three-measure extension of the third phrase, the high b^2.

That pitch, b^2, had been missing in the original version. Indeed, Beethoven may have eliminated two similar ascents from the instrumental introduction, because they would have taken away from the singular effect of the climax. And by splitting the overextended second phrase of the melody into two, moreover, he allowed the singer to catch her breath, while letting the horns invigorate the voice to bring the prayer to its apex. This climax in the middle of the *Gebeth* motivates the exuberant call to action in the Allegro, whose final flourish (the only one that Beethoven kept there) culminates on the same pitch. That note— luminous like those exposed b^3s in the Adagio of the second Rasumovsky quartet—is noteworthy. This is not merely because of its sonorous brilliance (as Berlioz remarked in his 1860 review of *Fidelio* while suggesting that many melodies by Rossini suffered from lacking *"la note"*),[99] but also because we will not hear it again until Florestan and Leonore reunite happily in the so-called *Jubelduet* ("O namenlose Freude"). Despite the different tonal contexts, the b^2 inspires a different kind of Schenkerian *Fernhören* where the pure absolute *Klang* transcends its immediate tonal context to articulate the dramatic link between hope and fulfillment.[100] Here, the breathlessly broken chords of "O namenlose Freude" almost appear like a programmed version of the horn figure in the opening Allegro section of Leonore's aria that Berlioz found so striking.[101] By cutting the original duet nearly in half and eliminating its recitative, Beethoven turned it into a true *Augenblick*, consumed in a flash as the lovers rush to the final climax, where the high B flares up only once, compared with the excessive outcries in 1804.[102] The composer of *Fidelio* seems to have become more sensitive to the strategic placement of vocal highpoints. And while this does not mean that the opera's dramatic work is done solely through extreme notes, they did highlight their respective numbers and the dramatic connections between them.

"Tödt erst sein Weib!" Few moments in opera match the dramatic power and immediacy of this scream. Throwing herself between Pizarro and her husband in the act 2 Quartet of *Fidelio*, Leonore exclaims on a bb^2: "Kill first his wife" (ex. 1.2). If Leonore's vision of the star was the inner peripeteia in act 1, this moment is the outer one in act 2. Here the high Bb sponsors a long-range connection, when it fulfills Florestan's vision of Leonore as the angel of rescue in the grand *Kerkerszene*, which moved from utmost despair to the fast section of delirious hope that Beethoven added. As Florestan hallucinates how his wife will lead him "to freedom, into the heavenly realm," the helpless husband hits his highest note, a bb^1, three times on "das himmlische Reich."

"Tödt erst sein Weib," then, would be—literally—"the angel's cry," to invoke the premise of Michel Poizat's book with the same title.[103] In *Fidelio*, the orchestra stops here with a marked shift from G major to an Eb-sixth chord on the downbeat. Leonore, it seems, must pierce through the music and silence it in order to effect a dramatic reversal. The pause

Example 1.2. Fidelio No. 14 Quartet mm. 77–86: Leonore's scream

Example 1.2. (cont.)

thus creates a caesura in Hölderlin's sense, altering the rhythmic flow of the music. Over the stunned responses of the three men ("Mein Weib?" "Sein Weib?") begins a striking double eighth note plus quarter note pulsation on Db/Eb in the oboes and bassoons—the very rhythm that drove the development of the E-major Overture toward the recapitulation. Its anapestic pulse counters the dactylic blows at the climax of Pizarro's opening solo: "as an avenger I stand before you" (see ex. 2, mm. 83ff. and ex. 1.3, mm. 42–48). But after Leonore's intervention, Pizarro's renewed fury is confronted by the same rhythm, now reinforced by the brass (mm. 106–14). If his was the rhythm of rage, hers is the rhythm of rescue: "Ja, sieh' hier Leonore!" Beethoven seems to have adjusted that line to make it scan onto this rhythm. (ex. 1.4). What is more, it becomes the rhythm of the trumpet call which Beethoven seems to emphasize by the extra repetitions in the revisions of the signal (ex. 1.5). Like the scream, the trumpet call again disrupts the quartet, announcing the arrival of Don Fernando. Hence the two caesuras function like cause and effect—with Bb to make that connection. Having silenced the orchestra with her scream, Leonore now silences Pizarro: "One more sound and you are dead."[104] Now we can hear the trumpet call.

Don Fernando's arrival, then, is no *deus ex machina*. Where Florestan had equated freedom with the *Himmelsreich*, Leonore's scream radically demythologizes the divine. The trumpet signal is no sign of heavenly intervention, but a consequence of human action.[105] It is Leonore who summons the minister, or in eschatological terms, the Messiah. The echo of her scream is the sound of the trumpet—whether it heralds Don Fernando or becomes the *tuba mirum spargens sonum* that Bloch heard here in analogy to the requiem liturgy.[106] Indeed, the scream reverberates through the orchestra until it is answered offstage. To do so, it takes on

Example 1.3. Fidelio No. 14 Quartet mm. 39–49: Pizarro's "rhythm of rage"

Example 1.4. Fidelio No. 14 Quartet mm. 84–85:
Leonore's "rhythm of rescue" 1805 and 1814

Example 1.5. Fidelio No. 14 Quartet mm. 127–29:
Trumpet call 1805 and 1814

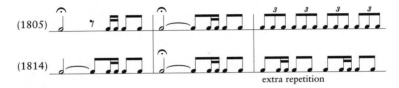

the rhythm of rescue: "Ja, sieh' hier Leonore!"

Between Leonore's scream and the trumpet call, then, the dialectic of vocal nature and instrumental reason comes to a standstill. It articulates the opera's moment of truth. Its power is that of the Name. At the moment when Leonore names her true identity, her cry abrogates the division between the noumenal and the phenomenal, between the autonomous and the functional, between will and representation, between the human and the divine, and between voice object and voice subject. For Wagner, the "indescribable effect" of this moment upon the listener is "the headlong plunge from one sphere to the other," and "its sublimity consists in our being given, as by a flash of lightning, a sudden glimpse into the nature of both spheres, the one the ideal, the other the real."[107] Yet Leonore's scream—turning the Schopenhauerian need into deed—is not just a moment of vocal *jouissance* (as Poizat would have it), but foremost one of dramatic action, whose effect is the trumpet call. This is no longer play, but politics; no longer music as "name in the state of absolute impotence," but music in the state of absolute power that can turn unfreedom into freedom. "The vocal is inalienably *preserved* in all instrumental music," we recall from Adorno: "only angels could make music freely." For a moment, Leonore seems to make that music to free Florestan.

This, then, is the opera's *Augenblick,* not the one Leonore named as such in the public sphere of the act 2 Finale as she removes Florestan's chains, singing, "Oh God what a moment!" and he answers, "Oh what unspeakably sweet happiness!" That moment, so celebrated by Bloch, already has an air of commemoration, and this not merely because the oboe's *Humanitätsmelodie* stems from Beethoven's cantata on the death of Emperor Joseph II, where it was associated with the words "Now mankind reaches to the light."[108] *Fidelio* possesses "a hieratic, cultic quality" Adorno wrote in the notes for his Beethoven monograph, adding in the margin: "The unity of the hieratic and the bourgeois in Beethoven is his *Empire* quality."[109] Hence in the opera "the Revolution is not depicted but reenacted as in a ritual. It could have been written to celebrate the anniversary of the Bastille. No tension, just the 'transformation' [added in margin:] '(Sacrifice!)' in Leonore's moment in gaol." [in margin:] "No 'conflict'. Action as mere working out."].[110]

The marginalia expose the cathartic instant of "Oh God what a moment" as empty commemoration. For the celebration of Leonore's *Augenblick* is no more than a ceremony recalling her original deed. It is introduced by the very deceptive cadence (Bloch's "sudden switch to a distant key") that introduced the first trumpet call. And the melismatic ascent to the high Bb that concludes the communal prayer is no more than an echo of the highpoint in Leonore's *Gebeth*. As a reprise of sorts, the public prayer is not only—in Adorno's words—"the seal of *idealism*" in Beethoven's music and "the pinnacle of the bourgeois spirit," but also as "aesthetically dubious" as the "thesis of identity in Hegel."[111] The opera's ostensibly intended moment of truth becomes its moment of untruth, its readiness to slip back into myth. Hence *Fidelio* fails to be "[a]n image of hope without the lie of religion."[112] To belie that lie, the opera's affirmative identity would have to be exploded from within, by the moment of the nonidentical.

How?

"Tödt erst sein Weib." In *Leonore,* Beethoven composed a B♮ on *Weib* creating a jarring dissonance against the Db/Eb in the woodwinds and second violins as well as the G in the basses (ex. 1.6).[113] Not until the piano score of 1810 did the B become Bb. An oversight by the composer, so prone to be inaccurate in his sketches and scores? Here this seems unlikely because the B appears not only in both the first violins and the violas, but Beethoven writes the pitch, as Helga Lühning has shown, with a letter "*h*" in the top margins of the autograph (fig. 1).[114] An elimination of a note difficult to sing in tune given the leap up from E♭ and the underlying harmony? Since Leonore's scream is an unheard-of dissonance in a diatonic context, Wilhelm Seidel has cast doubt on Beethoven's choice for a purely expressive dissonance: contemporaries would have heard it as a mistake and hence as a disturbance, rather than reenforcement, of the drama.[115] The chord surely is incorrect, but not necessarily meaningless (perhaps even not unintended). It is

Example 1.6. Leonore's scream in *Leonore*

Example 1.6. (cont.)

Figure 1. Leonore's "Tödt erst sein Weib" in Beethoven's autograph
of *Leonore,* D-Bsb Mus. ms autogr. Beethoven 3 B1. 77v reproduced with
permission of the Staatsbibliothek zu Berlin—Preußischer
Kulturbesitz—Musikabteilung mit Mendelssohn Archiv

not unlike the one in the middle of the *Eroica*'s first movement before
the onset of the "new" theme (mm. 276–79), where an "evil chord"
pronounces a "catastrophic impasse" and seeks to break it.[116] It stands
on the brink between the preceding G major (as V of C major) and the
first inversion of an E♭ dominant seventh.[117] While the G and B of the
voice belong to the former, E♭ and D♭ belong to the latter, turning the
merely ornamental chromatic neighbors C♯ and D♯ in the violins of mm.
77–79 into a sustained chord throbbing away in the woodwinds. Embedded in the harmony of the scream is the augmented triad (G-B-E♭),
spelled out in the ensuing questions of Florestan, Rocco, and Pizarro.
Significantly, B does not lead *up* to C, but *down* to B♭, on the last
syllable of "Ja, sieh hier Leonore!"—the very moment Fidelio reveals
himself/herself as Florestan's wife. To this extent it functions as C♭,
though never notated as such, leading to the E♭ dominant seventh,
whose long-range implications as a Neapolitan become apparent only
when the dominant has been firmly reached with the second statement
of "I swore solace to him, destruction to you."

In *Leonore*, the B♮ could be heard as a link between hope (her Aria), action (the Quartet), and fulfillment (the duet), where it resolves upward to the local tonic of C major (sometimes even considered the "tonic" of that version of the opera). Yet with the change to B♭ in *Fidelio*, Leonore's scream no longer connects with her private prayer, but with the public one (Table 1). True, it is only when the early and the later versions of this moment are laid over one another, like transparencies creating a palimpsest of sorts, that the philological detail speaks to the philosophical sense. It is only in hindsight that this whimsical difference might be perceived by the persistent eye, or ear, and speak to an impossible project: the futile reconciliation of personal happiness and political action that Georg Lukács saw in bourgeois literature, which "never found an artistically adequate means to unite the public and private spheres of life in its creations."[118] This impossibility is also reflected in the tension between Leonore's passive resistance and her active aggression, between shielding her husband and drawing a pistol on Pizarro. When Leonore "summons" Don Fernando, she also summons the king. However legitimate the hope of personal happiness envisioned in her aria, the liberation of Florestan is ultimately legitimized by higher authority. And however progressive the idea of a constitutional monarchy at the time, this endorsement from above puts *Fidelio* into the orbit of the Vienna Congress. Hence the resonance between "O Gott welch ein Augenblick" and the cantata *Der glorreiche Augenblick*, op. 136, celebrating that occasion. If anything, *Fidelio* only sharpened the drama's fundamental contradictions between its Jacobean and Josephinian aspirations, between its status as a *Revolutionsoper* and a *Kongressoper*, between its idealization of conjugal love and the realization of political engagement.

TABLE 1
Leonore's B and B♭

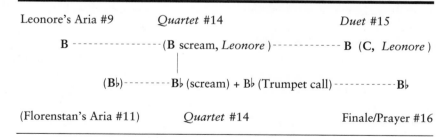

Leonore's Aria #9	Quartet #14	Duet #15
B - - - - - - - - - - - -(B scream, *Leonore*)- - - - - - - - B (C, *Leonore*)		
(B♭)- - - - - - - -B♭ (scream) + B♭ (Trumpet call) - - - - - - - - -B♭		
(Florestan's Aria #11)	Quartet #14	Finale/Prayer #16

Thus we might see Leonore as the mirror image of Zerlina, Adorno's *Moment musical* on the other side of the revolution. This was one of his most provocative insights: Zerlina is "no longer a shepherdess, but not yet a *citoyenne*"; she "reflects a humanity which both could not be mutilated by feudal force and would be protected from bourgeois barbarity."[119] Hence the light that she sheds on her seducer. Does she not learn the art of seduction from him, as Mozart implies, by molding her two arias on the two-part form of the Duettino? Are they not duets of sorts, as the first one suggests in the obbligato cello of an angry Masetto, who joins later— reconciled—into her melody? Does not Don Giovanni, for once poised between libertine and liberator, awaken her sexuality and create that moment between licence and liberty where the beating of the "Batti, batti" can turn into the "sentilo battere"—the beating of the heart in "Vedrai carino"? Where Zerlina "halts the rhythm of rococo and revolution," Leonore would seem to halt the rhythm of revolution and restoration. In that sense, she too could be "forever the image of history standing still," just as "natural beauty is suspended history" (*sistierte Geschichte*).[120] But Leonore's *moment musical* is no musical moment: its utopia lies suspended in the impossible connection between her prayer for hope and the communal prayer of thanksgiving; or between what Benjamin called the elegiac and the hymnic forms of happiness; or between the *not yet* and the *no longer* of the opera's star. To connect these two, there would have to be a note that is both B and B♭. That is the measure of the nonidentical.

But even if we consider the impossible tone B♭/B merely as an improbable conclusion (certainly not as the foundation) of such a reading of *Fidelio,* a nagging question remains. Has the interpretive power of such a nonexisting note not already evaporated under the interpretive pressure generated by a Benjaminian overdetermination, whose despair calls for a desperate hermeneutic: one that is driven not by the past, but the present? "To articulate the past historically," wrote Benjamin in the sixth of his *Theses on the Philosophy of History,* "does not mean to recongnize it 'the way it really was' (Ranke). It means to seize hold of a memory as it flashes up at the moment of danger. Historical materialism wishes to retain that image of the past which unexpectedly appears to the historical subject at the moment of danger. The danger affects both the content of the tradition and its receivers. The same threat hangs over both: that of becoming a tool of the ruling classes. In every era the attempt must be made anew to wrest tradition away from a conformism that is about to overpower it. The Messiah comes not only as the redeemer, he comes as the one who overcomes the Antichrist. Only *that* historian, who is firmly convinced that even the dead will not be safe from the enemy if he wins, will have the gift of fanning the spark of hope in the past. And this enemy has not ceased to be victorious."[121]

At first glance, the rejection of historicism in favor of materialist historiography has ripe and ready ramifications: to show solidarity with the oppressed.[122] The materialist historian, who seizes a memory "which unexpectedly appears to the historical subject at the moment of danger," is like Leonore, who seizes the rainbow. The materialist historian, who will have "the gift of fanning the spark of hope in the past" and "is firmly convinced that even the dead will not be safe from the enemy," will be like Leonore, who does not know whether her husband is dead or alive. And if this memory of Leonore reminiscing configures a messianic moment for us, we too could be materialist historians.

But a disturbing threat hangs over those who pin as much hope on Leonore as she did on the rainbow: "that of becoming a tool of the ruling classes." Or worse, of the dictators. As Thomas Mann noted in September 1945: "What amount of apathy was needed [by musicians and audiences] to listen to *Fidelio* in Himmler's Germany without covering their faces and rushing out of the hall!"; or what kind of dullness needed to attend the performance Furtwängler was to conduct to celebrate the liberation of Germany from Jewry.[123] Asking "with whom the adherents of historicism actually empathize," Benjamin remarked upon the *tristesse* that results from the answer: "with the victor."[124] One cannot underestimate the power of sympathy in the hands of those in power. In that sense especially, *Fidelio*'s message remains deeply ambiguous. The sudden conversion of the dutiful public servant, Rocco, should at least make skeptical those who believe too firmly in the opera's—and history's—happy end. "There is no document of culture," Benjamin believed, "which is not at the same time a document of barbarism. And just as such a document is not free of barbarism, barbarism also taints the manner in which it was transmitted from one owner to another. A historical materialist therefore dissociates himself from it as far as possible. He regards it as his task to brush history against the grain."[125] Although the resurrection of historical materialism is passé, the critical project of exposing art's barbaric motivations and appropriations has not lost its urgency. Still, not all art is an accomplice to barbarism. It can also document barbarism itself: by laying it bare.

To conclude, then, the other poem, a sonnet written by Albrecht Haushofer, who was an "eminently gifted, indeed brilliant, man with considerable artistic gifts.[126] He followed in the footsteps of his father, Carl Haushofer, "the well-known founder of the German school of 'geopolitics' which, combining a hard-nosed correlation of geography and politics with expansionist designs, exerted a considerable influence upon Nazi ideologists." Albrecht was "determined to play an active part in the formulation of the foreign policies of his country during the Third Reich." Indeed, "[h]is disdain of National Socialism, its vulgarity as well as its brutality, in part precipitated by the fact that his mother was of half-Jewish ancestry, was not to stand in the way of his sense of mission, let alone ambition. In fact, he owed his position of prominence largely to Rudolf Hess, the Führer's deputy, who, a grateful disciple of Haushofer's *père*, took it upon himself to declare Albrecht and his younger brother Heinz honorary Aryans." Thus "Haushofer's way through the labyrinth of agencies concerned with the formulation of Nazi foreign policy gave him direct access to the highest leaders of the Third Reich, especially Hess, Ribbentrop, and even Adolf Hitler." But Haushofer's "deep misgivings about the Nazis" had led him "as early as 1940 into the orbit of the Resistance," where he established contact with the Communist *Rote Kapelle* group as well as the Kreisau Circle. With the failure of the July 1944 coup on Hitler "Haushofer's fate was sealed. After spending more than four months in hiding as a fugitive, he was hounded down by the Gestapo early in December." Because of his expertise in foreign policy, however, "he was kept alive by Himmler throughout the early months of 1945 in the expectation that he might be useful in negotiations for a separate peace with the Western Allies."

"A story goes that when as a young boy he was asked what his aim was in life, Albrecht Haushofer responded that he wanted to become a German foreign minister." While in Gestapo custody, Haushofer told a fellow inmate after a hearing "that he was confronted with two menaces: 'either the firing squad or the appointment to be the last foreign minister of the Nazi Reich.'" "But finally, in the night of 22–23 April 1945, as the Russian troops were closing in on the German capital, having been formally released from the Moabit gaol together with seven of his fellow prisoners, Haushofer was herded by an SS gang to a nearby bomb site and brutally shot in the back of the neck." Three weeks afterwards, Heinz Haushofer found his brother's body at the execution site, holding in one hand a bundle of papers. They were a collection of eighty sonnets which Albrecht had written in prison. Number 21 bears the title "Fidelio":

Fidelio

Albrecht Haushofer

Ein Kerker. Einer, der das Böse will.
Ein Todgeweihter. Kämpfend, eine Frau.
Ein heller Klang durchdringt den dunklen Bau,
und einen Atem lang sind alle still.

In allem Zauber von Musik und Bühne
wird keinem Ruf so reiner Widerhall
wie diesem herrischen Trompetenschall:
Dem Guten Sieg, dem Bösen harte Sühne.

Geborgen steigen sie empor ins Licht,
gegrüßt von denen, die gefesselt waren,
geleitet von befreienden Fanfaren.

Im Leben gibt es diese Töne nicht.
Da gibt es nur ein lähmendes Verharren.
Danach ein Henken, ein Im-Sand-Verscharren.

Fidelio

A dungeon. Someone who wants evil.
A man fated to die. Fighting, a woman.
A bright sound pierces the dark building,
and for a breath's length everyone is still.

In all the magic of music and stage
no call reverberates with such pure echo
as this imperious trumpet blast:
triumph to the good, hard penance to the evil.

They climb securely up into the light,
greeted by those who were in fetters,
accompanied by liberating fanfares.

In life there are no tones like these.
There is only a paralyzing perseverance.
And then a hanging, a burying-in-sand.[127]

In an uncanny way, this poem anticipated the fate of its author, who understood the dilemma of being caught between resistance and collaboration as a distant reflex of *Fidelio's* dilemma. The caesura that separates, with an almost lapidary matter-of-factness, the final tercet from the rest of the sonnet not only stands between *Fidelio* and reality, but points back to the opera itself. It demarcates death and dystopia—what Bloch called *Nicht-Utopie*. If the trumpet call is the most decisive breaking-in of utopia into reality, Haushofer's sonnet has the sobering effect of reality breaking into utopia. This is suspension suspended; the moment of the whole undone by the moment of the particular. After reading the poem, it will be impossible to hear *Fidelio* ever again as an untainted representation of utopian humanity, nor the *Siegessymphonie* that makes Egmont's head fall *freudig*—happily—as an example of heroic death.

And yet, this does not spell the end of art after Auschwitz. Haushofer's sonnet speaks for the necessity of art against art for the sake of utopia. We may—must—cling to it in the way its author clutched the poems to his heart at the moment of his murder. "In life there are no tones like

these." Only this line, perhaps, might warrant the interpretive pressure put on the nonexisting note which could undercut Beethoven's heroic opera from within. It gives a terrible ring to that impossible tone, which is less a tangible symptom than an intangible symbol of the work's many contradictions. There is no microscope strong enough to resolve it, no telescope large enough to capture the ray of its falling star. It makes the opera, in Benjamin's words, "destined for sublime irony," which gathers a glimpse of messianic light from the inaudible trace of musical matter: "Only for the sake of the hopeless have we been given hope."

Chapter 2

SCHUMANN'S DISTANCE

Philosophy is prose. Its consonants. *Distant* philosophy sounds like poetry—because every call into the distance becomes a vowel. On both of its sides or, surrounding philosophy, lies + [*sic*] and minus poetry. Thus, in the distance everything becomes *poetry—poem. Actio in distans.* Distant mountains, distant people, distant events, etc., everything becomes romantic, quod idem est—from this results our essentially poetic nature.[1]

In these few fragmentary phrases, Novalis gives a definition of the Romantic, where distance does not make all the difference, but the difference for all: "in the distance everything becomes . . . romantic." This is a rather large claim. How could one possibly define the Romantic from a single perspective? As a pan-European phenomenon, Romanticism constitutes an unstable constellation of aesthetic categories (such as the arabesque and the fragment), poetic images and tropes (the blue flower, the wanderer, and the lost love), themes and genres (landscape painting, the song cycle, and the gothic novel), figures of thought (irony and *Witz*), utopian ideologies (the united Christendom), nationalist fantasies (the unification of both Italy and Germany), and modes of social behavior (the autonomous artist, the salon, and the *Davidsbund*). In this larger context, any attempt to define the Romantic through distance would seem to dissipate. Romantic distance is primarily a poetic trope and an aesthetic category. No more.

And no less. Novalis's use of distance captures the imagination of the musician: distant philosophy *sounds* like poetry. Dying away into the distance, prose turns into poetry, speech into vocalise, language into music. Distance, then, effects on a material level what has become a commonplace of romantic and romanticizing aesthetics: that "all art," as Walter Pater famously put it, "constantly aspires towards the condition of music."[2] That music reigned supreme in Romanticism hardly needs new confirmation, but it seems worthwhile to pursue how the new prestige of music grew, in part, out of the aesthetics of sound dying away in the distance. Therefore, the first section of this chapter will demonstrate the deep affinity between Novalis's definition of the Romantic through distant sound and Jean Paul's *Aesthetics* as well as his novel *Flegeljahre*, which, in turn, inspired Robert Schumann's own musical manifesto of Romanticism, *Papillons*, op. 2.

"In the distance everything becomes . . . romantic." Again, not everything. Yet with distant mountains, distant events, and distant people, Novalis chose to illustrate romantic distance with three archetypical experiences: spatial distance in landscape, temporal distance in recollection of the past, and personal distance in separation from the distant beloved. While romantic distance has prompted musicological studies of what Richard Kramer has called "a poetics of the remote"—from Beethoven's *An die ferne Geliebte* to Franz Schreker's *Der ferne Klang*—the focus of this chapter will remain on the music and aesthetics of Schumann as inspired by Jean Paul and, by extension, Novalis.[3] Indeed, Novalis's three examples for romantic distance resonate with some of Schumann's most emphatically romantic piano compositions examined below in sections 3 to 5: "distant events" with the textuality of musical memory in the "Aria" from the Sonata in F♯ Minor; "distant mountains" with the relation between music and landscape in "Wie aus der Ferne," the penultimate piece from *Davidsbündlertänze;* and "distant people" with the attempt to overcome the separation from his beloved Clara in the *Fantasie* and the *Novelletten.*

But how can the link be made between the Romantic defined through distance to romantic distance embodied in Schumann's music—in other words, from philosophy to *distant* philosophy? Distant philosophy, or for that matter distant prose, retains what the term they stand for— poetry—inevitably erases: namely, that poetry is a kind of prose, but transformed. Whereas the conjunction of poetry and prose appears to be a strict dichotomy, prose and *distant* prose seem closer: there remains a gap between the latter two, but the gap might be bridged. Such a bridge is of particular importance when it comes to music, which romantic aesthetics has tended to privilege as an untranslatable language: there is, as Carl Dahlhaus has shown, an inner kinship between the music of *poésie absolue* and the language of absolute music.[4] Physically, distance makes music out of language, creating, metaphysically (not necessarily in a transcendental sense), the language of music. But a language it is, albeit a distant one. Distance may transform language into music, yet music remains under the spell of language, which must spell out its meaning when trying to bridge that distance. At the beginning of the nineteenth century, that task became more complicated, since it was on the level of language *about* music that the dichotomy between prose and poetry returned: in the opposition between prosaic analysis and poetic criticism. Because Schumann, as a very self-conscious music critic, struggled with this issue, section 2 of this chapter will reexamine his strategies as a way of preparing our dealings with the distance between composition and commentary, as well as analysis and criticism in his own works. Whether or not music is an untranslatable language or a translatable text, however, this chapter seeks to illustrate that the link between music and *logos,* either severed or sutured, continues to be the lifeline of musicology.

Defining the Romantic Through Distance: Novalis, Jean Paul, Schumann

Novalis: actio in distans

"*Distant* philosophy sounds like poetry." The opening quotation stems, again, from Novalis's *Das allgemeine Brouillon,* whose poetic epistemology[5] juxtaposes two different ideas under the rubric *Philosophie:* the transformation of language into sound and the concept of *actio in distans* (action at a distance). In combining the two, Novalis arrived at a definition of the Romantic. The source for his idea of transforming language into sound was a 1791 treatise by Christian Gottlieb Schocher, who proposed a new kind of declamation based on a "scale" of the vowels a, e, i, o, u, with the *Umlaute* ä, ö, ü equivalent to half steps.[6] Schocher's treatise resonates with early nineteenth-century manuals instructing mothers how to teach their children to read. The new pedagogy no longer treated language as a visual phenomenon, but rather as an aural one—a tendency that coincided with efforts to eliminate dialects in favor of a universal German *Hochsprache.*[7] Novalis appropriated Schocher's idea of a melody of vowels for his own notion of speech, reasserting its original primacy over writing. The dichotomy between prose and poetry functioned within the context of a triadic historical model in which prose represented a transitional stage from the naive and natural Golden Age to the poetic era of the future. Thus the music of pure vowels, which surrounds philosophical prose as "+ [sic] and minus poetry," not only is reminiscent of the childlike *Ursprache,* but also anticipates the universal language: "Our language—it was originally more musical and has only gradually become prosaic—so *toneless.* It has become now more a kind of *reverberation [Schallen]—noise [Laut],* if one wants to debase this beautiful word. It needs to become *song* again. *Consonants* transform *tone into reverberation.*"[8]

Novalis may have encountered the concept of *actio in distans,* which sought to explain the attraction and repulsion of noncontiguous bodies, in Newton's theory of gravity. Kant later defined it in his treatise

Metaphysische Anfangsgründe der Naturwissenschaft (1786) as follows: "The action of one matter upon another outside of contact is action at a distance (*actio in distans*). This action at a distance, which is also possible without the mediation of matter lying in between, is called immediate action at a distance, or the *action* of matters on one another *through empty space.*"[9] Novalis's understanding of action at a distance was undoubtedly influenced by Friedrich Wilhelm Schelling's *Ideen zu einer Philosophie der Natur,* published in 1797, whose sequel, *Von der Weltseele,* he studied immediately upon its appearance in 1798. In the preface to *Von der Weltseele,* Schelling gave an idealist reading of *actio in distans:* "Idealism, which philosophy is gradually introducing into all the sciences . . . still seems intelligible to few. The concept, for example, of *action at a distance,* which to many is still a stumbling-block, rests entirely on the idealist conception of space."[10] Inspired by this idealist fusion of natural science and philosophy, Novalis combined it with Schocher's system of articulation in order to create a poetic system of all sciences that would supersede a work of seminal importance to the *Frühromantik:* Johann Gottlieb Fichte's *Die Grundlage der gesammten Wissenschaftslehre* of 1794–95. Thus Novalis noted, "Words are partly vowels—partly consonants—valid and nonvalid words. Application to scientific constructions. Substantial (vocalic) principles and sciences—accidental (consonantic) principles and sciences."[11]

Novalis mapped this phonetic classification onto philosophy: "*distant* philosophy sounds like poetry—because every call into the distance becomes a vowel." This "vocalic" philosophy is opposed to philosophy as prose, or "consonantic" philosophy. "Not until the philosopher appears as Orpheus" will history organize itself into a true and meaningful system of sciences.[12] When the philosopher becomes a musician, one might say, science sings. Shortly before *Das allgemeine Brouillon* breaks off, Novalis acknowledged *actio in distans* as a universal principle of poetic transformation: "All actions, even those of thinking, will be traced back to *actio in distans.*"[13]

Jean Paul: Beautiful Infinity

The Romantic is beauty without limit, or *beautiful* infinity, just as there is a *sublime* infinity. . . . It is more than an analogy to call the Romantic the undulating hum of a vibrating string or bell, whose sound waves fade away into ever greater distances and finally are lost in ourselves, and which, although outwardly silent, still sound within. In the same way moonlight is both image and instance of the Romantic.[14]

Thus Jean Paul defined the Romantic in his 1804 *Vorschule der Ästhetik*. In October 1798, he had met Novalis, who was then busily working on *Das allgemeine Brouillon*. They might have exchanged ideas. Notwithstanding the differences between Novalis's speculative esotericism and Jean Paul's more vivid and concrete imagery, they each placed distance at the heart of the Romantic. To be sure, Jean Paul's definition also relied on a quite different tradition. His notion of "beautiful infinity" was a paradox in terms of eighteenth-century aesthetics: for Burke and Kant, infinity belonged to the realm of the sublime, itself distinguished from the beautiful. Moreover, whereas Kant had associated the beautiful with definite boundaries (*Begrenztheit*), and the sublime with boundlessness (*Unbegrenztheit*),[15] Jean Paul's example for beautiful infinity—the dying sound—forges their formal distinction into a contradictory closure within open form. His solution is a *double* ending. Because the sensual perception of the dying sound is limited, it is projected through the power of imagination into an ideal infinity, so that it, "although outwardly silent, still sounds within."

As a corollary to this suspension of the boundary between the phenomenal and noumenal worlds, Jean Paul also obliterates the difference between metaphor and event, or between the figurative and the real. The sound fading away is "more than an analogy"; like moonlight, it is both image and instance (*Bild* and *Beispiel*), both emblem and embodiment of the Romantic. Jean Paul spelled out this metaphysics of presence when he expanded on his understanding of the dying sound in his *Kleine Nachschule zur ästhetischen Vorschule* (an accumulation of afterthoughts to his *Vorschule* which he did not prepare for publication until 1825, the year of his death):

> Music . . . is romantic poetry for the ear. Like the beautiful without limit, this [romantic poetry] is less a delusion of the eyes, of which the boundaries do not fade away as indeterminably as those of a dying sound. No color is as romantic as a sound, since one is present at the dying away only of a sound but not of a color; and because a sound never sounds alone, but always threefold, blending, as it were, the romantic quality of the future and the past into the present.[16]

In comparison with visual perception, then, the auditory is superior. This was one reason why romantic aesthetics considered music the most privileged of the arts, and believed all arts should aspire to music's expressiveness. Like the extension of tone into ideal space, the resolution of future and past into the present results in the unlimited expansion of time within a single instant of the temporal continuum. Jean

Paul's notion of musical time as both moment and movement—a paradox that phenomenologists have wrestled with since Husserl—originates in the acoustics of specific instruments. The bell, for instance, is "calling the romantic spirits" because its sound reverberates the longest, just as the horn and the flute carry over long distances.[17]

Since distance narrows the gap between the phenomenal and noumenal, distant music—fading away or coming from afar—often evokes memories in Jean Paul's novels, as if he had composed out his own (and implicitly Novalis's) program of romantic distance—whether generally:

> The distant bells of the village were calling, like beautiful, dying-away times, over into the dark shouting of the shepherds in the fields.[18]

or specifically evoking memories of distant people or events:

> Suddenly an old, familiar, but wonderful chiming of the bells at midday emanated from the distance, an old sounding as from the starry morning of his dark childhood; . . . full of yearning he thought of his distant parents, the still-life of his childhood—and the gentle Wina.[19]

Often Jean Paul even joins landscape with sound, which—dying—holds distance and nearness in suspension:

> From the thunderstorm he turned again toward the multicolored sunny countryside—a breeze from the east carried the sounds—swam with them to the sun—on the flowering evening clouds the little echo, the lovely child, repeated quietly his playing. . . . Heavy and slumbering the sun swam on the sea—it was drawn down—its golden aura glowed away in the endless blue void—and the echoing sounds lingered and died away on the glow.[20]

Thus emblematic of the Romantic in Jean Paul's aesthetics and embodied in his novels, sound, both dying and distant, surely did not go unheard by one of his most avid musical readers, and certainly the most prominent: Robert Schumann.

Robert Schumann: The Dying Sound

"The Romantic is beauty without limit, or *beautiful* infinity, just as there is a *sublime* infinity." Schumann chose these lines as a motto for the *Neue Zeitschrift für Musik,* only three weeks after his famous proclamation of a "young poetic future" in the editorial of the 1835 New Year's issue (he had just taken over the journal as sole editor).[21] These mottos have attracted little attention, although they had been announced as an integral part of the journal.[22] Schumann assiduously collected maxims, aphorisms, and striking phrases for this purpose in the so-called mottobook, a fascinating source of information about his reading habits, literary preferences, and aesthetic views.[23] His choice of this very excerpt from Jean Paul's *Vorschule* is remarkable because he noted in the margin of the mottobook, "Definition des Romantischen" ("Definition of the Romantic").[24] Jean Paul's definition not only epitomized Schumann's idea of a "young poetic future," but also encapsulated the aesthetic background of its first *musical* manifesto, the *Papillons,* op. 2, inspired, in turn, by his favorite of Jean Paul's novels, *Flegeljahre,* itself the poetic *pendant* to the *Vorschule.* Indeed, it appears that Jean Paul's definition of the Romantic, as formulated in the *Vorschule,* left its mark on the ending of *Flegeljahre* and was, by extension, composed out in the ending of Schumann's *Papillons.*

As is well known, Schumann's own copy of *Flegeljahre* bears annotations associating individual numbers of *Papillons* with passages in the novel's penultimate chapter.[25] Here, the main protagonists, the brothers Walt (a poet) and Vult (a musician), attend a masked ball with the woman they both love: Wina. The ball is the dénouement of the novel, where Wina finally settles for Walt, after which Vult wanders off into the world. Schumann marked ten passages: most of these do not relate easily to musical details, let alone account for the two remaining numbers of the dozen in the cycle; moreover, it is unclear whether Schumann annotated his copy before or after he finished the work.[26] If Schumann's marginalia fail to yield an explicit correspondence between *Flegeljahre* and *Papillons,* his choice of the novel's last sentence as the cycle's motto does: "Enchanted, Walt heard the vanishing sounds still speaking from afar: for he did not notice his brother vanishing with them. End of J. Paul's *Flegeljahre.*"[27] Although deleted from the published score, the motto provides access to the work's aesthetic subtext.

To facilitate the critical reception of his daring new work, Schumann advised his friends, family, and potential reviewers to read the ending of *Flegeljahre* as a key to understanding the unusual cycle. As he wrote to Friedrich Rellstab, music critic of the *Vossische Zeitung* and editor of *Iris im Gebiet der Tonkunst:*

> Less for the sake of the editor of *Iris* than for the poet and kindred spirit with Jean Paul, I take the liberty of adding a few words about the origin of *Papillons,* since the thread that connects them is hardly visible. You will recall the last scene of *Flegeljahre*—dance of the masks—Walt—Vult—masks—Wina—Vult's dancing—the exchange of masks— confessions—anger—revelations—running away—final scene and then the brother's walking away.[28]

If, however, in a letter to Ignaz Castelli of the *Allgemeiner musikalischer Anzeiger Wien,* Schumann even quoted the last sentence of the novel, his original motto,[29] why, then, did he abandon it before publication? His remarks to Henriette Voigt suggest a possible answer:

> If you ever have a free minute, please read the last chapter of Flegeljahre, where everything stands in black and white even to the giant boot in F♯ minor (at the end of the Flegeljahre I feel as though the play (to be sure) were over but the curtain not fallen.)—I will mention also that I have set the text to the music, not the reverse—otherwise it seems to me a "foolish beginning." Only the last one, which playful chance formed as an answer to the first, was inspired by Jean Paul. Another question. Are not the *Papillons* clear to you in themselves? I am interested in learning this.[30]

How sure was Schumann that the *Papillons* were clear "in themselves"? He had certainly been willing to publish them without the motto, but his assertion to Voigt, that it was foolish to begin a composition with a text, seems to mask his ambivalence about the matter, since his music was (and continued to be) at least partly inspired by texts. Moreover, he repeatedly manifested curiosity about the correspondence between some musical language and the verbal responses to it. In directing some listeners to the ending of *Flegeljahre,* what did he expect them to find in *Papillons?*

Worth pursuing is Schumann's hint to Voigt that only the last piece was actually inspired by Jean Paul. A trace of that inspiration might be found in the seemingly insignificant change he made by replacing the novel's "aus der Gasse herauf" (from the street) with the motto's "aus der Ferne" (from afar). Since this variant also occurs in the letter to Castelli, it may be more than a slip of Schumann's memory, to which Gustav Jansen attributed it.[31] The alteration adds a more poetic flavor to the way Walt hears Vult's vanishing music: as distant music, thus highlighting its specifically "romantic" dimension. Indeed, the explicit invocation of distance suggests a reading of *Papillons*'s ending that not only takes the usually neglected last chapter of *Flegeljahre* into account, but also connects it with Jean Paul's definition of the Romantic in both the *Vorschule der Ästhetik* and, as we will see, the *Kleine Nachschule.*

The last chapter of *Flegeljahre* concludes with a dream that Walt recounts to his brother during the night after the ball. As a fantastic tour de force overflowing with the mixture of allegories and symbols typical of Jean Paul's virtuosic style, the dream effectively resists easy interpretation and thwarts an unequivocal conclusion to the novel (Jean Paul had originally planned a continuation). In a dense stream of images, Walt dreams of the changing relationships among the three protagonists played out at the ball. Schumann must have been struck by their eventual metamorphosis into tones—separating and uniting. Symbolizing separation and departure, flowers first become children engaged in the play of love (an image of the ball), and then stars, of which the departing star is further transformed into the fading evening glow: "'Stay with me, my child, when you leave me,' the staying child said. Then, in the distance, the departing child turned into a small evening glow; then into a little evening star; then, further into the countryside, into merely a shimmer of the moon without the moon; and, finally, further and further into the distance, it faded into the tone of a flute or a philomela."[32] Jean Paul's choice of the flute is not surprising: it is Vult's instrument. And distance, as another passage of *Flegeljahre* has it, "is the foil of the flute."[33] But the puzzling alternative—"the tone of a flute *or* a philomela"—renders the passage ambiguous, which, after all, is only characteristic of a dream (Walt does not yet know the outcome of the ball). Since Vult had compared Wina with the tone of a philomela earlier in the novel, the departing glow-become-tone could stand for both Vult and Wina: Vult leaving his brother, and Wina leaving Vult.[34] For all three of them, however, nightfall symbolizes the irreversible change from adolescence to adulthood. Then comes dawn, but doubled—the new couple, Walt and Wina:

> Facing dawn, another dawn arose. Uplifting the heart, both were rushing toward each other like choirs, with sounds instead of colors, as if un-known, radiant beings would sing their joyful songs from behind the earth. . . .

> Now the choirs of dawn were thundering toward each other, and every thunderbolt ignited a more powerful one. Two suns were to arise, in the sound of morning. Behold, when they wanted to come, the sound became softer and softer, then quiet everywhere. Amor flew from the East, Psyche from the West, and they met in the middle of the sky. And both suns were rising—they were only two soft tones, two tones dying and awakening to each other; perhaps they sounded: "You and I."[35]

The difference between dusk and dawn in the dream holds a special place in Jean Paul's view of the Romantic; it could well be that a passage as prominent as this one in *Flegeljahre* may have prompted him to specify the aesthetic implications of this difference in the *Kleine Nachschule*, in the very section (quoted above) that had begun "Music . . . is romantic poetry for the ear." He continues:

> To the eye, beauty without limit appears best as moonlight, this wonderful light of the spirit, which is akin neither to the sublime nor to the beautiful, and which penetrates us with a painful longing, like an eternity that can never dawn on earth. Therefore, the evening glow is romantic, but the dawn sublime or beautiful. And both are banners of the future: the former announcing the most distant, the latter the nearest, future. Thus a bound-

Example 2.1. (a) *Papillons,* op. 2, no. 1 mm. 1–4

less green plain is as romantic as distant mountains; while near mountains and the desert are sublime.

The realm of the Romantic is, in fact, divided into the morning realm of the eye and the evening realm of the ear, and in this it compares to its relative, the dream.[36]

Again, Jean Paul maps poetic images onto aesthetic categories, associating dawn with the old dichotomy between the sublime and the beautiful, and evening glow with the new aesthetics of the Romantic. Its dying color inhabits the realm of the ear and that of the dream, just as in *Flegeljahre*'s dream the evening glow mutated into the tone of the flute.

Flegeljahre does not end with the dream, but with Walt waking up to hear, enraptured, how his brother fulfills the dream: playing his flute, Vult goes away. Thus the novel literally closes on a romantic note, not only with sound dying away—Romanticism as defined in the *Vorschule*—but also with moonlight metamorphosing into sound: Romanticism as refined in the *Nachschule*. Was Schumann aware of the connection? He knew the *Vorschule* as early as 1828,[37] drawing the motto from it for the *Neue Zeitschrift* in 1835. It is not certain when he read the *Nachschule,* but it has not been noted previously that Schumann marked in his own copy the very passage that follows up on the motto. Thus it can be safely assumed that he understood the complementary connection between the passage he marked and the motto he took from the *Vorschule*. And one may reasonably speculate that he also understood how the dream in *Flegeljahre* embodied the distinction drawn in the *Nachschule* between sublime or beautiful dawn on the one hand and romantic dusk on the other.

Given the musical symbolism of the dream and its aesthetic implications, the ending of *Papillons* appears in a new light. It begins when the unexpected return of the first number suspends the music of the Finale, the so-called *Großvatertanz* (ex. 2.1a). Since Walt is the protagonist of the passage Schumann had marked in the previous chapter from *Flegeljahre* as number 1, and since Schumann names Walt first in the narrative sequence offered to Rellstab, one can safely associate Walt

Example 2.1. (b) *Papillons,* op. 2, no. 12, "Finale" mm. 47–91

with the first number of *Papillons*. But Walt's music is only his mask—a papillon—like the "psyche fluttering up over the withered body."[38] The difference is important in light of the ball's ending and its symbolic replay in the dream. To recapitulate, the ball ends with Vult first trading his mask with Walt, then taking the last dance with Wina, and finally pressing her into a declaration of her love—to Walt's mask. Thus the return of the first number in the Finale is a double reminiscence: both of the past and of Walt. Moreover, when the last dance returns in the left hand in measure 31, both tunes seem to dance together, as if representing varying constellations (because Vult is wearing Walt's mask): Wina and who she thinks is Walt, or Wina and who she does not know is Vult. Since the two tunes die away together over a tonic pedal to which Schumann added the six strokes of the clock announcing the end of the ball at dawn (ex. 2.1b), he might have heard this ending through the symbolism of the dream: "two tones dying and awakening to each other; perhaps they sounded: 'You and I.'" The "perhaps" points to the ambiguity of this "You and I." What the two tones/tunes do depends on the double meaning of Walt's mask: whereas the love between Wina and Walt is awakening, the love between Wina and Vult is dying.

In an earlier version of the ending, preserved in one of Schumann's sketchbooks, he closed here by adding a chromatic descent over two and a half octaves in the bass, colorfully harmonized with ascending chords in the right hand.[39] The rejected ending was just as daring and experimental as the final version is poetic: after a general rest in measure 73, the melody outlines the tonic triad rising to a held A, which mirrors, suspended, the tonic pedal from before. A sustained arpeggio of the dominant seventh chord follows, with the keys gradually lifted so that it terminates in a single held A. In light of Schumann's motto or the last sentence of *Flegeljahre,* the passage can only be Vult's departure, but heard, like the ending of the ball, through the aural imagery of Walt's dream: a flute fading away into a single tone. Thus, in terms of Jean Paul's aesthetics, the two tunes awakening at dawn are sublime or beautiful, like their closure on the tonic. But dying at dusk, far in the distance, the tone of Vult's flute is sublime *and* beautiful, or romantic, like its open ending on the dominant. The novel ends, but the story goes on. This doubleness persists through Schumann's final measure, when, beneath Vult's distant dominant, the wind wafts the waltz rhythm back to close nearby on the tonic.

How fitting, then, that Hugo von Hofmannsthal concluded his little-known essay on Jean Paul with a reference to the doubleness of distance and nearness, foretelling what would return again and again from Jean Paul's forgotten novels: "*to make what is close so distant, and bring what is distant so close, that our heart could embrace them both.*"[40]

Schumann's version of this embrace became the ending of *Papillons*—a model of his musical Romanticism to which he, too, would return again and again.

A "Heavenly Guest" and "Distant Analysis"

Schumann's 1840 review of Franz Schubert's Great C-Major Symphony, D. 944—a work he had discovered in Vienna in the composer's large *Nachlass* of unprinted music and whose performance and publication he had arranged in Leipzig—is probably best known for its comparison of the symphony's "heavenly length" to novels by Jean Paul. Framing the review with a report of his trip to Vienna in search of Schubert, Schumann closes in on the meaning of the symphony by describing his impressions of the city and their relevance for understanding the work:

> Often when I contemplated [the city] from the heights of the mountains, it occurred to me how Beethoven's eye had doubtless strayed restlessly across those distant Alps time and time again, how Mozart may often have pursued dreamily the course of the Danube . . . and Father Haydn may often have gazed at St. Stephen's steeple. . . . And if now this whole charming landscape stands alive before us, strings also will be set into motion inside us that otherwise would not have begun to sound. On hearing the Symphony of Schubert, with the bright, blossoming romantic life it contains, the city again arises before me more distinctly than ever, and again I find it perfectly clear how such works can be born precisely in these surroundings. I will not attempt to give the Symphony a foil; different times of life choose too differently in the texts and pictures they attribute to music: the youth of eighteen often hears an international event in a composition, where the adult sees only a provincial incident, while the musician has thought of neither the one nor the other and just has produced no more than his music as he found it in his heart. But that the external world . . . often takes hold of the inner life of the poet and musician we must indeed believe, and that in this Symphony there lies hidden more than mere beautiful song, more than mere sorrow and joy as music already has pronounced them hundreds of times, indeed that it leads us into a region we nowhere can remember having been before: to acknowledge this we have only to hear such a symphony. Here is, besides masterly musical technique of composition, also life in every fiber, the most subtle shading of color, meaning everywhere, the most acute expression of each single idea, and, finally, a Romanticism poured over the whole, which is known from elsewhere in Franz Schubert. And the heavenly length of the Symphony, like a thick, four-volume novel, for example

by Jean Paul, who can also never come to an end, and for the best reasons: to allow for later re-creation by the reader.[41]

After a general appraisal of the work's overall form, Schumann concluded:

> It will not give us or others any pleasure to analyze the separate movements; one would have to copy the entire symphony in order to give an idea of its pervasive novella-like character. Yet I cannot take leave without a few words about the second movement, which speaks to us in such touching voices. There is a passage in it where the horn is calling as if from afar; this appears to me as if it had come from another sphere. Here everyone is listening, as if a heavenly guest were creeping through the orchestra.[42]

According to Edward Lippman, Schumann's review betrays a striking ambivalence toward external (literary or cultural) influences on the creation of music as well as their relevance for its reception—an issue that had been of concern not only for the composer, but for the critic as well.[43] My reading of Schumann's rich and complex review, however, will focus on the larger interpretive implications of the two poetic fantasies that frame the excerpts given above: the image of the distant Viennese landscape that allegedly inspired Schubert's symphony, and the image of the distant, "heavenly," guest that the symphony inspired in the critic. These images are, of course, romantic clichés,[44] but in the context of Schumann's self-conscious criticism they resonate with Paul Ricoeur's notion of hermeneutic "distanciation." To be sure, poetic distance appears remote from Ricoeur's rather prosaic notion of distanciation, despite the obvious metaphorical connection. Yet Ricoeur's theory of interpretation may draw closer the critical framework of Schumann's interpretive practice.

To summarize: Ricoeur's *Hermeneutics and the Human Sciences,* an ambitious attempt to combine Hans-Georg Gadamer's historical hermeneutics with its subsequent critique by Jürgen Habermas, proposes four different forms of distanciation.[45] In spoken language he already perceives a distance opening up between the "saying" and the "said," between "event" and "discourse," or between the Saussurian *parole* (speech) and *langue* (language). A further distanciation occurs, once spoken discourse becomes fixated as a written text: "What the text signifies no longer coincides with what the author meant; henceforth, textual meaning and psychological meaning have different destinies."[46] From this, a third form of distanciation results: the inevitable "decontextualization" of the text from the original cultural and historical conditions of its production, so that, as a "closed" or "proposed" world of its own, it becomes open to a potentially unlimited number of interpretations. In its fourth form, finally, distanciation takes place between the text and its reader. Ricoeur describes it as a changing dialectic between distanciation and appropriation (*Aneignung*).[47] In the nineteenth century, appropriation was guided by the premise of historicism, which sought to overcome cultural distance and historical alienation. With the shift toward phenomenological, and later structuralist, analysis in the twentieth century, however, this historical distance was no longer an obstacle, but the very condition for an explanation of the text as a world of its own. While Ricoeur welcomes both the liberation from historicism, which sought the world "behind" the text (such as the author's intentions), and the advances of phenomenology and structuralism, which sought to explain the closed world "in" the text, he proposes that interpretation nevertheless renew the original dialogic relationship between the reader and the text: "To understand is *to understand oneself in front of the text*."[48] Ricoeur insists, however, that the reading subject has no more control over the text than the authorial subject it replaces: "The matter of the text becomes my own only if I disappropriate myself, in order to let the matter of the text be."[49] Moreover, this "*distanciation of the self from itself* . . . implements all the strategies of suspicion, among which the critique of ideology is a principal modality. Distanciation, in all its forms and figures, constitutes *par excellence* the critical moment in understanding."[50]

Where, then, does Schumann stand with respect to Ricoeur's theory? As an acutely self-conscious critic, Schumann not only used different strategies, but also perceived their limitations. Initially, he sides with the romantic hermeneutics of congeniality: in the distant view of the Viennese landscape he looks for the authorial intention behind Schubert's symphony, suggesting "how such works can be born precisely in these surroundings." But by remarking that "different times of life choose too differently in the texts and pictures they attribute to music," he also admits the possibility that music is open to multiple readings, even if these are relative to the original vision of the authorial subject. Furthermore, with his assertion that music "leads us into a region we nowhere can remember having been before," Schumann would seem to subscribe to the aesthetics of autonomy, to what Ricoeur considered the work as a proposed world of its own, accessible through phenomenological or structural analysis. Yet Schumann feels uneasy about analyzing the symphony as a self-contained whole. Instead, he offers his own subjective response, which emerges in Ricoeur's terms *vis-à-vis* (in front of) the musical text. It is the poetic vision of the distant horn call as a heavenly guest that seems to have descended from that very "region we nowhere can remember having been before"—the realm of absolute music. Thus

Schumann rehearses and reflects upon various interpretive approaches: the historicist and psychological search "behind," the phenomenological investigation "within," and the listener's response "in front of" the musical text. But where is the critical moment in his own understanding? To answer that question, we need to observe how Schumann situated himself within the two interpretive modes that emerged in early nineteenth-century German writings about music: formalist analysis and hermeneutic criticism.

As an attempt to translate the untranslatable into words, E.T.A. Hoffmann's famous 1810 review of Beethoven's Fifth Symphony inaugurated, as it were, modern music criticism. Combining technical and literary language, Hoffmann both carried on the rationalistic tradition of the Enlightenment and followed the impulse of the emerging Romanticism: the former seeking to determine the musical material of the composition, the latter to make explicit its poetic idea.[51] The difference between prosaic analysis and poetic criticism counts among the most enduring legacies of early nineteenth-century writings about music, having persisted through Hanslick and Hausegger, Kurth and Kretzschmar, to Babbitt and Boretz—to say nothing about its far-ranging institutional implications. Not surprisingly, nineteenth-century theories of interpretation reflected the dualism: while Schleiermacher distinguished between the more objective comparative method and the more intuitive divinatory one, so did Dilthey between scientific explanation and historical understanding.[52] More recently, the revival of hermeneutic criticism (in search of music's cultural meaning) has sought to unburden present-day musicology from the legacy of formalism (in search of music's autonomous structure). The relationship between the two approaches continues to be negotiated in both interpretive practice and theory—as it was in the early nineteenth century.[53]

Soon after his *Neue Zeitschrift für Musik* had rolled freshly off the press in 1834, Schumann defended himself against the reproach of having "emphasiz[ed] and extend[ed] the poetic side of music at the expense of its scientific side": "We hold it as the highest kind of criticism that which itself leaves an impression similar to the one created by the subject that stimulated it."[54] The critical stance behind this statement was Friedrich Schlegel's famous fragment beginning, "Poetry can only be criticized by Poetry."[55] In a footnote, Schumann gave an example of how to approach such creative criticism: "In this sense, Jean Paul could possibly contribute more to the understanding of a Beethoven symphony or fantasia through a poetic counterpart (even without talking about the symphony or fantasia alone) than a dozen critics who lean their ladders against the colossus to take its exact measurements."[56]

Schumann, of course, did not completely shun analysis. In his well-known 1835 article about Berlioz's *Symphonie fantastique*, he offered, on the one hand, a poetic counterpart of the symphony in a poem by Franz von Sonnenberg (which appeared in the introductory installment) and, on the other hand, the most detailed technical analysis of a major symphonic work since Hoffmann's review of the Fifth.[57] In fact, Schumann's review of the *Symphonie fantastique* seems to have enjoyed its later status as a textbook classic primarily for its wealth of analytical detail, and not for its more adventurous poetic introduction, which he eliminated from the version that appeared in his *Collected Writings*. As Leon Plantinga has noted, Schumann gradually moved away from his extravagant early writings toward a "soberer style of the later 1830s and the 1840s."[58] Despite that tendency, or precisely because of it, Schumann remained uneasy about the relationship between technical analysis and poetic criticism. His review of Schubert's C-Major Symphony would have provided an opportunity to refine the critical model of the Berlioz article. But Schumann distanced himself from analysis. Why?

According to Sanna Pederson, Schumann, in his later music criticism, struggled to maintain his rapport with a general audience in promoting high-quality music without having to demonstrate its intrinsic qualities through "a more specialized, technical, and professional stance that cut off most readers."[59] His early poetic criticism had successfully established an imaginary public forum in quite a revolutionary way: by staging a fictive dialogue among different subjective personae, Florestan and Eusebius, thus stepping out of the very private space so valued by romantic sensibilities. In the review of Schubert, however, Schumann's "illusion of representing public opinion" appears under pressure both from "the growing consumption of popular music" by a widening middle class less willing to plumb emotional depths, and from the increasing specialization of music professionals more interested in purely technical matters.[60] Schumann's attempt to strike a middle ground in the review appears ambiguous, however: he speaks with his own personal voice, but one that appears subtly authoritative; he invokes the objectivity of the score and proposes its study,[61] but omits it from the review as being "no pleasure" for the critic and the reader; he refrains from a literary extravaganza, but allows for a poetic moment at the end. That moment stands out because Schumann, touched by the music, sought to touch the reader. Instead of "validating autonomous music" by explicitly analyzing its intrinsic qualities, he fell back on poetic paraphrase, which realized "the opportunity [the music] afforded for some type of metaphysical revelation or sublime experience."[62]

Schumann thus proved susceptible to the "dilettantish" picking and choosing that has stigmatized musical hermeneutics to this day. Surely he knew that passage from *Flegeljahre* in which Vult, the *Kenner,* ridicules Walt, the *Liebhaber:* "How, then, do you listen? Forwards and backwards, or only to what is right in front of you? The folk, like cattle, only hear the present, but not the two poles of time; only musical syllables, no syntax. A good hearer of the word memorizes the antecedent of a musical period, in order to grasp beautifully the consequent."[63] In light of Adorno's distinction between atomistic and structural listening,[64] Schumann's indulgence in a hermeneutics of the moment amounts to a breaking of the hermeneutic circle, spinning not only between the whole and the part, but also between the objective and the subjective, between the comparative and the divinatory, between explanation and understanding, between the material and the psychological, in short, between analysis and criticism. Moreover, the distance opening up between artwork and beholder resonates with Benjamin's distinction between trace and aura: "The trace is the appearance of closeness, however distant that which left the trace behind. The aura is the appearance of a distance, however close that which created it. In the trace we get hold of a thing, in the aura the thing gets hold of us."[65]

Benjamin's distinction is rooted in romantic hermeneutics. The goal of analysis is to be close to, to grasp, the music. But the distant aura of art, like that of nature, grasps *us:* "If, while resting on a summer afternoon, you follow with your eyes a mountain range on the horizon or a branch which casts its shadow over you, this means breathing the aura of those mountains, of this branch."[66] If, in turn, Schumann's eyes followed the distant mountains of the Alps, the Danube, and St. Stephen, he wanted to breathe the aura of Vienna and, by implication, that of Haydn's, Mozart's, Beethoven's, and Schubert's music. And as a critic, he wanted to let his readers also breathe that very aura.

Had it involved any pleasure, Schumann, in closing his review, might have "traced" the entire symphony—literally tracking its text by copying it. But he did not even analyze that horn call in the second movement, which occurs during the transition leading from F major to the re-entry of the main theme in A minor (ex. 2.2). Here the horn enters when the thematic material has decayed into the basic pulse of alternating quarter notes in the horn and strings; the sustained half notes of the latter are composed as an echo between lower and upper strings. For six measures (mm. 151–56), the harmony rocks back and forth between the V^7 of F major and the V^6_5 of D minor, until the latter eventually resolves into the Neapolitan sixth that pulls the cadence to the A-minor tonic. Until the G in the horn is tied over to form a suspension with this Neapolitan, however, it belongs to neither key. This gestural and harmonic in-between state suspends time and space and expands—as the horn call is dying away—into a small eternity.

Example 2.2. Franz Schubert, Symphony in C Major, D. 944,
"Andante con moto" mm. 144–62

In the parallel passage, this magic has disappeared (mm. 319–32): a direct move from A major to A minor; a quick arrival on the dominant; pervasive sixteenth-note figures binding the passage into the figuration of the surrounding sections; and finally, the clarinet taking over the horn part, no longer calling from afar. Nor did Schumann further pursue the link to the horn calls at the opening of the symphony and in the final movement (mm. 577–613). Such a simple analytical (or as Schleiermacher would say, comparative) exercise might have disturbed the poetic aura that he needed in his review to envoice the horn with the divine presence of a heavenly guest. As a distant caller, disembodied from the orchestra,

Example 2.2. (cont.)

the horn became for him the transcendent "other"—a visitor from that "region we nowhere can remember having been before." Given Schumann's claim that "this symphony . . . had an effect among us like no other after the ones by Beethoven," perhaps he did, subliminally, remember.[67] Perhaps that visitor was Beethoven, whose alternating chords in the first movement of the Fifth (second half of the development, mm. 210–27 and 233–39) seem to hover—nameless, but with a divine aura— over Schubert. Perhaps Schumann, visiting the graves of the two composers, heard Schubert (re)do that desirable moment he himself wished to have: "looking into the face of a great man, grasping his hand."[68]

Thus, on the level of language about music, the poetic moment with which Schumann takes leave of the virtual analysis of Schubert's symphony parallels Novalis's vision of philosophical prose dying away into *distant* philosophy. Analysis is prose; criticism is poetry—or *distant* analysis. The expression is a reminder that criticism grows, or should grow, out of analysis; that analysis and criticism are deeply related modes of musical perception.[69] As a composer, Schumann knew that one needs to know the notes. But as a critic, trying to address a wider audience, he did not want to detach the work, through phenomenological or structural analysis, from both the author and the reader. Instead, he suspended the interpretive dialectic between distanciation and appropriation to follow the impulse behind the latter: "the actualisation of meaning as addressed to someone."[70] Feeling for his readers, Schumann felt addressed by the "heavenly length of the Symphony" that would, like a novel by Jean Paul, "allow for later re-creation by the reader." Incomplete, the work creates the dialogic situation that is the premise for interpretation as appropriation, which "releases something like an event, . . . an event in the present time."[71] This event is the moment of understanding. Thus, if a critical impulse lies behind Novalis's distant philosophy and Schumann's distant analysis, it is—paradoxically—that poetic distance can undo prosaic distanciation by overcoming—momentarily—the gap between the saying and the said, between speech and writing, between author and text, between composition and commentary, between one reader or listener and another. This is how *we* might understand why Schumann chose his heavenly guest to speak for the heavenly length of Schubert's symphony.

Distant Events and the Textuality of Musical Memory

I left on the 21st. With a melancholy heart, I took leave of the whole precious home with a long, silent look down from Mosler mountain; the autumnal morning was shining like a mild day in spring, and the illuminated world was tenderly and cheerfully smiling on my beautiful, lonely wandering. The moment of separation from loved ones, and of farewell, gives our soul the gentle melancholic minor chord, which is seldom heard. All the bells of past childhood, the present, and the future flow into *one* chord—the shining future would like *to drive out* the past, and so tender, undefined feelings are *gently* fighting in our breast. . . . The evening was wonderful, and the soul was as it is on a still Friday; before Altenburg I sat down for a few hours and rested peacefully, and followed the setting sun with my eyes, and the image of the *süße Heimath* [sweet home] appeared shy and tender before my eyes and sank like the parting and reddening sun, like its last ray, still and stiller into the graves of the past. Therese stood before me and sang softly: sweet home. And while I was dozing off in the evening, every minute of the day and of the past was darkly wafting by again, and like the gentle echo of the soul, I heard the sounds melting and dying away and the last one trembling softly: sweet home.[72]

Thus the eighteen-year-old Schumann reworked a letter to his mother for his diary, shortly after leaving home to continue his studies in Leipzig. In resorting to literary reverie as an antidote for homesickness, Schumann and his self-indulgent nostalgia may seem hypersentimental today; but for the young composer in search of his vocation as a romantic artist, life was literature. Slipping into romantic imagery, he endowed a real event with a poetic aura: the wanderer, the gaze into the distant landscape, the dying sound. The relationship between the images is dynamic: the experience of spatial distance (Schumann's gaze on the setting sun) conjures up the memory of distant music (a Lied sung by his sister-in-law Therese). In an earlier letter from 31 August 1828, Schumann had suggested to his mother, "Have Therese sing to you Reissiger's song *süße Heimath;* I warble it to myself all the time."[73] The song in question, the first of Carl Gottlieb Reissiger's op. 50 published in the same year (ex. 2.3), was in fact entitled "Heimweh" ("Homesickness"), but Schumann referred to it with the words from its *adagio* envoi, *süße Heimath,* which seem to have remained in his ear. The fate of these words will concern us.

Manfred Hermann Schmid has drawn attention to the striking connections between Reissiger's "Heimweh" and Schumann's "An Anna," one of the young composer's early efforts in the genre of the Lied between 1827 and 1829 (ex. 2.4a).[74] The two songs share the same meter, a somewhat generic accompaniment of repeated eighth-note chords, and chromatic passing notes that provide the touch of sentimentality prescribed in Reissiger's performance indication (*mit Gefühl*). These parallels hardly suffice to establish an intertextual relation, but more direct melodic allusions (discussed below) suggest that Schumann was

Example 2.3. Carl Gottlieb Reissiger, "Heimweh," op. 50, no. 1

Example 2.3. (cont.)

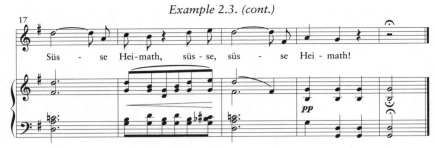

Süs - se Hei-math, süs - se, süs - se Hei - math!

2.
Warum ist es denn das Sehnen
Nach der Heimath trautem Heerd,
Das mit süsser, stiller Schwermuth
Mir das arme Herz beschwert?
In der Heimath wohnt die Liebe,
In der Heimath weilt die Lust,
In der Heimath athmet freier
Wieder die bedrängte Brust.
Süsse Heimath!

3.
Seh' ich hier die grünen Fluren,
Dort der Schiffe Wimpel weh'n,
Denk' mit Wehmuth ich der Heimath
Wo mir alles doppelt schön:
In der Heimath wohnt die Liebe,
In der Heimath weilt die Lust,
Und so bange, ach so bange
Klopft das Herz hier in der Brust
Süsse Heimath!

4.
Seh' ich Arm in Arm hier wandeln
Ein beglücktes Liebespaar,
Denk' ich, wie ich einst so glücklich
In der lieben Heimath war;
In der Heimath wohnt die Liebe,
In der Heimath wohnt die Lust,
Und so bange, ach so bange
Klopft das Herz hier in der Brust.
Süsse Heimath!

5.
Vater! lieber Vater droben,
Lass es einmal noch gescheh'n,
Meine traute Heimath lass mich
Nur noch einmal wiedersehn;
In der Heimath wohnt die Liebe,
In der Heimath weilt die Lust,
In der Heimath athmet freier
Wieder die bedrängte Brust

indeed influenced by Reissiger's song when composing "An Anna" on 31 July 1828, four weeks before he told his mother to have Therese sing Reissiger's song to her.

After Johannes Brahms incorporated Schumann's early songs in the 1893 supplement of the *Gesamtausgabe*, it became public knowledge that Schumann reworked "An Anna" as the slow movement of his Piano Sonata in F♯ Minor, op. 11 (as he did with another early song, "Im Herbste," for the Sonata in G Minor, op. 22). In the sonata, Schumann gave the now textless song the title "Aria" and made a number of changes. Besides the transposition from F major to A major, immediately notable is the melody moving to the lower register in the middle section, where it is accompanied by arpeggiations in the right

Example 2.4. Robert Schumann, "An Anna" vs. Piano Sonata in F# Minor, op. 11, "Aria" hand. Schumann also smoothed out the transition to the flat submediant of the middle section by substituting the song's blunt V–I cadences with progressions employing semitonal voice leading. That the Aria appears more refined results from Schumann's growing awareness of the potential of the piano, as well as his greater experience as a composer. Keeping the melody and form of the vocal model largely intact, however, the sonata movement retained much of its original identity and character: indeed, the Aria had literally become a "Song without Words." Schmid therefore discussed it in connection with Schumann's June 1835 review of Mendelssohn's *Lieder ohne Worte,* opp. 19 (1834) and 30 (1835), quoting the following passage:

> Who has not once sat at the piano in twilight (a grand piano would already sound too courtly) and in the midst of fantasizing sung to himself a soft melody? If one can fortuitously connect the melody with the accompaniment in the hands alone, and if one is mainly a Mendelssohn, then the most beautiful songs without words will come into being. It would be easier, however, if one would set texts to music in the first place, eliminate the words and present the result to the world. Yet this would not be the right thing, but, in fact, a kind of fraud [eine Art Betrug].[75]

Schmid insisted that a text could no longer be added to the Aria: its now wordless expression had become part of a purely musical remembrance (*musikalische Erinnerungshaltung*) in which Schumann transformed into sound the memories described in the letter to his mother. Schumann, thus acquitted, would not be guilty of fraud. "This music," according to Schmid, "is not graspable" (*ungreifbar*), but grasps the listener through its specifically romantic tone—the tone from afar.[76] Schmid concluded that this "metaphysical trait" of the Aria is apparent "without having to know its real subject, the song."[77] To summarize Schmid's conclusion: the text left no trace on the musical memory.

While Schmid offers fascinating information about the Aria's layers of sources, his interpretation places the piece too securely in the category of absolute music. Has the song—the real subject—really become obsolete in the Aria? Or is not the sonata movement, in a literal sense, more equivocal, shot through with other voices, half-heard and half-remembered? How, then, did the composer hear the Aria, and how do we hear it now, knowing what lay behind it? At issue is what might be called the textuality of musical memory in a Song without Words—one that originated as a song. Clearly, Schumann felt ambivalent about this textuality, as is evident from the two alternative origins of melody he imagined for this new genre. Whereas the origin in improvisation is difficult but authentic, the origin in stripping a song of its text is facile but fraudulent—or, to use Schumann's phrase about *Papillons,* "a foolish beginning" (see his letter to Henriette Voigt quoted above). He alluded to the problem in the continuation of his review of Mendelssohn, which is not quoted by Schmid: "Still, one could test how definitely music can express feelings by asking the poet (who would not be told about his own words) to lay a new text under his song. If the new text were to coincide with the old one, then this would be yet another testimony to the sureness of musical expression."[78]

Schumann's experiment betrays a deep concern about the relationship between musical and linguistic expression. His hypothetical tone seems to call into question "the sureness of musical expression," precisely because of his uncertainty about successfully setting words into music and then putting music (back) into words. Moreover, if we replace in the review the word "poet" with "critic," the experiment encapsulates what had become one of Schumann's major challenges during the time he was working on the sonata: the task of the critic, who "lays a new text" under the music for his readers. As noted earlier, Schumann was an extraordinarily self-reflective critic, enjoying both the benefit and the burden of being a composer himself. Thus his view of the alternative origin of Songs without Words may well have been informed in part by his own compositional experience. Strikingly, however, the Aria exemplifies not just one, but both possible origins of melody, and thus falls, uneasily perhaps, between two kinds of musical memory: with words and without.

First the words. Reissiger's simple and strophic song matches the one-dimensional mood and frequent internal repetitions of its poetry. The word *Heimath* occurs six times in the first strophe and twenty-eight times altogether in the five strophes, including the repetitions of the last line. If Schumann remembered "Heimweh" sung by his sister-in-law and also "warbl[ed] it to [himself]," the song would indeed have gone around in his head for days, perhaps weeks. Thus Schumann may have been inspired to set the phrase "süße Heimath" in Justinus Kerner's poem "An Anna" (a soldier's farewell to his bride from the battlefield) to the same sweet 2–1 appoggiatura that Reissiger used in the *adagio* envoi of his song (ex. 2.4a).[79] The appoggiatura is prefigured in measure 9 of Reissiger's song, setting the refrain-like fifth line—"In der Heimath wohnt die Liebe"—and thereby also repeating "Heimath" through all five stanzas. Schumann may have heard more: the four-note turn at the beginning of Reissiger's envoi saturates the melody of "An Anna": the figure recurs transposed in measure 4, it shapes the opening of the Db-major middle section in measure 16, and it blends into the *Abgesang* of Schumann's outer sections, when the melody descends from f^2 to a^1. ("du süsses Leben, denk' ich dein"). In Reissiger's song, the corresponding descent from $f\sharp^2$ to b^1 in the third measure had "Heimath" only in the first stanza, but the related descent in measure 11 (starting with g^2) carried the word throughout the song in the equally refrain-like sixth line, "In der Heimath wohnt die Lust." In short, Schumann's ostensibly arbitrary melodic allusions to the song that he had been warbling to himself may well have been guided by the very word ringing in his ears and reverberating in his soul: *Heimath.*

If Schumann had originally sought to recapture the mood of Reissiger's "Heimweh" in his own "An Anna," he may no longer have cared much for the poem's sentimental content when reworking the song into the Aria half a decade later. Yet his setting of the word "Heimath" in the Aria would suggest otherwise. The most marked moment in this respect is the return of the song's first occurrence of "Heimath" in the third section: in "An Anna," the melody reaches the tonic third immediately, but the Aria postpones that melodic resolution until the end (ex. 2.4b). Here, in a coda added by Schumann, the opening phrase returns twice (ex. 2.4c). First stated in the original register, the melody finally touches the tonic third $c\sharp^3$ on "Heimath." Thus the Aria's "vocal" line resolves into the A-major tonic triad, suggesting that "süße Heimath" are the last words to be heard, not sung, but sweetly transfigured. Moreover, unlike the song, the melody of the Aria ends on the fifth scale degree. This segment of the melody is echoed once again: first hidden in the accompaniment's middle register and then—finally—leaving its last three notes dying away alone. One could hear this ending with Schumann's letter to his mother in mind: his poetic account of Therese singing Reissiger's song first transformed into "An Anna" and then into the Aria. "And like *the most distant echo* of the soul, I heard the sounds melting and dying away and the last one trembling softly: sweet home."[80]

Did Schumann *hear* these words? If so, they must have struck him—by his own critical standards—as "a kind of fraud": a Song without Words created by stripping a preexisting song of its text. So long as "An Anna" remained unpublished, Schumann had, of course, no reason to fear detection of its fraudulent appropriation in the sonata, let alone any deeply hidden private association. Nor would naming its slow movement after a vocal genre have necessarily aroused the listener's suspicion; after all, "airs" were part of the eighteenth-century suite.[81] More importantly still, in the sonata's fantasia-like *Introduzione,* the melody of the Aria already emerged, *sotto voce,* from the many rising seconds that prefigure the characteristic anacrusis of its incipit and gradually approach its entrance on e^1/e^2 in measure 22 (ex. 2.4b). Tentative and fragmentary, as well as severed at its seams, however, this is not yet the sweeping line that Schumann brings under a single slur in the Aria by smoothing out the double dotting and suturing the segments. Melody in the process of creation?

The *sotto voce* melody never returns in the first movement, even when the introduction reemerges in F minor during the development (mm. 268–79). Its later return as the Aria does not obey the rationale of reprise, but follows the irrationality of reminiscence: no longer voluntary composition but involuntary memory, which appears, as the performance marking has it, *senza passione ma espressivo.* If, then, according to his review of Mendelssohn, Schumann himself had produced a fraudulent Song without Words, he might have wanted to conceal that very fraud by having the Aria originate in the introduction of the sonata from improvisation: from sitting "at the piano in twilight . . . and in the midst of fantasizing [singing] to himself a soft melody"— surely a method of composition he cherished.[82] Thus created in the first movement, this *sotto voce*, this soft voice, is remembered in the second. Caught between the aesthetics of vocal and absolute music—between song and sonata— the Aria descended from song, but *appears* to have sprung from music alone. For the listener, the Aria was purely instrumental music, its metaphysics a logocentrism without *logos.* But in Schumann's soul, the words "süße Heimath" may still have died away with their melody. And now that we know those words, might we not hear them as well?

Distant Mountains and the Musical Landscape

Standing thus on the very top of the mountain, recognizing nothing in the cold clouds, and gazing upon immense oceans of fog, I felt an inexpressible melancholy and thought I was the only human being on earth.[83]

Thus Schumann recalled an impression from his Italian Journey in a letter he drafted in Mantua on 27 September 1829. His experience of the sublime landscape is archetypally romantic (as painted, for instance, in Caspar David Friedrich's famous *Der Wanderer über dem Nebelmeer*). Numerous descriptions of Alpine journeys by eighteenth- and early nineteenth-century writers, among them Lord Byron, could have provided the traveling student with the vocabulary—already a cliché—for his own impressions of the mountains. But for the young composer, personal experience nourished his inclination toward aesthetic reflection, and vice versa. Thus "mountaintops" figured prominently in an aphorism that he jotted down in his diary for his Jean Paulesque treatise, *Die Tonwelt: Aus dem Tagebuch der heil. Caecilia,* written the year before. In it, Schumann made an explicit association between music and landscape on the grounds of their ability to express the inexpressible: "In human beings reposes a great, immense Something which no tongue can proclaim, because it is too unearthly; but we feel it on high mountains, or during the sunset, or when hearing soft sounds."[84]

In a monograph-length chapter of his book *The Romantic Genera-tion,* Charles Rosen documented the affinity between landscape painting and music in late eighteenth- and early nineteenth-century aesthetics.[85] Drawing upon a variety of literary sources, theoretical texts, and land-scape descriptions, he reappraises the romantic genre of the song cycle and concludes, climactically perhaps, with a discussion of Schumann's *Davidsbündlertänze* as a song cycle without words. I will take an alter-native route toward that same goal, namely, the cycle's ending with a piece entitled "Wie aus der Ferne" ("As from afar"). While crossing Rosen's path, however, I will pursue different sources closer to Schumann's environment—sources that deal specifically with the relationship be-tween the temporal and spatial dimensions of romantic distance. Finally, new evidence about the musical origins of *Davidsbündlertänze* will pro-vide a surprising step beyond the goal.

Within the larger shift from imitative to expressive aesthetics in the late eighteenth and early nineteenth centuries, the increasing prestige of in-strumental versus vocal music paralleled that of landscape versus history painting. At issue in music was the status of verbal language, in paint-ing, the position of the human subject within the world on the canvas. Traditional history painting—depicting heroic, tragic, or fateful mo-ments in history, mythology, and religion—had served the collective needs of a particular community involved with that moment in a direct or allegorical way. But the representation of nature in landscape paint-ing became both a reflection of, and a foil for, individual experience. According to Rosen, landscape was now experienced through a "double time scale," in which the "long-range time" of natural history merges with the "fleeting sensation of the moment" that belongs, as it were, to the personal history of the beholder.[86]

In this sense, Schumann's experience of loneliness facing the Alps speaks to his isolation from the human collective, thus making him susceptible to being overwhelmed by incommensurable, sublime nature. Such isolation had its melancholic side, but the absence of human action from nature made room for a different experience of landscape. On 16 May 1832, the almost twenty-two-year-old Schumann copied into his diary this excerpt from the *Kunstblatt,* a forum for the discussion of current aesthetic issues:

> What has been taken really deeply *out of nature* is more deep and univer-sal than the artist himself knows; for it also awakens responses in such spheres he could not know: it opens for everybody different perspectives on life, just as everybody, in meaningful, characteristic nature, becomes lost in those perspectives, together with different images and feelings, when the landscape opens toward a beautiful distance.[87]

The passage may have caught Schumann's eye because it describes how nature elicits from the beholder a sense of being lost. When landscape "opens toward a beautiful distance," it creates a double opening: without and within. Yet this opening can be filled with individual memory, replacing or superseding the collective commemoration of history painting. To illustrate how landscape triggers personal memories, Rosen cites from Louis Ramond de Carbonnières's 1789 *Observations faites dans le Pyrénées* a passage describing the descent from the glacier above the circus of Gavarnie during sunset:

> I took pleasure in this vague reverie so near to sadness, aroused by the images of the past; I extended on to Nature the illusion that she had caused to be born, by uniting with her, in an involuntary movement, the times and the events of which she had stirred up the memory; I ceased to be isolated in these wild places; a secret and indefinable intelligence established itself between them and me; and alone, on the banks of the torrent of Gedro, alone but under that sky which saw all the ages flow away and which encompasses all the climates, I abandoned myself with emotion to a security so sweet, to this profound sentiment of coexistence inspired by the fields of one's own country.[88]

If, in this proto-Proustian experience, landscape stirred up the *mémoire involuntaire,* music did so as well. Compare Ramond's visual feast with this passage from the 1785 *empfindsam* novel *Andreas Hartknopf* by Karl Philipp Moritz:

> Everyone will have noticed at least a few times in their life that some otherwise utterly meaningless tone, heard, say, in the distance, has a quite wonderful effect on the soul if the mood is right; it is as though a thousand memories, a thousand dim ideas had awakened all at once with this tone and transported the heart into an indescribable melancholy.[89]

Melancholy, the indescribable, a thousand memories: here music and landscapes converge in *Poesie,* which August Wilhelm Schlegel captured in Novalis's and Jean Paul's spirit as "music for the inner ear, and painting for the inner eye, but half-heard music, but painting fading away."[90] It is not simply landscape and music, then, that are poetic, but *distant* landscapes and *distant* music.

For early nineteenth-century composers and music critics, the elective affinity between distant landscape and distant music went both ways: from landscape to music and vice versa. Consider first the musical experience of a distant landscape in this little-known passage from Carl Maria von Weber's unfinished novel *Tonkünstlers Leben:*

The contemplation of a landscape is to me the performance of a piece of music. I feel the whole, without dwelling on the details which produce it; in a word, the landscape is moving within me, strangely enough, in time. It is a successive pleasure. . . . While standing still I look fixedly into the distance, this picture almost always conjures up a parallel musical image from the related spirit world of my fantasy, one which I may perhaps then take a fancy to, secure, and develop.[91]

Weber's transformation of sight into sound is inverted by Franz Brendel, Schumann's successor as editor of the *Neue Zeitschrift für Musik*, in his tribute to Schumann's early works for piano:

Schumann's compositions can often be compared with landscape paintings in which the foreground gains prominence in sharply delineated clear contours while the background becomes blurred and vanishes in a limitless perspective; they may be compared with a misty landscape, in which only here and there a sunlit object stands out. Thus the compositions contain certain principal passages, then other passages that should by no means stand out clearly, and are intended only to serve as background; some passages are points lit by rays of sunlight, others fade away in blurred contours. To this inner peculiarity corresponds the exterior one that Schumann is very fond of playing with the constantly depressed pedal, so that the harmonies do not emerge with particular clarity.[92]

For both Weber and Brendel, then, the creative transformation of music into painting, or the comparison between them, hinges on the experience of distance that dissolves space into time and vice versa, such that ontological time and space become a psychological fusion of space–time—the realm of romantic synesthesia. Early nineteenth-century aestheticians surely knew how much this subverted the division between temporal and spatial arts in Lessing's *Laocoön*.[93] If Brendel compared Schumann's piano music and landscape paintings by means of the *Fantasiestücke,* op. 12 (notably "Des Abends" and "In der Nacht"), the analogy is apt given that night and twilight tend to confound our sense of space and time. But his image is equally fitting, perhaps even more so, for the first half of "Wie aus der Ferne," the penultimate number of Schumann's 1838 *Davidsbündlertänze,* op. 6, published in two books of nine dances.[94] The most direct invocation of distance in "Wie aus der Ferne" is the echo of the opening melody in the lower register (ex. 2.5).[95] The sense of depth, moreover, results from layers added to the melody and its echo: a bass pedal and a sustained voice pulsating in the middle register. Executing this texture on the piano requires those permanently lifted dampers that Brendel and others observed when they heard Schumann playing.[96] Therefore the overall impression of "Wie aus der Ferne" easily compares to Brendel's image of a landscape with a

Example 2.5. Robert Schumann, *Davidsbündlertänze*, op. 6,
Book 2, no. 8, "Wie aus der Ferne" mm. 1–58

Example 2.5. (cont.)

Example 2.5. (cont.)

blurred harmonic background against which melodic shapes stand out like sunlit objects.

But representation of distance in the piece appears to exist primarily on the surface, as *spatial* distance. Indeed, in sketching some fundamental aspects of how we experience time and space in music, Robert Morgan noted that in music "variations in texture . . . produce an effect that is unmistakenly 'spatial' in quality."[97] Schumann thus seems to imitate, or to paint, with sound. In his essay "On Some Relations Between Music and Painting," Adorno remarked about such imitation:

> Music that "paints" . . . nearly always suffers a loss of temporal organization, [and thereby] lets go of the synthesizing principle through which, alone, it assumes a form approaching space. . . . The moment one art imitates another, it becomes more distant from it by repudiating the constraint of its own material, and falls into syncretism, in the vague notion of an undialectical continuum of arts in general. . . . The arts converge only where each pursues its immanent principle in a pure way.[98]

Primarily a reaction against Debussy and Stravinsky, Adorno's stance is a remote reflex of Lessing's firm boundary between the arts. Thus Adorno claimed, "In a picture, everything is simultaneous. . . . The more emphatically a painting presents itself, the more time is stored up in it."[99] By rejecting the purely impressionistic depiction of space in music, Adorno advocates what Morgan has called logical space or conceptual space in music, which is essentially a space of relationships that draws on the notions of pitch space, harmonic space, or formal space.[100] Morgan illustrates this logical space with Schenker's conceptualization of tonal space: "a space that is at once unique, in that it encompasses the particular set of structural–temporal relationships found in that single work; and general, in that these relations are shown to derive from and exist within the unchanging space of the background."[101] Adorno posits a similar paradox: when the synthesizing principle connects diachronically different motivic, thematic, and tonal events (what Morgan described as "a fixed set of synchronic connections"),[102] time is stored up, as it were, in structure, so that Adorno's structural listener "hears the first measure only when hearing the last, which redeems it."[103]

The extent to which Adorno's (and for that matter Schenker's) ritualistic reception of unity in Beethoven's symphonic music from the heroic phase was entrenched in a long-standing historical master narrative becomes evident from remarks by Brendel (quoted in chapter 1), setting up Beethoven's ability "to develop an overriding perspective," which controls the different "parts and forges them into a unity," as the foil for his discussion of Schumann and Mendelssohn: "Beethoven created the most richly structured totality; he was led in this direction by historical necessity."[104] For Brendel, this historical necessity eventually led Beethoven from the highest peak attained in the genre of the symphony to the more characteristic, often word-based music of his late style, which the younger generation of composers, including Schumann, emulated by creating "self-contained tone paintings" that captured definite (i.e., poetic) sentiments "in a smaller frame."[105] (I will discuss the aesthetic category of the "characteristic" in chapter 4.) From this point of view, Beethoven would be a history painter, one who does not merely *represent* a heroic moment—for instance in his cantata *Der glorreiche Augenblick*, Op. 136, written for the Vienna Congress in 1814 and often dismissed by embarrassed critics as a casual work—but who actually *presents* his own heroism in the *Eroica*: what Wagner called Beethoven's *unerhörte Tat*, his "unheard-of deed."[106]

Today, however, we tend to look upon Beethoven's musical heroism with an ambivalent mixture of admiration and resistance—admiration for the music, but resistance to its formalist, universalist, and nationalist reception. To be sure, we no longer believe, as Brendel did, in the historical necessity of such heroism, nor do we uncritically endorse the cultural values attached to it. The critical move, then, is to differentiate, as Scott Burnham put it, between Beethoven's hero and Beethoven Hero.[107] In terms of Ricoeur's hermeneutic theory, we can "distance" ourselves from Beethoven Hero as a figure too invested with ideologies of different kinds. But we may appropriate Beethoven's hero to understand Schumann's music as *non-heroic*— not anti-heroic, since Ricoeur's interpretive dialectic is not the historical dialectic that the Hegelian Brendel invoked when he portrayed Schumann and Mendelssohn as heirs to the subjective and objective Beethoven, respectively.[108] Thus, if Beethoven "mastered" the tension within the "'Romantic Hero of Sensibility': the urge to be subsumed in a greater organic whole struggl[ing] against the urge to be passionately individual and self-assertive"; if he created "the 'superclosure' effect of the 'organically unified musical masterpiece,'" so that "there is no world beyond the piece, no fading horizon, no vanishing point of perspective,"[109] then Schumann's Romanticism painted a different picture in "Wie aus der Ferne": a world beyond the piece, a fading horizon, and a vanishing point of perspective.

"Wie aus der Ferne" is run on from the B-minor Trio of the preceding "Mit gutem Humor" (a scherzo by definition of its programmatic title), thus thwarting the expected return of its A section in G major. When the Trio gradually loses momentum and sinks into the lower register, it leaves F♯ dying away both as a sustained note and as a syncopated repetition; this will be the most pervasive gesture for the next fifty measures, the first half of "Wie aus der Ferne." Its unmarked beginning seems odd, yet appropriate for a musical representation of a distant landscape. The impression is that of a painting without a frame, which, of course, suits the boundlessness of its subject. Schumann traverses the boundary between the formal scherzo and the following musical painting by invading the Trio with three F♯ octaves, hammered out against the *pianissimo* chords, rising to A, and eventually turning into the transitional F♯ pedal. The gesture belongs to what Peter Kaminsky has called a network of "cross reference between movements" in *Davidsbündlertänze*, in which the threefold F♯s establish "the surface motivic relationship" between Book 1, no. 3, "Etwas hahnbüchen" ("A bit rough"), and the Trio of "Mit gutem Humor."[110] In "Etwas hahnbüchen," the repeated F♯s occur in measures 7–8, emphasized rather markedly with three consecutive *forte* signs. With the return of the opening section, they appear first in the left hand followed by the right hand (exx. 2.6c^1 and 2.6c^2). This enigmatic gesture, which Schumann concealed so cleverly, seems to hold the key to the remarkable double invocation of musical distance in "Wie aus der Ferne" and Schumann's new, non-heroic, vision of musical form.

As is well known, Clara Wieck was the primary inspiration for *Davidsbündlertänze,* which Schumann began on 20 August 1837, "less than a week after receiving Clara's 'yes'" that sealed their engagement.[111] His letters to his fiancée speak warmly of her presence in the work:

> There are many wedding motifs in the *Tänze*—I wrote them in the most wonderful state of excitation that I can ever remember. I'll explain them to you sometime.

> My Clara will find out what's in the *Tänze;* they are dedicated to her more than anything else of mine—the story is a bachelor's party, and you can imagine the beginning and the end. If ever I was happy at the piano, it was when I composed them.

> You haven't looked deeply enough into my *Davidsbündlertänze;* I think they are *quite different* from *Carnaval* and are to the latter as faces are to masks. But I can be mistaken since I haven't forgotten them yet. One thing I know: they were conceived in joy while the other one was often difficult and painful.[112]

Commentators to date have located Clara's musical involvement with the cycle in the "Motto by C.W." taken from the Mazurka in her *Soirées musicales,* op. 6. This was surely not the first instance of Schumann's borrowings from her compositions: the theme of her *Romance variée,* op. 3 became the theme for his *Impromptus,* op. 5; the "Scène fantastique" from her *Quatre Pièces caracteristiques,* op. 5, no. 4 inspired motivic connections to the F♯-Minor Sonata; and the "Valse allemande" in *Carnaval* took its opening gesture from Clara's 1835 *Valses romantiques,* op. 4 (marked *x* in exx. 2.6a and 2.6b; see also ex. 2.7). Given that Robert and Clara exchanged musical ideas to the point that, in Nancy Reich's words, "it is often difficult to determine the origin of many musical ideas they shared,"[113] we may hear Clara's *Valses*—varying in mood, key, and gesture, and organized as a cycle (the opening dance returns at the end)—as a creative response to *Papillons.* But they may well have inspired Schumann to write his own cycle of dances.

Aside from the "Motto by C.W.," one trace of that inspiration seems to have been Clara's first waltz, which Schumann had already used in *Carnaval.* In *Davidsbündlertänze,* however, Schumann alludes more obliquely to the opening figure of the waltz. The repeated F♯s and the following descent to A (later to A♯) in "Etwas hahnbüchen" change the eighth notes in Clara's extended upbeat into quarter notes, but because Schumann preserves the metric position in triple time, the connection remains audible (exx. 2.6c^1 and 2.6c^2). Moreover, he realizes the harmonic implications of the original figure, beginning on the third scale degree, differently: as a V–i (F♯/b). He thus begins, as in the "Valse

Example 2.6. (a) Clara Wieck, *Valse Romantiques,* op. 4;
(b) Robert Schumann, *Carnaval,* op. 9 ("Valse allemande");
(c) Robert Schumann, *Davidsbündlertänze,* op. 6 ("Etwas hahnbüchen");
(d) Schumann, *Davidsbündlertänze* ("Mit gutem Humor");
(e) Schumann, *Davidsbündlertänze* ("Wie aus der Ferne")

Example 2.7. Clara Wieck, *Valse Romantiques*, op. 4 mm. 1–32

Example 2.7. (cont.)

allemande" from *Carnaval,* on the fifth scale degree, but unlike in *Carnaval,* he keeps the melodic scale intact. Strikingly, Clara herself makes an unusual move to an F♯ pedal as the dominant of B minor in the middle section of her waltz.[114] While she expands the descent from F♯ to A♯ in measures 17–20, her gesture of hammering out the F♯s in the retransition to the first section (mm. 21–24; ex. 2.7), may have rung in Schumann's ears—loudly enough, as it were, to intrude into "Etwas hahnbüchen" and, more distantly, into the Trio of "Mit gutem Humor" (ex. 2.6d).

This intrusion helps to assert the new tonal area, linking the B-minor Trio with the B-major "Wie aus der Ferne," which seems to prolong F♯ endlessly. This prolongation compares to the unlimited perspective in Brendel's landscape painting, and the more animated middle section, touching on F major, stands out as a passage "lit by rays of sunlight" (mm. 17–34; see ex. 2.5). The fleetingly articulated ternary form, however, is different from the one projected by the preceding scherzo, which it truncates. Because F♯ never descends in the first part of "Wie aus der Ferne" (even though there are cadences to the tonic), closure is denied at the end. The structural listener is deprived of a last measure that would redeem the first and create an image of completeness.

This lack of closure may indeed indicate the "loss of temporal organization," lamented by Adorno for "music that paints." Yet Adorno's rhetoric is problematic: the "loss of temporal organization" does not correspond to a lack of musical logic in the conceptual space of Schumann's cycle. In Schenkerian terms, extended pedals, like the F♯ dominant pedal, often articulate in the foreground a background prolongation. What looks like an infinitely extended painted background on the surface of "Wie aus der Ferne" corresponds to the underlying shift in the tonal background: from the G tonic of the Scherzo to a B tonic in the Trio. In the abstract—inner—"space of relationships," the move from G to B duplicates Schumann's extension of Clara's motto from G to B at the beginning of the cycle.[115] In the sensual space of the surface, on the other hand, the shift seems to be triggered by the repeated F♯s from outside: from "Etwas hahnbüchen" and, by extension, Clara's "Valse." Clara, as it were, inhabits both spaces: inner and outer. Through this combination of logical space and painted space, music and painting converge in "Wie aus der Ferne"—not, however, through the antithesis of extremes, which Adorno's negative dialectic dogmatically posited, but as their synthesis.[116] Instead, music and painting, time and space, merge in the distance of a common vanishing point.

This merging of inner space and outer space marks the moment of the cycle that is most poetic in August Wilhelm Schlegel's sense: "music for the inner ear, and painting for the inner eye, but half-heard music, but painting fading away." After the seemingly infinite expansion into the distance of musically painted space, a temporally distant past emerges in measure 51 with the unaltered return of the second number of *Davidsbündlertänze*, "Innig" ("Deeply felt")—the voice of Eusebius (see the end of ex. 2.5). Apparently at a late compositional stage, while preparing the *Stichvorlage* in September 1837, Schumann decided to cut the sheet that contained the piece, pasting its first part (to become Book 1, no. 2) in an earlier place in the manuscript (fol. 2v) and marking it with a "0." The second part, a coda (from mm. 74 to the end of Book 2, no. 8), he pasted right after "Wie aus der Ferne" (fol. 9r), telling the engraver to insert the music marked "0" before the coda.[117] Since Schumann often shuffled pieces around in his cycles, the procedure becomes indicative of his conception of large-scale form.

Thus the reemergence of Eusebius is, as Rosen put it, "a genuine return of the past—not a formal return, or a *da capo* or a recapitulation, but a memory."[118] Reminiscence is not produced by a predetermined structure or "abstract pattern";[119] it does not result from the coercive construction of form that forces a reprise to happen voluntarily. Instead, Schumann's musical gaze into the distance conjures up a musical memory in the manner of the *mémoire involuntaire*. To use the words Schumann copied into his diary, the compositional subject "becomes lost . . . together with different images and feelings when the landscape opens toward a beautiful distance." But much is gained with that loss in distance: lost, the self opens up toward the other—Clara's distant voice. Nearby, her repeated F♯s had interrupted the Trio, causing a change of perspective as its sound waves, in Jean Paul's terms, "fade away into ever greater distances and finally are lost in ourselves, and . . . although outwardly silent, still [sound] within." Within, then, F♯ finally descends to A♯ to become an inner voice that even continues across the augmented second a♯^{1}–g^1, just as Clara's variant of the opening waltz did when returning in the A♭-major *scherzando* that prepares the reprise of her first number in measure 201 (cf. exx. 2.6a^2, mm. 173–75, and 2.6e). The return of No. 2 in *Davidsbündlertänze*, however, endows Clara's procedure with a distinctly poetic aura. As a distant memory flashing back closely, it is the most magical moment of the cycle: not a mask, as Schumann said, but a face—Clara's face.

"Wie aus der Ferne," however, does not end with Eusebius, whose vision of Clara vanishes. Fleeting and fleeing, her half-heard music accelerates after measure 67 (*nach und nach schneller*) and transforms into that of Florestan, exuberantly closing this number. (It was signed "F. und E." in the first edition.) If the mood swing toward the more passionate mood recalls, however remotely, the octave cascades from the middle section of "Mit gutem Humor," distant reminiscence turns into a distant recapitulation that would seem to bring the whole opus to a more "formal" close. Still, even here the cycle does not end. There is another piece, which extends the progression from G major to B minor (the cross-referential relationship that Kaminsky called P) to C major. Again, Schumann took this from Clara's opus 4: his pivotal introductory dominant seventh on G is the same one that she had used to return from the hammering F♯s to the concluding C-major section of her opening waltz (ex. 2.7, mm. 24–25). Just as Clara herself had composed out the chromatic decent from G through E that is inherent as an inner voice in the six-measure motto of her cycle (ex. 2.7, mm. 1–6/7), Schumann finally leads the $f\sharp^1$ he had left hanging at the end of "Wie aus der Ferne" (itself extending the G major of "Mit gutem Humor") to e^1, which becomes the third of the C major of his final waltz. In Clara's cycle, the return to C completed the ternary form of her first *valse*, and rounded off all her *valses* with a virtuosic coda (from m. 291 to the end). Yet Schumann's ending in C (a key of symbolic significance as the *Fantasie*, op. 17 will show) expresses formal closure differently. Labeled a "superfluous" addition,[120] his coda is neither dazzlingly brilliant nor self-assertively Beethovenian, but rather a bachelor's blissful dream.

Distant People: Exchanging Voices with the *ferne Geliebte*

Schumann conceived his *Fantasie,* op. 17 during the summer of 1836 as a contribution to a musical fund-raiser for the planned Beethoven monument in Bonn. Since then, the *Fantasie* has enjoyed perhaps the richest reception of any romantic piano work, having become, in a sense, a monument to Romanticism. Interpretations of the first movement, especially, have drawn upon quintessential categories of romantic aesthetics: fragment, *Witz,* and arabesque.[121] Romantic distance, however, embraces these categories in a special way, bringing to light striking new evidence for Schumann's public homage to Beethoven, as well as for his private lament for Clara in the first movement. In it, moreover,

Novalis's varieties of distance—distant mountains, distant events, distant people—coalesce.

Schumann's letters to Clara leave no doubt as to the *Fantasie*'s personal dimension:

> I have also completed a fantasy in three movements which I had drafted in detail in June [18]36. The first movement of it is possibly the most passionate I have ever written—a deep lament for you—the others are weaker, but have nothing to be ashamed of.

> The *Fantasie* (of which you know nothing), which I wrote during our unhappy separation and which is excessively melancholy . . . it is dedicated to Liszt.

> You can only understand the *Fantasie* if you imagine yourself back in that unhappy summer of 1836, when I was separated from you.[122]

As a motto for the first edition, Schumann chose a quatrain from a poem by Friedrich Schlegel:

> Durch alle Töne tönet
> Im bunten Erdentraum
> Ein leiser Ton gezogen
> Für den der heimlich lauschet.

> Through all the sounds
> In earth's many-colored dream
> There sounds one soft long-drawn tone
> For the one who listens in secret.[123]

Upon publication of the work, Schumann wrote to Clara:

> Write to me what you think about the *first* movement of the *Fantasie*. Doesn't it stimulate a lot of images in you? This melody

> I like the most. I suppose that *you* are the "tone" referred to in the motto. I almost believe it.

And Clara wrote back:

> It is strange that my favorite passage in the first movement of the *Fantasy* is your favorite passage, too. I like to dwell on that passage; it is so pleasant [*gemütlich*], so peaceful! Yes, my Robert, many images come to my mind as I play the *Fantasy*, and I think they coincide with yours.[124]

Example 2.8. Robert Schumann, *Fantasie,* op. 17, first movement mm. 295–309

While Schumann's humorous "almost" should send up a red flag, we should not exclude, in light of the earlier letters, what Nicholas Marston has called Clara's "very real 'presence' in the composition."[125] Still, the precise nature of the lament for Clara and the homage to Beethoven remained obscure until they were heard to coalesce in Schumann's alleged reference to Beethoven's *An die ferne Geliebte* in the coda of the first movement (ex. 2.8).

Opinions, however, vary. Charles Rosen testifies that he learned of the Beethoven reference from his teacher Moritz Rosenthal, a pupil of Liszt, who in turn "knew" it from Schumann himself.[126] Anthony Newcomb, on the other hand, remains more skeptical, noting that the reference appears in the Schumann literature only in 1910 with the second edition of Hermann Abert's *Robert Schumann* (it was lacking in the first).[127] Newcomb thus felt forced to wonder whether the Beethoven reference was made by Schumann or created by a more recent critical tradition. The possible Beethoven quotation at the end of the first movement of op. 17 is not extraneous to the rest of the music—is not embedded in musical quotation marks, so to speak, as is the quotation from *Papillons* in "Florestan" of *Carnaval* or the "Stimme aus der Ferne" in the last *Novellette*.[128]

On the matter of thematic coherence, therefore, Newcomb concurs with Rosen, who maintained that "the reference becomes self-reference: the phrase from Beethoven seems as much to derive from what has preceded as to be the source. In fact, one cannot take the full measure of Schumann's accomplishment in this work without observing that the quotation from *An die ferne Geliebte* sounds as if Schumann had written it."[129] Indeed, most commentators have focused primarily on the reference in the coda as the source for the movement's thematic material. Can we break the impasse between Rosen's reliance on an oral tradition and Newcomb's insistence on further corroboration for this reference?[130]

I will approach the problem from a different angle. When Schumann asked Clara to describe the images that the first movement of the *Fantasie* evoked in her, he appears to seek confirmation (as with Henriette Voigt and *Papillons*) of the poetic vision that had inspired his music. The composer's query is not unlike the experiment he proposed in his review of Mendelssohn's *Songs without Words* for a song stripped of its text: to test the definiteness of musical expression by observing whether newly underlaid words match the original poem. Moreover, as we know from his review of the *Symphonie fantastique*, Schumann chided Berlioz for unfolding before the public a sentimental story by means of a program, though he eventually enjoyed how the story was "almost invariably clothed in vibrant, living, sound."[131] Since there is a hypothesis regarding what might have been the text, or program, behind the *Fantasie*'s first movement, I shall pursue Schumann's experiment from the other end, by assuming that the composer's original poetic vision was indeed Beethoven's *An die ferne Geliebte*.

The imagery of the first poem in Beethoven's cycle begins with the now familiar example of romantic distance: the gaze into a blue, misty landscape:

An die ferne Geliebte, no. 1

Auf dem Hügel sitz ich spähend
In das blaue Nebelland
Nach den fernen Triften sehend,
Wo ich dich Geliebte fand.

Weit bin ich von dir geschieden,
Trennend liegen Berg und Thal
Zwischen uns und unserm Frieden,
Unserm Glück und unsrer Qual.

Ach den Blick kannst du nicht sehen,
Der zu dir so glühend eilt,
Und die Seufzer, sie verwehen
In dem Raume, der uns teilt.

Will denn nichts mehr zu dir dringen,
Nichts der Liebe Bote sein?
Singen will ich Lieder singen,
Die dir klagen meine Pein!

Denn vor Liebesklang entweichet
Jeder Raum und jede Zeit,
Und ein liebend Herz erreichet,
Was ein liebend Herz geweiht!

[On the hill I sit and gaze upon the blue, misty country toward the distant valleys where I found you, beloved. Far from you have I been separated, mountain and valley lie between us and our peace, our happiness and our suffering. Alas, you cannot see my gaze that so ardently rushes to you, and my sighs die away in the space that lies between us. Is there nothing that can reach you, nothing to be love's messenger? I will sing, sing songs which will tell you of my sorrows! For all time and space must yield to the sound of love, and a loving heart will attain what a loving heart has offered.]

The poem unfolds the topos of lament transformed into song, which the male lover sends into the distance to overcome what separates him from his beloved. But only in the last song of Beethoven's cycle, as the sun sets over a blue lake, will the beloved sing these songs. Only then does their *Liebesklang* have the effect of *actio in distans:* the spiritual communion of hearts bridging the gap between their physically distant bodies.

An die ferne Geliebte, no. 6

Nimm sie hin denn diese Lieder
Die ich dir, Geliebte sang,
Singe sie dann Abends wieder
Zu der Laute süssem Klang.

Wenn das Dämmrungsrot dann ziehet
Nach dem stillen blauen See,
Und sein letzter Strahl verglühet
Hinter jener Bergeshöh;

Und du singst was ich gesungen,
Was mir aus der vollen Brust
Ohne Kunstgepräng erklungen,
Nur der Sehnsucht sich bewußt:

Dann vor diesen Liedern weichet,
Was geschieden uns so weit,
Und ein liebend Herz erreichet
Was ein liebend Herz geweiht!

[Take, then, these songs which I sang for you, beloved; sing them again in
the evening to the sweet sound of the lute. Then, as the twilight's glow
moves toward the still, blue lake, and the last ray dies away behind that
mountaintop; and as you sing what I have sung, the songs that sprang
from my full breast without artificial pomp, knowing only longing: then
these songs will overcome what separated us, and a loving heart will
attain what a loving heart has offered!]

Thus the outer poems of *An die ferne Geliebte* frame the cycle with
hopeful presentiment and anticipated fulfillment. This may well have led
Beethoven to begin the last song with a melodic variant of the first,
while matching the actual textual return of "then these songs will overcome what divided us" with a literal return of the opening song in the
passage beginning in measure 295 specially marked *Ziemlich langsam
und mit Ausdruck*. Apparently Beethoven was struck fairly late in the
compositional process by the ingenious idea of initiating this return,
without text, in the accompaniment, which he squeezed into the autograph before the return of the voice.[132] Such a gesture would surely not
have escaped Schumann's notice. But did it also leave its mark on the
composition of the *Fantasie*?

It apparently did.

The passage marked *Ziemlich langsam und mit Ausdruck* seems to
have been Schumann's source for the beginning of the second theme (ex.
2.9b).[133] But there is more: Schumann based almost the entire second

theme on passages from the last song of *An die ferne Geliebte* in a way
hitherto unrecognized. Since his creative appropriation ranges from almost literal transfer to scarcely recognizable variation, an imaginary
melodic line may help to delineate some of the song's basic melodic
shapes recurring in the *Fantasie* (ex. 2.9a). Schumann draws his material
for the second theme from different parts of the song (ex. 2.9b). While
he begins with alternating eighth notes, the analogous pendulum of
sixteenth-note chords in Beethoven's song came only after the vocal
entry. The chromatic passing notes in the left hand (segment w^1) also
derive from a later passage in the song (mm. 44–45). In addition,
Schumann reverses Beethoven's distinct melodic incipit, the ascent from
b♭^{1} to e♭^{2} (segment *z*), into a descent (segment y^1), which also appears
later in the song. Whereas the *Ziemlich langsam und mit Ausdruck*
passage accelerates beginning at measure 301 (*nach und nach
geschwinder*), Schumann slows down to expand Beethoven's melodic
line around the rise from A♭ to C, thus turning the song's initial four plus
four measures (punctuated by a half cadence and a full cadence at mm.
301 and 305) into an extended period of seven plus four measures
(*Fantasie*, mm. 254–60 and 261–64). The lyrical expansion of his antecedent produces the very passage of which Schumann was so fond that
he copied it into the letter to Clara (see above). As if in response to this
expansion, Schumann condenses even more segments and elements from
Beethoven's melody into his consequent (ex. 2.9c). It breaks down into
two two-measure variants of the characteristic descent, leaping down
from e♭^{2} to b♭^{1}, which stemmed from the beginning of Beethoven's sixth
song and recurs intact in Schumann's coda. Strikingly, as if to make up
for the missing anacrusis, the bass line repeats four times the ascent from
B♭ to E♭ from the incipit of Beethoven's first song (segment *z*), which, to
recall, was recapitulated in the *Ziemlich langsam und mit Ausdruck*
passage. What is more, an inner voice sings out the chromatic progression from B♭ through G that lent such a characteristic flavor to Beethoven's
melody (segment w^1). Finally, the triplets, with which Schumann created
the second two-measure variant (*Fantasie*, mm. 263–64), seem to have
spilled over from the source (Beethoven, mm. 317–18).

At this point, the second theme of the *Fantasie* appears to approach
full closure, which, however, is denied. What follows disintegrates into a
striking series of fragments that can be traced back, once again, to
Beethoven. Set off by the tonic turning into a dominant seventh, a series
of *portato* chords rises, mostly chromatically, to c^2 (mm. 265–66). Though
initially unrelated to the song (its function in the *Fantasie* will become
evident later), this ascent finally ruptures into an isolated b^1 and c^2,
ritardando (ex. 2.9d). The gesture strongly evokes the magical *molto
adagio* measure with which Beethoven launched the transition from the

Example 2.9. Schumann, Fantasie, op. 17, second theme vs. Beethoven, An die Ferne Geliebte, op. 98

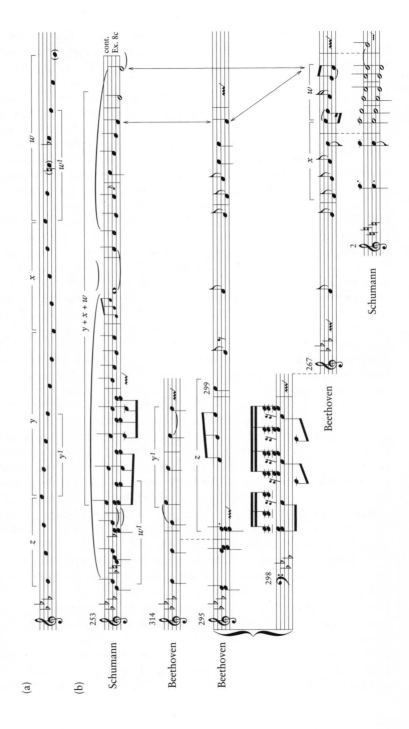

Example 2.9. (cont.)

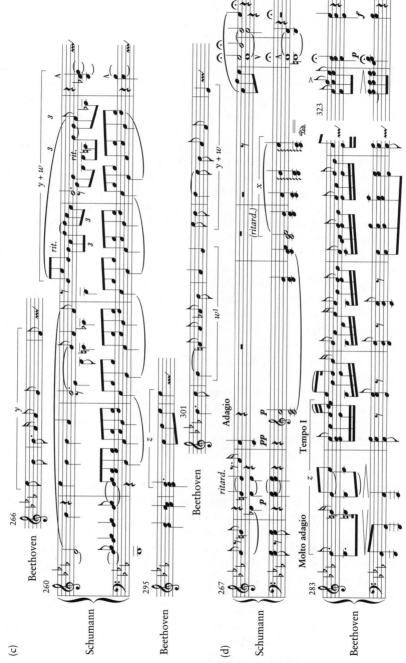

second strophe to the third, beginning so suggestively "And you sing what I have sung." Indeed, the *adagio* passage that follows in the *Fantasie* is an eerily distant echo of Beethoven's melody. Laid bare in the left hand, it picks up the song's A♭ major, descends to the c–e♭–f chord that omits Beethoven's bass note A♭, and rises back to c^2 over F minor (ex. 2.9d). Here Schumann hears the song's melody as a prolongation of the subdominant. Over an open pedal and against the blurred background of the fading *adagio* measures, the subdominant blends into a small melodic segment that stood out as Beethoven's penultimate cadence in the final song. Yet if both the song and the *Fantasie*'s theme return to their initial $e♭^2$, their closing gestures point in different directions. Beethoven resolved his *piano* leading note, prolonged by a fermata, into a weak, but *forte,* tonic sixth chord, as if taking a breath before rushing toward the final cadence (ex. 2.9d). But Schumann's deceptive cadence, using an accented diminished seventh on B♮, leads to a single $e♭^2$: isolated by three fermatas, it dies away to a *pianissimo.*

To be sure, there are other fragments from Beethoven's song in the first movement which are not directly related to the reference in the coda, notably the opening melody that begins so characteristically on the sixth scale degree (segment *w;* ex. 2.9b).[134] Since it is precisely this sixth scale degree that is exposed in the segment Schumann inserted in the letter to Clara, why did he weave the most intricate web of allusions around what he considered the emotional center of the movement? A possible answer lies in Schumann's idiosyncratic contribution to the romantic "poetics of the remote": the way in which distance embraces other romantic categories of fragment, *Witz,* and arabesque.

Given that the fragment was the romantic response to the classical aesthetics of the whole,[135] the various Beethoven fragments in the *Fantasie,* including the one alluding to the Seventh Symphony in the third movement, would appear as ruins, whose wholeness has been lost. Indeed, Schumann's early title of the *Fantasie, Ruinen. Trophaeen. Palmen. Große Sonate f. d. Pianof. für Beethovens Denkmal* ("Ruins. Trophies. Palms. Grand Sonata for the Pianoforte for Beethoven's Monument"),[136] expresses a historical distance to a musical culture inevitably gone. Given that Schumann's musical ruins are references, historical distance manifests itself as referential distance. Yet his second theme bridges that distance to Beethoven's *An die ferne Geliebte* by recovering the cycle's lost wholeness in a filigree of fragments framed by its beginning and end. Schumann's theme begins with an allusion to the very passage marked *Ziemlich langsam und mit Ausdruck* that refers to the opening of Beethoven's cycle in the final song, and it ends with a cadential gesture from the end of that final song. In other words, the *Fantasie*'s lyrical theme encapsulates the entire song cycle. Of course, later names of the *Fantasie,* among them *Dichtungen* (Poems), suggest that Schumann deliberately distanced the piece from its direct association with Beethoven.[137] Yet if Schumann had veiled the ruins that he had preserved in his own way, his new motto by Schlegel encouraged his listeners to pursue their traces—if only in secret.

This search for the *Fantasie*'s secretly intertextual tone (as carried out above) ties into another, more conceptual, facet of distance: that of romantic *Witz* (the German word for the Latin *ingenium*). Jean Paul defined *Witz* as "the ability to discover a *distant similarity,*" but he saw a contradiction in this traditional definition: if distant denotes dissimilar, *Witz* would detect a seemingly impossible "dissimilar similarity."[138] To resolve the dilemma, Jean Paul drew on the distinction between wit and judgment, established in eighteenth-century aesthetics by John Locke and Edmund Burke. For Jean Paul, then, *Witz* "discovers the relation of similarity . . . hidden beneath a greater dissimilarity," while judgment, which he called acumen (*Scharfsinn*), "discovers the relation of dissimilarity . . . hidden beneath a greater similarity."[139] Traditionally, wit (establishing resemblance) was regarded as creative and poetic, and judgment (establishing difference), as rational and prosaic.[140] But Jean Paul's ideal was the combination of the two, called profundity (*Tiefsinn*), which "seeks similarity and unity of everything that wit connected by perception and that judgment separated by reason."[141] Profundity thus collapses the difference between wit and judgment (and the distance between similarity and dissimilarity) to arrive at the highest level of knowledge and being: the identity of subject and object. Schumann seems to have had this profundity in mind when, in his diary, he referred to Jean Paul's "profound, brilliant wit" (*tiefen, geistreichen Witz*).[142] In this sense, we might understand Schumann's Jean Paulesque transformation of Beethoven's music in the *Fantasie:* his compositional wit creates a distant similarity with the song cycle and thus plays with our analytical judgment fixated on dissimilarity. Both wit and judgment, however, combine in the work's musical *Tiefsinn.*

Distance, finally, embraces the third romantic category, the arabesque, which John Daverio suggested as a possible key to the formal function of the famous "Im Legendenton" section in the middle of the first movement.[143] In the romantic master genre of the novel, the arabesque compares to the permanent "parabasis" (a multiplication of interlocking levels of narration through ongoing digressions), which Friedrich Schlegel regarded as typical of the novel's form.[144] Thus "Im Legendenton" digresses from the main plot of the piece, even though it draws upon its material: the characteristically solemn opening stems from the syncopated inner melody of the transition between the first and second groups (mm. 33–40); and the melody that prefigures the second theme in measures 41–48 reappears in the remote tonal area of Db, woven into a more thickly textured accompaniment (mm. 181–94). Containing music removed from its original context and placed in a new one, "Im Legendenton" is like an arabesque interpolation that manifests *discursive* distance. I will digress to discuss this discursive distance, for it will help demonstrate Schumann's reference to Beethoven's *An die ferne Geliebte* by means of a yet unknown reference in "Im Legendenton" to his own distant beloved, Clara.

Marston has pointed out that in the autograph of the *Fantasie,* "Im Legendenton" was originally entitled "Romanza," a vocal genre "which narrates a tragic or amorous incident in a lyric verse form."[145] He draws attention to Sterndale Bennett's 1837 *Drei Romanzen,* op. 14 as an instrumental form of the genre.[146] What has not been remarked is that Schumann had a model close at hand: Clara's own *Romance variée,* op. 3. The *Romance* begins with a short five-measure "Introduzione," followed by a "Romanza," whose theme (also attributed to Schumann himself) he had used in his *Impromptus über ein Thema von Clara Wieck.*[147] The similarity between Clara's "Romanza" and "Im Legendenton" (formerly "Romanza") would seem remote (exx. 2.10a and 2.10b). But after a series of *brillante* variations and before the final virtuosic section, Clara brings back her "Romanza" theme in a C-minor *adagio* as a distant memory in a different—melancholy— tone. Thus Clara's meter, key, melody, and above all her formal procedure are either the same as, or closely resemble, Schumann's (exx. 2.10b–d).[148] In that sense, "Im Legendenton" might be another "Imptromptu." Like Clara, Schumann also has a "brilliant" variation of his/her theme, using her techniques of the sustained melodic notes in the middle register (cf. *Romance variée,* mm. 53–88, and *Fantasie,* mm. 195–203). It even appears that Schumann recalls at the ensuing climax the C–F–G–C, his famous counterpoint to Clara's theme in his *Impromptus:* C is prolonged from measures 201–3 and then leads to F–G–C in measures 204–6 (ex. 2.10e).

Schumann's appropriation of Clara's "Romanza" is hardly surprising, especially in light of the both amorous and melancholy circumstances that he associated with the composition of the *Fantasie*'s first movement.[149] But why did he replace the autograph's "Romanza" heading in the *Stichvorlage* first with "Legende" and then with the even more idiosyncratic "Erzählend im Legendenton" (later stripped of the "Erzählend")?[150] Perhaps he sought to veil the source: just as he had formerly eliminated the outdated advertisement of Beethoven in the title of the *Große Sonate,* he concealed any hint of an amorous meaning. Is the "Legende" the "lament" mentioned in the letter to Clara? Indeed, as in *Davidsbündlertänze,* the music from Clara's *Romance* intrudes into

Example 2.10. (a–c) Clara Wieck, *Romance variée*, op. 3;
(d–e) Robert Schumann, *Fantasie*, op. 17 ("Im Legendenton")

the composer's fantastic improvisation (mm. 33–40) before it becomes distant music recalled as a memory, finally dying away with a double echo (ex. 2.10e). And like the Aria (a movement), "Im Legendenton" (a movement within a movement) is a Song without Words, but one even more removed from the vocal genre from which it sprang. Yet if the Aria's tone was lyrical, the tone of "Im Legendenton" is narrative (*erzählend*). What does it tell?

Marston, inspired by Carolyn Abbate (herself inspired by Paul Ricoeur), argued that "Im Legendenton" can only narrate, because music, in Abbate's words, does not "possess *narrativity* without the *distance* engendered by discursive formulation," which becomes manifest only in a disjunction with the "music that constitutes its encircling milieu."[151] Given that Schumann's interpolation is a quasi-phenomenal narrative song that digresses from the main body of the movement and evokes a distant time, his final choice for a heading, "Im Legendenton," would seem to speak eloquently to that distance. Strangely enough, though, it is not the narrative that is most telling, but a single moment that breaks it open (ex. 2.11). After an eruption stilled by a fermata, this passage rises like a *fata morgana,* one of the *Fantasie*'s early titles that Schumann suggested to Breitkopf.[152] Here, Beethoven's cycle appears as if compressed into its most cryptic cipher: the opening anacrusis of the last song combined with the downward-leaping sixth of the first—at their original pitch level. While the melody immediately vanishes when a sequential pattern draws it back into the body of the legend, it has flashed, however briefly, and exposed, like a print without a negative, its source: Beethoven's song, written, as it were, in the air. The resulting *écriture,* distant and disappearing like a shooting star, is arguably the most telling event of "Im Legendenton"—not the disrupting narration, but the narration disrupted. This moment is not pastness—not the distant reminiscence of Clara's "Romanza" or the melody anticipating the second theme in D♭ and A♭—but presence. This moment slits open the body of the narrative song as if to foretell urgently what we will learn only in the coda: that both "Im Legendenton" and the movement it disrupts grew out of improvisation, which itself grew out of song. Finally, this moment, now only a mirage, gestures tonally and motivically beyond the discursive distance of "Im Legendenton" toward the double ending of the movement. Here all the varieties of distance—distant mountains, distant events, and distant people—will coalesce into the message that distance—spatial and temporal—may be overcome.

The first closure occurs with the end of the recapitulation of the second theme, which dies away into the distant landscape like the lover's song in the first poem of *An die Ferne Geliebte.* If E♭ is seen as a kind of second tonic folded into the movement, the recapitulation of the second

Example 2.11. Robert Schumann, *Fantasie,* op. 17, first movement mm. 154–60

theme in this key is much less surprising than its "absolutely unclassical" appearance in the subdominant F major (if seen from C as the tonic).[153] Since Schumann often composed at the piano, would he not have begun improvising on the final song of *An die Ferne Geliebte* in its original E♭—an improvisation eventually becoming the *Fantasie's* first movement? Thus, in a sense quite different from the classical recapitulation, Schumann's reprise of the second theme would function—intertextually— as a "recapitulation" of Beethoven's music in *its* home key. Dying away with the *adagio* into the space opened by the lifted dampers (perhaps signified by the two horizontal lines in mm. 79 and 271), as if toward the distant mountains, the single E♭ is the last note of Beethoven's song (assimilated by Schumann) heard at its original pitch level. Yet the diminished seventh leading to this E♭ implies a resolution to C minor, deflected abruptly to the *fortissimo* C-major chord that will lead to the second closure of the movement in the coda.

The coda is marked by the first full appearance of C major in the movement, resolving, at last, the dominant from its very beginning. Tonal closure coincides here with the revelation of the sonata's source: Schumann's theme on Beethoven's song. In the coda, Schumann's melody, repeated four times, stands exposed and resembles most closely—it is almost a literal quotation—the incipit of Beethoven's final song. This incipit complements (in reverse) the movement's passionate opening, which had begun, *in medias res,* with a later segment of Beethoven's melody (ex. 2.9b). In the coda, then, Schumann does not run the risk of revealing his source, because it sounds indeed as if he had composed it—as if it had grown out of improvisation and not been taken, fraudulently, from a song stripped of its text. But now Beethoven's song no longer needs words, since Schumann encoded their meaning into his music. Key signatures provide the key to unlocking this code. If, as Linda Correll Roesner suggests, the C in the final C major stands for the first letter in Clara,[154] this is not the C minor of her sadly remembered—legendary— "Romanza." Instead, as in the associated line of the poem, "And you sing what I have sung," Clara finally sings back, in "her" key, Beethoven's song, which, having broken through the Romanza's tone and become Schumann's song, has died away on E♭, that is, "*Es,*" for the first letter in *S*chumann.[155] The distance between E♭ and C is mediated through that enigmatic ascent from E♭ to C which stood out in the second theme. Now we may hear that ascent as a projection of Schumann's voice into the distant landscape, prolonging c^2 over the eerie *adagio,* but then dying away on $e♭^2$. In the coda, this gesture is picked up as the ascent turns into similarly gestured *portato* chords, first descending in the bass from C to E^1 (mm. 299–300), and then, in the original register, from c^2 to $e♭^1$, just before the very last, augmented, statement of Beethoven's melody.[156] Superimposed, descent and ascent create a voice exchange between E♭ and C (ex. 2.12)—as if Schumann's distant beloved had received the song and finally made his voice her own.

But Schumann also made her voice his. In a letter of 6 February 1838 he described to her the *Novelletten,* op. 21:

> Then I have composed a terrible lot in the last three weeks—humoristic things, stories of Egmont, family scenes with fathers, a wedding, in brief most lovely things—and the whole is called Novelletten because your name is Clara and "Wiecketten" does not sound well. . . . I have lived with you a long time, and there is really little difference between husband and wife and us. I talked like you. . . .[157]

Five days later Schumann wrote to Clara about the "Notturno" from her *Soirées musicales,* op. 6: "Do you know what the most precious thing of yours is for me—your Notturno in F major in six-eight time. What do you think about that? It is sufficiently melancholic, I believe. Then the Trio from the Toccatina."[158] Schumann used the beginning of the "Notturno" (whose melody resembles the Trio from the preceding Toccatina) in the last of his *Novelletten,* marking it explicitly in the score as "Stimme aus der Ferne" ("Voice from afar," ex. 2.13b). The last Novellette seems to have originated in a pair of Novelletten in D major and B♭ major, written between 11 March and 10 April 1838,[159] which Schumann combined, later adding the F♯-minor introduction (written in

Example 2.12. The voice exchange between "S"/E♭ and C

Example 2.13. (a) Clara Wieck, *Soirées musicales*, op. 6 ("Notturno");
(b–d) Robert Schumann, *Novelletten*, op. 21, no. 8

his own hand into the *Stichvorlage* that was prepared by a copyist).[160]
The result is a series of interlocking Novelletten within a Novellette,
setting up the "Voice from afar" in different tonal and expressive contexts. Indeed, what was originally the beginning of an independent piece
is now the D-major Trio 2. It opens with a section reminiscent of the
more forceful D-minor middle part in Clara's "Notturno." Her piece
would thus seem to have been turned inside out, since Schumann does
not recall her opening melody until the Novellette has settled on the
long D pedal, eventually giving way to an underlying accompaniment
reminiscent of the "Notturno" (ex. 2.13a).

Example 2.13. (cont.)

According to Jeffrey Kallberg, audiences would have recognized Clara's emulation of Chopin, so that Schumann cherished her "Notturno" in part for its generic association with the feminine.[161] In the Novellette, however, Schumann removed most of Clara's Chopinesque embellishments and added some of his own touches, as if her voice should sound different, more simple, when heard from afar. Prepared by an added trill, the expressive octave anticipation, for example, is realigned to fall squarely on a downbeat ("Notturno," m. 7, vs. *Novelletten,* mm. 207–8); or the opening harmonization includes a C♯ that obscures Clara's augmented triad. Schumann apparently felt entitled to appropriate his sources—a delicate situation with respect to his performing fiancée, who had her own ambitions as a composer.[162] Yet if Schumann exerted creative control over Clara's music, as he did over Beethoven's, he may have done so because they shared a melancholic quality he particularly cherished. Moreover, he seems to have ended the *Novelletten* with a poetic vision complementary to the *Fantasie:* a voice exchange between lover and beloved.

While arranging the Novelletten into a cycle of coherent tales (*zusammenhängende Geschichten*), Schumann realized only at a very late stage that the multiple closure of the composite Novellette in F♯, D, and B♭ could be used for such a deeply poetic ending.[163] Indeed, when the *Stimme aus der Ferne* fades away in a drawn-out descent, the work would seem to come to a close, since D major has been the key around which the *Novelletten* revolve. But Schumann continues with what is labeled in the score as *Fortsetzung* (beginning in m. 228) and *Fortsetzung und Schluß* (beginning in m. 282).[164] This could be a humorous reference to the practice of publishing novels in installments, but Schumann's vision seems to have been more serious. The first *Fortsetzung* evokes—again—Jean Paul's definition of the Romantic as the sound which, after having died away in the distance, continues to vibrate inwardly. If Schumann was drawn to Clara's "Notturno" for its "sufficiently melancholic" mood, he sings out Clara's melody (even more than Beethoven's song in the *Fantasie*'s second theme) in a kind of continuous inner expansion, replaying her now ornamented octave leap three times before it closes again in D major (ex. 2.13c). Schumann may have had this first—inner—*Fortsetzung* in mind when writing to Hermann Hirschbach that the *Novelletten* are "on average joyful and upbeat, except for particular moments, where I got to the bottom."[165] As if the "voice from afar" and its inner transformation had suspended time and space and reached to the bottom of his heart, Schumann resumes with the cadential gesture that preceded the double interpolation, again settling on D major (*Tempo wie im vorigen Stück,* mm. 255–81).

Once again, the piece seems to have come to an end. But when the *Fortsetzung und Schluß* strike a new tone, a "new" Novellette opens another narrative level. As in Schlegel's novelistic parabasis, Schumann accumulates arabesque-like frames that culminate in the climax, not merely of the last Novellette, but of the entire cycle. As if responding to the melancholic introversion before, he now passionately plays back the "Voice from afar" with utmost extroversion (ex. 2.13d). Here Clara's music appears at its original pitch level, her melody so amplified that it could be heard far away and "suggest a symbolic reunion with Clara."[166] As in the *Fantasie,* there is a striking conjunction between the main tonic and music from outside in the flat mediant, though their order is reversed and not connected to a symbolism between keys and name initials. Still, Clara's conspicuous move from her tonic, F major, to its relative minor in the middle part of the "Notturno" may have inspired Schumann to hear a bridge to his tonic, D major, where, after the quick close of the B♭-major digression, the *Novelletten* end exuberantly. Complementing the poetic vision of the *Fantasie,* Schumann, hearing the voice of his beloved from afar, finally sang himself "what you have sung."

The "voice exchange" between Robert and Clara, then, constitutes a rare case where analysis and criticism work together in a way that seems to undo the distance between them; it also seems to close the gap between a historically distant composition and its modern commentary. This, one might say, takes place when, on the one hand, the—poetic— expression "exchanging voices" assumes a precise technical meaning, and, on the other, the technical—prosaic—term "voice exchange" regains its original metaphorical quality. Collapsing the difference between technical and nontechnical language, analysis and criticism exchange voices themselves, capturing Schumann's profound attempt (in Jean Paul's sense) to overcome in his music the distance between the similar and the dissimilar, artwork and reality, lover and beloved. In that sense, his *Fantasie,* especially, is romantic *actio in distans.* Stripping Beethoven's tune of its text, Schumann folded its *logos* into the musical logic of the first movement. He thus turned music, literally, into a language, where sounding letters metamorphose into singing lovers, whose musical dia-*logos* creates the otherwise impossible event of understanding: when they exchange the tonic of a single song.

Epilogue

The nobleman soon took a great liking to him, although he often confessed that he felt rather uncomfortable in his presence, and that ice-cold shivers ran through him whenever the stranger, over a full cup of wine, *spoke of the many distant and unknown lands and strange men* and beasts he had become acquainted with during his far-flung travels. At such times his speech faded into a [miraculous sound], in which he wordlessly rendered obscure and mysterious things comprehensible.[167]

However accidental the connection to this passage from E.T.A. Hoffmann's "Johannes Kreisler's Certificate of Apprenticeship," the poet in Schumann's *Kinderszenen* begins his stories similarly with "Von fremden Ländern und Menschen." And at the end, in "Der Dichter spricht," his musical language, like that of Hoffmann's stranger, dies away when the chorale gradually transforms into free melody—abso-

113

lute music. Other than in Novalis's definition, however, prose is not surrounded by poetry, but poetry by prose that abruptly returns to secure closure. In "Der Dichter spricht," Schumann seems to suggest that making music of language is romantic utopia. The poet–composer may transform prose into poetry, but may not easily exchange poetry for prose again without re-creating between them the difference that distance has made. Usually, the poet as well as the critic speak. Sometimes they *sing*.

ELSA'S SCREAM

I will examine the story of two stories, both by Richard Wagner: a story of Lohengrin, knight of the Holy Grail, and of *Lohengrin,* the opera. Lohengrin's story is well known: Elsa of Brabant, accused by her former suitor, Friedrich of Telramund, of having killed her brother and heir to the throne, prays for help from the unknown knight in her dreams, promising herself as wife in exchange for his assistance. Miraculously, the knight appears in a boat pulled by a swan and accepts her offer, with the condition that she never ask about his origin, name, or nature. But political and personal intrigue, spun by Friedrich and the gypsy woman Ortrud, nourish doubts about the knight's magical existence, doubts that ultimately drive Elsa to ask the forbidden question on her wedding night. Lohengrin publicly discloses his identity and leaves Elsa, though not without returning her brother, whom Ortrud had transformed into the swan, to power.

The story behind *Lohengrin,* composed in 1846/47 and premiered in 1850 in Weimar, exists only as fragments scattered throughout Wagner's writings. It can be reconstructed, however, because it is part of a larger, well-known, and problematic story: Wagner's account of his own artistic evolution and its role in the history of music, in which Western art reaches its pinnacle and fulfillment in music drama, as the fusion of Shakespeare's drama and Beethoven's symphony. *Lohengrin* figures prominently in this master narrative, first told in Wagner's 1851 autobiographical essay, *A Communication to my Friends,* which was to accompany an edition of his libretti for *The Flying Dutchman, Tannhäuser,* and *Lohengrin.* Wagner wanted primarily to communicate that these operas should not be heard in light of his recently completed *Opera and Drama,* but as preliminary, yet necessary, stations on a path to the work that would put his new theory into practice: the *Ring.* Arthur Groos has shown that Wagner constructed *The Flying Dutchman* as his first attempt to transcend the generic constraints of traditional romantic opera.[1] Yet *Lohengrin* held an even more important place in the trajectory of Wagner's oeuvre, because:

> the tragedy of Lohengrin's character and situation was confirmed as one
> deeply rooted in modern life: it repeated itself with the work and its
> creator, precisely in the same way as it was presented through the hero of

this poem. The character and situation of this Lohengrin I now recognize, with clear conviction, as the *type of the true and only tragic subject, the tragic element of life, of modern times.*[2]

Lohengrin's story thus prefigured *Lohengrin's* story. Just as the hero was misunderstood, Wagner claimed in hindsight, so had the opera and its author. Yet he considered Lohengrin's tragedy not merely analogous to his artistic situation, but an essential part of it:

> This woman [Elsa], who with clear foreknowledge rushes on to her doom for the sake of love's necessary nature . . . this glorious woman, before whom Lohengrin had to vanish because he . . . could not understand her—I had found her *now*: and the lost shaft that I had shot towards this precious discovery . . . was precisely my Lohengrin, whom I had to abandon, in order to discover the *truly feminine*, which should one day bring me and all the world to redemption . . . Elsa, the woman . . . made me a total revolutionary.[3]

The overblown rhetoric conceals that the ending had been a trouble spot in the opera's genesis. In *A Communication*, Wagner took great pains to diffuse the critique of an unidentified "friend" (the writer Hermann Franck), who had found Lohengrin a cold and forbidding figure, and his departure—as Wagner recalled later in his autobiography *My Life*—an unseemly punishment of Elsa.[4]

Franck touched a nerve. In fact, Wagner admitted to him in a letter of 30 May 1846 (during work on the first complete musical draft) that his criticism had been "of great help in forcing me to consider ways of making Lohengrin's involvement in the tragic outcome clearer than had previously been the case."[5] As John Deathridge has shown, the changes between the first complete musical draft and the final version indicate that Wagner realized "the necessity of heightening Lohengrin's participation and of inventing a clear motivation for his departure."[6] Yet in public accounts of the incident Wagner congratulated himself for having considered, but ultimately rejected, Franck's criticism. In other words, he sought to justify *Lohengrin's* problematic dénouement and thereby place the opera in his artistic trajectory. Elsa, Wagner implied, opened the door for Brünnhilde and the artistic revolution of the *Ring*.

To be sure, Wagner's portrayal of his early operas as inevitable stages in the evolution of music drama (and Elsa's role as the catalyst of the breakthrough to the music of the future) smacks of special pleading. Cleary he attempted to press his life and work into an historical scenario, whose "mode of emplotment" (as Hayden White would say) was romance: "a drama of self-identification symbolized by the hero's transcendence of the world of experience, his victory over it, and his final liberation of it."[7] Most historians agree that history is some sort of storytelling (narrative being a central theoretical problem of historiography), but insist on the distinction between stories and true stories—the former being based on fictional events, the latter on real ones.[8] In the same way, musicologists have come to differentiate between Wagner's life and *My Life,* as the latter is interlaced with self-serving fictions and myths.[9] Yet given Wagner's lifelong insistence on the close relationship between history and myth, it is hardly surprising that he would see his life mirrored in the mythological subjects of his operas, and vice versa. Indeed, if Wagner's primary ploy was to plot himself into the history of music, he did so in part by making his characters do the job for him, a process perhaps most obvious in *Lohengrin,* whose conjunction of a fairytale subject and historical drama Carl Dahlhaus considered the opera's central paradox.[10] This paradox is the crux of the drama, embodied in Elsa being torn between her belief in the knight of the Holy Grail and her love for the hero of Brabant. For Wagner, this conflict became deeply symbolic: in Elsa, the revolutionary, the story of Lohengrin (hero) and the (hi)story of *Lohengrin* (opera) come together. They should, in some sense, be told together.

How?

Wagner criticism has recently taken a turn towards reading his operas and theoretical oeuvre as what Jean-Jacques Nattiez called "interlocking texts."[11] The approach is not entirely new, having originated with two essays on *Lohengrin* from the early 1850s.[12] Yet the recent studies by Nattiez and Thomas Grey have sought to do more: to interpret Wagner's operas as allegories of his most conspicuous theoretical concept from *Opera and Drama:* music as woman, poetry as man.[13] Thus, in the *Ring,* as a "mythic account of the history of music," the union of Siegfried and Brünnhilde figures as that of poetry and music—a union of which Tristan and Isolde are a variation and Parsifal and Kundry the antithesis.[14] But Lohengrin and Elsa have not inspired similar readings, even though Wagner described the couple in the terms he also employed for the relationship between music and poetry:

> In "Elsa" I saw from the outset my desired antithesis to Lohengrin—not, of course, the absolute antithesis far removed from his own nature but, rather, the *other half* of his own being—the antithesis that was contained within his own nature and that is only the complement of his specific masculine essence, a complement he necessarily longs to embrace. *Elsa* is that unconscious, involuntary element in which Lohengrin's conscious, voluntary nature longs to be redeemed; but this *longing,* in turn, is itself the unconscious, necessary, involuntary element in Lohengrin, through which he is related to Elsa's being.[15]

Poetry will easily find this path [to intimate union with music], and acknowledge its own deep longing for an eventual merging with music as soon as it realizes that music itself has a need which only poetry can fulfill.[16]

According to Nattiez, "the figure of androgyny takes the form of a double" with Elsa and Lohengrin.[17] But what did their unfulfilled union—their failed dialectic—imply for the opera's stance on the relationships between music and poetry, for its position in Wagner's dramatic oeuvre, and for its place in his history of music?

This, then, will be *my* story: how Wagner mapped the story of his last romantic opera onto his history of opera. My narrative hinges on two moments whose meaning emerges through the union of musical hermeneutics and historical hermeneutics. In these moments, Lohengrin's and *Lohengrin's* story do not merely "interlock," but coalesce into a single event cutting across not only the fictional and the real, or myth and history; but also across the distinction between absolute music and opera. This event is the birth of music drama. These two moments are two screams: when Elsa cries out to Lohengrin for help, he comes; and when she cries out for his name, he must depart.[18]

Elsa's First Scream

In 1879 Wagner wrote three short articles for the *Bayreuther Blätter,* the final contribution to his aesthetics of opera.[19] In the third article, "On the Application of Music to the Drama," he dealt, for the last time, with the central issue of his theoretical writings: the difference between symphonic and dramatic music. While Wagner's discussion is unusually specific, using musical examples from the *Ring,* he concludes with an even more remarkable gesture, choosing two passages from *Lohengrin* act 1 scene 2 to demonstrate the "characteristic difference" between symphonic and dramatic music: "not only the transformation and use of motifs—as demanded by the drama, but prohibited by the symphony—but in the first creation of the motif itself." The passage deserves to be quoted in full:

The motif, which the composer of "Lohengrin" employs as the closing phrase of a first arioso of his *Elsa,* sunk in memory of a blissful dream, consists almost solely of a web of remote harmonic progressions. In the Andante of a Symphony, this progression would strike us as far-fetched and highly unintelligible; here, in the opera , it does not seem strained, but arising out of itself, and therefore so intelligible that to my knowledge it has never been decried as the contrary. This has its grounds, however, in the scenic action. *Elsa* has slowly approached, in gentle grief, her head bowed bashfully; one upward glance of her transfigured eye [ex. 3.1] informs us what is in her soul.

Example 3.1. First harmonic progression from *Lohengrin* as it appears in Wagner's article

Questioned, *Elsa* replies only with the vision of a dream that fills her with sweet confidence: "With virtuous conduct he gave me consolation." That upward glance had already told us something of the kind. Now, boldly passing from her dream to the assurance of fulfillment in reality, she adds: "That knight I will await then; he shall be my champion." And after further modulation, the musical phrase now returns to its original key [ex. 3.2].

Example 3.2. Second harmonic progression from *Lohengrin* as it appears in Wagner's article

At the time a young friend of mine, to whom I had sent the score for arrangement as a piano-vocal score, was much astonished by the look of this phrase which has so many modulations in so few bars, but still more when he attended the first performance of "Lohengrin" at Weimar and found that this selfsame phrase appeared quite natural.[20]

Wagner's (self-)analysis reaffirms a central thesis of *Opera and Drama*: devoid of dramatic motivation, absolute music remains an end in itself and thus incomprehensible. The anecdote about his friend drives the point home: because the explanatory view of the stage was lacking in a mere reading of the score, the modulation in question—from the dominant of A♭ minor to A major with a characteristic mode change from G♭ major to F♯ minor as pivot chords—appeared "unnatural."[21] This had been an unchanging principle in Wagner's aesthetics: harmonic progressions that deviate from those warranted by the fixed forms of traditional instrumental music require a *raison d'être*—drama.

But why *Lohengrin*? Since Wagner, in *A Communication*, had cautioned against reading his pre-*Ring* operas as an application of his theoretical writings, why, towards the end of his career, did he not use the *Ring* or *Tristan* to exemplify the complex combination of alliteration and modulation developed in *Opera and Drama*?[22] Apparently, Elsa's dream held special significance for him. Joachim Raff, for instance, considered the second scene of *Lohengrin* a "poetic masterpiece," which alone would "secure Wagner an honorary place among the poets of all time."[23] Raff's hyperbole aside, it seems that for Wagner the scene marked a key moment in evolution of his operatic aesthetic and practice and that it therefore functioned as a model when he postulated in *Opera and Drama* the ideal form of a dramatic unit.

To recapitulate: when, in the first scene of *Lohengrin*, King Heinrich arrives to reinforce his troops, Friedrich of Telramund seeks a public trial to establish his claim on Brabant. Elsa's grief thus stems not only from the disappearance of her brother, but also from the charge of fratricide. Summoned by the king, she enters at the beginning of the second scene with an eight-measure period in A♭ minor, punctuated with interjections from the men of Brabant: "Seht hin! Sie naht, die hart Beklagte" ("Behold, here comes the heavily accused"; ex. 3.3). Its consequent begins with Wagner's first musical example in the article, the four measures modulating to A major. The stage direction prescribes that Elsa advance with a bashful expression, suggesting that her eyes be cast down during the A♭-minor phrase—not least because Wagner describes the modulating continuation of this phrase as "an upward glance." The Brabantian men are struck and begin weighing this impression against the gravity of Friedrich's accusation. Their response blends into a variant of the Elsa motif, transposed up a whole step:

Ha! wie erscheint sie so licht und rein!
Der sie so schwer zu zeihen wagte,
wie sicher muß der Schuld er sein!

[How fair and pure she seems! The one who dared to bring this heavy charge: how certain he must be of her guilt!]

Example 3.3. Lohengrin, act 1, scene 2, Elsa enters

Example 3.3. (cont.)

Raff noted that the chorus in *Lohengrin* often functions as a surrogate for the audience, playing a double role as both character and commentator.[24] Indeed, the second scene shows Wagner on the way to his grand project of, in Hegelian terms, "sublating" the chorus of Greek drama into the orchestra of modern (music) drama.[25] Initially, chorus and orchestra operate as distinct agents, but gradually they converge. The voices blend into the harmony of Elsa's motif played by the orchestra, but since they do not yet take over its melodic line, it seems as though the Brabantians do not fully understand her. Can they *hear* Elsa?

Example 3.3. (cont.)

Of course they cannot, and the distinction is crucial for understanding the scene.[26] We, as the audience share the men's gaze, but Elsa's motif tells only us—by means of music—what lives inside her. As if Wagner had Elsa in mind, he wrote in *Opera and Drama* how such a situation is ideal for dramatic development:

What is offered to our eye by a . . . still and silent human figure . . . [instrumental] music can present to our emotions in such a way that, starting from the moment of repose, it moves this emotion towards a state of suspense and expectation which the poet needs, so that we can assist him in the revelation of his intent.[27]

In *Lohengrin*, then, the drama starts to move at the moment when Elsa's upward glance moves the crowd and, by implication, us. Wagner seems to have taken the image of the glance from his own stage directions. When the king asks whether she accepts him as her judge, "Elsa wendet ihr Haupt nach dem König, blickt ihm ins Auge und bejaht dann mit vertrauensvoller Gebärde" ("Elsa turns her head towards the king, looks into his eyes, and assents with a trusting gesture"). Here, her motif recurs at its original pitch level. In an even more pertinent passage from *Opera and Drama,* Wagner describes how the music figures such a gesture:

> The orchestra expresses musically [in *Tonfiguren*] . . . what is revealed to the eye by means of gesture, and speaks it out *so far* as there was no need for mediation through verbal language. . . . We commonly say: "I read it in your eye"; which means: "In a way intelligible to it alone, my eye perceives in the look of yours an involuntary feeling in you, which I involuntarily, in turn, now feel with you."[28]

Thus the king sees and senses what only we hear. Yet to both him (visually) and us (aurally), Elsa's glance communicates what Wagner called an "involuntary feeling." These involuntary emotions:

> . . . in which a human being speaks so truly, are solely those of most perfect repose or highest agitation: what lie between these extremes are transitions, which are determined by genuine passion only in so far as they either approach the state of highest agitation, or return therefrom, appeased, to a harmonious repose. These transitions consist of a mixture of voluntary, reflective action of the will with unconscious, necessary emotion: the determination of those transitions towards the direction of involuntary emotion—with an unflagging flow towards, and final flow into, true emotion— . . . is the subject of the poetic intent in drama.[29]

We have come to associate Wagner's "art of transition" with *Tristan*,[30] though it is also present in his earlier aesthetics and practice. Thus, after the perfect repose of Elsa's silent appearance, her glance touches off a dramatic transition. This seemingly inconspicuous *Augenblick* initiates the king's request: "Sag', Elsa! Was hast du mir zu vertraun?" ("Elsa, what do you have to confide to me?"). She must tell him what is behind that glance: her dream.

Elsa's dream narration is in two parts: the events leading up to the dream, and the dream itself. Two moments concern me here: the melodic climax in the first part and the motivic working in the second. Elsa begins:

> Einsam in trüben Tagen
> hab' ich zu Gott gefleht,
> des Herzens tiefstes Klagen
> ergoß ich im Gebet.
> Da drang aus meinem Stöhnen
> ein Laut so klagevoll,
> der zu gewalt'gem Tönen
> weit in die Lüfte schwoll:
> ich hört' ihn fernhin hallen,
> bis kaum mein Ohr er traf;
> mein Aug' ist zugefallen,
> ich sank in süßen Schlaf!

[Alone in gloomy days I made entreaty to God. The deepest anguish of my heart I poured forth in prayer. Then from my moaning burst forth a sound so sorrowful, which, becoming a powerful tone, swelled far into the air; I heard it resound in the distance until it scarcely reached my ear; my eyes closed, I sank into sweet sleep.]

Elsa begins calm and composed: two lines of text, a four-measure phrase, a melodic descent from eb^2 to ab^1, and a full cadence to the tonic, Ab major. When she elaborates, composure and composition crumble: another four-measure phrase, again in the tonic, but a more chromatic descent from eb^2 thus closing not on the first but the fifth scale degree (eb^1). The change seems small, yet with it Elsa's narration slips into reliving the original experience: her square phrasing opens up into a nine-measure string tremolo, over which her melody rises back to eb^2 at "Laut." Repeating eb^2, she crescendos, climbs to fb^2, gb^2 and finally—*fortissimo*—reaches ab^2 (over Cb major), the climax of the entire narration.

Relating how the sound broke loose from her moaning, Elsa's voice breaks as well: her sorrowful sound splits off from her body into the orchestra, which holds eb^2 over eleven measures, swelling and then dying away. No singer can sustain such a sound, but the winds prolong it almost infinitely to reach the infinite.[31] In the *Lohengrin* epos, Elsa takes from a falcon a *schelle* (bell), whose sound, as an extension of her prayer, reaches out to King Arthur's realm in France:

> Ir cappelân die messe sanc.
> Eines tages in dûht wie der glocken klanc
> in doners wîse breche durch der wolken grüfte.
> Der galm gein Fránkrìche gienc,
> In sîn herze erz vür manige wunne enpfienc.
> Von irem dône teilten sich die lüfte. (Stanza 38)[32]

[Her chaplain sang Mass, when one day it appeared to him that the sound of the bell broke through the clefts of the clouds. The sound went to France, giving manifold pleasure to his heart. The sound of the bell divided the air.]

Singled out in one of Wagner's sources, this passage must have stirred the composer's imagination.[33] His decision to split the cloud-splitting sound is both practical and poetic. The climactic $a\flat^2$ pierces the air (and our ears) as the *Laut* that is *loud*. It gestures ahead towards the tonic, where Elsa will begin the actual dream, but to bridge the distance between reality and vision, between Brabant and France, between the tonic of the narration and the tonic of the dream, Wagner prolongs the dominant. Telling how she "sank into sweet sleep," Elsa's voice descends to $e\flat^1$, where the flute picks it up and literally lifts it from her body by rising chromatically to $e\flat^3$ (see the beginning of ex. 3.4). Thus recalling her call for help, Elsa triggers the effect of its original sound dying away: the state of somnambulistic clairvoyance. In it, she recounts:

In lichter Waffen Scheine
ein Ritter nahte da,
so tugendlicher Reine
ich keinen noch ersah.
Ein golden Horn zur Hüften,
gelehnet auf sein Schwert,
so trat er aus den Lüften
zu mir, der Recke wert.
Mit züchtigem Gebahren
gab Tröstung er mir ein:
(*mit erhobener Stimme*)
des Ritters will ich wahren,
er soll mein Streiter sein!
(*schwärmerisch*)
Er soll mein Streiter sein!

[In the shine of bright armor approached a knight of such virtue as I had never seen before. A golden horn at his side, leaning on his sword, thus the worthy warrior came out of the air to me. With virtuous conduct he gave me consolation. (*with raised voice*) That knight I will await; he shall be my champion! (*enthusiastically*) He shall be my champion!]

What Elsa sees, we hear as a series of three motifs. All will eventually be associated with Lohengrin's appearance, but in her dream, each has a different status according to Wagner's theory of how dramatic music must be motivated:

A musical motif into which . . . the thought of the word–verse of a dramatic actor has been poured before our eyes, is necessarily determined; on its recurrence, a *definite* emotion is perceptibly communicated to us.[34]

Given this scheme (which Wagner handled with considerable flexibility), the motif that opens Elsa's dream stems from the opening of the prelude (see the end of ex. 3.4), but is still without words and therefore

Example 3.4. Lohengrin, act 1, scene 2, Elsa's dream narration (beginning of second half)

Example 3.4. (cont.)

indefinite. Equally indefinite is the music accompanying Elsa's description of Lohengrin. Although never heard before, its distinctly regal character immediately links up with his image (hence its popular label as the Lohengrin motif). Finally, at the end of her dream narration, Elsa's own motif returns (Wagner's second example, see ex. 3.2). No longer wordless, however, it has become the "verse melody into which the thought of the word–verse of a dramatic actor has been poured before our eyes" (see the first part of ex. 3.5).

Example 3.5. Lohengrin, act 1, scene 2, Elsa's dream narration (end)

Example 3.5. (cont.)

If, in light of Wagner's discussion of the passage, the creation of Elsa's motif took place at the beginning of the scene, the end of her dream gives us its use and transformation. The first half of the motif is nearly the same. Though transposed, it moves a tritone toward what Wagner, in this context, would have considered the bright side: from A♭ to D major—"Mit züchtigem Gebaren, gab Tröstung er mir ein" ("with virtuous conduct he gave me consolation"). But then, as Wagner put it, Elsa passes boldly from dream to reality, from the past relived to the

Example 3.5. (cont.)

future envisioned: "des Ritters will ich wahren, er soll mein Streiter
sein!" ("that knight I will await then; he shall be my champion"). Here
after the characteristic pivotal mode change from D major to D minor,
the motif modulates *back* to the tonic A♭—Elsa's key. Wordless, her
motif has been played by the higher woodwinds. But when it is determined through the words of her voice, the lower strings—as Adorno
heard it—"affix the music, which was, as it were, transfixed in the air,
onto the body of the dreaming woman."[35]

Elsa's closing gesture does more than wrap up her narration: instead,
it is pushed beyond the traditional boundaries of the operatic adagio.

Now the people ("very moved") take over her motif completely, praying for the grace of heaven and their own clear vision for a just judgement. Can they hear Elsa *now?* Whatever the case, her refrain and its collective echo suggest that she has the crowd behind her (see the second part of ex. 3.5). Initially powerless, she is now in control: Friedrich accepts the challenge of her vision, and the king surrenders his secular jurisdiction to a divine one. Determining her motif, she determines the nature of her trial, an ordeal by battle. As Adorno put it, Elsa's vision attracts the entire action.[36]

Formalities of the ordeal follow, its nodal points punctuated by Elsa's motif. When the king asks her, "Wen wählest du zum Streiter?" ("Whom do you choose as your champion?"), the first part of her motif from the end of her dream returns—but without text. As the property of pure, but now determined, music, the motif gestures towards a definite answer. Again that musical answer is for our ears only, not the king's, since her official response comes with the motif's original text: "des Ritters will ich wahren, er soll mein Streiter sein" ("That knight I will await then; he shall be my champion"). Continuing where she left off at the end of her dream, she modulates from Ab major to Gb major, which surely resonates with the pivotal Gb in the original "upward glance." Launching into a short arioso, Elsa increases the stakes, offering her champion the crown and—on another climactic ab^2—herself as his future wife.

Yet the herald's two calls for Elsa's knight remain unanswered. And so she sinks to her knees, praying:

> Du trugest zu ihm meine Klage,
> zu mir trat er auf dein Gebot:
> O Herr, nun meinem Ritter sage,
> daß er mir helf' in meiner Not!
> (*in wachsender Begeisterung*)
> Laß mich ihn sehn, wie ich ihn sah,
> wie ich ihn sah,
> (*mit freudig verklärter Miene*)
> sei er mir nah!

[You imparted to him my lament, he came to me by your command: O Lord, now tell my knight to help me in my distress! (*with increasing enthusiasm*) Let me see him as I saw him, as I saw him (*with an expression of happy rapture*) let him be nigh!]

Elsa exclaims "Herr" ("o Lord") again on the same ab^2 that once pierced the air to reach the divine and, moments before, rang out her promise of marriage. At the prayer's climax, finally, her motif returns in its original form (ex. 3.6). Begging that the past may become present, and dream become reality, Elsa exclaims: "Let me see him as I saw him, as I saw him let him be nigh!" Only now do we know for sure that she *sings,* for her prayer is—by operatic convention—phenomenal song.[37] Having narrated her prayer before, she now reenacts it. Unlike Senta's Ballad, her former dream narration was not performed song. While her many highpoints on ab^2 gestured towards song and came increasingly close, they remained mimetic. Only when Elsa sings her prayer do operatic and (re-)enacted narrative, epos and drama, dream and reality, become one.

At this climax, then, Elsa's motif conjures up Lohengrin's and with it his actual appearance on the horizon, in a boat pulled by a swan. And now her original motif finally stays in the new tonic of A major. Sung, her a^2 is the highest note in the scene: the extreme moment of utmost agitation that Wagner set forth as the goal of a dramatic unit. Elsa's narration could not have effected the advent of her savior; only song, as the embodiment of her involuntary agitation, can bring this about. Thus, at the climax, the ear must join the eye to achieve true aural vision. As Wagner suggested in *Opera and Drama:*

> If we imagine the infinitely agitated impression which the sight of the dramatic individuality must produce on our powerfully captivated eye, then we also understand the desire of hearing . . . completely in accordance the one that affects the eye . . . for "(only) at the mouth of two witnesses shall the (whole) truth be known."[38]

Here, then, Wagner's theoretical text does not merely interlock, but coalesces with the opera's plot. Just as music drama requires our senses to bear witness to visual and aural action, Elsa needs the witness of both eye and ear in her trial: the people have to hear the inaudible in her upward glance; and see the invisible narrated in her dream. And so her a^2, the "final flow into true emotion" that brings about Lohengrin's arrival at the moment of her greatest distress, is carried over—through the chorus describing Lohengrin's arrival—to the beginning of the third scene. Only now does Elsa turn around and, seeing him for the first time face to face, scream.[39] Strangely, the scream is drowned in a deafening cymbal clash. As a reflex of the original *schelle,* the clash carries the symbolic resonance of distance overcome: its explosion marks the fusion of sight and sound in music drama.

Screaming, Elsa's voice becomes her will and her will brings Lohengrin into the world. This is the opera's *Augenblick* of the whole—the moment of fulfillment that brings (like Leonore's scream) the two spheres, the ideal and the real, together. Could Wagner have avoided appropriating Schopenhauer's metaphysics of the will a decade later? Later still, in his

Example 3.6. Lohengrin, act 1, scene 2, Elsa prays

Example 3.6. (cont.)

introduction to the Zurich writings for the 1871 edition of his prose words, Wagner urged his readers to replace his earlier Feuerbachian *Unwillkür* (the involuntary) with Schopenhauer's *Wille* (will).[40] The terminological swap is shrewd, authorizing a rereading of *Opera and Drama* in Schopenhauer's terms, which Wagner claimed were latent in the treatise. This correlates with a well-known remark to Cosima Wagner in 1872:

> Of *Opera and Drama*, which he is correcting, he says: I know what Nietzsche didn't like in it—it is the same thing . . . that set Schopenhauer against me: what I said about words. At the same time I didn't dare to say that music produced drama, although inside myself I knew it.[41]

The contradiction between *Opera and Drama* (1850), according to which music "cannot, of itself, determine the aim of drama," and *Beethoven* (1870), where music reigns supreme as "man's a priori capacity for fashioning drama," has baffled generations of Wagner scholars.[42] Given Wagner's history of fabricating history, it might be dangerous (as Nattiez suggests)[43] to believe Wagner's remark to Cosima, and accept his switch from the involuntary to the will in the new preface to *Opera and Drama*. But the risk of believing him carries its rewards. These rewards will not do away with the contradictions between Wagner's early and later writings, which he admitted to Cosima. Yet if Wagner's notoriously enabling fictions are not true, they are plausible—and this plausibility enables them to sustain their historical force, and our historical interest. If drama, according to one of Wagner's most famous aphorisms, is indeed "deeds of music become visible," then Lohengrin is born out of music: out of Elsa.

Lohengrin the Absolute Artist

Lohengrin, as Wagner saw him, had a male half and a female half, Elsa. Given the slippage between Lohengrin and *Lohengrin,* those parts become wholes—operatic characters—who seek to come together. But why does their union fail? Why does the *Augenblick* of Lohengrin's aesthetic appearance, the moment of the beautiful artistic whole, have no future?[44]

Lohengrin enters the world of opera in a scene that seems a perfect model for Wagner's notion of organic dramatic form: "By presenting his artwork in continuous organic becoming, and making us ourselves organically participating witnesses of that becoming, the poet frees his work from all traces of its creation."[45] Behind this organicism looms Kant's notion that art (second nature) had to appear like (first) nature.[46] But Wagner went a step further: he understood the *Dichter* as a *Verdichter,* who compresses otherwise diffuse human action into a moment, "which, taken for itself, appears indeed unwonted and miraculous, yet shuts its own . . . magic within itself, and is in no way taken by the spectator *for a miracle* but apprehended as the *most intelligible* representation of reality."[47] Wagner called this the "poetic miracle": the poet has to begin with an ordinary situation in which we could find ourselves—such as Elsa's being wrongfully accused.[48] Then he can "ascend gradually towards the formation of situations whose force and magic remove us from everyday life, and show us human beings at the height of their powers"—such as Elsa's conjuring up Lohengrin.[49] Indeed, the entire scene becomes a giant transition from the natural to the supernatural: from the Brabantians' initial whispering "How miraculous" about the silent Elsa to their exclaiming "A miracle" about Lohengrin's arrival. But there is one problem: the poetic miracle, "the most intelligible representation of reality," has come to represent something entirely unreal: a true miracle.[50]

Wagner was aware of the paradox. In *Opera and Drama*, he distinguished between the poetic miracle and what he called the "dogmatic" or "Judeo–Christian miracle":

The Judeo–Christian miracle tore the connection of natural phenomena apart, allowing the divine will to appear as standing *above* nature. . . . The *fundamental negation of understanding* was therefore a precondition by the one demanding a miracle and the one who carried it out: *absolute belief* was demanded by the one making the miracle happen and granted by the one receiving the miracle.[51]

The passage reflects Wagner's reception of Ludwig Feuerbach's *Essence of Christianity* (1841), which posits belief as built on the special revelation of God, who does not arrive (like Lohengrin) through the common—human—way. Feuerbach devoted a chapter to "The Contradiction between Belief and Love," stating that:

Love identifies man with God, God with man, and, therefore, man with man; belief separates God from man, and, therefore, man from man. . . . Belief isolates God, it turns Him into a *special, other,* being; love . . . turns God into a *common* being, whose love is at one with the love towards man. Belief disunites man *intrinsically with himself,* and, therefore, externally, too; it is love, however, which heals the wounds that belief has inflicted on the heart of man.[52]

Wagner could have used these terms to spell out Lohengrin's dilemma in his relationship with Elsa:

Lohengrin sought the woman who would *believe* in him: who would not ask who he was and whence he came, but love him as he was . . . who would *love* him unconditionally. Therefore, he had to hide his higher nature, for precisely in not uncovering and revealing this higher . . . nature lay his only guarantee that he was not adored and marveled at, or humbly worshiped as something incomprehensible. . . . He wanted to become and be nothing other than a . . . *human being,* not God, i.e., absolute artist. . . .

> Undisputably there clings to him the telltale halo of heightened nature; he cannot but appear like a miracle; the gaping of the common people, the poisoned trail of envy throw their shadow even across the loving woman's heart; doubt and jealousy show him that he has not been *understood,* but only *worshipped,* and force from him the avowal of his divinity, where-with, destroyed, he returns into his loneliness.[53]

In the figure of the absolute artist, then, Wagner elides the spheres of Lohengrin (hero) and *Lohengrin* (opera). In the Zurich writings, "abso-lute" denotes a negative extreme: isolated, egoistic, metaphysical—in short, not communist. Within Wagner's gendered imagery of the rela-tionship between music and poetry, Lohengrin, the absolute artist, would seem to stand primarily for the absolute poet:

> The poetic intellect . . . is not at all interested in *belief* but only in *understanding through feeling.* It wants to display a great combination of natural phenomena in an easily perceptible image, and this image must therefore correspond to these phenomena in such a way that involuntary feeling may absorb it without reluctance, and not be asked to explain it. The characteristic of the dogmatic miracle, on the other hand, consists in despotically subjugating the search of understanding for such an explana-tion, while seeking its effect precisely in this subjugation. The dogmatic miracle is therefore unfit for art, while the poetic miracle is the highest and most necessary product of the artistic power of perception and repre-sentation.[54]

In theoretical terms, Lohengrin's dilemma is that he wants to be that poetic intellect, but behaves dogmatically. He therefore tells Elsa not to ask him to explain himself, despotically subjugating her "search of understanding for such an explanation, while seeking its effect precisely in this subjugation." Paradoxically, Lohengrin uses the demand of abso-lute belief to conceal his own absoluteness.

But what of Elsa, Lohengrin's other half? The Elsa-half of Lohengrin is the absolute musician. Indeed, in labeling Lohengrin the absolute artist, Wagner may have had primarily his musical half in mind. In *A Communication,* he noted that the:

> . . . *absolute* artist [will develop] along the path which we must designate as the feminine, i.e., that which embraces alone the feminine element of

art. On this we meet all those artists of the day who define modern art. Separated from life it is the art world, where art plays with itself . . . we find above all painting, and pre-eminently music.[55]

Absolute music, then, was for Wagner a kind of feminine fantasy, which becomes in *Lohengrin* a fantasy of love. In his program note for the prelude, written for a series of 1853 Zurich concerts including highlights from the opera, Wagner alluded to the myth of the Grail as a product of "enchanted imagination" that "set both source and goal of this incomprehensible desire for love outside the actual world."[56] Similarly, Wagner saw the archetype of Lohengrin's story in the legend of Zeus and Semele: "Who had taught man that a god could burn with love for earthly woman? For certain, only man himself."[57] The notion that God is an unconscious product of human consciousness is again Feuerbach's, who sought to collapse the difference between God and human beings, between the metaphysical and the physical.[58] The "essence of love," Wagner echoed Feuerbach in *A Communication*, "is the *desire for full physical reality*."[59]

As a fantasy of love, then, the prelude to *Lohengrin* begins that process towards physical reality, gradually shaping pure sound into distinct motifs, allegorically compressing indefinite desire into a more definite vision. Indeed, the prelude can be heard as the dream that Elsa recalls in act 1. Strikingly, however, the motif that opens that dream (the Grail motif) remains undetermined—absolute. In terms of Wagner's aesthetics:

> . . . the omission of this determination sets a musical motif before the feeling as something indefinite; and no matter how often something indefinite returns in the same way, it will remain a mere recurrence of the indefinite, so that we cannot justify it by any felt necessity of its appearance, nor, therefore, associate it with anything.[60]

Lohengrin's actual appearance in the world is a major step towards physical reality. And it would seem that this alone would suffice to "determine" the Grail motif that continues to hover over him like a halo: when Lohengrin arrives at the shore (high strings), when he bids farewell to the swan and orders it back (solo voice), when he tells the king that he is sent to fight for Elsa (again the strings), when he asks Elsa whether she will keep her promise (both voices and strings). Nonetheless, this saturation is suspicious. Lohengrin's conspicuous musical aura throws into relief the evasiveness of his words that refuse to reveal who he is. He neither says where the swan should return to, nor responds to the king's enquiry whether he was sent by God. Lohengrin's many words do not satisfy the need of the music: to be determined by them. Elsa's aural vision of Lohengrin is a nameless image into which only Lohengrin can inscribe himself.

But Lohengrin is unwilling to do so, and thus is unable to undo his miraculous—absolute—appearance. When he asks Elsa whether she will "entrust" herself to his "protection," she "sinks to his feet with an overwhelmingly blissful feeling." The musical gesture that accompanies her surrender—"Nimm mich hin! Dir geb' ich Alles was ich bin" ("Take me! to you I give all that I am")—resembles the long descent after the climax in the prelude (Prelude, measures 58ff.). In fact, Wagner's description of this passage varies the stage direction: after the revelation of the Grail, the beholder "sinks down in devotional annihilation" (ex. 3.7).[61] Since Lohengrin's appearance on the horizon, A major has been the dominating key. But, strikingly, Elsa now returns to A♭, using her motif, which originally led from A♭ to A. Even though her desire for love enabled her to bridge the gap between A♭ (her world) and A (his world), she wants him in the former. Thus the often noted tonal opposition between Elsa's A♭ and Lohengrin's A marks the symbolic gap between the human and the divine, over which the bond between the couple must be negotiated. Elsa's love is unconditional: take me as I am—in my key. But Lohengrin's love is conditional: swear that you will never ask about my origin, nature and name—in both my key and yours (ex. 3.8).

As has often been remarked, the motif of the forbidden question contains striking connections to Elsa's music. In the first half of its eight-measure period, the plagal cadence in C♭ major evokes the same progression from Elsa's motif at the visionary end of her dream (see ex. 3.2, cited above by Wagner). Although the melody leaps upward a fourth (not a third), the double-dotted rhythm reinforces the connection. The second half of the motif approaches its cadence with a formulaic, yet quite distinct, eighth-note figure (e♭-d♭-c♭-d♭, see ex. 3.6). This figure is prominent in Elsa's prayer and relates to the cadential flourish in her motif as it appears in the prelude, where it resolves the suspended f² (Prelude, m. 29). Manfred Hermann Schmid has shown that this formula found its way into the prelude through its musical model, Lohengrin's act 3 Grail narration, where the motif of the forbidden question appeared in a passage Wagner later abandoned:[62]

> Nun höret noch, wie ich zu euch gekommen!
> Ein klagend Tönen trug die Luft daher,
> Daraus im Tempel wir sogleich vernommen,
> Daß fern wo eine Magd in Nöten wär.

[Now hear also how I came to you! The air carried a lamenting sound, from which we, in the temple, learned at once that far from us a young woman was in distress.]

Example 3.7. Lohengrin, act 1, scene 3, Elsa surrenders

(Elsa, die, seitdem, sie Lohengrin erblickte, wie im Zauber, regungslos festgebannt war,
sinkt, wie durch seine Ansprache erweckt, in überwältigend wonnigem Gefühle zu seinen Füßen)

Lohengrin's taboo, then, names by way of music that which he for-
bids to be asked. The twofold prohibition—stated first in her key, then
in his—is reminiscent of a marriage pledge, though perverted: instead of
an exchange of vows, there is a unilateral imposition of conditions that
Elsa must finally accept on his terms. Although she surrenders to
Lohengrin freely, he subjugates her by force.[63] The imbalance is striking:
while he always calls her by name, she can address him only with
substitute names: savior, lord, protector, angel, redeemer—invoking the

Example 3.8. Lohengrin, act 1, scene 3, the forbidden question

Example 3.8. (cont.)

her   ich kam   der Fahrt,_____ noch wie mein Nam'   und   Art!

divine aura that Lohengrin tries to hide. Lohengrin's condition is that his music remain unconditioned. Yet the absolute artist's most absolute music—the Grail motif—continues to pose the opera's central question: Whence came Lohengrin?

Elsa's Second Scream

> The whole interest of *Lohengrin* lies in an experience taking place in the heart of Elsa which reaches down to the mind's very depths. The blissful spell, which casts its magic so convincingly over the whole setting, can last only so long as she does not ask where it comes from. The question bursts forth like a cry from the troubled depths of her womanly heart—and the spell is broken. It will not escape you how singularly that tragic "Whence?" coincides with that theoretical "Why" referred to above.[64]

This passage from Wagner's *Music of the Future* (1860) does it all. In Elsa's second scream, her "Whence?" and Wagner's "Why?", operatic practice and operatic theory, as well as the stories of Lohengrin and *Lohengrin,* collapse into one. Together, "Whence?" and "Why?" create a symbol in the way Wagner, rehearsing the *Ring,* remarked about *Siegfried* act 3 scene 3: "Here everything is symbolic."[65] To unfold the symbolism of Elsa's "Whence?," however, we need to ask: What was Wagner's "Why?"[66]

Music of the Future tackles the perennial problem: how the relationship between music and poetry is nested into the difference between symphonic and dramatic music. Although Wagner saw the infinite power of music revealed in the symphonies of Beethoven, he demanded its union with poetry for the sake of music drama:

> Poetry will . . . acknowledge its own deep longing for an eventual merging with music as soon as it realizes that music itself has a need which only

poetry can fulfill. To explain this need we have to remind ourselves of the human mind's ineradicable impulse, when confronted by an impressive phenomenon, to put the question: Why? Even when we are listening to a symphony the question cannot be completely suppressed and, since the symphony is least of all able to provide an answer, the question puts the listener . . . into a state of confusion. . . .

Drama, through its scenic representation of an action imitating real life as faithfully as possible, instantaneously arouses in the audience a feeling of intimate participation, and this participation induces a state of ecstasy in which that momentous "Why?" is forgotten and one willingly abandons oneself to the guidance of those new laws which enable music to make itself so miraculously comprehensible, those laws which—in a profound sense—provide the only right answer to that "Why?" . . .

The character of the scene, the legendary tone, transport the mind into a dream-like state which soon becomes a clairvoyant vision: the phenomena of the world are then perceived as possessing a coherence they do not have for the enquiring mind in its ordinary waking state, forever asking "Why?" in order to overcome its fear of the incomprehensible world— that world it now perceives so clearly and vividly. How music should consummate the magic of this clairvoyant vision you will readily understand.[67]

This, then, is the paradox: absolute music instigates the quest for a raison d'être, but once the poet, through drama, has made us forget the question, it is music that gives the answer. In opera, Wagner heard the question posed by the overture, stirring up a spectator's expectation that the drama satisfies. In this sense, the *Lohengrin* prelude arouses our interest through its two main musical ideas: the Grail motif, which modulates gradually to the sharp side (mm. 5ff.), and the Elsa motif, which modulates rather abruptly to the flat side (mm. 28ff.). Both pose the question of Lohengrin's origin and, with it, the origin of drama. But they provide fundamentally different answers.

Wagner theorized the origin of dramatic expression in two stages. First, language comes into being when sound, as the maternal element, is "fructified" by a "natural, real object that lies outside of it."[68] In the second stage, male poetry (the poetic intent in general, and the libretto in particular) "fructifies" female music: "Just as understanding must . . . fructify feeling . . . so the word of reason is impelled to recognize itself in sound, while the language of words finds itself vindicated in the language of music."[69] Wagner's notion of music as the mother of language supports his later claim always to have "known" that music produced drama. Yet in *Opera and Drama,* music is not only the mother from which language originates, but also the woman with whom it seems to reunite for the purpose of drama. Wagner addressed the paradox in a footnote: "Would it be thought trivial of me if I were to remind the reader—with reference to my account of the relevant myth—of Oedipus, who was born of Jocasta and who fathered the redeeming figure of Antigone by her?"[70] Assuming that Lohengrin was born out of Elsa's musical fantasy, in terms of the Oedipus myth the forbidden question—the condition of his (re-)union with Elsa—masks the incest taboo. Thus, if the drama revolves around the political legitimacy of the forbidden question, the struggle is about the role of the female element in the origin of drama, and, deeper still, about the primacy of divine patriarchy or human matriarchy. The question shifts the opera's meaning from the historical to the mythological and from the public to the private sphere. When Friedrich and Ortrud challenge Lohengrin at the end of act 2, he makes clear that the only person who may ask him is Elsa. In public, she stands firm, yet as Wagner remarked in a letter to Liszt the orchestra blares out: "you will *nevertheless* break the taboo."[71] She will do it in private— during the wedding night.

The so-called Bridal Chamber Scene in act 3 begins with post-wedding bliss, but ends in despair when Elsa puts the forbidden question to Lohengrin. According to Grey, the duet shows Wagner on his way from "the classical hierarchical organization of periodic structures" to the "evolutionary" principle of music drama.[72] Building on Dahlhaus's observation that "schematic periods [eight- or sixteen-measure phrase pairs] exist alongside more differentiated ones, tending to dissolution of conventional structure," Grey remarks:

> Indeed, precisely this juxtaposition contributes to the overall sense of a dialectical progression: just as Elsa parries Lohengrin's sharp-side keys with flat keys, and . . . answers his tonal closure with tonal indecision, so do her periods increasingly tend toward metrical instability.[73]

One can go a step further: the duet interlocks with Wagner's aesthetics in the form of an argument between Lohengrin, the "conservative," and Elsa, the "progressive." At stake is the second stage of Wagner's origin of drama: the reunion of poetry and music, which, however, fails to take place.

Wagner stages the escalating argument by drawing on the Franco-Italian model with alternating "static" and "kinetic" sections, handled with great flexibility.[74] Thus the duet opens with a self-enclosed slow movement in E major ("Fühl ich zu dir"), strongly reminiscent of those middle movements in Italian and French duets. After alternating statements, the couple ends up in thirds and sixths, but the blissful presence is too sweet to last. It slips away almost imperceptibly from that static state into the past (and the subdominant) when Lohengrin and Elsa look back on their first encounter:

LOHENGRIN:
Wie hehr erkenn' ich uns'rer Liebe Wesen!
Die nie sich sahn, wir hatten uns geahnt;
war ich zu deinem Streiter auserlesen,
hat Liebe mir zu dir den Weg gebahnt.
Dein Auge sagte mir dich rein von Schuld,
mich zwang dein Blick zu dienen deiner Huld.

ELSA:
Doch ich zuvor schon hatte dich gesehen,
in sel'gem Traume warst du mir genaht:
als ich nun wachend dich sah vor mir stehen,
erkannt' ich, daß du kamst auf Gottes Rat.

[*Lohengrin*: Now I recognize the noble essence of our love! Having never seen each other, we felt each other; though I had been chosen as your champion, it was love that showed me the way to you. Your eyes told me that you were free of guilt—your glance made me serve your favor.

Elsa: But I had seen you before in a happy dream in which you had approached me. When I, waking, saw you stand before me, I knew that you came by God's command.]

This is a remarkable exchange of perspectives on the past: while Lohengrin felt commanded by Elsa's glance, she knew he came by God's command. How does she know? We need to keep in mind that this is *before* their false marriage pledge. Elsa's recollection is a distant echo of her act 1 narration, replaying the Lohengrin motif and the characteristic turning figure from her prayer, whose original climax marked the shift from A♭ to A. But she now moves in the opposite direction: passing through the pivotal F♯ minor in her original glance-up she goes from A major to G♯ (A♭) major, and then on to D♭ (ex. 3.9). Elsa thus recalls the difference underlying their first encounter, recalling her vision of marriage on *her* side of the tonal realm:

Da wollte ich vor deinem Blick zerfließen,
gleich einem Bach umwinden deinen Schritt,
als eine Blume, duftend auf der Wiesen,
wollt' ich entzückt mich beugen deinem Tritt.

[Then I wished to melt before your look, like a brook to wind around your steps, like a fragrant flower in the meadow to bow delighted before your step!]

146

Example 3.9. Lohengrin, act 3, scene 2,
Elsa recalls her first encounter with Lohengrin

This was Elsa's surrender—the surrender to the man–poet that Wagner praised as the ideal of woman–music: not the strumpet, coquette, or prudish woman of Italian, French, or German opera, but a flower bending under Lohengrin's tread. Yet Elsa's surrender to Lohengrin turned into his subjugation, forbidding the name Elsa now longs to utter:

> Wie süß mein Name deinem Mund entgleitet!
> Gönnst du des deinen holden Klang mir nicht?
> Nur wenn zur Liebesstille wir geleitet,
> sollst du gestatten, daß mein Mund ihn spricht.

[How sweet my name escapes your mouth! Will you not grant me the noble sound of yours? Only in the seclusion of love's peace you may permit me to pronounce it.]

But Lohengrin responds:

> (*umfaßt Elsa freundlich und deutet durch das*
> *offene Fenster auf den Blumengarten*):
> Atmest du nicht mit mir die süßen Düfte?
> O wie so hold berauschen sie den Sinn!
> Geheimnisvoll sie nahen durch die Lüfte,—
> fraglos geb' ihrem Zauber ich mich hin.—
> (*mit erhobener Stimme*)
>
> So ist der Zauber, der mich dir verbunden,
> da ich zuerst, du Süße, dich ersah;
> nicht brauchte deine Art ich zu erkunden,
> dich sah mein Aug'—mein Herz begriff dich da.
> Wie mir die Düfte hold den Sinn berücken,
> nah'n sie mir gleich aus rätselvoller Nacht:—
> (*feurig*)
> so mußte deine Reine mich entzücken,
> traf ich dich auch in schwerer Schuld Verdacht.
> (*Elsa birgt ihre Beschämung, indem sie sich*
> *demütig an ihn schmiegt*)

[Lohengrin (*embraces Elsa kindly and points through the open window to the flower garden*): Don't you breathe with me these sweet fragrances? Oh, how delightfully they intoxicate the senses! Mysteriously they approach us through the breezes, and unquestioning I surrender to their spell. (*with a raised voice*) Thus is the magic that bound me to you when I first saw you, my sweet. I needed not to question who you are, since as my eyes saw you my heart knew you. Just as the fragrances sweetly enchant my senses when coming near me as from the mysterious night, (*passionately*) so your purity had to charm me, although I found you charged with heavy guilt. (*Elsa hides her embarrassment by humbly nestling close to him.*)]

As Grey puts it, Lohengrin tries to "uphold" the "orderly domestic idyll of the duet opening—reflected in a regular periodicity and tonal closure."[75] The formal gesture is symbolic: a set piece of operatic style modeled on the fixed forms of traditional opera. Later, in *Opera and Drama*, Wagner employed the flower metaphor to express how words and music were once unified in folk melodies, but are now corrupted in operatic practice:

> Whereas the melody was the enchanting *fragrance* of the flower, the word verse was its *body* with all its tender reproductive organs. And so the hedonist, who merely wanted to consume with the sense of smell, but not in communion with the eyes, removed the fragrance from the flower and artificially distilled the perfume, which he bottled in order to carry it with him at will.[76]

Absolute—Rossinian—melody, then, is bodiless perfume. Yet Lohengrin does not portray himself as a hedonist, because he can consume Elsa *fraglos,* without asking "Why?" He would seem to be Wagner's ideal listener, because he has it all: her body, her name, and her music—which is *Zukunftsmusik*. Its meandering modulations—mixing major- and minor-third progressions, augmented triads, mode changes, and secondary dominants—seem to exude the fragrance of progressive music, but he encases it in yet another closed movement that shuts away his name, which is his body.

Elsa's rejoinder, a more "kinetic" section, pushes harder for this name, forcing the music again towards the flat side. In response, Lohengrin manages one more time to launch into an A-major arioso, attempting to secure his hold on her: "An meine Brust, du Süße, Reine!" ("To my breast, pure one," mm. 244–329). But his arioso is finally invaded by the motif of Ortrud's doubt from act 2 (mm. 314ff.). Lohengrin's casing of tonal closure cracks precisely when he invokes his divinity, seeking to secure it against Elsa's pressure: "Drum wolle stets den Zweifel meiden, / dein Lieben sei mein stolz Gewähr! / Denn nicht komm ich aus Nacht und Leiden, / aus Glanz und Wonne komm' ich her" ("Always avoid doubt, let your love be my proud warrant! For I come not from night and sorrow, but from light and happiness"). The more Lohengrin tries to hold on to Elsa, however, the more he exposes the lack of a real bond. And the more he clings to the aura of absolute music, the more he underscores the metaphysical magic that nourishes her question "Why?":

> Ach! Dich an mich zu binden,
> wie sollt' ich mächtig sein?

Voll Zauber ist dein Wesen,
durch Wunder kamst du her:—
wie sollt' ich da genesen?
wo fänd' ich dein' Gewähr?
(*Sie schreckt in heftigster Aufregung zusam-*
men und hält an, wie um zu lauschen)

[Ah, how could I have the power to bind you to me? Your being is full of magic; you came here miraculously. How could I recover? Where could I find assurance? (*She starts in most violent excitement and pauses, listening*)]

Lohengrin's coming had been Elsa's original dream. It came true, but has now turned into the nightmare of the swan returning to carry Lohengrin away, its music ominously oscillating between C♭ major and the G♯ (A♭) minor of her original misery. The passage is uncanny, for it appears as if the sound once projected into the distance has come back, undoing its original modulation from A♭. To awake from this nightmare, Elsa screams—again. In extreme agitation, rising above the a^2 of act 1, she reaches the double climax of the scene on b^2 at "Wo fänd ich dein Gewähr?" and at "Wie deine Art?" This is Elsa's revolutionary act, and it is on a b^2, a liminal note, like that of Leonore's original scream. Crying out for Lohengrin's name, Elsa breaks the spell of his magic and demands the impossible from the absolute artist: to unite his name with her music.

Here Elsa's second scream links with Wagner's most explicitly Schopenhauerian essay, *Beethoven*, which appropriates the philosopher's dream theory to describe how the gap between the world of sound and the world of sight might be bridged:

From the most terrifying of such dreams we wake with a *scream,* the immediate expression of the anguished will, which thus at first makes definite entrance into the sound-world, in order to manifest itself out-wards. Now if we take the scream in all the diminishings of its vehemence . . . and if we cannot but find in it the most immediate utterance of the will . . . then we have less cause to wonder at its immediate intelligibility than at an *art* arising from this element.[77]

This primal scream becomes not only the origin of music, but also of music drama. In one of Wagner's most notorious historical fictions, Beethoven made the leap from instrumental to vocal music in the last movement of the Ninth:

What we experience here is a certain overcharge, a vast compulsion to unload outwards, comparable only with the stress of wakening from an agonizing dream; and the important issue for the genius of mankind is that this special stress called forth an artistic deed whereby that genius gained a novel power, the qualification for begetting the highest artwork.[78]

Like Beethoven breaking the spell of his own music by exclaiming "Freude," Elsa breaks Lohengrin's spell by demanding his name. At the moment of her scream she enters Wagner's master narrative of music history. Like Beethoven, however, Elsa only gains the "qualification for begetting the highest artwork"—not the work itself. She succeeds in creating Lohengrin, but she cannot save *Lohengrin*. Neither can Lohengrin. When he finally matches his name to music in the Grail narration, its dramatic effect falls flat. Raff accorded the highest praise to Elsa's dream in act 1, but placed the heaviest blame on Lohengrin's Grail narration:

> . . . a miscalculation of the poet which he will pay for with the yawns from a large part of the audience and the silent curses of the singer . . . The mystic content of the narrative is exhausted in the prelude. The singer can do nothing more than declaim to the music of the prelude.[79]

The Double Frame

Lohengrin, then, is doubly framed (in a double sense): by the prelude and Grail narration, and by two screams. Wagner critics, distracted by the formalist aesthetics of absolute music, have privileged the outer frame, seemingly holding the opera together through reprise and tonal closure, the devices of the symphonic principle. Wagner's ambivalence is evident: on the one hand, he struggled free of what he considered the square syntax of instrumental music; on the other hand, he sought to justify the great recapitulation of Lohengrin, who lives while Elsa dies. Only in retrospect did another view dawn on him—one that could reconcile his most unreconciled ending as historical necessity. *Lohengrin* became the opera of Elsa, the progressive. The outer frame is Lohengrin's, the inner, Elsa's. But they connect only in the beginning, when her first scream joins her A♭ and his A—her sound and his sight. Her second scream explodes that connection, killing herself like the other Wagnerian heroines. Her death, however, became sacrificial only later: as the destruction of *Lohengrin*. Lohengrin's absoluteness is logo-centric without *logos* or, as it were, phallo-centric without phallus. Lohengrin's *logos* is not just the missing link between the lovers' bodies; it also became symbolic for the link lost between music and drama. Nameless, Lohengrin is no man. As an impotent poet, he becomes—to use Wagner's most notorious metaphor—the seed that fails to fertilize. In the Grail narrative, Lohengrin will deliver his *logos*—but lonely, lamely, and too late.

Example 3.10. Lohengrin, act 3, scene 3,
Elsa's resignation and Lohengrin's arrival

Elsa's Scream

Example 3.10. (cont.)

(Der König hat seinen Platz unter der Eiche wieder eingenommen. - Lohengrin, ganz so gewaffnet wie im ersten Aufzuge, tritt ohne Gefolge feierlich und traurig auf und schreitet ernst in den Vordegrund).

153

When Elsa enters for this final revelation, her second trial where Lohengrin, not Friedrich, will be her accuser, the men of Brabant note that her inner light is gone:

> DIE MÄNNER:
> Seht, Elsa naht, die Tugendreiche!
> Wie ist ihr Antlitz trüb und bleiche!
>
> KÖNIG:
> Wie muß ich Dich so traurig seh'n!
> Will dir so nah die Trennung geh'n?

[*The Men:* Behold, Elsa, full of virtue, comes! How troubled and pale is her face! *King:* How sad you seem to me! Does the departure affect you so deeply?]

The king can no longer read Elsa's downcast eyes: "Elsa versucht vor ihm aufzublicken, vermag es aber nicht" ("Elsa tries to look up to him, but cannot"). When her motif appears for the last time, it no longer connects two keys (ex. 3.10). The pivotal mode change from G♭ major to G♭ minor has become a diminished seventh that does not lead to A major, but to her original A♭ minor. The organic transition is lost. There is no *Augenblick*. Nothing could show this more drastically than the bald juxtaposition of Elsa's resignation and Lohengrin's triumphant entry in A major:

> Macht Platz dem Helden von Brabant!
> Heil! Heil dem Helden von Brabant!

[Make way for the hero of Brabant! Hail! Hail! the hero of Brabant!]

Cheering Lohengrin's arrival, the crowd unwillingly points to the great irony of this twofold story: Lohengrin, the lost shaft, is already gone. So is *Lohengrin*—opera as failure. But because Elsa screamed, music drama will be born.

LISZT'S PRAYER

When a new age dawns, in which art should undergo a thorough change, make great progress, and move with hitherto unknown power and force on a new track, then such a great moment is usually heralded by portentous signs. Rarely, however, does mankind understand the prophetic sense of these signs at the moment of their revelation; rather they are seen as isolated events, indeed often as abnormal apparitions, as more or less attractive phenomena. Only when the sun of such a new day already stands high in the sky does one recognize that the scattered rays, which heralded its light like dawn, all came from the same center.[1]

Indeed, this "Mountain Symphony" is the greatest and the most epoch-making among all of *Liszt's* symphonic poems. You understand what this means! This symphony is a true revelation towering so far above the musical present that it cannot be measured through parallels or comparisons; a *Mountain* Symphony in the most sublime sense of the word.[2]

The claim Liszt made about Beethoven's *Egmont* Overture, Richard Pohl made about the performance of Liszt's first symphonic poem on 7 January 1857 in Weimar: the recognition of a great work in the history of music. Based on an ode from Victor Hugo's 1831 *Les feuilles d'automne, Ce qu'on entend sur la montagne* (or Mountain Symphony—*Bergsinfonie*—as the composer liked to call it) was the leading work in Liszt's ambitious project to create a new orchestral genre during his tenure in Weimar. With it he sought to combine the legacy of the Beethovenian symphony with the heritage of European literature—nothing less than an effort to spearhead the renewal of German instrumental music and to assert its universality. Although Pohl celebrated the work accordingly, neither its extensive proportions nor its privileged place as the first of twelve symphonic poems have made it as popular as *Tasso* and *Les Preludes,* not to speak of the Faust and Dante symphonies. If the Mountain Symphony aspired to be a watershed work, it failed to enter the canon.

There is, of course, no need to lament such a failure now that the pantheon of Western music seems to be a thing of the past. Still, the genealogy of the canon deserves critical attention, because the mechanisms of validation prove to be more persistent than the objects validated. The concept of what Alfred Einstein called "greatness" in music has shown the greatest wear and tear, yet newness, originality, and influence (even quality) remain decisive criteria in artistic (and academic) production—postmodern disclaimers not withstanding. Of Liszt's symphonic poems, the Mountain Symphony drew the most intense barrage of critical commentary because it failed to negotiate successfully what might be called a canonical contract, which mediates between momentuous presence and monumental past. If the work was to renew the historical momentum of German music, it remained caught between autonomy and function, traditional and avant-garde techniques, personal and public expression, as well as art religion and religious art.

Apart from the work's long gestation (itself symptomatic of the birth pangs of the new genre), the most decisive symptom of these inner contradictions is a particular passage in the Mountain Symphony that for some has been precious and for others precarious: an "Andante religioso" which disrupts the musical process and runs counter to the literary program (ex. 4.1). In the first edition of the work, Liszt had inserted a note stipulating that "these words indicating the content are supposed to be added to the programs of the concerts in which the following symphonic poem is performed":

> The poet hears two voices; the one immense, magnificent, and full of order, roaring a jubilating song of praise towards the Lord—the other dull, filled with sounds of pain, swelling with crying, blasphemy, and malediction. One voice spoke *Nature,* the other *Humanity!* Both voices struggle towards each other, struggle and merge, until they finally enter into solemn contemplation and die away.[3]

In addition to this note, Liszt printed Hugo's ode which ends rather differently: "And I asked myself . . . why the Lord . . . forever blends, in a fatal marriage the song of nature into the cry of mankind?" This discrepancy has surely been noticed before. In the perhaps most provocative study of the work, Carl Dahlhaus sought to explain it, claiming that the Mountain Symphony is a "paradoxical structure" where neither scepticism nor belief has the last word.[4] Although Dahlhaus's thesis hardly squares with the composer's stated intention to go beyond Hugo's poem, the discrepancy between philosophical speculation and philological evidence need not be resolved one way or the other. On the contrary, its very tension may arguably become a source of insight. When the Mountain Symphony was performed in Sonderhausen in June 1886 during the *Tonkünstlerversammlung* of the *Allgemeiner Deutscher*

Example 4.1. *Ce qu'on entend sur la montagne:*
"Andante religioso" (first section)

Example 4.1. (cont.)

Musikverein on the occasion of Liszt's seventy-sixth birthday (he was the honorary president), his student August Göllerich recalled how Liszt "spoke about the Mountain Symphony, this gigantic monument of the *Zeitgeist* of a whole cultural epoch. 'The piece'—he said—'is in its conception the *first* of my symphonic poems and goes back to the year 1830, when I got the idea from *V. Hugo's* poem. I did not complete the work until 1857. With the *song of the anchorites,* I was thinking of hermits in the mountains, Carthusian monks near *Grenoble* in southern France. Hugo did not have the 'prayer.' I needed it."[5]

The anecdote's inconspicuous constellation of particular and whole practices, unwillingly, a hermeneutics of the moment, which is less a source of historical information than a reflection of historical consciousness. Consider the large claim that the work would represent "an entire epoch." Where the piece represents its time, the single part that represents the piece is the added prayer, which carried, for Hans Joachim Moser, the epithet of "a truly great moment."[6] But Liszt's prayer is not only poised between the two poles of Schleiermacher's hermeneutics (particular passage and whole epoch), it also punctuates the very moment where the centrifugal and centripetal forces of the work and its reception enter into a peculiar balance between public monument and personal moment. Their mutual suspension suggests, again, a Benjaminian "dialectics at a standstill" whose uneasy mélange of Marxism and Messianism touches on central concerns of Liszt's first symphonic poem. In hindsight, we can hear the Mountain Symphony as an allegory of the clash between historicist and materialist conceptions of historiography: the former based on the notion of a historical continuum, the latter on the idea of exploding this very continuum.

Historicism, to recall Benjamin's *Theses on the Philosophy of History,* recognizes the past "the way it really was" (Thesis 6) empathizes "with the victor" (Thesis 7); subscribes to the "conception of progress" (Thesis 13); and holds to a "continuum of history" that "culminates in universal history" (Theses 16 and 17).[7] The Mountain Symphony does all this; or rather, historicists could do all this with the Mountain Symphony. The work, in a word, could signify historical progress and be celebrated as an integral part of continuous history. But Benjamin's historical materialist, on the other hand, seeks to recognize in the structure of a historical subject "the sign of the messianic standstill of what happens, or a revolutionary chance in the fight for the oppressed past. He takes cognizance of it in order to blast a specific era out of the homogeneous course of history—blasting a specific life out of the era, or a specific work out of the life's oeuvre"(Thesis 17).[8] And, it should be added, *a specific moment out of the entire work.* Once the detail has become, as it were, an absolute fragment, the dialectical movement of

Benjamin's hermeneutics reverses, so that (in Hegelian terms) "the life's oeuvre is preserved [*aufbewahrt*] in this work and at the same time canceled [*aufgehoben*]; in the life's oeuvre, the era; and in the era, the entire course of history" (Thesis 17).[9] Materialistic historiography thus no longer reconstructs history, but constructs it in such a way that its dialectic movement comes to a standstill.[10] It does not situate the particular—moment, work, oeuvre, era, epoch—*within* historical continuum, but *without*. The critical element that explodes the universal history declares its solidarity with the oppressed and tries to bring them justice. In doing so, the historical materialist liquidates the epic moment and replaces it with a messianic moment.

Although they were partly written as a response to the disillusionment over the Hitler–Stalin pact, Rolf Tiedemann noted that Benjamin's *Theses* are also a late reflex of his youthful enthusiasm for a "spirit of social labor" that was nurtured "in the ideas of the deepest anarchists and in monastic communities of Christianity."[11] Thus the opening of Thesis 10: "The objects which monastic discipline assigned to friars for meditation were designed to turn them away from the world and its affairs. The thoughts which we are developing here originate from similar considerations."[12] Benjamin's uneasy blend of communist and theological ideas shares its concerns with the mix of revolutionary and religious ideals behind Liszt's lifelong commitment to social reform.[13] Yet if the Mountain Symphony—at some point even entitled *Méditation Symphonie*—mingles anarchic and cloistered contemplation, it is also subject to similar problems. According to Tiedemann, Benjamin's vision of history faced the danger that "the re-translation of materialism in theology" could "result in a double loss: the dissolution of the secularized content and the evaporation of the theological idea."[14] Similarly, Liszt's project of social and religious reform through music was caught between an art religion overreaching itself, and a religious art becoming trivialized. This dilemma is the hermeneutic crux of the Mountain Symphony, which unfolds not merely in the contest between the voices of nature and humanity, but in contesting attitudes vis-a-vis this contest.

This all crystallizes in the "Andante religioso": first, the general trend in nineteenth-century aesthetics away from the unified whole towards a particular that nevertheless seeks to recover this whole; second, the concomitant deformation and reformation of formal conventions in German symphonic music; and third, the conflict between the secular sublime (embodied in a climactic chorale) and the sacred sublime (embodied in the contemplative hymn). But it is only after illuminating these inner contradictions of the Mountain Symphony that we might justify subjecting the work to Benjamin's physiognomic gaze; because it is only after this gaze "recognizes the monuments of the bourgeoisie as ruins even before they have fallen apart," that it may reconstitute the configuration of its scattered particulars as the very "monad" in which the work's messianic moment was to become manifest.[15]

A Program for the Particular

In the mid-1850s Liszt brought program music into the center of aesthetic discussion, drawing serious critical attention to his own works. Yet if Liszt made history, that history was to a good measure the making of Franz Brendel, the leading critical voice of the New German School. Though full justice has yet to be done to Liszt's and Brendel's eclectic appropriations of philosophical aesthetics, my primary concern here is how their embrace of the category of the characteristic clashed with Hegel's idea of beauty, while at the same time their idea of program music fell in line with Hegel's adherence to a traditional content-based aesthetic.[16] In pushing the particular, both Liszt and Brendel attempted to promote an agenda of progress, while preserving the values of classical art. And here the "Andante religioso" stood in the middle, between heterogeneity and unity, as well as between private expression and popular appeal.

Given his progressive outlook, therefore, Brendel had to walk a fine line *vis-à-vis* Hegel's classicist bias, which took the deepening discord of romantic art as a symptom of its decline, exemplified by the isolation of "*particular* characterizing passages" that disturb "the flow and the unity in a disastrous way."[17] Brendel pointed to A.B. Marx's theory of harmony, which had posited the characteristic as a new principle, and in which an unusual harmonic progression (*Combination*) can no longer be justified through a technical analysis based on traditional rules, but must be explained "*directly* through the idea."[18] (Wagner, to recall his self-analysis of *Lohengrin*, made the same point about dramatic modulation.) In short, the program was to redeem the particular, and vice versa. Hence Brendel justified the stylistic development from middle to late Beethoven, and further to Mendelssohn, Schumann, and Liszt, as a movement from whole to part: "What occurred in Beethoven's rich world only as a moment, now appears as a particular artwork; a particular mood seems fixated and cast in a smaller frame."[19] Just as Schumann adapted the subjective particularity of the character piece to the "objective" world of the symphony, Mendelssohn gave orchestral music a poetic impulse with his programmatic overtures and symphonies.[20] While Beethoven's music could still reconcile extreme opposites and contrasts through an underlying basic mood (*Grundstimmung*), this all-encompassing unity eventually receded into the background in Liszt's music. Quite in the spirit of Jean Paul's definition of the Romantic as "beautiful infinity" (discussed in chapter 2), Brendel claimed that Liszt possessed traits of both beauty *and* the characteristic. But now the musical surface was dominated by "moments set apart in the extreme and juxtaposed: spirit and sensuality, tender enthusiasm and heroic force . . . a universal view of the world and mystic rapture."[21] The last opposition clearly alluded to the Mountain Symphony, which opens with a panoramic view of the entire world and concludes with a prayer—a totalizing vision with a particularizing perspective. However pre-dominant the individual moments in Liszt, Brendel assured, they would not sever "the general bond."[22]

Thus Liszt's famous remark that *Tasso* and *Les Preludes* were constructed from a single motif has been a staple in discussions about his compositional technique, summarized best by Johann Christian Lobe's formulation that Liszt "introduced thematic work [*thematische Arbeit*] before the theme [*Thema*]."[23] That was the basis of Wagner's praise in his *Letter on Franz Liszt's Symphonic Poems:* that the composer's "ingenious grip of the musical conception" is so evident at the very outset of the piece, "that after the first sixteen bars I often had to cry out with astonishment: 'Enough, I have it all!'"[24] And the composer and critic Felix Draeseke—who, as a member of Liszt's Weimar circle, wrote the most detailed reviews of the symphonic poems that were authorized by the composer—noted that the application of the thematic art not only averted the specter of disunity and confusion from a programmatic composition, but that the "artful variation and transformation of a single musical idea" would allow the composer to "generate new and contrasting motives . . . which are capable of expressing a full range of emotions and yet always reveal their common origin."[25] Given Wagner's predilection for material that he submits to large-scale musical processes, there is of course a similarity between the *Uranfang* of the *Rheingold* prelude and the E♭ that emerges at the beginning of the Mountain Symphony from the vibrations of the bass drum depicting the "wide, immense, and confused noise" in Hugo's poem (line 13).

In that sense Liszt's compositional technique resonates deeply with Hugo's romantic manifesto in his *Preface to Cromwell*, in which the "modern muse" will "set about doing as nature does, *mingling in its creations—but without confounding them*—darkness and light, the grotesque and the sublime; in other words, the body and the soul, the beast and the intellect; for the starting-point of religion is always the starting-point of poetry. All things are connected."[26] But connection is not synthesis. Hugo's infusion of grotesque comedy into *Cromwell* was to contradict the neo-classical style of serious drama.[27] Truth was to trump beauty. Inspired by Chateaubriand and Lamartine, Hugo proclaimed a "harmony of opposites"—what Liszt called "*diverse* unity" (*vielförmige*

Einheit).[28] In *Ce qu'on entend sur la montagne,* written two years after *Cromwell,* the voices of nature and humanity mingle; they do not merge.

Although there have been plenty of explanations about how the diverse voices of nature and humanity in the Mountain Symphony originate in one sound, there has been one point of contention: the "Andante religioso."[29] In response to Alfred Heuß's claim that almost every measure was related to the opening figure *except* the "self-explanatory" *religioso,* Dahlhaus traced the incipit of the hymn both to the rhythm of the third theme of Nature and the contrasting Humanity themes (ex. 4.2). As an integral, not extraterritorial, part of the work, the chorale exemplified Liszt's technique of working with "thematic configurations," composites of independent durational and pitch patterns which create a coherent musical language.[30] One could go further: the triplets, which first surface in the horn chords of the introduction (ex. 4.2b), later become a binding element between themes of both voices—for example H3 (ex. 4.2h) and variants of N3 (at mm. 632ff.) and N1 (at mm. 764ff. and 816ff.). All this may be heard as entering into the chorale's meter. And when the hymn dies away on its augmented cantilena (*dolce espressivo*), the bass maintains that original rhythm (*un poco marcato*), eventually settling for almost three measures on a faint echo of the introduction. What aspect of the "religioso," then, matters more? Do the thematic connections make it a moment held by a general bond below the musical surface, or does its topical and generic otherness mark the intrusion of extraneous particularity?

"To introduce a foreign element into instrumental music . . . appears for many to be an absurd, if not profaning endeavor," Liszt stated in his manifesto on program music, the 1855 article "Berlioz and his Harold Symphony," itself a response of sorts to Hanslick's 1854 *On the Musically Beautiful.*[31] Although the clash between *Formästhetik* and *Inhaltsästehtik* is a well-known chapter in nineteenth-century musical aesthetics,[32] it is worth pointing out that the philosophical underpinnings of the debate were a mixed blessing for both parties. If Hanslick sought to bolster his notorious claim that musical content consisted of *tönend bewegte Formen* with the Hegel-like conception of music as *Arbeiten des Geistes in geistfähigem Material,* he knew all too well that, for Hegel, instrumental music suffered from what Eduard Krüger so poignantly called a "curse of contentlessness" in his 1842 review of the *Lectures on Aesthetics* for the *Neue Zeitschrift.*[33] Nonetheless, Hegel's conservative assertion that "purely musical structure" was "empty," "meaningless," and unable to aspire to "true art" because of this lack of "spiritual content and expression" proved to be perfect propaganda for Liszt's cause.[34] If Hanslick had read Hegel one way, Liszt could read him the other way.[35]

Example 4.2. Ce qu'on entend sur la montagne:
Themes of Nature and Humanity

But Liszt wanted to have it both ways. A program, he submitted, was not meant to renounce "the old belief" that "the heavenly art does not exist for its own sake."[36] The new Weimar could not afford to downplay the high prestige and autonomy that music alone had gained in Romanticism as the "pinnacle" and the "most absolute utterance of our art."[37] Yet, although the "essence" of instrumental music was to "speak the unspeakable," the "indefinite" should be "fixated through the program" and "the roaming imagination guided towards a definite object."[38] As Dahlhaus put it so well, in Hegel's aesthetics, "music as art loses what it gains as music while losing as music what it gains as art."[39] Brendel was caught in the same dilemma, having studied with Hegel's student Christian Hermann Weisse, who propagated—against his teacher—the freedom of instrumental music from subject matter, nature, human voice, and language as the absolute or modern ideal.[40] Taking from Weisse the endorsement of instrumental music as the vehicle of progress, and from Hegel the desire to reconnect its inwardness with external reality in the manner of poetry,[41] Brendel and Liszt sought to continue *and* transcend the Beethovenian tradition; to negate the old *and* preserve it, that is, *sublate* it, in the new.

The introduction of the programmatic particular through the historically necessary union of music and poetry was for Brendel also part of a process of liberating artistic individuality. It had begun with Bach and culminated in Liszt as the "pinnacle of subjectivity" and the symphonic poem as the "truest expression of individuality, no longer restricted by former shackles."[42] Liszt himself had praised Berlioz's *Harold* Symphony for introducing, into the "absolute impersonal symphony," a "definite individuality" instead of expressing the "laments" and "hopes" of "all."[43] Moreover, he explained the rise of program music as resulting partly from hermeneutic interpretations of Beethoven's non-programmatic compositions, the "desire to designate precisely the main idea of great instrumental music."[44] Like Schumann, however, Liszt was concerned that programmatic, or associative listening would further increase the growing division between lay and expert cultures during the nineteenth century.[45] Indeed, fearing that a composer might not "trouble himself with such content consisting of ideas and feelings and instead make the principal thing the purely musical structure of his work," Hegel had complained that the hermetic world of music made it possible "to indulge in such a purely rational analysis for which there is nothing in the work of art except the skill of a purely virtuosic fabrication [*Machwerk*]." Because music's "mysterious enigmas" were "capable of all sorts of interpretations," the amateur had the "desire" to "supplement" it with "specific ideas and a more definite meaning."[46]

Quoting such passages served Liszt well in branding formalism as

purely mathematical calculation, and technical analysis as mere gram-
matical commentary, while promoting a Schumannesque "poetic appraisal" (*poetische Schätzung*) of program music for reaching a wider
audience.[47] But if Liszt was eager to add that "the artist, more urgently
than the amateur, has to demand of form an emotional content,"[48] it
was because nothing would have troubled the legendary titan of the
piano more than Hegel's fear that instrumental music would become a
"purely virtuosic *Machwerk*." Having achieved a "breakthrough" towards "transcendental execution" in piano technique,[49] Liszt's
Durchbruch towards the symphonic poem nevertheless aspired to the
status of the autonomous tone poet. Countering the charge that Liszt
"played the orchestra, as he formerly did play the pianoforte," Brendel
insisted that he was not "misusing it for the purpose of virtuosity."
Instead, the forms of orchestral composition were no longer "an objective power," but they would fit the personality "like a light garment."[50]
In short, the symphonic poem was not art for art's sake, but art for the
artist's sake.

Because of this superiour position of the creative artist, Liszt strove to
reconcile his notion of specific programmatic composition with the practice of unspecific programmatic listening. While granting that "each
person silently take pleasure in revelations and visions for which there is
no name and no designation," he nevertheless asserted that "the master
is still master of his work and may create it under the influence of
certain impressions, of which he would like to make the listener fully
and completely conscious."[51] That was the task of the program. Liszt's
search for the right balance between creative control and interpretive
freedom (as well as between the freedom of creation and the control of
interpretation) points to the aporia inherent in modern subjectivity, which,
according to Jürgen Habermas possesses "the unprecedented power to
produce the formation of subjective freedom and reflection," but which
is not powerful enough "to regenerate the religious power of unification
via the medium of reason."[52] Yet "[w]ho and what," Andrew Bowie
rightly asked, "legislates on the issue of whether my freedom is not your
enslavement?"[53] Because the "absolute impersonal symphony" spoke
for all and merely gave the individual listener the license to all kinds of
different interpretations, Liszt needed to legislate. Caught between the
creative and receptive subjects, he sought to wrest absolute music from
the programmatic listener back to the programmatic composer. Liszt
acknowledged, even prized, the freedom of subjective readings in non-
programmatic music as part of the artwork's universal appeal. But when
it came to the symphonic poem, he asserted the primacy of authorial
intention—that "the master is still master of his work."[54] Reading into
absolute music was not the same as reading out of program music.

For Liszt, then, the listener's act ultimately depended upon the composer's, who had put down the rules of the hermeneutic game—and had put them down for all listeners. Where the "absolute impersonal symphony" had expressed the laments and hopes of all, all should now understand the "definite individuality" expressed in the symphonic poem. Even when pressing for the particular, neither Liszt nor Brendel was willing to give up the universal. "The program" wrote Brendel, "is that which connects the individual with the general and the former appears therefore *now in itself and as such as the vessel* of the general lying outside of it."[55] Given that Schumann had chided Berlioz in his review of the *Symphonie fantastique* for providing programs "in the French spirit that offended German feelings, as they were tasteless in giving too specific hints about what the music should express," Brendel proposed that "we should content ourselves with grasping the general idea, while leaving the particular to the free play of the imagination."[56] Although he had claimed that "the subjective side, the side of artistic pleasure, of personal experience" had to be "the first and foremost point of departure," hermeneutic divination would still have to start with the whole: "the eternal characteristic of the human mind is that one has to *believe* first, so that one can later *understand*"—"only from the viewpoint of the whole can the parts be explained."[57] Liszt, in other words, was to do away with the bad particularity of the isolated listener and reinstate the general bond that ties together his bourgeois audience.[58]

All this would seem of less immediate concern for *Ce qu'on entend sur la montagne* were it not a piece about listening; about what one hears on the mountain, about what Liszt heard, and about what we hear. Perhaps the most provocative conceit of the work lurks behind its gesture of double listening—one manifest in the musical process as perceived by all in the manner of the absolute symphony; the other in the way the individual subject makes sense of that process in the one movement that seems to disrupt this symphony from outside. In fact, this double perspective will prove to illuminate, if not answer, the question about the work's hermeneutic crux: whether thematic integration trumps the topical otherness of the "Andante religioso," or vice versa.

The Dialectics of the Double Chorale

In a trenchant critique of the Mountain Symphony, Peter Raabe bemoaned Liszt's failure to free himself enough from formula. While Raabe found it "fair to assume that Liszt's devout feelings rejected *doubt* as the last word when thinking about God and the world, and that it was therefore not for musical reasons that he altered the ending," he was disturbed that "something purely musical curtails the clarity and hence damages the overall impression of the piece, namely, *repetition.*"[59] And to underscore his point, Raabe quoted Liszt's assertion "that repetition is indispensable for an understanding of the idea from the audience's point of view; while it nearly accords with the demands for clarity, construction, and effect from an artistic point of view."[60] Yet reading Liszt against himself, Raabe concluded that:

> [t]his is true for absolute music, but false for program music. In the first half of the Mountain Symphony, Liszt developed, in a picturesque and vivid way, those two voices out of an indefinite noise, and then made it sufficiently clear, with a devotional movement, how they 'unite in solemn contemplation.' Yet in the second half he brings back everything again and thus confronts the listener with the enigma, why now, after the redeeming prayer, all the laments reemerge, and why, once again, there is rejoicing and blasphemy until, finally, the same prayer leads to the conclusion, but thereby offers nothing at all different from what has already been emphatically said before."[61]

The question has been tackled before, notably by Dahlhaus, who took Raabe to task for not making enough sense of Liszt's progressive understanding of form; and by Richard Kaplan, who, conversely, challenged Liszt's reputation as a revolutionary by asserting that "Liszt's sonata form makes constant references to those of earlier composers."[62] But the problem is worth tackling again, especially when taking into account new evidence about the genesis and the contemporary reception of the Mountain Symphony, as well as the hermeneutic implications of what James Hepokoski has called "generic or structural deformation" in nineteenth- and early twentieth-century orchestral music.[63] The "Andante religioso" cannot be heard in isolation; it must be heard in conjunction with another chorale—the one at the climax of the work—thereby throwing into relief its formal significance and programmatic meaning. Between the chorale at the climax and the one at the end unfolds the dialectical movement of the work, which, when brought to a standstill, releases its meaning.

In an oft-quoted passage, Liszt defined the essential difference between the "so-called classical" music of the past and that of the program music of the future, noting that in the latter "repetition, alteration, variation, and modulation of motives are determined through their connection with a poetic idea. . . . All purely musical considerations, though not disregarded, are subordinated to those of the plot and the given subject.[64] The symphonic poem, therefore, is no genre sui generis, but an effort to advance what Adorno would call the symphony's "state of material." Aspiring to the cultural prestige of the symphony, Liszt had to rely on its conventions in order to design large-scale form and to communicate programmatic content. In the context of the new genre, however, the vestiges of the symphony could cause confusion, if not irritate. Thus Hanslick noted that the form of Liszt's symphonic poems "stands between Mendelssohn's expanded overture form and the symphony in several movements. With Liszt, the three to four sections that make up his symphonies are sharply distinct in character, and overlap without constraints, as in a free fantasy, so that they are performed as an ostensibly uninterrupted whole. This, however, does not prevent these sections from frequently appearing strung together like a mosaic, or often chaotically mixed together."[65] Joachim Raff, Liszt's copyist and assistant, came down much harder on his employer: "it is time that Liszt stops . . . making a veritable heap of rubble out of the edifice of beautiful forms we inherited."[66]

According to Hepokoski, the term "deformation" is "most appropriate when one encounters a strikingly nonnormative individual structure, one that contravenes some of the most central defining traditions, or default gestures, of a genre while explicitly retaining others."[67] The "normative practice" invoked here is that of "the *Formenlehre* traditions, for better or worse a fundamental frame of reference for the institution of German art music at least from the time of A.B. Marx onward."[68] Formal theory made thus explicit what was implicit in the works of the Viennese masters, above all Beethoven.[69] Although Liszt (and later Richard Strauss) sought to create new forms in part by rejecting old ones, they continued to work with the formal template of the symphony while adhering to fundamental principles of classical aesthetics: beauty, unity, and perfection. Their hope was, as Liszt said about Beethoven's *Egmont* Overture, that the "abnormal apparitions" or the "scattered rays" of the sun at dawn, would by posterity be perceived as all coming "from the same center."

Hepokoski lists five "deformation–procedure families," noting "that any single musical structure may combine aspects of two or more families": (1) "the breakthrough deformation"; (2) "the introduction–coda frame"; (3) "episodes within the developmental space"; (4) "various strophic/sonata hybrids"; and (5) "multimovement forms in a single movement."[70] All these procedures, to varying degrees, can be heard in the Mountain Symphony, making the work a veritable laboratory of formal experimentation (parallel to its laborious genesis) and explaining its mixed reception. Although both Dahlhaus and Draeseke read the Mountain Symphony as an attempt to express the program through a "telling" modification of sonata form, they differed fundamentally about whether the result is a two-part or a three-part structure (see table 2). The placement of the chorale is decisive. Dahlhaus saw the first "Andante religioso" as the dividing line between two full-fledged movements in sonata form, of which the second, the finale, becomes the goal of the overall process, quite in the way Ernest Newman spoke of "double-function form" in the B-minor Sonata—a special case of a multi-movement-within-a-single-movement structure (Hepokoski's fifth category) which was noted as early as 1855 by Liszt biographer William Neumann.[71]

While Dahlhaus's scheme rested on a thematic perspective (thus skirting tonal considerations and the question of whether the slow movements stand within or between sonata form and cycle), Draeseke saw a single sonata form, noting that in the third section (mm. 600–1012), "the poetic idea of the work nevertheless demanded a deviation insofar as the reprise simultaneously had to continue with the development of the ideas, which was far from having been completed. After taking this deviation into consideration, however, there is no difficulty tracing the form of the whole work back to Liszt's sonata form, which he often expands and endows with interpolated movements."[72] With the program speaking through manipulations of form, the twofold occurrence of "Andante religioso" was part of a larger trajectory: while "the two powers . . . only measure their forces against each other" during the development section, "the real battle" takes place with further development during the recapitulation. In between, the first "Andante religioso" rises "like a *fata morgana* before the warriors of the two armies, seemingly promising a peaceful resolution to the conflict"; but because it is only "a lovely, fleeting delusion," it "must vanish immediately as we are deceived into a hope of almost having reached it."

Purple prose? This was the moment that meant the most to Draeseke, like the horn call in Schubert to Schumann: "to be marvelled at as one of the revelations in which the muse herself, the divinity of art, speaks to us without further mediation, embellishment, or veiling."[73] Draeseke was touched. And, like Schumann, he sought to touch the reader. However shopworn the cliché, the "Andante religioso" figured as a voice from the beyond whose sudden apparition the critic divined from the linguistic void of the textless chorale. Indeed, Draeseke struck gold with the image of the *fata morgana* as a way to describe two extravagant incarnations of Hepokoski's strophic/sonata hybrid: either two stanzas of a chorale or an extraneous refrain articulating two giant strophes. The image of the *fata morgana* joins formal function and programmatic meaning: the first "religioso" in the upper mediant is a mirage of the tonic—distant enough in diatonic space to suggest non-identity, but close enough in chromatic space to suggest identity. The sharp mediant is the first step towards an equal major-third partition of the octave, going far enough to require a chromatic alteration of the fifth scale

TABLE 2

Alternative Sonata Forms in Liszt's *Ce qu'on entend sur la montagne*

Dahlhaus		Draeseke		Tonal Centers
PART 1 (Sonata 1)		**PART 1** (Exposition)		
Introduction	1–96	Introduction (nh0)	1–34	E♭, C, A, G♭, B♭
		N1 (1st Group)	35–67	E♭, C, A, F♯
Exposition		N1, N2	68–96	V/F♯
Main Theme	97–132	N3	97–132	F♯
Transition	133–157	H1, H2 (2nd Group)	133–157	A, C, g♯, f♯
Second Theme	158–180	H3	158–180	b♭, f♯/B
Closing Group	180–206	Closing Group	180–206	B♭
Slow Movement		***Slow Movement***		
and Introduction	207–308	H2, N1	207–308	g, B♭, g, B
		PART 2 (Development)		
Development	308–401	Development		
		H1, H2	308–365	g♯, b♭ (begin.)
Reprise		H3	366–401	g, b♭, e♭
Main Theme	402–423	N3	402–423	B, e♭
Transition	424–442	H2, N2,	424–	f♯*dim7*
Second Theme	442–454	H2, H3	–453	e♭/G
Closing Group	454–478	Closing Group	454–478	G
Hymn	479–520	***Religioso***	479–520	G
PART 2 (Sonata 2, Finale)		***Slow Movement***		
		N1, H2	521–599	G, d, E, b
Slow Mvt., Intro.	521–631	N1, N2 (c.f 68–96)	600–631	V/E♭
		PART 3 (Reprise)		
Exposition				
Main Theme	632–677	N1, N2, N3	632–677	E♭, E, A, F♯,
Second Theme	678–718	N1, H1, H2, H3	678–718	E(!), A, C, E♭
Main Theme	718–742	N3, H1, N2, H2, N1	718–763	C, E♭
(Pt.1)		N2, H2	764–779	E♭
Development	743–795	N1, N2	780–795	E♭, C, A, F♯
Reprise				
Second Theme	796–811	N1, H1	796–812	E♭, A♭, D♭
New Theme	812–848	New Theme		
		(N1, N3, H1, H2)	812–848	D, E♭, G♭, V/E♭
Main Theme	849–876	N3, H2, N2	849–876	E♭/F♯
New Theme	877–890	New Theme H1	877–890	E♭, V/E♭
Closing Group	891–919	Closing Group	891–919	E♭
Area of liquidation	920–947	H1, H2, H3	920–947	E♭, G♭
Hymn	948–989	***Religioso***	948–989	E♭
Coda	990–1012	N3	990–1012	C, E♭

degree, but staying close enough not to require an enharmonic exchange.[74] Less abstractly, perhaps, the G-major of the first "religioso" stands midway between the tonic, E♭ major, and the dominant, B♭ major, whose prolongation is the traditional function of the development section. In that sense, the chorale would also serve as an "episode within developmental space" (Hepokoski's third category). It appears topically close, but remains tonally distant.

Draeseke's analytical instincts must be credited—not least because of his closeness to the composer. This is borne out in the context of other long-range harmonic relationships in the Mountain Symphony sponsored by the striking progression—from E♭ to C, A, and F♯—which structures the first sixty-eight measures.[75] Taken by itself, it has long been seen as a token of Liszt, the progressive, emerging from his predilection to compose sequences in exact transposition and to modulate and transpose by thirds. Asked by Lina Ramann to point out innovative uses of harmony in his music, Liszt listed it along with other Skalen on two different fly leaves.[76] In fact, the octatonic progression based on this tetrachord may well have been his first musical idea for the Mountain Symphony, jotted down in the so-called Ce qu'on entend sur la montagne sketchbook.[77] The programmatic implications of the progression are suggestive: the symmetrical division of the octave, a product of humanity; the non-symmetrical relations, a product of nature. Yet the harmonic dichotomy cuts across the thematic conflict: the triumphant Nature 3 stands in F♯ major, whereas the forceful Humanity 3 is in B♭ minor. Clearly, Liszt was less interested in forging concrete associations than in exploring a more abstract symbolism of diatonic and chromatic relationships. These emerge with full force at the work's climax—the second chorale.

Draeseke remarked on the octatonic progression in the introduction that "in the third part of the work . . . this simple, purely musical device has come to represent, in a fascinatingly brilliant way, the utmost emotional struggle."[78] He heard the latter as an increase in harmonic tension: "after the initial harmonic basis of the pure E♭-major chord has gradually changed into the minor ninth chord on F♯, Liszt returns—symbolizing a superhuman effort—to the original unspoilt harmonic basis with the following unprepared E♭-major sixth chord. This is a very bold musical experiment, which nevertheless, because of its convincing and apparent poetic truth, can if need be do without a theoretical justification."[79] Today, to be sure, a theoretical explanation seems easier to come by than a programmatic meaning. The difference accords with the way Howard Cinnamon distinguished between "incipient" and "true" equal octave divisions in Liszt's music, depending on whether a dominant tonicizes one of its centers (as happens in measures 31 and 69), or

not (as happens in the reprise).[80] Because of the limited invariance between the octatonic and diatonic systems, the dominant triad or seventh
chord cannot be derived from the octatonic scale; neither can the flat
submediant (B/C♭) nor the sharp mediant (G). The "poetic truth"
Draeseke heard in the unprepared return to an "unspoilt" E♭-major
triad spells out the "struggle" in harmonic terms: the octatonic progression unfolds against the sharpening of the prolonged tonic third and
against an incomplete diatonic cadence of a mere B♭–E♭ in the timpani
(mm. 646–668). Moreover, in the build up towards the climax (the
passage he had excerpted for Ramann), Liszt condenses the octatonic
progression into a loop of repeating four-measure phrases with Nature 1
in diminution rising up (mm. 780–96). Its nondiatonic circling, sign of
that endless struggle, is cut short by the *grandioso* augmentation of
Nature 1 moving diatonically from E♭ down by fifths through A♭ to D♭,
until the new theme enters with a stunning semitonal shift to D major
(ex. 4.3). For Draeseke this was "not only the climax of the whole
work, but at the same time a climax in the entirety of musical literature":

> As a counter piece to the "Seid umschlungen!" this thundering call, "Stürzet
> nieder Millionen," seems to force us to our knees. Or can the reader name
> many passages which—more powerful in their appearance, more magnifi-
> cent and logical in their continuing build-up— radiate more sublimity
> combined with the uplifting power?[81]

In his attempt to carve out a place for the composer in the evolving
canon, Draeseke made the compositional climax coalesce with a historical highpoint, which could be heard only with a heightened sense of the
past as posterity (in the way Liszt viewed Beethoven's *Egmont* Overture). "At a later time," Brendel claimed in his *History of Music,* "this
whole epoch will appear as *one giant mountain range with various
peaks.*"[82] The Mountain Symphony was to be one of those peaks, perceived in a mixture of criticism and historiography close to the spirit of
a Burckhardtian history of culture, where moments of greatness result
from a genius coming at the right time in the evolution of art.

But how extraordinary is this moment in the Mountain Symphony? It
has been compared with a similar peak in the Finale of Mahler's First
Symphony, where the sudden appearance of a D-major chorale, in
Mahler's oft-quoted words, "must sound as though it had fallen from
heaven, as though it had come from another world."[83] In a breakthrough (de)formation, Hepokoski defines, "an unforeseen inbreaking
of a seemingly new (although normally motivically related) event in or
at the close of the 'developmental space' radically redefines the character
and course of the movement and typically renders a normative, largely

Example 4.3. *Ce qu'on entend sur la montagne:* Climactic Chorale

Example 4.3. (cont.)

175

symmetrical recapitulation invalid."[84] Draeseke would have concurred, as he found that Liszt was "perfectly right" to choose for the climax "a completely new idea capable of both intensification and refreshment." And ever eager to prove Liszt's adherence to the organicist paradigm, he praised him as "the sensitive formalist" who would connect the new theme with the other material of the tone poem" (i.e. the descending scale from Nature 1 with the dotted rhythm from Nature 3).[85] By both being part of the formal process and by going beyond it, the breakthrough proposes to be a transcendent moment where artistic intuition from inside seems to connect with divine inspiration from outside. Draeseke's pun—the juxtaposition of *erhaben* and *erhebend*, or *sublimitas* and *elevatio*—places in a nutshell the link between the aesthetically incommensurable and the religiously tremendous.

Still, John Williamson has argued that the unifying impulse of the new theme at the climax overtakes "the apparent identity of intent between poem and symphonic poem," providing "an image of the transcendent, embracing, in its accompanying configuration of motives, both voices."[86] Although Liszt's recapitulation is "an intended going-beyond," Williamson suggested, "the dialectical movement between restatement and transformation, translation and gloss, aporia and faith" derails, so that "an unintended, perhaps 'obtuse' image, in Barthes' sense of the term, subverts the intent."[87] But still: the subversion of the intent is intended. Unable to come to a rest in the tonic or in G♭ (the key of nature's first highpoint in the exposition), the new theme remains shot through with human interjections. In fact, Liszt brings the polarity between E♭ and G♭ (F♯) to a head in the next section, *animato,* where E♭ and F♯ alternate in a stretto of gradually shortening phrases until they are only a quarter-note apart (mm. 849–876). "The contact of the two powers," Draeseke remarked on this passage, "is ultimately so close that there is no more room for motives, only the sharply contrasting triads can battle against each other."[88] Indeed, this conflict grinds down the thematic material (foremost Nature 2) to a purely harmonic clash between the tonic and F♯ minor—the work's most prominent subsidiary center from the octatonic collection. Granted, the final statement of the new theme that follows does finally cadence in the tonic, but even there the structural downbeat remains haunted by human interjections. This unresolved conflict between nature and humanity is the hermeneutic crux of the symphonic poem, which unfolds between the chorale at the climax and the chorale at the end.

The second "Andante religioso" is part of a coda—itself part of an introduction-plus-coda frame, which effects the final "deformation" that puts the whole piece into an entirely new light. Enclosed by three timpani strokes on E♭, the coda corresponds to the "dying away" in the composer's program note. The voices of humanity fade first: a faint echo of the formerly piercing B♭ trumpet blasts of Humanity 3 (m. 158ff.), now in E♭ and subdued in the horns; the "cry of humanity" (Humanity 2) in the double basses and cellos; a "sigh" in the bassoons reminiscent of the once aggressive interjections of Humanity 1; and a trumpet call on B♭ recalling the very first figure that had emerged from the wide noise at the beginning (it merges now into the melody of the "Andante religioso," as the triplets become the meter of the chorale).

Taking a Schoenbergian perspective on thematic unity, Dahlhaus heard the dotted rhythm, emphasized on the second and third beats of the chorale's first measure, as a rhythmic cell belonging to both voices. Draeseke, however, was more interested in the effect of the hymn's tonal return: "no longer a mirage, but blissful certainty, its effect is indescribable." "Pouring balsam on the wounds of the heart. . . the "Andante religioso" belongs to the few pieces of music which possess and use their transfiguring, resolving, and peace-giving power in a perfect way."[89] These were (or became) Liszt's words, who later wrote of the piece as a palliative against worldly pain.

Whose voice is this? Norbert Miller has argued that the "Andante religioso" is only one of two related instances where the composer changes the program by eliminating the conspicuous presence of the speaker from the ode.[90] First, the music moves back in time to recount the actual acoustical events (the Mountain Symphony begins with line 13, not line 1, so that enactment can eclipse narrative mediation).[91] Second, Liszt omits the ode's concluding question and with it the striking moment of the speaker falling from a godlike position on the mountain top that grants total (aural) vision into the inner abyss of the meditating mind, unable to fathom the meaning of a divided creation. According to Miller, only a solo voice (as in Berlioz's *Harold en Italie*) could have marked the role change from the experiencing to the discursive subject. Echoing Dahlhaus, he saw the thematic integration of the chorale as a return to the *hymne éternel,* from whose *symphonie* the different voices sprang (vv. 25ff.).[92]

But the suggestion that Liszt eliminated any trace of the discursive subject flies in the face of other attempts to locate moments of narration in varied repetition, alteration of formal archetypes, or a change of voice. In the Mountain Symphony all of these fracture the music's immediacy with discursive distance. Like the speaker's formulaic "Now, as I have said" which initiates a further description of the conflict in the middle of the poem (v. 43), the rhetorical strategy of *elaboratio* in the second half of the Mountain Symphony (or Draeseke's third part), is a sign of reflective retelling, achieved through "epic synthesis."[93] Hence the developmental reprise and its breakthrough climax, brought about by such a synthesis, function as a telling deviation from the underlying narrative archetype of sonata form.[94] The enunication of a narrative voice in the "Andante religioso," on the other hand, is an intrusion of what Abbate called "phenomenal" as opposed to "noumenal" music, appropriating Kant's distinction between *noumenon* (the thing itself) and *phenomenon* (the thing as experienced by the senses).[95] However smooth its entry, however integrated its thematic material, however logical its position in the tonal structure—none of these can mitigate the chorale's generic otherness.

But who is speaking? Given the program, all music other than the "religioso" emerges from the *large bruit,* developing into ever more elaborate rejoicings of nature and cries of humanity. Despite the realistic rumbling in the opening bass drum (which Liszt added as late as the *Stichvorlage*), the acoustical panorama of the Mountain Symphony is only an idealized scenario: "while dreaming . . . I listened . . . and never had a similar voice/ emanated from a mouth nor touched an ear." If we are invited to eavesdrop on this unheard-of music, Liszt's portrayal of the two voices is not, however, strictly representational. Instead, what we hear on the mountain reaches, like absolute music, beyond the phenomenal world. Their culmination in the new theme figures as the *telos* of a purely musical process. In that sense, the breakthrough at the climax remains, as Adorno might have said, *formimmanent* (immanent to form).[96] Moreover, true to the poem, the breakthrough does not bring peace. The "Andante religioso," by contrast, is twice extraneous. It is not the product of the formal process, but its suspension. It is twice removed from narrative immediacy. It is not the narrator's voice, but the composer's.

The two moments, then, that matter most in the Mountain Symphony—the new theme and the "Andante religioso"—can be heard as relating to each other dialectically: the disruptive culmination of an objective formal process against the smooth suspension of that process; an overstated secular chorale against an understated sacred one; modern autonomous music against traditional functional music; bourgeois individuality against pre-bourgeois collectivity; idealized humanity against monastic community; in short: art religion against religious art. While the new theme fails blatantly to bring about thematic synthesis, generic otherness of the "Andante religioso" does. While the spectacular breakthrough of the secular chorale has merely a dramatic effect, the gentle intrusion of the sacred chorale effects a profound change in perspective. And while the most prestigious vehicle of free subjectivity—autonomous instrumental music—depicts the limitations of mankind, the vehicle of communal worship—a functional hymn—harbors the possibilities of personal redemption. Since the secular chorale is inverted by the sacred one, the "religioso" becomes the antithesis of the new theme. But it was only after introducing the hymn into the work at a later stage of its genesis that Liszt created this sublime suspension of the sublime.

The Sublime Suspended: From Overture to Symphonic Poem

"Perhaps in none of his works did Liszt struggle so much with the material before mastering it" wrote Peter Raabe in 1916 about the genesis of the Mountain Symphony.[97] Still, although the work went through at least three revisions (or four versions), only the second revision is so substantial that one should speak of an early and late conception of the work, clearly distinguishable by their overall proportions, which more than double from 482 to 1012 measures. The difference is one in kind, reflected in the change of titles from the *Ouverture* and *Méditation Symphonie* (first worked out in 1849–50) to *Poème Symphonique* (reconceived and refined in 1854–57).[98] Liszt felt so confident about this new version that it served as the basis for the *Stichvorlage*, a set of parts (A1e–g), and—as Pohl indicates—the arrangement for two pianos (W1a).[99] Despite further changes, the Gotha version is so close to the final version that the latter can serve as the basis for comparison with the *Méditation Symphonie* (see table 3).[100]

A comparison of the two conceptions shows first that Liszt retained the main thematic material, including the characteristic opening of the work and the exposition of Nature 1, the closing group, the beginning of the reprise as modeled on the octatonic progression, and the passage with the octatonic cycle leading to the augmented theme of Nature 1 (mm. 780ff. in the final version). The two early versions already possess a clear three-part structure (with two slow movements flanking a development) and they both move in the middle to the upper mediant. Finally, Liszt always envisioned the substantial third part to function as a developmental reprise leading to a climax, to which he added in *Méditation Symphonie* the D-major breakthrough with the New Theme followed by statements in E♭ and G♭. But this alone would not justify regarding the two early versions as two different conceptions, as the rousing conclusion does not lead to a reconciliation between the voices of nature and humanity. Instead a variant of Humanity 2 in F♯ minor interrupts the tonic affirmation of Nature 1 (in the *Ouverture*) and Nature 2 (in the *Symphonie*). Just as this harmonic contrast would later intensify immensely, the New Theme already bears in the *Méditation Symphonie,* the mark of a "diverse unity," by combining the head motive of Humanity 3 from the second group with the augmented version of Nature 1.[101]

If the creation of a divided climax had been one of Liszt's main

TABLE 3
Synopsis of Correspondences in the Different Conceptions
of the Mountain Symphony

Original Conception				Final Conception
Ouverture (ca. 1849)	*Méditation Symphonie* (ca. 1850)			*Poème symphonique* (1854/57)
1–27	Introduction (nh0)	1–27	Eb, C, A, Gb, Bb	1–34
A–B+	**Exposition** *A–B+*			
28–67	N1 (First Group)	28–75	Eb, C, A, F#, V/F#–F#	35–83
68–80	H3 (Second Group)	76–88	bb/Bb/Gb	*158–171
81–108	Closing Group	89–116	Bb/E	180–206
C+	<u>Slow Movement *C+*</u>			
110–160	H2 and N1	117–176	g, Bb, g, B	≈209–308
D, E, F+	**Development** *D, E, F+*			
161–173	H2	**178–205	(modulating)	
174–207	H2	206–235		
208–244	H3	236–273		
245–266	Closing Group	273–294	G	454–475
G–H+	<u>Slow Movement *G+*</u>			
267–309	N1, H2	*295–341	G, d, E, b	≈521–599
310–327	N1 (Retransition *H+*)	342–363	V/Eb	600–631
I–L+	**Reprise** *I–L+*			
328–375	N2/N1	364–406	Eb, C, A, F#	632–676/7
376–417	N1/H2, N2	407–455	E, A, modulating	≈678–683
418–	N1/H2 (Stretto)	456–471	Eb	[684–776]
–445	N1/H2 (Octatonic Loop)	472–483	Eb, C, A, F#	780–795
446–459	N1(augmented) *M+*	484–507	Eb, Ab, Db	796–810
(no New Theme)	New Theme (3x)	498–542	D, Eb, Gb	813–848
460–482	N2, nhO, H2 (Concl.) *N+*	533–542	Eb/f#	

Notes
** considerable differences
* some differences
+ original rehearsal numbers
≈ equivalent section

objectives from the start, resituating this climax within a new overall trajectory became a central concern when he reconceived the work in the mid 1850s. Apart from the tendency to expand at every juncture (doubling, for instance, the length of the slow movements), the most substantial changes include (1) the addition of the majestic theme Nature 3 together with its recurrence in both the development section and the reprise; (2) the addition of a fourth statement of the New Theme followed by another statement of the closing group; (3) the creation of a coda; and (4) the interpolation of the "Andante religioso." Most of these additions appear in the autograph score within an almost seamless stretch from the beginning of the reprise until the very end of the coda (pp. 20–39 in A1a).[102] There is, however, one exception: the "Andante religioso." Although Raabe correctly noted that both "religioso" sections are inserted on single leaves into a bifolio, only the concluding "religioso" appears on an inserted leaf that is numbered consecutively with the outer bifolio, while the first "religioso" is numbered 17a and 17b (fig. 2). Liszt crossed out six measures at the end of page 17, instructing the copyist to go to pages 17a and 17b. Inserting these measures at the end of the "religioso" he told the copyist to continue on page 18 (*geht weiter Seite 18*). Thus, what was to cause the greatest point of contention in the later readings of the work's overall form—the first occurrence of the chorale—had indeed come as an insertion from outside.

By increasing the Mountain Symphony to gargantuan proportions, Liszt seems to have tried not merely to match the vastness of the acoustical vision in Hugo's poem, but to capture its incommensurability as one that exceeds the speaker's comprehension. The "too much" that confused Raabe, overwhelmed Pohl, stirred Draeseke, and intrigued Dahlhaus, was meant to bring the listener to the point of literally loosing sight of the work's formal horizon, in the same way that the aural gaze of the divided world exceeds the moral horizon of the speaker. If the half-hour piece that Pohl heard was a "true revelation towering so far above the musical present that it cannot be measured through parallels or comparisons," he could indeed not have helped but speak of it as "a *Mountain* Symphony in the most sublime sense of the word." However casual the characterization, it touches on the deeper cultural concerns of the piece. And although the distinction between the beautiful and the sublime in Kant's *Critique of Judgement* has had some currency in music criticism since the early nineteenth century, Kant's lesser known notion of a sublimity of the mind helps to get to the bottom of these concerns.[103]

To recall: for Kant, the mathematical sublime of immeasurable magnitude and the dynamical sublime in terrifying nature bring imagination

Figure 2. (a) Franz Liszt, *Ce qu'on entend sur la montagne,* inserted "Andante Religioso," D-WRgs A1a, p. 17. Reproduced with permission of the Stiftung Weimarer Klassik, Goethe and Schiller Archiv

(*Einbildungskraft*) to its limits, resulting in the paradox of a pleasurable displeasure (what Burke called "relative pleasure").[104] Hence "nature is called sublime [*erhaben*] merely because it "elevates [*erhebt*] our imagination, [making] it exhibit those cases where the mind can come to feel its own sublimity, which lies in its vocation and elevates it even above nature."[105] This sublimity of the mind ties Kant's aesthetics into his transcendental philosophy, which is "occupied not so much with objects as with the mode of our knowledge of objects in so far as this mode of

Figure 2. (b) Liszt, D-WRgs A1a, p. 17a. Reproduced with permission of the
Stiftung Weimarer Klassik, Goethe and Schiller Archiv

knowledge is to be possible *a priori.*"[106] What mattered most to Kant
was not the unease or terror of the sublime object, but how its effects
testify to a moral being. Consider the famous peroration (and epitaph)
of the *Critique of Practical Reason* (which impressed Beethoven so
deeply): "Two things fill the mind with ever new and increasing admiration and awe, the more often and the more steadily we contemplate
them: the starry heavens above me, and the moral law within me."[107]
Later, in the *Critique of Judgement,* Kant asks us to do this: when

Figure 2. (c) Liszt, D-WRgs A1a, p. 17b. Reproduced with permission of the
Stiftung Weimarer Klassik, Goethe and Schiller Archiv

calling "the sight of the starry sky sublime, we must not base our
judgment upon any concepts of worlds that are inhabited by rational
beings, and then [conceive of] the bright dots that we see occupying the
space above us as being these worlds' suns, moved in orbits prescribed
for them with great purposiveness; but we must base our judgement
regarding it merely on how we see it, as a vast vault encompassing
everything. . . ."[108] Facing the sublime, therefore, the sublime mind is
not lost in an infinity of particulars, but can understand that infinity in
relation to an absolute whole.

When Friedrich Christian Michaelis adapted the notion of the sublime for the purposes of music criticism, he made two important distinctions: (1) between a musical sublime manifest in a lack of variety and a musical sublime manifest in an excess thereof; and (2) between music imitating the sublime through its structure and music imitating the effect the sublime has on us.[109] In Michaelis's musical sublime, the imagination "is elevated to the plane of the limitless, the immeasurable, the unconquerable," thus preventing "the integration of one's impressions into a coherent whole."[110] In taking the symphonies of Haydn, Mozart, and Beethoven as prime examples, Michaelis followed Sulzer's *Allgemeine Theorie der schönen Künste*. Sulzer not only took the symphony to be "most excellently suited to expressions of grandeur, passion, and the sublime," but also held that the symphonic allegro was analogous to the Pindaric ode, which "elevates and profoundly moves the soul of the listener, and to be successful, demands the same spirit, the same sublime imagination, and the same knowledge of art."[111] Thus the Mountain Symphony had dual ties with the symphonically sublime: as a symphony it presents a sublime object, difficult to understand; and as an ode—a genre that blended enthusiasm with reflection—it offered that object to the sublime mind for meditation.[112] Because sublime effects in music rely on temporal phenomena, James Webster suggested that "the musical sublime can arise even through the effects of a single moment: such a moment can 'reverberate' long afterwards, on different musical and hermeneutic planes. It is this multi-layered temporality that constitutes the analogy to Kant's *Bewegung* of the spirit, and therefore generates the musical sublime."[113]

In the Mountain Symphony the two chorales are two such moments. While the first moment is the climactic representation of the sublime object, the second moment appears, initially at least, as a representation of the sublime mind. The repetitive rumble depicting the first ruminations of the acoustical universe in Hugo's ode would surely have suited the sublime as excessive uniformity. And the abundance of thematic ideas and timbres, the huge proportions, and the convoluted form of the entire Symphony certainly qualified for the sublime as excessive diversity. If we trust Pohl that Liszt's first symphonic poem was more admired than understood; and if we trust contemporary critics (however malevolent) that it appeared chaotic—that is, as particulars not fitting into a whole—then the piece did challenge listeners, in terms of Kant's mathematical sublime, to comprehend "in one instant what is apprehended successively" and thus to cancel "the condition of time in the imaginations's progression and [to make] *simultaneity* intuitable."[114] To understand chaos as an organized whole requires the analytical ear to hear in a single instant what I have called earlier in this book the "moment of structure"; and not, in Pohl's terms, "to lose sight of the imposing overall impression" of what appeared at first as a "formless object."

Correspondingly, the equivalent of Kant's dynamical sublime may be understood as the structural moment that breaks through the form at the highpoint of the work. Nowhere does the voice of nature sound more glorious, but nowhere is the disruption of the climatic chorale more disturbing. The moment articulates not only the fissure between humanity and nature, but also between the finite and the infinite. The speaker in Hugo's poetry and the narrator implicit in Liszt's music are elevated enough to discern the diversity, but they cannot perceive them as a *harmony* of opposites or a diverse *unity*. The speaker's divine perspective lacks divine insight; being on top of the mountain is near heaven, but not heaven itself. In Hugo's ode, the *tremendum* of the sublime prompts the speaker's question, but provides no final answer. Neither does the breakthrough in the symphonic poem, which only exposes, but does not explain, the gap between the voices of humanity and nature. The breakthrough is a transcendent moment, not a transcendental one. It is a showing of the sublime object, but not of the sublime subject.

Only in the "Andante religioso," it appears, does the meditating mind aspire toward the equivalent of a transcendental perspective, exposing at the same time the distance between Enlightenment philosophy and romantic religiosity. For Kant, God's sublimity was to be matched by that of man, which expressed itself in reverence (*Ehrfurcht*), not fear (*Furcht*); respect, not submission; true religion, not superstition.[115] Kant's notion of the "*sublimity* of a religion" was hardly that of someone who would "prostrate himself on the flagstones before a *Muttergottesbild*" as Raff observed Liszt rediscovering his faith in the Protestant Weimar.[116] Of course, Liszt's faith should not be reduced to prayer as palliative (an easy target for a Marxist critique of religion as opium for the masses). The young follower of Abbé Lamenais—who once demanded that "art must leave the sancturay of the temple" and that through music such as the Marseillaise "*all classes* will at last melt into one religious magnificent, and lofty unity of feeling"—remained committed to the Saint-Simonian ideal of the artist's mission in society.[117] Liszt's religiosity is marked by a tension between progressive and regressive impulses; between a public activism for social reform and a retreat into the community of the church—"*se rejetter fortement dans le système catholique,*" as the composer put it in 1851.[118] Thus the Weimar Liszt wrote his Gran Mass in the most advanced symphonic style, yet heard it as "but a humble prayer to the Almighty."[119] And the Abbé Liszt composed the avant-garde *Via crucis*, yet considered it as the "simple reflections of my youthful emotions—which remain indestructible across all the trials of the years."[120]

Since the Enlightenment's critique of religion had put man on a par with God, it seemed to have opened forever the rift between belief and reason. The concommitant rift between the sacred and the secular runs through many of Liszt's works—whether sutured as in the early *De Profundis,* which weaves the chant into the fabric of the work; or exposed as in the late *Unstern,* where the diatonic invocations of the concluding *quasi organo* appear removed from the austerely chromatic first part, but then fragment into the opening tritone. Like the Protestant Brendel, Liszt remained torn between the critique of religion by the "Left" Hegelians and the attempt to rescue religion by the "Right" Hegelians. If the final question of *Ce qu'on entend sur la montagne* expressed Hugo's inability to fathom a divided creation, Liszt sought to comprehend the division not within a larger whole, but from a different perspective altogether: the "Andante religioso" was not there to undo the division; it was there to soothe the pain.

The ending of the Mountain Symphony is thus a distinct variant of the narrative archetype that Liszt used elsewhere to impose closure onto a programmatic conflict, be it the Faust Symphony or *Die Ideale,* where the rousing resitution of the Ideale theme seals the triumph of the sublime mind with the conviction of the Ode of Joy: "Überm Zelte *muß* ein guter Vater wohnen." From this the "religioso" of the Mountain Symphony could not be further removed. Within the larger trajectory of nineteenth-century culture, the chorale at the climax is a double product of the autonomous symphonic process and its surrogate art religion. Yet it does not achieve what the chorale at the end achieves, momentarily at least, as a residue of functional religious art. As a soothing episode, the "Andante religioso" does not follow any formal imperative; instead of fulfilling a demand, it responds to a longing. In his answer to Hugo, Liszt reached deep into the prelapsarian reserve of his robust childhood religosity, derived from such formative experiences as the nostalgic trips he took with his father to the Franciscan monastery that Adam Liszt had once sought to enter.[121] While the Kantian sublime was meant to prompt the power of reason that must measure it against the idea of an absolute whole, Liszt was calling out for a different whole, long lost and only momentarily within reach as the future vision of a better world. But this substitution for the Enlightened sublime mind was more than the sentimental childhood memories, called up by his later visit to the Carthusian monks near Grenoble. Recalling a personal reminiscence, the composer's individual voice was submerged within the collective choir of a utopain community.

The "Andante religioso," in this sense, would be the moment that falls out of the historical continuum of the Mountain Symphony. When the monumental work breaks into ruins in the coda, its scattered particulars surround the sacred chorale as the very messianic moment that the secular chorale at the climax could not be. The principal condition of messianic time, as Benjamin understood it, is the recognition of a historical object which "becomes citable in all its moments", that is, when "a redeemed mankind receives the fullness of its past."[122] Under the condition of messianic time, the "religioso" can be heard as a citation whose citability is made possible by the *fata morgana* finally become reality.[123] Whereas Dahlhaus heard the last measures of the work as a retreat from that which had been achieved, Draeseke heard the chorale separate the fragmentary voices of humanity from the voice of nature, which appears in the end "untroubled and solely in praise of the Lord."[124] Yet it seems that the coda does both by suspending the dialectic between topical otherness and thematic sameness; between rupture and reconciliation. Liszt's conclusion suggests an image of a "dialectic at a standstill" that brings both together and disengages the voices of humanity and nature. Just as for Benjamin, a life's oeuvre is both "preserved" and "canceled" (both *aufbewahrt* and *aufgehoben*) in the work, the era in the life's oeuvre, and the entire course of history in the era, we could hear the historical conflict between Enlightened reason and romantic religiosity to be *aufbewahrt* and *aufgehoben* in the moment of Liszt's prayer. When the method of materialistic history takes a piece of religious art to explode the continuum of art religion; when the messianic moment of the future configures presence by citing the past; when the elegiaic happiness of paradise projects the hymnic happiness of Parousia, then Liszt's prayer is indeed a paradox.

SCHOENBERG'S GAZE

S hortly after the end of World War I, Darius Milhaud paid Arnold Schoenberg a visit at his Mödling home in Vienna. Milhaud recalled the experience almost a quarter of a century later:

> We had coffee in a dining room, the walls of which were hung about with Schoenberg's paintings. Faces and eyes, eyes, eyes everywhere.[1]

A glimpse of Milhaud's experience, Reinhold Brinkmann has suggested, might be gleaned from a photograph taken much later in Schoenberg's Brentwood home, in which the composer is sitting in front of a wall hung with three of his paintings.[2] Perhaps the most striking aspect of this photograph, one might add, is the way Schoenberg's figure fits into the arrangement. The triangular shape of his face provides a link between the painting right above his head and the one to the lower left, the famous *Red Gaze* from 1910. This painting appears as a self-portrait of sorts, meant to bring out a particular aspect in the painter's view of himself, that is, as someone who gazes. Indeed, these "self-portraits" belong to a large group of similar paintings in the composer's output, which display, according to Brinkmann, "Schoenberg's central pictorial idea: the human being's existence concentrated in open eyes—eyes of a specific intensity, direct, active, burning, confronting, questioning."[3] Nowhere is this more apparent than in a handful of paintings entitled *Vision* and *Gaze*, whose striking originality and power has earned Schoenberg a small, but notable, niche in art history as an expressionist painter.

Milhaud's impression of seeing "eyes, eyes, eyes everywhere" testifies to Schoenberg's obsession with the sense of sight, and brings to mind, albeit in a starkly different way, Hegel's idea of the beautiful artwork as "a thousand-eyed Argus." But Schoenberg's self-portraits, visions, and gazes hardly square with the ideal of beauty; rather they appear as the ultimate outgrowth of the characteristic and the subjective also found in paintings by Schoenberg's friend, Richard Gerstl, or drawings by their Viennese contemporary, Egon Schiele.[4] Caught between Argus-eyedness and *Augenblick*, Schoenberg's expressionist portraits afford an opportunity to revisit the central paradox of the composer's historical position between progressive and regressive, or revolutionary and reactionary tendencies. Adorno sought to capture this paradox in the image of Schoenberg as a "dialectical" composer, whose most authentic voice comes through only during his expressionist phase—the "pregnant moment" (in Lessing's sense) where the expressive and rational tendencies in Schoenberg's oeuvre mutually suspend each other to create the music of free atonality. In the *Augenblick* of Expressionism, Schoenberg's dialectics are at a standstill. This was the particular moment of German music that transcended the moment of German music as a whole.

1910, wrote Gottfried Benn, was "the year when all scaffolds began to crack." Hence it seems more than intuitive to use Schoenberg's *Red Gaze* from the same year as the most eloquent emblem for the "emancipation of dissonance."[5] The impetus to draw connections between his paintings and his music was spurred by Schoenberg himself, who remarked that painting "was the same to me as making music."[6] Given the similarities that Courtney Adams saw between Schoenberg's expressionist paintings and the evolution of his atonal music, Brinkmann also noted the deep ambivalence with which the composer saw himself in the *Self-Portrait from Behind* as "leading his generation, at a critical moment within the historical process and through the paradigmatic art form music, into the future."[7] Speaking of the light of genius that shines in the darkness, Schoenberg wrote in his passionate 1912 speech on Mahler: "We ought to remain blind until we have acquired eyes. Eyes that see the future. Eyes that penetrate more than the sensual, which is only alikeness; that penetrate the supersensual: Our soul should be the eye."[8] The moment of Schoenberg's music, as it were, hangs in the balance between the refused gaze of the composer's back and his many eyes that stare at us; or, as I will argue later, between the utmost despair in *Erwartung* and the spiritual optimism of *Die Jakobsleiter*.

Enucleated Eye and Total Vision

"I never saw faces but, because I looked into peoples' eyes, only their 'gazes'. . . . A painter . . . grasps with one look the whole person—I, only his soul."[9] That he was able to grasp the soul, and the soul only, in the gaze of a person is perhaps Schoenberg's most pithy expressionist manifesto. Utmost subjectivity is literally the reverse image of the utmost objectivity that Benjamin saw in the "opening of the eyes," through which baroque iconography does "not so much unveil material objects as strip them naked."[10] Schoenberg dragged the Hegelian soul of the subject before our eyes. "The eye," noted Karl Linke in the introduction to the 1912 Schoenberg *Festschrift,* "places the soul on the outside and the things of this world disappear."[11] If many of Schoenberg's self-portraits appear as if the figure of the composer is under erasure, a series of paintings all dating from 1910 are strongly suggestive of this process: the head gradually becomes detached from his body and gradually dissolves until only the eyes are left, as in the second painting entitled *Red Gaze* (fig. 3). Not that these paintings were necessarily created in this order; rather they arrange themselves that way under the "persistent eye" of the beholder, whose hermeneutic gaze—like Goethe's *aperçu* or Adorno's *Augenblick*—suddenly perceives them as a sequence in the manner of a critical constellation. The gradual erasure of the human figure, ending with the eyes as its essence, appears as an act of enucleation—of removing the eye from the socket. An enigmatic painting from 1910, entitled *Hands,* might yield its secret when viewed as the very image of enucleation, with one hand reaching for the eye as if to remove it (fig. 4a).[12]

Given the supreme status the eye has enjoyed among the senses in Western culture, the extraction of the eye from its privileged place in the center amounts to its most radical critique. Martin Jay has pointed out that fantasies of enucleation were anticipated by Odilon Redon, whose images of single eyes as ballons, flowers, or Cyclops became particularly prominent in surrealism. Artists like Giorgio de Chirico, Ernst, Dali, Man Ray, and Magritte created "a rich ocular iconography" in which the eyes (or often the single eye) were enucleated, blinded, mutilated, or, as in Georges Bataille's transgressively pornographic *Story of the Eye,* "transfigured . . . into other shapes like eggs, whose liquid could easily be spilled."[13] For example, Man Ray's *Object of Destruction* (original version, 1923), where the eye is "cut from a photograph of a lover and mounted on a metronome," or the "chilling mixture of images of castration and enucleation" in Dali's *The Lugubrious Game* (1929), "typify the violent denigration of the visual" culminating in the "slashing razor" that slits the eye at the beginning of Buñuel's surrealist masterpiece *Un chien andalou* in a still shocking "rupture of visual pleasure accompanying experiences of imagistic wholeness."[14] Such treatment of the eyes in surrealism has prompted the notion that in twentieth-century painting they "are not alive": "[w]hen the viewer looks at them, they do not have the power to look back and see. So the individual or divine spark of contact does not exist in the missing or mutilated eye. In place of contact there is rejection; instead of sight, there is complete blindness."[15]

Schoenberg's gazes resist such generalization. They oscillate between vision and blindness, thus illuminating the central paradox in his oeuvre, which is torn between a critical moment and an affirmative one: the death of tonality and the life of the organic artwork. On the face of it,

(a) *Self-Portrait*, 1910

(b) *Blue Self-Portrait*, 1910

(c) *Green Self-Portrait*, 1910

(d) *Self-Portrait*, 1910

Figure 3. Schoenberg's Gazes and the Enucleated Eye.
Copyright VBK, Vienna 2001

(e) *Self-Portrait*, 1910

(f) *Red Gaze (Face)*, 1910

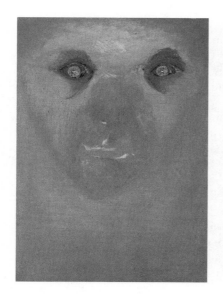

(g) *Gaze*, 1910

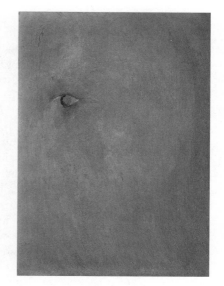

(h) *Red Gaze (Eyes)*, 1910

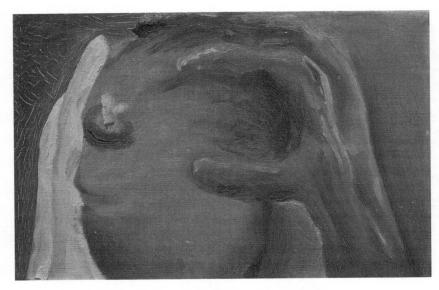

Figure 4. (a) Arnold Schoenberg, *Hands.*
Copyright VBK, Vienna 2001

literally, the fantasy of enucleation in a painting like *Vision* shows the right side of the head dissolving as if the eye had been cut open, so that the white leaking out makes the figure sag like a punctured sack of flour (fig, 4b). Yet the white is also painted like beams of light, just as the tears in Schoenberg's painting *Tears* stream from the eyes like rays, in a gesture that links lament with illumination and turns sorrow into a source of insight (fig. 4c) "Formerly, sound had been the radiation of an intrinsic quality of ideas, powerful enough to penetrate the hull of the form," Schoenberg asserted later in "Composition with Twelve Tones (1)": "Nothing could radiate which was not light itself; here only ideas are light."[16] Indeed, in a picture called *Thinking*, the piece of white that Schoenberg painted on the top of (presumably) his head to represent the idea might even be seen as an eye, itself radiant like a star.

Seen as a pictorial analogue to the changes and continuities in Schoenberg's compositional technique and aesthetic, the absoluteness of the enucleated eye is Janus-faced, caught between the revolutionary renunciation of a central tonal perspective for the sake of new expression, and the regressive regime of an omnipresent, panoptical, *Grundgestalt* for the sake of aesthetic coherence. While the severed nucleus becomes an image of the fluctuating tonality that Schoenberg described in his theory of harmony, the disembodied eye (or ear) is now

Figure 4.
(b) Arnold
Schoenberg,
Vision.
Copyright
VBK,
Vienna
2001

Figure 4.
(c) Arnold
Schoenberg,
Tears.
Copyright
VBK,
Vienna
2001

also free to explore changing perspectives, inspect from varying viewpoints, in short: to seek utmost transparency. Thus Schoenberg wrote about his orchestral songs op. 22, that "one must provide each tiniest element—as in an aphorism, or in lyric poetry—with such a wealth of relationships to all other component elements, that the smallest change of position will bring forth as many new shapes as might elsewhere be found in the richest development section. The various shapes find themselves as in a hall of mirrors, continually visible from all sides, and displaying their connections in all directions."[17] If aural vision aspires to be this total, the difficulty of hearing this totality has earned music composed that way the label *Augenmusik*—music for the eyes. The conceptual and cognitive labor that goes into its aesthetic perception is that of the "persistent eye" as much as that of the persistent ear.

This, at least, was Schoenberg's ideal, which he formed in response to the revival of the spiritual in art by the Russian painter Wassily Kandinsky and the Viennese architect Adolf Loos. On the occasion of the latter's sixtieth birthday, Schoenberg wrote about the "imaginative faculty" with which Michelangelo "carved his *Moses* right out of the stone": "when I then saw the *Moses*, I recognized the great artist's singular perception of space: he sees the object from all sides simultaneously, sees through it so speak, as if it were made out of glass."[18] Loos' contribution to architecture lay, for Schoenberg, in the very same qualitative shift from a mere successive experience to a simultaneous conception: "as if the spiritual eye beholds the space in all its parts and in its entirety at the same time."[19] "[T]he unity of musical space," Schoenberg wrote in an oft-quoted passage from "Composition with Twelve Tones (1)," "demands an absolute and unitary perception."[20] Just as the eyes are everywhere, one can hear everything. If expressionist music remained organic, Adorno argued in the *Philosophy of New Music,* this "drove [it] . . . again in the direction of totality."[21] The moment of absolute freedom takes a dialectical turn (*Umschlag*) to the moment of absolute control. If the two moments from *Erwartung* and *Die Jakobsleiter* discussed here seem to articulate that turn from expression to construction, as well as from particularity to totality, they also articulate the suspension of Schoenberg's compositional dialectic as a moment of musico-historical standstill.

Ariadne in the Labyrinth

In the *Philosophy of New Music,* Adorno noted how *Erwartung* "unfolds the eternity of the second in four hundred measures," echoing Schoenberg's comment that the work's aim had been "to represent in *slow motion* everything that occurs during a single second of maximum spiritual excitement.[22] The remarks are as evocative as they are contradictory. If Expressionism is, as Adorno defined it, "the definite negation of traditional musical means," *Erwartung,* of course, could not be the *Augenblick* of the traditional artwork, which is "the fusion of its particular moments into a whole."[23] Neither was it the moment of structure of Beethoven's symphonic movements "whose virtual effect is as if they lasted only one second," nor the instantaneous conception of the creative genius composing *aus dem Stegreif,* as Schenker had it.[24] The expansiveness of *Erwartung,* moreover, flies in the face of the notion that "contraction" and "inexorable brevity" are hallmarks of the expressionist style," which Schoenberg captured so succinctly in his preface to Webern's *Bagatelles for String Quartet* op. 9: "You can stretch every glance out into a poem, every sigh into a novel. But to express a novel in a single gesture, joy in a breath—such concentration can only be present in proportion to the absence of self-pity."[25] This had been Schoenberg's expressionist credo: "it is *impossible* for a person to have only *one* sensation at a time. One has *thousands* simultaneously." What Schoenberg proclaimed in 1909 to Busoni amounts to perhaps his most radical confession of artistic belief: that he sought "complete liberation from all forms" and "from all symbols of cohesion and of logic"; that he had to do away with "motivic working out," with "harmony as cement or bricks of a building," with "Pathos" and with protracted ten-ton scores"; that music "must be *brief.* Concise! In two notes: not built, but '*expressed*'!!"[26] "Compressed into a moment," Adorno said about such aphoristic works, music "is true as a reflection of negative experience. It pertains to real suffering."[27]

Schoenberg's "actual revolutionary moment," Adorno thus had reason to assert, "is the change in function of musical expression. Passions are no longer simulated, but rather embodied emotions of the unconscious, shocks, and trauma are registered in the medium of music. . . . Schoenberg's formal innovations were closely related to the change in the content of expression. They serve the breakthrough of its reality. The first atonal works are reports in the sense of psychoanalytical dream transcripts."[28] Hence one might plausibly explain the temporal paradox of *Erwartung* as that of an enacted nightmare. As Paul Bekker put it in the most perceptive contemporary "study" of the work (apparently a springboard for Adorno's ideas), *Erwartung* is "a dreamlike abbreviation of what should actually be the content of the musical stage play."[29] Although Bekker had stressed the continuity with the expressive tradition of Wagner, he argued that "the vision-like unfolding of a single moment of highest emotional intensity" necessitated a "new harmonic design," which occurs "through the sudden rupture of the harmonic organism at the moment of utmost energetic concentration," and thus allows "a look into the hidden, intrinsically moving and working elements of its nature."[30] Yet a closer look at what appeared to be "harmonic chaos" nevertheless revealed an "organic stringency", whose "resolution is, of course, not given through the tonic triad, but through a chromatic dissolution, in which all sonorities, from the searching beginning through the great climaxes of a futile finding, are lost."[31] If Schoenberg expressed the inner drama of *Erwartung* through the disorder of a new harmonic order, for Bekker, the central "*formal* difficulty" of the work—"to render this real momentary event as a *temporal* structure and process comprehensible"—could only be made possible through the "opposition" between this new harmonic language and traditional tonality. And their difference hinged on the different perception of time. "Harmonic music" (that is, tonal music), "intensifies the experience of time," so that "the most primitive progression tonic-dominant-tonic flows around a temporal event, whose significance exceeds incomparably the temporal span it requires; the whole process of the Egmont or Coriolan overtures takes place within a period of minutes."[32] But, Bekker continues:

> In contrast to this concentration of a complex event through harmonic music, here the task was to transform the temporality of a momentary event, as expressed in the title *Erwartung,* into a musically *expansive* form. This could only be gained through the multiplication of harmonic regions [*harmonische Vorstellungskreise*], their expansion not through particular chromatic gradation, but through the creation of changing tonal regions of movement [*wechselnder tonaler Bewegungskreise*]. Their mutual crisscrossing, mixing, overlapping without the tendency toward unification arrests the imagination in the perception of a still-standing moment; it prevents the consciousness of a real development of time and thus enables that *continuity* of the musical formal process, which makes the listener experience half an hour as a minute.[33]

Bekker's "minute" of *Erwartung* became Adorno's "second." In contrast to the actual length of symphonic movements by the middle Beethoven which "virtually" appear like an instant, *Erwartung* occupies in reality only a short period of time, although it "virtually" lasts much longer. The temporal paradox of *Erwartung* thus inverts the temporal paradox in the *Eroica*. The aesthetic appearance (the Hegelian *Schein*) of Beethoven's music is its heroic fusion of an expansive reality into the eternal moment of "good infinity," which is associated with the closed circle. In *Erwartung,* however, this dream is turned into a nightmare, whose inner reality expands into the terrible moment of "bad infinity" associated with the unending line: "*Ich suchte,*" the last words the *Frau* stammers.

Whereas Bekker's belief in historical continuity bespeaks his desire for musical continuity, for Adorno the "seismographic transcription of traumatic shocks" record in *Erwartung* "the law of formal technique," which *"prohibits continuity* and development."[34] From the perspective of *Philosophy of New Music,* written after Schoenberg had embraced dodecaphony, free atonality looked even more liberating. And later still, in the face of total serialism and aleatorism, it was *Erwartung* (and not the more constructivist *Glückliche Hand*), which held out the promise of a *musique informelle*. Such music "has discarded all forms which are external or abstract." It "should be completely free of anything irreducibly alien to itself or superimposed on it," but "should nevertheless constitute itself in an objectively compelling way, in the musical substance itself, and not in terms of external laws."[35] Schoenberg called this *musical prose,* which "presupposes the alert mind of an educated listener who, in a single act of thinking, includes with every concept all associations pertaining to the complex. This enables a musician to write for upper-class minds, not only doing what grammar and idiom require, but, in other respects lending to every sentence the full pregnancy of meaning of a maxim, of a proverb, of an aphorism."[36] That the moments of musical prose are meant for the structural listener is no less a paradox than that it fulfills the ideal of antimechanical organicism once proposed by romantic poetry. This musically unbound speech resonates, as Hermann Danuser has pointed out, with Adorno's attempt to conjure up song by shutting it off from regulated verse.[37] *Erwartung* promises a model for a *musique informelle* because it is not "running the risk of a new form of oppression."[38] The very lack of it, as it were, provides room for the repressed memories to surface without any formal dictate of repetition imposed from outside. If Schoenberg's new mode of expression helped the inner reality of a thousand simultaneous sensations to break through, its thousand moments, unfolded, no longer needed to unite into a thousand-eyed Argus. Instead, they coalesced into a single moment of despair.

Erwartung, as one of the most provocative readings of the piece by Karl Heinrich Wörner had it, is in *Momentform*. The *Frau* of *Erwartung* is "the Ariadne of the years around 1910."[39] Thus the monodrama— which Elizabeth Keathley has shown to be the product of intense collaboration between Marie Pappenheim and Schoenberg—is a free historical reprise of Georg Benda's melodrama *Ariadne auf Naxos,* whose 1775 premiere in Gotha was "epoch-making" for the *Sturm und Drang,* as the "Expressionism" of the eighteenth century.[40] Despite the anachronism of the analogy (not to mention the fact that Schoenberg probably did not know Benda's piece), it is intriguing enough to be pressed further, because both works make thematic the struggle of the abandoned individual at the "dawn" and the "dusk" of the self in bourgeois culture.[41] In both *Ariadne* and *Erwartung*, exterior action is stripped away in favor of an inner drama—the search for the lost lover. Although Benda's libretto by Johann Christian Brandes (based on a Cantata by Heinrich Wilhelm von Gerstenberg) begins with Theseus's inner turmoil over leaving his sleeping wife, the dramatic weight lies with Ariadne's subsequent monologue that ends in a quasi suicide.

Stockhausen's notion of *Momentform* helped Wörner capture the "centrifugal" formal tendencies of Benda's melodrama.[42] For Stockhausen, a work in *Momentform* no longer "tells a continuous story, is no longer composed along a 'red thread' that needs to be followed from beginning to end in order to understand the whole," so that "there is no dramatic form with exposition, expansion, development, highpoint and final effect (no closed form)," but "each *moment* exists on its own as a center connected with all other moments."[43] Though neither Benda's *Ariadne* nor *Erwartung* abandon a sense of temporal succession, the relationship between particular and whole is not governed by any rigid formal expectations. Hence Webern noted—in a probably unintended but telling allusion to Goethe's definition of the novella—that the score of *Erwartung* is "an unheard-of event," with which "all traditional architecture has been broken; always something new follows through the most sudden change of expression."[44] If that suddenness signifies modernity, *Momentform* does not mean formlessness, nor even the complete absence of tonal or motivic repetition. Instead, it expresses an absolute dependence on the dramatic present.

As a music of the moment, the formal freedom in Benda's melodrama stems from the accompanied recitative and the free keyboard fantasy, whose historical "moment" is located between the strict molds of the late baroque da capo aria and the standardized cyclical forms of Viennese Classicism.[45] Wörner's analogy between *Ariadne* and *Erwartung* is suggestive because of the comparable moment between tonality and dodecaphony in Schoenberg's music. Two moments in both works— quotations of sorts—are particularly evocative of this parallelism. In *Ariadne* it is the striking *Adagio* with a *concertante* solo violin, which occurs at the point when Ariadne recalls the "golden times" with her mother (and with it the opening key of E♭ major; ex. 5.1).[46] This is not a return of previously heard material, but a quotation of genre: a self-contained musical movement giving room for personal memories, now lost.

We may approach the equivalent moment in *Erwartung* through Wörner's consideration of the monodrama as a labyrinth similar to the melodrama.[47] This implies a critical conflation of the Crete and Naxos components of the Ariadne myth, along with unsettling inversions and

Example 5.1. Georg Benda, *Ariadne auf Naxos,*
Ariadne's memory with genre quotation

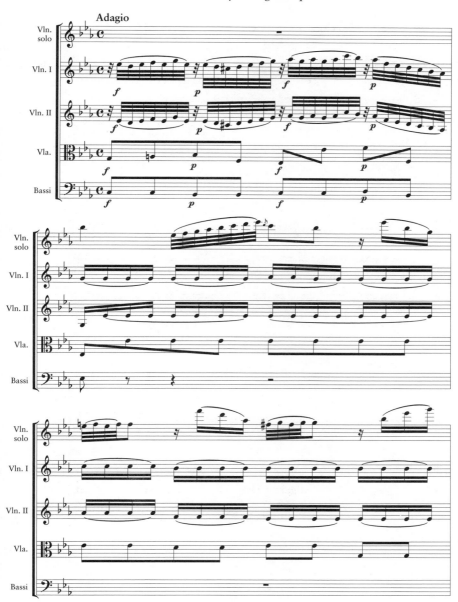

Example 5.1. (cont.)

Einst war ich schuldlos! Ohne
Kummer, ohne Thränen, heiter
und froh blühte mein Frühling,
noch unbekannt der Liebe.

(Once I was innocent! Without
sorrow, without tears, happily
and joyously my spring flowered,
still unknowing love!)

Example 5.1. (cont.)

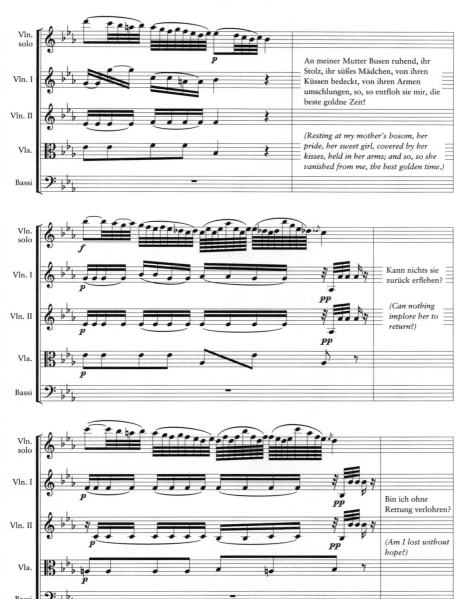

An meiner Mutter Busen ruhend, ihr Stolz, ihr süßes Mädchen, von ihren Küssen bedeckt, von ihren Armen umschlungen, so, so entfloh sie mir, die beste goldne Zeit!

(Resting at my mother's bosom, her pride, her sweet girl, covered by her kisses, held in her arms; and so, so she vanished from me, the best golden time.)

Kann nichts sie zurück erflehen?

(Can nothing implore her to return?)

Bin ich ohne Rettung verlohren?

(Am I lost without hope?)

Example 5.1. (cont.)

doublings. In *Erwartung,* it is Ariadne who finds herself in the maze, abandoned. Recall that the labyrinth had been designed to restrain the Minotaur, whose murder by Theseus is a typical heroic act in ancient mythology: man destroying the destructive drive of nature. Recall that Ariadne's thread helps Theseus escape the labyrinth. Here rationality doubles up in the service of progress and as a symbol of a new bond between humans based on reason (later exposed as an illusion when Theseus leaves Ariadne). Thus when the woman of *Erwartung* is lost in the labyrinth of human emotions, the damaging forces of nature—jealousy and murder—break through from within with an uncontrollable vengeance. And when she, in search of her lover, stumbles over his dead body, Theseus is mapped back, as it were, onto the slain Minotaur, and with it, man onto beast, legitimate desire onto taboo, object onto abject.

The terror of *Erwartung* unfolds in the woman's search for a way to her lover and to his life. Three of the four scenes open with a profound sense of disorientation in that search,[48] where the moonlight only helps the hallucination of a ghastly phantom with "wide yellow eyes, sticking out, as if on stalks . . . staring" like the glaring pupils of the red-rimmed eyes in Schoenberg's *Red Gaze* (scene 3, mm. 106–8). The terrifying look of the "shadow" foreshadows the essential link between the loss of life and the loss of vision: "look at me, beloved one, I am lying beside you. . . . Please look at me. . . . Oh your eyes are so glazed, so frightening" (mm. 231–34); "all light came from your eyes" (m. 267). The spiritual bond between the lovers was made through the eye and sealed with a kiss, in the manner of Goethe's "eternal *Augenblick* of love."[49] Vision lost means paradise lost. No *Augenblick,* no anagnorisis. Crying out at dawn in the final section of the monodrama, the woman relives the endless anxiety of separation, followed by an "endless day of waiting":

Liebster, Liebster, der Morgen kommt . . .
Was soll ich allein hier tun? . . .
In diesem endlosen Leben . . .
In diesem Traum ohne Grenzen und Farben . . .
denn mein Grenze war der Ort, an dem du warst . . .
und alle Farben der Welt brachen aus deinen Augen . . .
Das Licht wird für alle kommen . . .
aber ich allein in meiner Nacht? . . .
Der Morgen trennt uns . . .
immer der Morgen . . .
So schwer küßt du zum Abschied . . .
Wieder ein ewiger Tag des Wartens . . .
oh du erwachst ja nicht mehr . . .
Tausend Menschen ziehn vorüber . . .
ich erkenne dich nicht . . .
Alle leben, ihre Augen flammen . . .
Wo bist du?
Erwartung, mm. 389–416

Darling, darling, the morning comes . . .
What am I to do here alone? . . .
In this unending life. . . .
in this dream without boundaries and colors . . .
because of you my boundary was the place where you were . . .
and all the colors of the world broke out of your eyes . . .
The light will come for all . . .
but for me, alone in my night? . . .
The morning separates us . . .
always the morning . . .
So heavily you kissed me farewell . . .
Again an eternal day of waiting . . .
oh, you will no longer awaken . . .
A thousand people pass by . . .
but I do not recognize you . . .
They are all alive, their eyes shine . . .
Where are you?

In the *Philosopy of New Music,* Adorno was the first to point out what may have been common knowledge in Schoenberg's inner circle: that "*Erwartung* contains, towards the end, at one of the most exposed passages, a musical quotation with the words 'Tausend Menschen ziehn vorüber'. Schoenberg took it from an earlier tonal song, whose theme and counterpoint are woven with greatest artistry into the unrestricted texture of *Erwartung* without destroying the atonality."[50] The song op. 6 no. 6 is a setting of John Henry Mackay's "Am Wegrand" ("At the Wayside"). Its mixture of Art Nouveau and Expressionism is mirrored in Schoenberg's music, "which, in the use of Brahmsian technique of piano composition, disturbs tonality through independent chromatic auxiliary tones and contrapuntal collisions."[51]

Am Wegrand
John Henry Mackay

Tausend Menschen ziehen vorüber,
den ich ersehne, er ist nicht dabei!
Ruhelos fliegen die Blicke hinüber,
fragen den Eilenden, ob er es sei . . .

Aber sie fragen und fragen vergebens.
Keiner gibt ihnen Antwort: "Hier bin ich. Sei still."
Sehnsucht erfüllt die Bezirke des Lebens,
welche Erfüllung nicht erfüllen will,

und so steh ich am Wegrand-Strande,
während die Menge vorüberfließt,
bis erblindet vom Sonnenbrande
mein ermüdetes Aug' sich schliesst.

At the Wayside

A thousand people are passing by,
the one I long for is not among them!
Restlessly my glances fly that way,
they ask the one in haste whether it is he . . .

But they ask and ask in vain.
No one answers: "Here I am. Be still."
Longing fills the realms of life
which fulfillment will not fill.

And so I stand at the wayside-beach,
as the crowd flows by,
until, blinded by the sun's blaze,
my weary eye closes.[52]

The layering of Schoenberg's quotation suggests that the dream transcript records events in the manner of a palimpsest (ex. 5.2). Apart from the change of meter from $\frac{3}{4}$ time to $\frac{4}{4}$ time, the quoted segment of the

Example 5.2. Musico–textural counterpoint in *Erwartung*.
(a) "Am Wegrand" mm. 3–4, (b) "Am Wegrand" mm. 22–24,
and (c) *Erwartung* mm. 411–12

song's bass and melody resound in the bassoons, bass clarinet, and
clarinets. The voice, however, has a different melody whose words belong, as it were, to the bass line, which appeared in the melody at the
beginning of the song. Hence, we may hear behind the triple counterpoint of the music a threefold counterpoint of words, with the sung
words surrounded by those resonating with the instruments.

Both Herbert Buchanan and Alan Lessem took Schoenberg's self-quotation as a "key" to *Erwartung*—surely a large claim for a work in which tonality was at stake.[53] Without referring to Adorno, Buchanan observed (like Adorno) that "tonal material from *Am Wegrand* appears in *Erwartung* without disturbance to the stylistic consistency of the work," but suggested (unlike Adorno) "that *Erwartung* is more tonal than heretofore believed."[54] Lessem even asserted that D was the work's tonic, given that the music of *Erwartung* is "tonal insofar as fixed pitch elements recur throughout as structural and dramatic points of reference." Just as "the operation and effects of unconscious or subconscious motivations which, no matter how irrational or confusing they might appear, are, as Sigmund Freud was demonstrating at the time, strictly governed by discoverable controlling forces," the monodrama, for Lessem, "reveals formal procedures that, in their manner of working, can almost be described as compulsive, even if rarely perceptible as such."[55] *Erwartung* justified Schoenberg's own reservation, made in the *Theory of Harmony,* about his concept of "suspended tonality," namely that it allows for "the assumption of an operative center, even though it is not necessary, to help this center attain externally a power that it has, at most, internally."[56]

Such a search for tonal order betrays an anxiety similar to that of the woman's search for her lover in *Erwartung*. According to Michael Cherlin, "remembering shadowy fragments from a tonal song in another context does not make that later context tonal any more than moments of lucidity make the psychotic sane": if there are "recollections of tonality" in *Erwartung,* they are "evanescent" at best.[57] Schoenberg's self-quotation is a mere "specter of tonality"; it is "uncanny" (*unheimlich*) in the sense Freud, inspired by Schelling, defined the term as something "familiar" (*heimlich*) extended into its opposite: something which "ought to have been kept concealed but which has nevertheless come to light."[58] Tonality thus surfaces like a repressed memory of the hidden desire that the unsung words from *Am Wegrand* had expressed as a "longing" which "fulfillment will not fill." "All light came from your eyes," sings the woman, but in the end "the light will come for all"—that is, not her. This very phrase carries Schoenberg's first allusion to the song, initially in E♭ minor. Only when "all" those "thousand people" pass by, does it return in its original key. Because they "all" live, light shines from their thousand eyes. If we read this Argus-eyedness as traditional tonality, its thousand eyes, once everywhere, now flash only once in a fleeting allusion. Like the thousand people, the tonal moment passes by in an uncanny resemblance to Benjamin's suggestion that the end of aura can be dated to the moment in history when urban crowds grow so dense that people, passers-by, no longer return one another's gaze.

If the vain search for a tonal center is allegorized as a frustrated search for the lover, the trauma of *Erwartung* becomes deeply ambiguous by mapping tonal hierarchy on social patriarchy. If the lover's death is an act of liberation from the father by a "female lunatic," as Susan McClary has argued, Schoenberg's and Pappenheim's efforts at freedom would be slanted: since the woman's path through the forest—the *Weg*—is tinged with the tonality of D minor, it demarcates the line between regress and progress.[59] Liberation occurs at the price of loneliness. Sensitive to this tension, Adorno located the desparate search for security in the reference which represents authority: "the *angst* of the lonely one, who is quoting, seeks a foothold in what is valid."[60] This leads to the paradox that he worked out with Horheimer in the *Dialectics of Enlightment*. On the one hand, the anxiety of the lonely person has "emancipated itself from the bourgeois taboos"; on the other, "[t]he position of the absolute monad in art is both: resistance against the bad subsumption into society, and the readiness for a society that is worse."[61] Hence the meaning of Expressionism is "that the absolute subject is not absolute" so that "in its loneliness appears society"; hence every expressionist challenge to traditional categories "brings new demands of organization—demands of a coherence in terms of being-thus-and-not-being-otherwise"; hence "the absolute liberation of the particular from the universal renders it universal" once more.[62] That had been Schlegel's logic of the fragment: the ab-solute becomes absolute again. The new absoluteness, as detachedness, cannot absolve the emancipated subject from becoming subject to the totalizing regime of bourgeois barbarity. In that sense, perhaps, the dawn of *Erwartung* would also be the dusk of modernity.

What the Soul Sees

In December 1912, Schoenberg received a letter from Richard Dehmel thanking the composer for the music of *Verklärte Nacht* (which was based on a poem by Dehmel). In his answer, Schoenberg took the opportunity to ask the poet for a libretto for "a work that would fill a whole evening":

> I have long wanted to write an oratorio on the following subject: modern man, having passed through materialism, socialism and anarchism, having been an atheist, but still retaining the vestiges of his ancient faith (in the form of superstition), wrestles with God (see also Strindberg's *Jacob Wrestles*). He finally manages to find God and become religious. He learns to pray.[63]

Citing the letter in his essay, *Vers une musique informelle,* Adorno chided the composer's naivete in combining the "need to return to theological authority" with "the renunciation of political radicalism":

> The element of violence and rupture in the transition from the experiences of free atonality to the systematization of twelve-note technique, and the conception of religiosity as return, together with the finger-wagging admonition about learning to pray, all come together, not just historically, but also in terms of musical substance. In both dimensions order is derived from the need for order and not from the truth of the matter.[64]

For Adorno the changes of style, of expression, and of meaning appeared nowhere more glaring than in the gap between *Erwartung* and *Die Jakobsleiter*; between the frustrated search for human love and the successful prayer for divine love; between the lonely subject among the thousand people passing by and the thousand lives that unite in a single soul. Expressionism had been the golden moment of modern music. Its seal of authenticity was a paradox, manifest both on the level of content and on the level of compositional technique: by preserving hope through the negation of form and by articulating entrapment through free atonality. Hence his double verdict of *Die Jakobsleiter*: both as a progressive relapse into a rational order and as a false fusion of art and religion. This put the work in line with Wagner's *Die Meistersinger,* Mahler's *Symphonie der Tausend*, and Pfitzner's *Palestrina*—all instances of the bourgeois *opus magnum* which "takes refuge in the power and glory of what it dreads" and whose "official posture is fear deformed as affirmation."[65]

Thus Adorno perceived the imminent change of Schoenberg's compositional technique in *Die Jakobsleiter* as a return to the mechanics of oppression, sanctioned by a resurgent aesthetics of the whole that subjugates the particular. Schoenberg became suspect of falling back onto an aesthetics of identity. If "the smallest detail can become the whole, because it is already the whole," that could lead to the "negation of the details by the whole."[66] In *Die Jakobsleiter,* that smallest part consisted of a hexachord, whose employment became Schoenberg's first significant effort to organize pitch material in the new, systematic way that eventually led to dodecaphony. Or at least this was Schoenberg's own view, when he surveyed his artistic "evolution" at the age of 75, stating almost in a lapidary manner: "Time for a change had arrived. In 1915 I had sketched a symphony, the theme of the Scherzo of which accidentally consisted of twelve tones. Only two years later a further step in this direction was taken. I had planned to build all the main themes of my unfinished oratorio, *Die Jakobsleiter,* out of the six tones of this row."[67] Hence Jean Christensen felt justified to speak of Schoenberg's technique as "composing with tones" (rather than motives) and to use the terms "hexachord" and "6-tone row" interchangeably.[68] The implication: this was the beginning of serialism.

That which irritated the late Adorno in Schoenberg's turn to religion had already surfaced in his critique of Mahler's Eighth: "[t]hat the Spirit should come is a plea that the composition should be inspired"; and that Mahler "repudiated his own idea of the radical secularization of metaphysical words, uttering them himself."[69] As prayer proper, *Die Jakobsleiter* failed on Adorno's ideal of music as "demythologized prayer."[70] But Schoenberg could not have been clearer about his intentions: *Lernt beten* was the exhortation of a convert, not of an apostate. The ending of *Die Jakobsleiter* in prayer replays that of Honoré de Balzac's *Séraphita* which had become Schoenberg's main source of inspiration, itself inspired by Strindberg, who had experienced a turning point in his artistic and personal crisis during the 1890s precisely when encountering Balzac's novel. (This is vividly described in Strindberg's autobiographical *Jacob Wrestles*.) Based on the writings of the eighteenth-century Swedish scientist, philosopher, and mystic Emanuel Swedenborg, Balzac's story tells of the conversion of the couple, Wilfrid and Minna, by the androgynous figure of the angelic Séraphita/Seraphitus, which, in turn, echoes Swedenborg's own conversion through his visionary encounter with angels. Schoenberg was to have is own vision.

"It seems," the composer pencilled on a fly leaf attached to the final page of the revised libretto from 1917, "that the theosophes will resent this ending. But they overlook that the work was written *only* because of this ending. *From this* I began, only *this* was what I wanted to show: this prayer, beginning in greatest despair, quieting down through itself, elevating itself (!!) and the creation of the presentiment of a higher honoring. . . . I took my point of departure from God! They appear not to do this; but what they *believe*, I *don't* know; only what *I* believe."[71] That was Schoenberg's belief: "Learn to pray: Knock, and the door will be opened." This line ushers in the oratorio's finale, where as the composer's directions have it, "out of the depth, the prayers of the creatures become audible," sung by a "Chorus from the Depth" with "many individual voices and groups in vigorous motion and constant alternation," between despair and hope eventually coalescing in a version of the *De profundis* (ex. 5.3).[72] With the vocal groups distributed throughout in the concert hall "music was to stream into the room from all sides" and the audience, enveloped by sound, was to experience the omnipresence and omnipotence of divine unity.[73]

Adorno's critique aimed at such an all-encompassing ending because it created the illusion that a sublime subject alone can guarantee the sublimity of content. The text's "vulgarization of the Hegelian aesthetic of content" found its musical correlate in the Hegelian aesthetic of Argus-eyedness.[74] At the same time, Adorno argued that the unfinished state of *Die Jakobsleiter*, like the symphony out of which it grew, gave

Example 5.3. Die Jakobsleiter, conclusion of libretto
(Translation adapted from Jean Christensen,
"Arnold Schoenberg's Oratorio *Die Jakobsleiter* 1: 31–32 and 49–50.)

Chorus from the depths:
Lord God in heaven, free me from the unberable pressure - - - -
Lord, take from me the heavy burden - - - -
No more will I bear, O Lord, the terrible pain - - - - . . .
I can live only in beauty - - - -
My dream be fullled at least - - - -
I shall be honored as a high one - - - - . . .

Main Chorus:
Many thousand voices, thousand-fold different,
in wish and lament, in worry and hope,
in joy and suffering, in rage and fear,
strive towards God, press toward him,
who hears them all, receives them by one
as they had felt, thought and spoken.
And all the different voices,
different in motive and expression,
produce together the one sound.

Main Chorus and Chorus from the depths (together):
Lord God in heaven
Hear our plea,
Forgive our sins,
Have mercy on us
Grant our requests,
Fulfill our wishes
Yield to our laments
Give us eternal love and happiness.

Chorus from high alone:
A single great wave carries the desires to the Eternal One
who is merciful to deeply felt prayers.
Concession and denial are already present in the person and his prayer:
before him all desires are equal; he listens to everyone.
Their connection with him awakens by magnetism the streams of the spirit
    through induction
the spirit grows stronger, the more often they stream,
the stream grows with every prayer:
A moment of heavenly glory grants God's mercy to the prayer.

Chorus from the depth:	*Main Chorus:*	*Chorus from the height:*
Lord God in heaven	Lord God in heaven	Lord God in heaven
Hear our plea	Hear their plea	Hears your plea
Forgive our sins,	Forgive their sins	Understands your sins
Have mercy on us	Have mercy on them	Has mercy on you

Example 5.3. (cont.)

Grant our requests,	Grant their requests	Hears your requests
Fulfill our wishes	Fulfill their wishes	Notes your wishes
Yield to our laments	Yield to their laments	Gives room to your laments
Give us eternal love	Give them eternal love	Gives you eternal love
and happiness.	and happiness.	and happiness.

Amen.

testimony to the "social structure" and "the state of the aesthetic con-
stituents of form" that "prohibit[ed] the magnum opus."[75] Ultimately,
this prohibition is that of the graven image, the *Bilderverbot*. It creates
the impasse which Adorno called, in his late essay on Schoenberg's
unfinished opera *Moses and Aron*, "the impossibility of the sacred work
of art." If sacred music "cannot simply be willed,"[76] the illusion that it
can is the one "from which the bourgeois spirit has never been able to
free itself: that of the unhistorical eternity of art."[77] Karl Kraus captured
that unholy alliance between religious art and art religion in the poem
"Wiese im Park" (the first of Webern's op. 13). With inimitable irony its
first line, "How I become timeless," invokes the aspirations of a bygone
age, which is brutally canceled through Kraus's mixture of charm and
nonchalance: "A dead Sunday opens its eyes." Because the malaise of
the fin-de-siècle had already been exposed and exploded by Expressionism, Adorno argued that Schoenberg's failing in *Moses and Aron* (and
by implication in *Die Jakobsleiter*) was "to negate the message of negation which the historical conjunction proclaimed to him."[78] The problem of the opera (and hence the oratorio) was that it took "theological
truth" for the musical "purity of construction free of any intention"
which created "the expressionless." If the libretto of the opera creates
the theological scandal of speaking of the "One God as the idea
[*Gedanke*], then this is a scandal that is duplicated in the texture of the
music, though rendered almost unrecognizable by the power of the art.
The absolute which this music sets out to make real, without any sleight
of hand, it achieves as its own idea of itself: it is itself an image of
something without images—the very last thing the story wanted."[79]

Or rather, the last thing Adorno wanted. He expected Schoenberg to
suspend the "unified language and construction" that Wagner had per-
fected.[80] But Adorno could not find the "decisive caesura" that could
have rescued the opera in the pronounced difference between Moses's
Sprechstimme and Aron's *melos*, demanding instead that "rupture was
to become music."[81] Schoenberg, as Gary Tomlinson incisively put it,
not only "shares Moses' dilemma of representing the unrepresentable,"
but "[i]n the process of representing metaphysics through an integrated
musical totality" the composer also "loses *the possibility of representing*

the impossibility of representing metaphysics."[82] Tomlinson, too, protests against the routine of reading the ending of the operatic fragment as Schoenberg's representation of that very impossibility, when Moses utters the words "O Word, you Word that I lack". For Philippe Lacoue-Labarthe argued that Adorno should have located the caesura here—"had he remembered only that Kant gives the very prohibition of representation as the privileged example of the sublime"; and had he recalled only that Hegel considered the (Jewish) sublime as an affirmation of "the incommensurability of the finite and the infinite."[83] The "ultimate paradox" of the opera is that "the naked word—the language of signification itself—comes to tell of the impossible beyond of signification." Lacoue-Labarthe called this the "metasublime." It "tells the truth of the sublime in a sublime manner: that there is no possible presentation of the metaphysical or of the absolute."[84] Because Adorno insisted that the caesura had "to become music," he failed to register the breakdown of music itself at the moment when Moses laments his loss of the *logos* as the work's most sublime rupture.

It will be worth lingering over the notion of rupture and caesura, because Adorno had claimed that the opera "could not be completed," yet located its "success" in the "unity" that "truly does justice to the idea which forms the subject of the text."[85] Paradoxically, Adorno found the attempt to name God to be as much a betrayal as to keep silent about Him. But this "impossibility which appears intrinsic to the work" can only be "an impossibility which was not intended."[86] That struggle comes through in Adorno's twofold application of Benjamin's "expressionless": not only as particular moment, but also as structural whole, that is, as "purity of construction free of any intention." Although Adorno held that Schoenberg's *opera magna* could not be sacred works, that is precisely what they were. Hence Lacoue-Labarthe's idea of "the caesura of religion" assumes, unintentionally, a double meaning in both works: it is not only religion ruptured by reality, but also religion rupturing reality. In the former, the absolute is fragmented; in the latter, the fragment becomes absolute again.

Like the opera, the oratorio does both. Schoenberg, to recall, conceived *Die Jakobsleiter* in two parts, pertaining to life before death and life thereafter. Between them stands, both as a link and transition, what he called a Great Symphonic Interlude (*Großes symphonisches Zwischenspiel*). It breaks off after almost one hundred measures, despite Schoenberg's repeated attempts to complete it until the very end of his life. The finished libretto and the sketches suggest that he conceived the oratorio's grand cycle of life, death, and rebirth not as a circle, but as an ascending spiral: the labor of all at the beginning progressing to the lament of all at the end, where material from the Great Symphonic

Interlude was to be used, both in the Main Chorus ("Many Thousand Voices") and for the concluding "Amen."[87] The cyclic conception of the work thus breathes a giant formal and narrative rhythm, contracting and expanding between the fate of all at the beginning and end, and the fate of particular groups and individuals in the middle. *Die Jakobsleiter* thereby moves through what Schoenberg, inspired by *Séraphita,* imagined as a process of increasing perfection from a toiling humanity on the *Unterstufe* to a Soul ascending to the sounds of an angelic choir at the *Oberstufe*—all guided by the Archangel Gabriel (a variant of Seraphitus).[88]

In the more complex second part of the oratorio, the Souls ("first individually, later in groups") initially converse with their Demons, Genii, Stars, Gods, and Angels before leaving them behind to undergo transformation. Four individual "Voices" (sung by The Dying One, The Struggling One, The Called One, and The Protestor from the first part) give way to groups of souls in highly diversified categories: Submerged Souls (Rationalists, Lazy Ones, Sceptics, Cynics, Cunning Ones, Journalists, Impure Ones), Vacillating Souls (Helpless Ones, Needy Ones, Unhappy Ones, Unlucky Ones, Deceived Ones), Imperfect Souls (Enslaved Ones, Good-Natured Ones, Satisfied Ones, Indecisive Ones), Limited Souls (Arrogant Ones, Weaklings, Misguided Ones, Conventional Ones, Compromisers, Pliant Ones), Half-Knowers (Scientists, Successful Ones, Disbelievers, Fortunate Lovers, Upstarts, Intolerant Ones, Climbers), and, finally, Lost Souls (Inconsiderate Ones, Don Juan, Disloyal Ones, Hypocrites, Criminals). This is nothing less than a summation of humanity, summoned by Gabriel's extended monologue (itself an offshoot of Séraphita's great speech at the end of Balzac's novel) to learn to pray.

The most extraordinary moment of *Die Jakobsleiter,* however, is not the monumental ending (as Schoenberg imagined it), but the very moment of death and transfiguration in the middle of the work. Here the thousand voices that were, and the thousand voices that will be, are paired down, at the end of the first part, to the single voice of the Dying One: "Lord! throughout my whole life I waited for this *Augenblick*"—a word doubly underlined in Schoenberg's draft.[89] Already in his early synopsis of the piece, the composer had made this association: "The Dying One (a thousand lives)."[90] Death is the moment of the whole that allows the Dying One to embrace not only all former lives (as in the doctrine of reincarnation), but invoke a synthesis of humanity. Having been driven "through thousands of years," lived "a thousand lives," and died "a thousand deaths," *Der Sterbende* exclaims:

> Tausend Leben!
> Wer von ihnen weiß und sie überblickt,
> dem sind sie nichts Fürchterliches mehr.

Fürchterlich ist ein Leben; ein Leid!
Ein Schmerz, so groß, daß man nur ihn fühlt.
Wer, wie jetzt ich, tausend Schmerzen fühlt,
ist fast schon schmerzfrei.
Sie heben ihn, er wird leicht
und weiß, daß ihn seine verstorbenen Leben tragen.
Und er fliegt—
Ich fliege—
Der seligste Traum erfüllt sich:
fliegen!
Weiter! Weiter!
Zum Ziel—
Oh—
Die Jakobsleiter, mm. 540–63

A thousand lives!
For me who knows of them and looks over them,
they are no longer fearful.
It is only *one* life that is frightening; *one* suffering!
One pain so great that you feel only *it.*
Who feels, as I do now, thousand pains
is almost free from pain.
They raise him up, he becomes light,
and knows that he is borne by his departed lives.
And he flies—
to fly—
The most blissful dream is fulfilled: to fly!
Onward!—Onward!—
To the goal—
Oh—

The moment of death comes with a gasping glissando on an "Oh" that descends two octaves from $f\sharp^2$ to $f\sharp$: *die Seele aushauchen* ("to expire") must have been the idiom that Schoenberg had in mind. It befits the gesture of stripping the words from the melody, as bodily breath is transformed into spiritual *pneuma.* In two measures (originally planned as an even longer stretch to be played "most delicately in suspended motion"[91]), the soul is literally lifted from the body by a texture itself lifted from the corresponding moment in the last movement of the second string quartet: "Ich fühle luft von einem anderen planeten."

The textural allusion plays on the inner affinity to op. 10, where, in Adorno's words, "the individual, bereft of hope, breaks down and, without any transition, the imago of his ecstasy answers him."[92] The last line of the quartet, "ich bin ein dröhen nur der heiligen stimme," is the paradigmatic trope of transcendence in Schoenberg's oeuvre, marked by static iridescent textures, or *Klangflächen,* as well as a change from declamatory recitation to what Martina Sichardt has called "spheric singing."[93] We also find it in the middle of the central, and only, vocal movement of the *Serenade* op. 24, right at the caesura between the quatrains and tercets of the Petrarcan sonnet, where the "soul . . . leaves the body, freed from its cruel prison" and "flies" to the one who not only "destroys" with "her glances and words," but also causes "greater pain" by denying "the smallest glance from those sweet eyes." Or in the middle of *Herzgewächse* op. 20, where the lily "alone . . . rears up, its rise imperceptible over the grieving foliage" and sends "to the blue crystal"—heaven—"its mystical prayer." In *Die Jakobsleiter,* death is process suspended: "your ego is dissolved" between the end of physical particularity and the mystical state of wholeness; between the sung words of the dying one and the wordless song of the soul. And yet the oratorio's very *Augenblick* is not the change from song to vocalise. Its caesura is not the moment of death, but the moment of transfiguration: when the wordless voice becomes a voiceless violin—offstage.

Between the downward glissando of the voice on "Oh" and the upward glissando of the violin to e^3, the spirit *becomes* this melody. It takes flight from the dying body into the immortal soul; or from corporeal matter to immaterial *Geist.* Gabriel describes this at the beginning of his final monologue: "The spirit which is pressed between two infinities—space and time are foreign to its essence although generated by it—flees into the immortal soul."[94] And the soul, "dividing itself into a thousand particles, each of which, as a slave of the free will, is subjected to delusion, and becomes free only as matter, renewing itself, falls apart."[95] Hence, Gabriel must exhort the different groups of souls, whose thousand-fold variety is a mark of their materiality, to pray that God release them from it:

> Herr lass uns eingehn, aufgehn im Ganzen!
> Erlöse uns von unsrer Einzelheit!
> Nimm uns ab die Gefühle, die uns auf uns verweisen!
> Lass uns wieder ein Ganzes werden, mit jenem Ganzen,
>   dessen Teile wir jetzt sind!
> Herr, nimm uns gnädig zu dir.

> Lord, let us cease to exist, become part of the whole!
> Release us from our individuality!
> Take away the feelings that make us self-centered!
> Let us again become a whole, with that whole whose parts we
>   now are!
> Lord, receive us mercifully.[96]

Material is finite and particular; spirit is infinite and whole. No wonder
that Balzac, in the *Avant-Propos* (1842) to the *Comédie humaine,* had
defended himself against charges of belonging to the "schools of materialism and sensualism" by pointing to *Séraphita.*[97] No wonder that
Schoenberg, writing to Kandinsky in the summer of 1912, praised
Séraphita as "the most glorious work in existence" explaining in the
same letter that "[a]n inner vision is a whole which has component
parts," and whose "binding agent" is "the soul."[98] No wonder that the
composer reported still a decade later to the painter that he had been
working simultaneously on *Die Jakobsleiter* and the *Lehre vom
musikalischen Zusammenhang.*[99] For what Schoenberg had found in
Séraphita was the poetic parallel to Kandinsky's 1911 treatise *On the
Spiritual in Art.* "When we remember," Kandinsky had written, "that
spiritual experience is quickening, . . . that dissolution of matter is
imminent, we have reason to hope that the hour of pure composition is
not far away."[100] And more evocatively: "[t]he nightmare of materialism, which turned life into an evil, senseless game, is not yet passed; it
still darkens the awakening soul. Only a feeble light glimmers, a tiny
point in an immense circle of darkness."[101] That glimmer will be the
program for the ending of Adrian Leverkühn's *Lamentations of Doctor
Faustus*—a crack of white in total blackness; the flicker of a star.

Given Schoenberg's rediscovery of religion, hardly any commentary
on *Die Jakobsleiter* has failed to point out that the composer's new
conception of musical space as relationships between sets of pitches is
expressed, like an aesthetic manifesto, in Gabriel's opening speech:
"whether to the right or to the left, forward or backward, uphill or
downhill—one must go on, without asking what lies in front or behind.
It must be hidden; you ought to forget, you must forget, so that you can
fulfill your task" (mm. 11–19).[102] Schoenberg formulated its theoretical
correlate in his "Composition with Twelve Tones (1)," which we must
now cite in full: *the unity of musical space demands an absolute and
unitary perception.* In this space, as in Swedenborg's heaven (described
in Balzac's *Séraphita*) there is no absolute down, no right or left, forward or backward. Every musical configuration, every movement of
tones has to be comprehended primarily as a mutual relation of sounds,
of oscillatory vibrations, appearing at different places and times. To the
imaginative and creative faculty, relations in the material sphere are as
independent from directions or planes as material objects are, in their
sphere, to our perceptive faculties."[103]

The "space of relationships" that Robert Morgan has called "logical"
space in music, was for Schoenberg also a *spiritual* space.[104] He abandoned the tonal center as the Archimedean point of a single perspective,
only to replace it with a concept of a total vision that can comprehend

the new musical space simultaneously from *any* perspective. Hence the seeming contradiction between the demand for an "absolute" perception and the claim that there is no absolute down, no right or left, no forward or backward. When "[y]ou acquire alacrity of spirit," says Séraphita in Balzac's novel, "in one instant you can be present in every region; you are borne, like the Word itself, from one end of the world to the other."[105] In Schoenberg's renewed aesthetics of aural Argus-eyedness, the absolute relativization of time and space goes hand in hand with absolute perception.

Thus we may understand how Schoenberg conceived the melody of the soul as absolute in the two ways mentioned above: as the absolute that is fragmented, and as a fragment that becomes absolute again. In the textless vocalise ab-solute music becomes absolute music; and in the fragment of the hexachord it becomes the new whole accessible to "absolute" perception. In that sense, the caesura of *Die Jakobsleiter* comes closest to the final chapter of Balzac's novel, entitled "The Assumption," which dovetails into the ending of Séraphita's final speech, or rather his songs (*chant*s), which were:

> . . . not uttered in words, nor expressed by a glance, nor by a gesture, nor by any of the signs that serve humans beings as a means of communicating their thoughts, but as the soul speaks to itself [*mais comme l'âme parle à elle-même*]; for, at the moment when Séraphita was revealed in her true nature, her ideas were no longer enslaved to human language [*ses idées n'étaient plus esclaves des mots humains*]. The vehemence of her last prayer had broken the bonds. Like a white dove, the soul hovered for a moment above this body, whose exhausted matter was about to dissever.[106]

Among the few phrases that Schoenberg translated himself in his copy of the French edition of Balzac's novel, two (inserted into the quote in square brackets above) belong to this passage: "sondern so, wie die Seele mit sich selbst spricht"; and "war ihr Denken nicht mehr ans Menschenwort gebunden." They had been part, perhaps even the very core, of the earliest conception of *Die Jakobsleiter,* dated 27 December 1912, then still called *Séraphita.* Even if *Der Sterbende,* sung by a woman who continues as *Die Seele,* is no longer a direct representation of Balzac's androgynous Séraphita-Seraphitus, Schoenberg conceived of death and transfiguration in the manner of the angel's assumption: as spirit separating from matter, and as pure music separating from song.[107] It is tempting to hear that phrase—"the soul hovered for a moment above this body"—to be composed out in the violin solo, because it becomes the oratorio's *Augenblick,* the suspension of its process, the ultimate turning point in its formal rhythm. "Speaking to itself," the music of the soul corresponds to what Bloch described in his medita-tions "On the Thing-In-Itself in Music," as "the stage of pure self-hearing."[108] The music of angels is this autonomous and absolute. Or, as Adorno would say, "only angels can make music freely."[109]

Given Adorno's criticism that Schoenberg did not articulate the cae-sura *musically* in *Moses and Aron*, the *Augenblick* in *Die Jakobsleiter* would seem to do just this, albeit affirmatively. We may hear the solo violin mediate the very impasse between what Adorno considered the betrayal behind the desire to name the absolute and the sin to keep silent about it. It is the same impasse between the absolute and the programmatic that Schiller expressed so well in a distich, entitled *Sprache*, which Friedrich Kittler took to illustrate the romantic aporia of a lan-guage that stands in the way of communication:

> Warum kann der lebendige Geist dem Geist nicht erscheinen?
> *Spricht* die Seele, so spricht, ach! schon die *Seele* nicht mehr.
>
> Why can the living spirit not appear to the Spirit?
> When the soul *speaks*, then, alas, does the *soul* speak no longer.[110]

Where Schiller's "Ach" articulates the rift between the name and nam-ing, Schoenberg makes the soul *speak* and the *soul* speak. The paradox of its passage to heaven turns on Benjamin's conjunction of the messi-anic and the materialist; or Adorno's concurrence of the mimetic and the rational; or Bloch's "coincidence of expressive truth and constructional truth."[111] Implied is a twofold sense of the expressionless. On the one hand, what is neither expressed by a word, nor a glance, nor a gesture, perfectly exemplifies the expressionless that "shatters false totality." On the other hand, in making use of the hexachord, the passage also as-pires, however tentatively, towards a new totality: the expressionless as the "purity of construction free of any intention." The caesura of *Die Jakobsleiter* gestures at both: the expressionless as the moment of the particular and the moment of the whole.

A provocative way to illustrate this paradox would be to hear the hexachord of the solo violin melody, as Yonathan Malin has suggested, as an allusion to the opening of Wagner's *Tristan* (ex. 5.4).[112] Not only is the melodic contour (not pitch content) the same, except for the missing pickup; but the meter is also analogous ($\frac{6}{8}$ versus $\frac{6}{4}$). And although the register is higher and the rhythm is not exact (because the last two notes of Wagner's motif are squeezed into the rest of the measure), Schoenberg positioned the e^2, the very note whose equivalent Wagner harmonized with the famous Tristan chord, at the beginning of a bar. But after laboring considerably over this passage, Schoenberg abandoned any accompaniment and left the melody alone. It is played as the first of two

Example 5.4. Die Jakobsleiter mm. 602–607
with opening motif from *Tristan*

Fernmusiken, which he positioned as offstage ensembles, suggesting the transformation of the single soul (and later of the many souls) into spirit. The ensembles were to be arranged separately behind the stage, their sound projected through tubes into the hall, either from above, designated as H1 and H2 (H for *Höhe*), or from afar, designated as F1 and F2 (F for *Ferne*). If Schoenberg planned to bring back material from the Great Symphonic Interlude in the concluding choruses, the ethereal chorus of violins in *Fernmusik* H1 seems to anticipate such a chorus, especially the five notes of the choral texture in measures 634–36, whose cantus firmus works with the words "Herr Gott im Himmel" that Schoenberg sketched for the final prayer.[113] As the very first music from above, the violin solo creates the striking effect of an ethereal immateriality, not least because Schoenberg asks it to be played "very calmly and broadly, but without any prolongations and without any important crescendos."

The melody, then, initiates what Schoenberg described as "'generally-heavenly' motives" in the first part of the Interlude, whose occasional dotted barlines were meant to weaken any strong accents of a measure, "so that the character of 'hovering' is brought out."[114] It pervades the remainder of the interlude: as a counterpoint in the bassoon (mm. 622ff.);[115] in the *Fernmusik* H1 (mm. 648–50); as *Nebenstimme* in the piccolo (m. 653); in a four-part imitation in the trumpets and horn of *Fernmusik* F1 (m. 661); and in augmentation in *Fernmusik* F2 against its inversion in the violins in *Fernmusik* F1 (m. 668)—all products of Schoenberg's canonic experiments with the melody in the sketches. If the melody of the soul is not only the moment of the particular, but also the moment of the whole, then Schoenberg would try to make it truly visible from all sides—like the *Sehnsuchtsmotiv* that is the true "soul" of

Tristan, from the yearning start of the prelude to its resolution in the *Liebestod.* As the smallest part become whole, Wagner's motif unifies harmonic and dramatic structure, love and death, longing and fulfillment at the very *Augenblick* when Tristan and Isolde, having drunk the love potion, "look at each other with utmost emotion, but without changing their position, while their death-defiant expression changes to glowing love." If Wagner's *Tristan* is the paradigmatic inner drama, then its motivic "outer eye," as Schoenberg could have read it in the introductory essay to his copy of Swedenborg's theological writings, "is the mirror of the soul."[116]

Still, Schoenberg's allusion to Wagner, however pertinent to the themes of death and transfiguration as well as love and redemption in the oratorio, does not have to be an overt or conscious gesture in the manner of op. 11.[117] Indeed, it could be entirely unintended. But the composer certainly would have agreed, even if only in hindsight, that the similarity between the *Sehnsuchtsmotif* and the violin solo reveals itself to the persistent eye in the way he detected motivic connections in *Die Verklärte Nacht* years after the work was composed. Precisely by being not intended, the allusion collapses the "constructional truth" of the hexachord with the "expressive truth" of the Tristanesque gesture. Poised between the no-longer of chromatic harmony, and the not-yet of dodecaphony, the solo of the soul becomes emblematic of Schoenberg's historical position between the two different compositional paradigms, both of which he sought to embrace. As an unintended instance of programming the absolute, it is the absolute melody which, to use Nietzsche's words, "chooses" the program as a metaphorical expression of itself.[118]

It is here that Adorno clashed and concurred with Schoenberg. "The beginning of music, in the same manner as its end," Adorno postulated in the *Philosophy of New Music,* "extends beyond the realm of intentions—the realm of meaning and subjectivity."[119] That is why it is "closely related to the origin of tears." That is why the line from Goethe's *Faust,* "Tears dim my eyes: earth's child I am again," "defines the position of music" in the way "earth claims Eurydice again."[120] That is why the "gesture of return—not the sensation of expectancy—characterizes the expression of all music, even if it finds itself in a world worthy of death."[121] That is why "the whole system of bourgeois music" had to be seen "only as something vanishing from sight. As Eurydice was seen. *Everything* must be understood from that viewpoint."[122] Hence Monteverdi's Orpheus sings "O sweetest eyes, I see you now, I see . . . but what eclipse obscures your light?"; and the elipsis in his speech that articulates the eclipse of sight is musically marked, like Kundry's death, by the hexatonic pole which Richard Cohn has read as a figure of the death of tonality.[123] But Schoenberg would not hear everything from that viewpoint. Hence Gabriel, promising a new life (and by implication a new understanding of tonality), says to The Soul: "Do you approach the light again? To heal the wings that the darkness has burned?" When the hexachord of the violin solo binds the two halves of *Die Jakobsleiter* together, the ultimate paradox of this *Augenblick* is that the expressionless partakes of the very paradigm of expression precisely when the oratorio alludes to the two archetypal glances of all opera—the one that separated Orpheus and Euridice, and the one that united Tristan and Isolde.

If, in Adorno's words, the "harsh expressionist visions of loneliness," which Schoenberg painted around 1910 "also resemble *phantoms* of transcendence," then *Erwartung*'s image of such a *phantom* reverts back to a *fantasy* of transcendence in *Die Jakobsleiter*.[124] If the thousand people pass by irretrievably at the end of the monodrama while the soul's thousand lives soar to heaven in the oratorio, then Schoenberg would indeed negate the negation. Then these two visions would describe the dialectical turn in Schoenberg's oeuvre from the aesthetics of Argus-eyedness lost, to the aesthetics of Argus-eyedness recaptured. And yet: while the woman in *Erwartung* had been blind and the soul in *Die Jakobsleiter* had regained its sight, Adorno claimed that the former had seen what the latter could not. "The metaphysics of art," he wrote in the *Aesthetic Theory*, "requires its complete separation from the religion in which art originated. Artworks are not the absolute, nor is the absolute immediately present in them. For their methexis in the absolute they are punished with blindness that in the same instant obscures their language, which is a language of truth: Artworks have the absolute and they do not have it."[125] Having discovered his religious roots and that of his art, however, Schoenberg had come to cherish such blindness from a different perspective, confessing in 1922 that one "gains a feeling of truest duty when one does not do, despite wishing otherwise, what one considered holy in the past and betray what the future appeared to promise; and begins secretly to delight in one's blindness with seeing eyes."[126] That was Schoenberg's new-old gaze. What the soul sees at the beginning of the Interlude of *Die Jakobsleiter*, or what we see that soul see, would be such a moment of visionary blindness.

Chapter 6

ECHO'S EYES

> "I find," he said, "that it is not to be."
>
> "What, Adrian, is not to be?"
>
> "The good and noble," he answered me; "what we call the human, although it is good and noble. What human beings have fought for and stormed citadels, what the ecstatics exultantly announced—that is not to be. It will be taken back. I will take it back."
>
> "I don't quite understand, dear man. What will you take back?"
>
> "The Ninth Symphony," he replied. And then no more came, though I waited for it.
>
> Dazed and grievously afflicted I went up into the fatal room. The atmosphere of the sick-chamber reigned there, clean and bare, heavy with the odours of drugs, though the windows were wide open. But the blinds were almost shut, only a crack showed. Several people were standing round Nepomuk's bed. I put out my hand to them, my eyes already on the dying child. He lay on his side, his legs drawn up, elbows and knees together. The cheeks were very flushed; he drew a breath, then one waited long for the next. His eyes were not quite closed, but between the lashes no iris showed, only blackness, for the pupils had grown unevenly larger; they had almost swallowed up the colour. Yet it was still good when one saw the mirroring black. For sometimes it was white in the crack, and then the little arms pressed closer to the sides, the grinding spasm, cruel to see but perhaps no longer felt, twisted the little limbs.[1]

That the German composer Adrian Leverkühn intended to "take back" Beethoven's Ninth has been recounted many times. But the details of his motivation—the suffering and death of his nephew, Nepomuk Schneidewein, nicknamed Echo—has not. Not the "fresh vomiting, skull-splitting headache, and convulsions that shook his small frame"; not the "heartrending moans and yelling screams" of the "typical 'hydrocephalic shriek'"; not the "twenty-two hours of crying, writhing torture, of a child, of this child, who folded his twitching little hands and stammered: 'Echo will be good, Echo will be good'!"; not, finally, the "most dreadful" symptom of all: the squinting of the heaven's-blue

224

eyes, caused by the paralysis of the eye-muscles accompanying the rigidity of the neck."[2]

Nothing shatters human hope more than the death of a child. Echo's death made people cry.[3] The figure of Echo, Mann maintained, was "without doubt the best and the most poetic in the book."[4] "Working on Echo's fatal disease, with sorrow," he quoted his own diary in his account of the novel's genesis, reiterating: "With sorrow!" And when asked by his translator, Helen Tracy Lowe-Porter, "How could you do it?," he reported to have answered "that she could read my own feelings in Adrian's behavior, in his use of the phrase 'it is not to be,' in his break with hope and his saying, 'It will be taken back.'"[5]

Linking the loss of hope with the stylistic breakthrough in Leverkühn's last work had been Mann's idea from the beginning. He explained it later as a result of his musical mode of literary composition:

> The artist always carries a work of art as a whole within himself. Although aesthetics may insist that literary and musical works, in contradistinction to the plastic arts, are dependent upon time and succession of events, it is nevertheless true that even such works strive at every moment [*Augenblick*] to be present as a whole. Middle and end are alive in the beginning, the past suffuses the present, and even the greatest concentration upon the moment does not obviate concern for the future. Thus, while the story of the child seemed to absorb me completely, I was already looking toward what was to follow immediately, the depiction of Leverkühn's second major work, *The Lamentation of Dr. Faustus*. An entry at the time I was still busy with the first Echo chapter reads: "Drawing on the chapbook for ideas for the Faust oratorio. The whole thing to be choric, historically linked to the *lamento* of the seventeenth century, breakthrough from formal construction to expression." Around the same time: 'Talking with Adorno about the cantata. . . .'[6]

"The novel," wrote Mann to Gerhard Herz, "is a thoroughly constructed artwork and strives to be what its subject is, namely constructive [*konstruktive*] music."[7] If *Doctor Faustus* was "at every moment to be present as a whole," Mann conceived the novel not just as an analogy (and allegory) of musical composition, but to *total* musical composition. The ideal was that of a "strict" style, "the complete integration of all musical dimensions, their neutrality towards each other due to complete organization."[8] The formulation may well have been by Adorno, one of the novelist's neighbors during his Los Angeles exile and the major source of information on matters musical. In a letter to Adorno, Mann justified as "montage" his quoting *verbatim* passages from the draft of the *Philosophy of New Music* in Adrian's notorious conversation with the devil, noting also in a sentence from the draft of *The Story of a Novel*: "'Apparently I am the devil,' he [Adorno] said after having finished [reading] the chapter."[9]

All this is well-known and well-documented.[10] Hence my focus lies elsewhere: on Echo's eyes—once heavenly blue, but black at the moment of death. It is Echo's death that Benjamin would have called the caesura of *Doctor Faustus*: like the very moment in *Elective Affinities* where "hope shot down from the sky like a star" (after which, to recall, Ottilie drowns Eduard's child). As Mann's perhaps most poetic figure, Echo is caught—elusively—between the novel's dialectics of part and whole, *Augenblick* and Argus-eyedness, blueness and blackness, expression and construction, hope and despair, humanity and barbarism. Echo thus partakes in the principal allegory of *Doctor Faustus,* where the life of the German composer stands—*pars pro toto*—for the history of German culture narrated parallel to the destruction of Germany during World War II. But Echo's eyes meant more to Mann: they were to look at us as the particular *Augenblick* of German music that was to transcend the moment of German music as a whole.

Echo, then, is easily the most overdetermined figure in Mann's most German novel. Still babbling a child's language, but already reciting prayers in *Lutherdeutsch,* he helps shoulder the burden of Germany's guilt: "Echo prays for all gainst harms, May God hold him too in His arms."[11] We know that his is a sacrificial death, when the pastor presents him "with a colored picture of the Lamb of God."[12] His is the moment of the *puer senex,* both Christ as a child and Christ at the Cross, thus taking "refuge in the sphere of the mythical and timeless, the simultaneous and abiding, where in the Savior's form as a grown man is no contradiction to the Babe in the Mother's arms."[13] Refiguring the messianic caesura in salvation history, Echo also prefigures the breakthrough that Leverkühn's last work is meant to achieve in the history of music and in the history of mankind.

Mann's attempt to work through the trauma of Germany's (self-) destruction, returns us to the question of how hope can be possible when facing the fatal conjunction of German art and politics. Despite the doom and despair, Mann twice struck up a note of hope in his novel; twice the note took on meaning under the influence of Adorno; and twice humanity hinges on that single note: first at the end of the Arietta Variations from Beethoven's piano sonata op. 111 (discussed in the first section of this chapter), and second at the end of Leverkühn's *Lamentations* (discussed in the third section). But because Mann "composed" the *Lamentations* as an echo of the Arietta, we may (as discussed in the second section) hear the two notes as the *Augenblick* where the novel's philosophical, historical, and musical dialectic comes to a standstill. We may hear and see them as Echo's eyes.

The Twinkle of Beethoven's Star

Two of the most famous interpretations of Beethoven's music are also two of the most fabled ones: E. M. Forster's fantasy of the goblins in the Fifth; and the bizarre lecture on Beethoven's op. 111 by Wendell Kretzschmar, teacher of the young Adrian Leverkühn, stuttering cantor from that imaginary turn-of-the-century German town Kaisersaschern, and surely a parody of the most prolific musical exegete of his time, Hermann Kretzschmar (1848–1924). After Mann's diaries were published, we have come to know in detail that the novelist labored extensively over the episode from 4 August to 22 September 1943, drawing on such literature as Anton Schindler's Beethoven biography and Paul Bekker's *Beethoven* monograph; that Mann then read the draft to Adorno and reworked it between 30 September and 2 October; that Adorno played the sonata to Mann on the evening of the fourth, leaving the novelist a copy of his 1937 essay on Beethoven's late style; that Mann asked Adorno the next day for a written and annotated copy of the Arietta theme from the last movement, receiving it the day after; and that the revisions of that segment of the chapter were completed by 8 October.[14] Bruno Walter, to whom Mann read the episode in the summer of 1945, effused that "something this true had been never said about Beethoven's music"; never "anything this profound and illuminating" (though Mann admitted in the diary that "much of Adorno has been taken over as mine").[15] If the Arietta variations exemplified the late Beethoven as "an ego painfully isolated in the absolute" whose works contemporaries could understand "only at moments," Kretzschmar had illuminated such a moment. In the late style, he ventriloquized the gist of Adorno's essay, "the subjective and the conventional assumed a new relationship, conditioned by death."[16] That the cantor "stuttered violently" at this word suggests both a parody of contemporary hermeneutic practice and a radical effort to vindicate it. Paradoxically, the linguistic lapse triggers one of the most eloquent readings of music ever:

The arietta theme, destined to vicissitudes for which in its idyllic innocence it would seem not be born, is presented at once, and announced in sixteen bars, reducible to a motif which appears at the end of its first half, like a brief soulcry—only three notes, a quaver, a semiquaver, and a dotted crotchet to be scanned as, say: "heav-en's blue, lov-ers' pain, fare-thee well, on a-time, mead-ow-land" [*Wiesengrund*]—and that is all. What now happens to this mild utterance, rhythmically, harmonically, contrapuntally, to this pensive, subdued formulation, with what its master blesses and to what condemns it, into what black nights and dazzling flashes, crystal spheres wherein coldness and heat, repose and ecstasy are one and the same, he flings it down and lifts it up, all that one may well call vast, strange, extravagantly magnificent, without thereby giving it a name, because it is quite truly nameless; and with labouring hands Kretzschmar played us all those enormous transformations, singing at the same time with the greatest violence: "Dim-dada!" and mingling his singing with shouts. . . .

The characteristic of the movement of course is the wide gap between bass and treble, between the right and the left hand, and a moment comes, an utterly extreme situation, when the poor little motif seems to hover alone and forsaken above a giddy yawning abyss—a procedure of blanch sublimity to which then succeeds a distressful self-depreciation, an uneasy fear as it were, that such a thing could happen. Much else happens before the end. But when it ends and while it ends, something comes, after so much rage, persistence, obstinacy, extravagance: something entirely unexpected and touching in its mildness and goodness. With the motif passed through many vicissitudes, which takes leave and so doing becomes itself entirely leave-taking, a parting wave and call, with this D G G occurs a slight change, it experiences a small melodic expansion. After an introductory C, it puts a C sharp before the D, so that it no longer scans "heaven's blue," "mead-ow-land," but "O-thou heaven's blue," "Green-est meadowland," "Fare-thee well for aye," and this added C sharp is the most moving, consolatory, pathetically reconciling thing in the world. It is like having one's hair or cheek stroked, lovingly, understandingly, like a deep and silent farewell look. It blesses the object, the frightfully harried formulation, with overpowering humanity, lies in parting so gently on the hearer's heart in eternal farewell that the eyes run over. "Now for-get the pain," it says. "Great was-God in us." "'Twas all-but a dream," "Friendly-be to me." Then it breaks off. Quick, hard triplets hasten to a conclusion with which any other piece might have ended. . . .

A third movement? A new approach? A return after this parting—impossible! It had happened that the sonata had come, in the second, enormous movement, to an end, an end without any return. And when he said "the sonata," he meant not only this one in C minor, but the sonata in general, as a genre, as traditional art-form; it itself was here at an end, brought to its end, it had fulfilled its destiny, reached its goal, beyond which there was no going, it canceled and resolved itself, it took leave—the gesture of farewell of the D G G motif, consoled by the C sharp, was a leave-taking in this sense too, great as the whole piece itself, the farewell from the sonata. . . .

Most of us, as usual, as we put on our coats and hats and walked out, hummed bemusedly to ourselves the impression of the evening, the theme-generating motif of the second movement, in its original and its leave-taking form, and for a long time we heard it like an echo from the remoter streets into which the audience dispersed, the quiet night streets of the little town: "Fare-thee well," "Fare thee well for aye," "Great was God in us."[17]

We know that hearing this farewell as a farewell to the genre of the piano sonata was Mann's free, if not false, appropriation from Bekker.[18] We know that Mann learned of Beethoven's poetic inspirations through Schindler's biography and Julius Bahle's study on the creative process.[19] We know, finally, that Mann's obssession with the Arietta's three-note motif and its final variant was inspired by Adorno's comments on his copy of the Arietta theme, reproduced here as Figure 5, calling attention to the "original, 'objective' gestalt" of the former and the "'humanized,' leave-taking variant" of the latter. "The added, decisive note," Adorno had noted, "is C♯."

How *decisive* was that note musically? How could it assume such enormous significance hermeneutically? To answer these questions, we might reconsider the gap between musical analysis and musical hermeneutics, which could not have been greater than between the two "contemporaries" seemingly most at odds with each other: the fictive Wendell Kretzschmar and the real Heinrich Schenker. Yet two passages from Schenker's 1916 *Erläuterungsausgabe* of op. 111 resonate deeply with the reading by the Kaiseraschern cantor. In the "Introductory Remarks," Schenker lashed out against the arbitrary detachment of detail by the hermeneuts who might fear "that they could be deprived through analyses from the understanding of the whole and thus from the enjoyment of the artwork." If the hermeneut, he asked, "enjoys the middle tones of a motive—to illustrate it with language: the middle syllable of a word, such as the syllable 'ga' in the little word 'legato'—as a truly beautiful, independent word, will this not provoke laughter?"[20] Without question Schenker would have laughed at what Kretzschmar made of the C♯ as "middle tone" of the final appearance of the Arietta motif. Schenker accused the hermeneuts of creating the "quandary of having to build bridges of images to the work, and to babble affect," because they "cannot understand that it is impossible to grasp what (they believe) is great, unless one knows of the small and smallest, that is, of what (I believe) are the last musical causes."[21] How, then, could the 'Dim-dada' ever mean "Fare—thee well"?

And yet, in a trenchant comment exposing the contradictions within the ideology of absolute music as *serious* music, Bekker noted in 1925 that it was "instructive, and not without an involuntary comic side-effect, to observe how all these who repudiate hermeneutics—Schenker, Halm, Pfitzner, on down to the most recent generation with writerly ambitions—themselves become hermeneuts as soon as they start to speak

Figure 5. Fly leaf of the Arietta theme in Adorno's hand
with annotations for Thomas Mann.
Courtesy of the Thomas Mann Archive Zurich, reproduced
by permission of the Theodor Adorno Archiv, Frankfurt

seriously about music."[22] We can hear this very hermeneutic impulse in
Schenker's comment about the three-measure melody extending the fourth
Arietta variation (Tovey called it a "three-bar cadence"): "Here too, as
so often with Beethoven, these simple tones take on the meaning of
purest words, as it were, eternal *Ur*-words of deepest inner humanity,
which, transfigured by truth, can do without any embellishment."[23]
Precisely such *Ur*-words Wendell Kretzschmar seems to have spelled out.
Inasmuch as Schenker's analysis of op. 111 itself broke into hermeneutics,
Mann's poetic reading of the Arietta Variations grew out of Adorno's
analysis. And inasmuch as Schenker's attention to detail rested on the

aesthetics of Argus-eyedness, so Adorno's aesthetics of the *Augenblick* needed the whole as its foil. Both Schenker's classicism and Adorno's modernism associated the unified and autonomous artwork with the ideal of humanity as epitomized by Beethoven. Still, though rooted in the same aesthetic tradition, Schenker and Adorno differed fundamentally about whether to leave that tradition behind. How so is apparent in the way both seized upon a single note—Schenker on an F, and Adorno on the C♯. Drawing on the same analytical discourse, the implications of their hermeneutic reading of these notes could not be more different. This close were Schenker and Adorno; and this distant.

First, Schenker's F. On the second dotted-eighth note beat of measure 102, it tops the three-measure melody which, for Schenker, uttered those "eternal *Ur*-words" (ex. 6.1). He hears this f^3 as the "visionary tone" initiating what the composer labeled in the sketches as a cadenza beginning at measure 106 in sharp contrast to the surrounding serenity. For Schenker it was a strange dream. As in a dream, single measures of the Arietta "wander like a ghost" through this passage.[24] As in a dream, "the bridge of the key" is temporarily disrupted. And "where the dream is the deepest"—that is, where the harmony first shifts to the dominant seventh of E♭ major in measure 110—it appeared to Schenker that the very f^3, which had "cast a shadow" on the resolution of the $^6_4$ suspensions in measures 102 and 105, "would suddenly be mysteriously transformed into the fifth of the new sonority and with it at the same time into the F of the motif" in the left hand. As if the F had continued to "resound as the seventh of the dominant," it does not cede until "the new harmony (B♭) with its own seventh, A♭, has covered the dream with a new tension." At this point, instead of interpolating the fugue that he had already substantially worked out in the sketches, Beethoven chose to conjure up the Arietta's ultimate antipode in an *espressivo* section that forms the core of the cadenza. After a vertiginous fall through fourteen fifths (from A♭ to A♭ in mm. 125–29), it ends by recalling the *Maestoso* opening of the first movement, whose main pitches E♭-C-B (right hand, mm. 2–3) later hammer out the contour of the first theme. Hence, Beethoven's allusion articulates the reprise of the Arietta theme at the point of utmost contrast. But inasmuch as the sudden shift from C minor back to C major is startling, it is mitigated by the overlapping rhythmic pulse of the sixteenth notes, as well as the thirty-second-note triplets that will drive the whole recapitulation of the theme. If the moment is this dialectical, its inherent dichotomy is this mediated. For it is the darkness of the dream that the end of the movement promises to dispel.

The F, therefore, comes back at the end precisely when, in Schenker's words, "the uncanny power of the last *Augenblick*, as it were, recalls the dream lived through during the transition: a god of miraculous powers

Example 6.1. Beethoven op. 111, Arietta Variations mm. 100–130

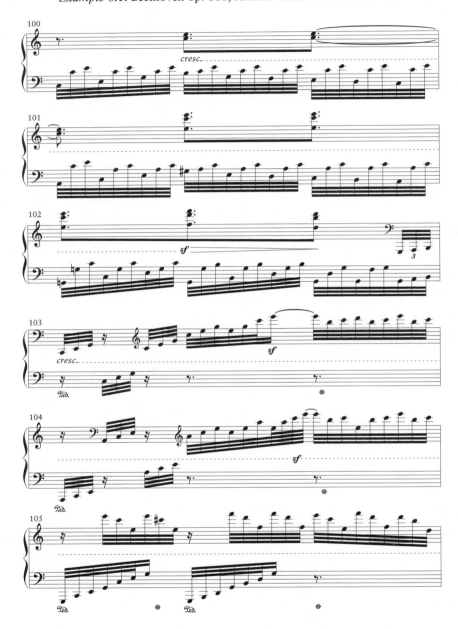

Example 6.1. (cont.)

Example 6.1. (cont.)

suddenly changes the second fifth of the dream [the F-B♭] as it befits the soul of the Arietta" to F-B.[25] In other words, F is a structural note. To hear it we must be structural listeners. Our *Fernhören* must connect the f^3 from the beginning of the dream to the f^3 in the penultimate measure. The *Ur*-word to be scanned to the unembellished F foreshadows the aesthetic of the *Urlinie* that Schenker would soon begin to develop. According to William Drabkin, the conspicuous linear ascent of the Arietta theme in measures 1–3 and 12–15 is not "balanced by a comparable linear descent" (one that includes F and D), which will not come until the extension of Variation 4 leading to Schenker's *Ur*-words.[26] This, then, had been Schenker's point about the dream as the antipode of the piece: "despite the shifting ground, despite the distance" one can still "feel the unity that once tied these measures together in the reality of the Arietta and the variations."[27] If Beethoven's cadenza culminates in the falling fifths as the "last reduction of the whole"; and if at the end "theme and variations finally had to become, as it were, one soul," then that soul, according to Hegel's aesthetics of Argus-eyedness, would still be visible all over the movement's musical body. If the composer becomes in the *Urlinie* "a seer," as Schenker later put it in *Der Tonwille*, then, by inserting the missing F into the Arietta's last utterance, the composer would seem to have seen to it that the *Urworte* finally articulate that *Urlinie*.[28]

Now Adorno's C♯. No analyst could endow it with the kind of structural significance accorded to the C♯ in measure seven of the *Eroica*, the impetus for the most elaborate symphonic argument to date.[29] Even if C♯ appears as the very first chromatic note in the first variation of the Arietta (m. 17); even if it is the grace note leading to the trill that opens the cadenza—it is only an ornament. The C♯ may well be all that remains of a detail that Beethoven added to one of his numerous sketches of the Arietta theme preserved in the sketchbook Artaria 201. Here, scattered among other variants, he inserted an isolated C♯ meant for the fifth measure of the melody and glossed it *zuweilen* ("at times").[30] Schenker had spotted the note in the sketches, suggesting about the remark that the composer "envisioned the chromaticism to occur only eventually in one or another of the variations."[31] True: C♯ is the leading tone of the newly interpolated secondary dominant that prepares the return of the D minor from measure six of the theme in all variations (see mm. 22, 37–8, 54, 77–78 and 135–36). And "at times" it does even creep into the melody that ends the first part of the theme (see m. 23 in Varation 1, m. 27 in Varation 2, m. 79 in Varation 4). However well-prepared, when Beethoven used the C♯ to embellish the final statement of the Arietta theme, it adds no more than a sparkle.

And as such it would be like that "evanescently fleeting association" of "trotting horse hooves" Adorno heard ending the first movement of the *Les Adieux* sonata, and which nevertheless carry "a greater guarantee of hope than the four Gospels."[32] If for Benjamin "the eternal is in any case rather a frill on a dress than an idea," then the C♯ flourish is such a frill.[33] Recall the premise of Benjamin's hermeneutics of the moment: the smaller the detail, the larger its promise. And recall Adorno's challenge: "Only a philosophy that could grasp such micrological figures in its innermost construction of the aesthetic whole would make good on what it promises."[34] In the first of two consecutive fragments of op. 111 that belong to the earliest layers of the Beethoven monograph, Adorno, listening to Benjamin's voice, had identified the disruptive E♭ passage of Schenker's dream as being "in shadow" and designated it as "one of Beethoven's most magnificent formal means": in shadow are the "moments of oppression in Beethoven . . . in which subjectivity 'seizes' the Being alien to it. 'Before you seize the body on this star,' oppression prevails."[35] And in the second fragment he noted:

> "[t]he close of the Arietta variations has such a force of looking back, of leavetaking, that, as if over-illuminated by this departure, what has gone before is immeasurably enlarged. This despite the fact that the variations themselves, up to the symphonic conclusion of the last, contain scarcely a moment which could counterbalance that of leavetaking as fulfilled present—and such a moment may well be denied to music, which exists in illusion. But the true power of illusion in Beethoven's music—of the 'dream among eternal stars'—is that it can invoke what has not been as something past and non-existent. Utopia is heard only as what has already been. The music's inherent sense of form changes what has preceded the leavetaking in such a way that it takes on a greatness, a presence in the past which, within music, it could never achieve in the present."[36]

With such words Adorno might have accompanied his playing of Arietta for Mann five years later. And he would continue to grapple through the late *Aesthetic Theory* with the aporia of aesthetic appearance or aesthetic illusion, or *Schein*. Since *Schein* is the creation of a unified whole from disparate elements, it both helps to cover up social antagonisms and promises the possibility to reconcile them.[37] Because *Doctor Faustus* is, as Fredric Jameson has argued, "[t]he most familiar and widely read version of Adorno's account of the crisis of art (or the emergence of modernism)" figured as a "crisis of *Schein*," it raises the question "how a music might be imagined which would resolutely attempt to confront the guilt of the fictional and the original sin of aesthetic appearance and to absolve itself of it."[38] Adorno saw Beethoven as having solved the problem in two ways: by making the shadow integral to the *Schein* through the "immanence of the opposition"; and by transcending that immanence at a particular moment.[39] However painful the remembrance of the past, Adorno's nostalgia (in a formulation by Andreas Huyssen) "is not the opposite of utopia, but, as a form of memory, always implicated, even productive in it."[40] Hence the farewell at the end of op. 111 is a source of both sorrow and solace. What has preceded the leave-taking is not lost to the past, but remains present. *Schein* is reconciled with the shadow.

"In what does the expression of the human manifest itself in Beethoven?" Adorno had asked, answering: "I would say, in the fact that his music has the *gift of sight*. The human is its gaze. But this must be expressed in technical concepts."[41] Hence he would find it "necessary in identifying expression in Beethoven to interpret minute variants like that in the second theme of the *Adagio* of op. 31.2, where the syncopation appears [in measure 36]. It causes the theme to 'speak,' in just the same way as something extra-human—starlight—seems to bend towards the human being as solace. It is the sign of *yieldingness*—just as transcendence is presented as something invoked (but then demonically entreated) in Beethoven. The expression 'humanized star' in a poem by Däubler comes very close to this. This sphere, and its symbols, are especially relevant to the great *Leonore* Overture."[42] If these examples—notably something as minuscule and inconspicuous as a mere syncopation in the *Tempest* sonata—constitute the foundational, Benjaminian, layer of Adorno's Beethoven project, the C♯ belongs right there.[43] Thus Adorno noted in the first of only four fragments jotted down in 1943 (and it is tempting to speculate about the relationship between this fragment and his copying out the Arietta theme for Mann): "the C♯ at the end of the variations (a 'humane variant,' a 'humanized star')."[44] While for Schenker "[t]he *Urlinie* is the composer's gift of sight" by virtue of its platonic ideality, for Adorno it is the minute variant that testifies to Beethoven's "gift of sight" by virtue of its modern particularity.[45] The former perceived through the all-seeing eye of the divine, the latter seen in a single human *Augenblick*. So similar were Adorno's and Schenker's metaphysics of music—and so different.

What Adorno heard as the "over-illuminated" coda of the Arietta movement is like as the shimmering tapestry of chromatic and diatonic notes Schenker observed as "a Milky Way of tones."[46] But whereas the C♯ would be for Schenker no more than the twinkle of Beethoven's star, for Adorno, it would be no less.

Good Glance and Evil Eye

Soul is not an invariant, not an anthropological category. It is a historical gesture. Nature, having become the ego, opens its eyes *as* ego (not *in* the ego, as its regressive part) and becomes aware of itself *qua* ego as nature. This moment—that is, not the breakthrough of nature but its remembrance of otherness—is closest to reconciliation as also to lamentation.[47]

If the descriptions of music in *Doctor Faustus* aspire to a panoptic view of Western music—from the simple canons of folk song to the cultured constructions of dodecaphony—they are also the moments where the novel is "being endowed with soul, over and over again." And if there are two moments whose "remembrance" of nature's "otherness" comes "closest to reconciliation as also to lamentation," these would have to be the Arietta Variations and the *Lamentations of Doctor Faustus*. The two works function as the musical frame of the novel, its *Auftakt* and *Abgesang*. Indeed, given that Echo's death is the raison d'être of the *Lamentations*, the two chapters devoted to Nepomuk Schneidewein provide an echo of the description of the Arietta movement.[48] We know, because Leverkühn and Zeitblom hum the Arietta motif "in its original and its leave-taking form" on their way home from Kretzschmar's lecture: "and for a long time we heard it *like an echo* from the remoter streets into which the audience dispersed, the quiet night streets of the little town: 'Fare—thee well,' 'Fare thee well for aye,' 'Great was God in us.'"[49]

In hindsight, therefore, we can hear the Arietta theme to be like a child: "destined to vicissitudes for which in its idyllic innocence it would seem not to be born"; we can hear the "utterly extreme situation" of the cadenza to anticipate the moment when Adrian, as Gunilla Bergsten put it, "watches heaven and hell fighting over the child"; and we can hear the words Kretzschmar scans to the "Dim-dada" as allusions to Echo: to the divine aura of his eye color—"heavenly blue"; to Adrian's deep feelings for him—"lover's pain"; to his ephemeral appearance—"on a time"; to his final departure—"fare-thee well"; and, of course, to the one who inspired them all—"meadowland" or *Wiesengrund*, Adorno's middle name. But it is only with the final reprise of the Arietta theme—whose "added C sharp" is the "most moving, consolatory, pathetically reconciling thing in the world," like "having one's hair or cheek stroked, lovingly, understandingly, like a deep and silent farewell look"—that the music seems to gesture unequivocally: I am Echo.

For the echo will be the compositional principle that governs *The Lamentations of Doctor Faustus* as the response to Echo's death. It grows out of the work's aesthetic premise that "all expressivism is really lament; just as music, so soon as it is conscious of itself as expression at the beginning of its modern history, becomes lament and '*lasciatemi morire*,' the lament of Ariadne, to the softly echoing plaintive song of nymphs."[50] Inspired by Ernst Krenek, Mann conceived Leverkühn's stylistic recourse to Monteverdi's "echo-effect" to articulate the two most important paradigmatic shifts in the history of Western music. The central part that Monteverdi had played in the change from medieval modality to modern tonality occupied, in Krenek's words, "a position analogous to the place held today by Arnold Schoenberg with respect to tonality in decay and the new language of atonality."[51] "Art," Schoenberg had written in his expressionist manifesto from 1910, "is the cry of despair uttered by those who experience at first hand the fate of mankind. . . . The world revolves within—inside them: what bursts out is merely the echo—the work of art."[52] Mann's equivalent of this echo— echoing the lament of Schoenberg's Ariadne in *Erwartung*—is Adrian Leverkühn's final breakthrough. Surely Mann knew that "Ariadne" was a metathesis of "Adrian."[53] Envoicing Adorno, he paid homage not only to the historical moment of radical Expressionism, but also made it the necessary goal of Western Music: "The echo, the giving back of the human voice as a sound of nature, and the revelation of it *as* sound of nature, is essentially a lament: Nature's melancholy 'Alas!' in view of man, her effort to utter his solitary state. . . . In Leverkühn's last and loftiest creation, echo, favorite device of the baroque, is employed with unspeakably mournful effect."[54] Note the italicized "*as*." That the echo reveals the human voice "*as* sound of nature" almost echoes Adorno's idea that nature "opens its eyes *as* ego." Adorno's "remembrance of otherness" is the ultimate goal of Leverkühn's last work—though no longer as reconciliation (as in the Arietta), but as lamentation.

The *Lamentations of Doctor Faustus* are the final product of the novel's pervasive historical dialectic, which Adrian inherits through the father's dominating speculative gaze (associated with rational coldness) and the mother's restrained voice (a mezzo soprano radiating corporeal warmth). On the level of narrative composition, this dualism functions analogously to the exposition of the masculine and the feminine themes in traditional descriptions of sonata form (just as the composer's final years at the Schweigestill farm recapitulate his upbringing at the Buchel estate). The inner affinity and antagonism between the two themes—the instrumental reason of the paternal mind and the vocal desire of the maternal body—work like the principle of "contrasting derivation" that Arnold Schmitz detected in Beethoven's sonata form.[55] This dialectic will concern us now, for it is the central aesthetic and philosophical axis around which Leverkühn's personal life and artistic evolution revolves— just as in his eyes the "pitch-black of the mother's eyes had mingled with the father's azure blue to a shadowy blue-grey-green iris with little metallic sprinkles and a rust-colored ring round the pupils."[56]

With the dichotomy of blue and black Mann revisited the problem of the artist as the other, raised first in *Tonio Kröger*. For blue eyes and blond hair are the very features that Tonio does not possess. Between the early novella and the late novel (or his Lübeck childhood and his Los Angeles exile) Mann worked through the clash between creative genius and the wish to belong to the very imagined community that the Nazis had perverted through the politics of racial purity: *blond und blauäugig*—features of the ideal German. Hence Adrian's impossible passion for the two archetypal hybrids of *eros* and *ars*—the blond and blue-eyed violin virtuoso Rudolf Schwerdtfeger, and the French-Swiss designer Marie Godeau, whose eyes are as black "as tar, as ripe black-berries."[57] Hence Berowne's attraction in Adrian's opera *Love's Labour Lost* to the "dangerous piece of female flesh" of Rosaline who has "two pitch-balls stuck in her face for eyes."[58] If the "musical predisposition" of the black-eyed Elsbeth Leverkühn had been associated with "desire," then, as Michael Beddow surmised, the "terrifying symbolism" of Adrian's fatal encounter with the syphillitic prostitute Esmeralda is "that it is a figure of incest."[59] Given Adrian's "weakness, for the magic of the eye, the black and the blue," the composer's own labors of love are lost in the dialectic between the two colors.[60] While death takes from him those he cannot have, taboo bars him from the ones he must not have.

The parental dualism, then, is part of a larger dialectic of artistic creation and musical composition. On the one hand, the father's experiments with chemicals purchased from an apothecary's shop called the "Blessed Messengers" (many of Mann's names are telltale) show that manipulating the crystallization of inorganic matter will make it appear like organic growth, just as art creates the illusionary second nature of aesthetic *Schein*. On the other hand, the maidservant Hanna, who is not afraid to use the voice that Adrian's mother had suppressed "in a sort of chaste reserve," shows him how vocal performance becomes subject to instrumental reason.[61] In the polyphony of her simple canons he experiences, for the first time, how the desire of horizontal melody is controlled through the ratio of vertical harmony.[62] Kretzschmar will later try to account for this very dialectic of difference and identity in his lectures on "Beethoven and the Fugue," on "Music and the Eye," and on "The Elemental in Music." To reconcile the double nature of music—its sensual body and its spiritual essence—will be the ultimate challenge of Leverkühn's work, where "heat and cold prevail alongside each other."[63] For only "in moments of the greatest genius they play into each other, the *espressivo* takes hold of the strict counterpoint, the objective blushes with feeling." But this exact equilibrium is reached spontaneously only once in the music-historical trajectory of the novel: in Adrian's expressionist phase, where the "[g]enuine and serious is only the very short, the highly consistent musical moment."[64] Only in the *Brentano Songs*—a fictive blend of texts from Mahler's *Wunderhorn* songs and the score of Schoenberg's *Book of the Hanging Gardens*—"music turns its eye upon itself and looks at its own being"; only here the notes "offer each other the hand" both "consolingly and grievingly."[65] It is this conjunction of spiritual glance and physical handshake that Adrian seeks to recapture after his evolution has passed through the expressionist moment of perfect balance between body and mind, nature and reason, the old and the new, the banal and the refined.

Struggling to bridge the ever-growing distance between construction and expression, Adrian's ideal of composing with twelve tones is a Benjaminian "constellation" where "reason and magic" may unite.[66] These are the terms with which he explains his conception of dodecaphony to Zeitblom during a walk passing the so-called "Cow Trough"—a small oval-shaped pond near the parental farm, whose bottom "was flat only near the edge," which "fell off rapidly into darkness," and in whose water Adrian finds it now "much too cold to bathe" in the autumnal evening.[67] The premonition is pivotal. Just as Adrian will see his parents for a last time—"pressing his father's hand in farewell" and "leaning his head on [his mother's] shoulder"—his music is about to loose its human touch.[68] Although serial composition is only "[b]ound by a self-imposed compulsion to order, hence free," once he will have chosen the material for the *Lamentations*, its "strict composition" will generate "no note, not one, which did not fulfill its thematic function in the whole structure"—"no free note" as Mann echoed the *Philosophy of New Music*.[69] With the twelve-tone row for Faust's twelve-syllable theme—"For I die as a good and as a bad Christian"—"the order of the basic material becomes total."[70] Yet if Mann imagined Leverkühn's final work as the final stage of the dialectical process between the moment of expression and construction, how could it be of "utmost calculation" and "*at the same time* purely expressive"?[71] How could the total order of the material come with a "perfectly conscious control over all the 'characters' of expressiveness which have ever been precipitated in the history of music"?[72]

That was the central issue of the *Philosophy of New Music.*

Dodecaphony had to avoid the double danger of a fatal regress to the manufactured pre-expressionist *expressivo,* or a false progress to the total mechanical control of serialism. How can construction, Adorno asked, "become expression without plaintively giving into lamenting subjectivity?" And how can music avoid "the blatant emptiness of the integral composition"?[73] While Schoenberg's oeuvre "in all its transitions and extremes" was "to be understood as a dialectical process between expression and construction," which had not been resolved in the New Objectivity, the solution was the very "breakthrough" the devil promises to Leverkühn: a sudden turn (*Umschlag*) in the "dialectical process by which strictest constraint is reversed into the free language of emotion, by which freedom is born out of bondage."[74] Paradoxically, it is only when the highest level of "intellectuality and formal rigor" has been achieved that the "reversal" can occur of "calculated coldness into an expressive sound of the soul, into the heartfelt unbosoming of the creature."[75]

Mann tied this dialectic between creative freedom and strict style into the larger theological dialectic between good and evil, figured so acutely as the good glance and the evil eye. As has often been noted, the novel's forty-seven chapters plus epilogue are not only composed in analogy, however contrived, to the musical technique of dodecaphony, but they also do so by having the main incarnations of the devil appear in every twelfth chapter: in the thirteenth chapter with the theologian Eberhard Schleppfuß; in the twenty-fifth chapter with the devil himself; and in the thirty-seventh chapter with the music publisher Saul Fittelberg.[76] In a conspicuous moment of self-reflection about the coincidence of the number thirteen with the Schleppfuß episode, Zeitblom admits to have been "almost tempted" to accept the influence of chance, but tries to convince the reader that he merely broke down the long thematic complex of Adrian's student years out of convenience.[77] But since the return of the devil in *Doctor Faustus* rotates with the row, the explanation is disingenuous at best. For Zeitblom, though having introduced himself in the first sentence of the book by asserting "not to bring my own personality into the foreground," barely hides his control over the counterpoint in his twofold tale. His narrative corollary to a double fugue, the double story of a German composer and of Germany ends, inexorably, when the composition of the final work converges in the destruction of both. At best Zeitblom is an accomplice, at worst another incarnation of the devil. His narrative composition has a foregone conclusion. Already at the end of the introduction, he compares Leverkühn's loneliness to "an abyss, into which one's feelings towards him dropped soundless and without a trace."[78] That is: without an echo.

The craft of epic narration, Mann wrote in his essay "The Art of the

Novel," is Apollinian, for Apollo is "the god of distance, the god of objectivity, the god of irony."[79] Turning Zeitblom into the utmost parody of the omniscient narrator, Mann's ultimate irony was to ironize that god and suggest that Apollinian enlightenment is just as deadly as the destructive forces of the Dionysian music it seeks to control. Hence the total vision of Zeitblom's story has itself a blind spot—a bottomless hole in the center which is as dark and cold as the Cow Trough. The novel's negative *kairos*, its moment of the constructed (w)hole, belongs not to the divine, but to the devil. For he occupies the center of the labyrinthic narrative like the middle of medieval mazes, which look like an eye where the minotaur has taken the place of the pupil. This is the evil eye that in popular imagination strikes animals and humans with disease and death. Recall the moment when Adrian first met his nephew: "He held Nepomuk's hand and gazed, quickly lost, into the sweet light of the azure smile of those starry eyes looking up at him."[80] This is why Leverkühn will fault himself for having inflicted the fatal illness on Echo: "I feasted my eyes on him"; the devil "slew" the child, "merciless, and used thereto mine own proper eyes."[81] At the moment of death, therefore, Echo's eyes are no longer *himmelsblau*, but instead "between the lashes no iris showed, only blackness." If blue is the moment of the good particular and black the moment of the evil whole, with Echo's death this dialectics takes a fatal turn towards the latter. Hence Nepomuck's gaze during his final moments will be played back in reverse by Adrian's gaze after having gone mad: "an Ecce-homo countenance . . . with woeful open mouth and vacant eyes"—a "mocking game" of Nature "presenting a picture of the utmost spirituality, just there whence the spirit had fled!"[82] This paradox becomes the terminal critique of art as false illusion. While Leverkühn's art strove to appear like nature, now his nature appears, mockingly, like art. That is the shadow's final ridicule of the *Schein*. "The subsumption of expression under a reconciling generality" the devil had claimed in his conversation with the composer, "is the innermost principle of musical appearance. That is over."[83]

And over it is for Germany to be reconciled with the world, because it possessed the hubris to rule the world. The parallel the devil draws between art and politics—"the artist is the brother of the criminal and the madman"—recapitulates the central thesis of Mann's 1939 essay "Bruder Hitler."[84] Both Leverkühn and Germany signed a pact with the devil to attain complete mastery over their subjects; both are going down into a bottomless hole, like the half-seeing sinner going to hell in Michelangelo's *Last Judgement*. As Zeitblom concludes the novel, "Germany was reeling then at the height of her dissolute triumphs, about to gain the whole world by virtue of the one pact she was minded to keep, which she had signed with her blood. Today, clung round by demons, a hand over one eye, with the other staring into horrors, down she flings from despair to despair. When will she reach the bottom of the abyss? When, out of uttermost hopelessness—a miracle beyond the power of belief—will the light of hope dawn? A lonely man folds his hands and speaks: 'God be merciful to thy poor soul, my friend, my Fatherland.'"[85]

If we read the last paragraph of *Doctor Faustus* like the structural listener who must hear the last measure to grasp the entire composition, the novel's moment of wholeness is indeed one of total negation, of total hopelessness, of total damnation. Mann's narrative construction appears to be afflicted by the same problem Adorno diagnosed for the composition with twelve tones: "As soon as this principle becomes total, the possibility of musical transcendence disappears."[86] We hear this denial of transcendence in the last chapter when Adrian performs his final work as a farewell to his friends, gathered on the day when the time the devil granted him is to run out. But here we also hear, simultaneously, *two* sounds from the composition that were "utmost calculation" and "*at the same time* purely expressive": a dissonant chord that stands for the twelve-tone construction; and a wail that stands for expression.[87] We hear, in Zeitblom's words, "the giving back of the human voice as a sound of nature, and the revelation of it *as* sound of nature . . . essentially, a lament: Nature's melancholy 'Alas!' in view of man, her effort to utter his solitary state."[88] We hear, in Adorno's words, how "music, compressed into a moment, is true as a reflection of negative experience" and hence "pertains to real suffering."[89] And we hear, in the words of the devil, the only thing that is "still permissible" and "not fictitious, not a game": "the unfeigned and untransfigured expression of suffering in its real moment."[90]

> Leverkühn . . . had sat down at the brown square piano and flattened the pages of the score with his right hand. We saw tears run down his cheeks and fall on the keyboard, wetting it, as he attacked the keys in a strongly dissonant chord. *At the same time* he opened his mouth as though to sing, but only a wail which will ring for ever in my ears broke from his lips. He spread out his arms, bending over the instrument and seeming about to embrace it, when suddenly, as through smitten by a blow, he fell sidewise from his seat and to the floor.[91]

Although Christ's words at Gethsemane ("Watch with me!" and "Forsake me not! Be about me at my hour!") had been Adrian's final plea; although collapsing at the piano he "spread out his arms" like Christ on the cross; and although Frau Schweigestill "lifted the head of the unconscious man . . . holding him in her motherly arms" like a Pietà—Adrian's musical death, this moment, where the dialectics between expression and construction comes to a standstill, threatens to be one without transfiguration.[92] Echoless.

"Modern music," Adorno said upon concluding the first part of his *Philosophy of New Music*, "has taken upon itself all the darkness and the guilt of the world. Its fortune lies in the perception of misfortune; all its beauty is in denying itself the illusion of beauty. . . . It dies away unheard, without an echo."[93] That is the negation of Leverkühn's final work: as the total echo of Echo, it falls silent to become the very aural image of the "abyss, into which one's feelings towards him [Adrian] dropped soundless and without a trace."[94] No one, perhaps, captured the compression of the *Lamentations* into a lone chord and a single sigh better than Schoenberg in the preface to Webern's *Bagatelles for String Quartet* op. 9, quoted in the previous chapter: "You can stretch every glance out into a poem, every sigh into a novel. But to express a novel in a single gesture, joy in a breath—such concentration can only be present in proportion to the absence of self-pity."[95] If Zeitblom indulged in such self-pity by expanding the German composer's whole life into a novel of such proportions, here his narrative would be distilled into the moment of Adrian's last musical utterance. That utterance was almost prescribed by Adorno in the *Philosophy of New Music*: "With Webern, the musical subject, falling silent, abdicates and delivers itself to the material, which, however, grants it no more than the echo of falling silent."[96]

It is in this spirit that the philosopher persuaded the novelist to change the last two pages about the ending of the cantata. For Adorno found them "too positive, too unbrokenly theological in relation to the structure not only of the *Lamentation of Dr. Faustus*, but of the novel as a whole. They seemed to lack what such a crucial conclusion required: the power of determinate negation as the only permissible figure of the Other."[97] And so Mann composed that "determinate negation" into the purely orchestral ending of the cantata, "a symphonic adagio, into which the chorus of lament . . . gradually passes over" and which becomes "the reverse of the 'Ode to Joy,' the negative, equally a work of genius, of that transition of the symphony into vocal jubilation."[98] Moreover, since the "revocation" of the Ode of Joy became "in every note and accent" an "Ode of Sorrow," Mann also followed Adorno's advice to abandon his original idea of letting Leverkühn leave the *Lamentations of Doctor Faustus* unfinished.[99] Where at the end of the work the "uttermost accents of mourning are reached," Mann would write, there had to be "up to the very end no consolation, reconciliation, transfiguration."[100]

But Mann did not end on that note.

Consider what had been at stake, for Mann and for Adorno. Just as Faust dies "as a good and as a bad Christian," Adrian Leverkühn dies as a good and as a bad German. In his programmatic address *Germany and the Germans* given before the Library of Congress and written in February and March 1945, right after he finished the conversation with the devil in Chapter 25, Mann insisted that Faust "had to be a musician."[101] Both "German metaphysics" and "German music," he argued, were products of German *Innerlichkeit* that stemmed from the "great historical deed" of Luther, the "musical theologian."[102] Although the musicality of the German soul meant a total separation of art and politics, the author of the notoriously aestheticist 1918 *Reflections of a Nonpolitical Man* had come to realize, by 1945, that such separation had been, in fact, utterly political. While Mann bought into the the popular explanation of the German catastrophe as one rooted in German culture (the Luther-to-Hitler line), he modelled Adrian Leverkühn not primarily after the image of Faust, but after that of Nietzsche, whose name, he later explained, "does not appear in the entire book—advisedly, because the euphoric musician has been made so much Nietzsche's substitute that the original is no longer permitted a separate existence."[103]

Through Nietzsche, Mann's reckoning with the past also became a reckoning with his own past, notably his friendship with Ernst Bertram, whose seminal *Nietzsche: Versuch einer Mythologie* (1918) had spoken of the "inner musicality that Nietzsche shared with the German soul."[104] Mann created Leverkühn's Janus-faced profile parallel to the "godlessly divine" philosopher who would mix dialectically, like Adrian in his *Apocalypsis,* the "burning scream for the eternal mysterium" with "the mocking laughter of intellectualism"; and whose theology "that man needs his most evil to create his best" was expressed in Schleppfuß's doctrine that God's "real vindication . . . consisted in his power to bring good out of evil."[105] Thus Faust's "For I die as a good and as a bad Christian" became Mann's "self-critical" refusal to separate the good Germany from the bad Germany.[106] If the bad Germany was the "good Germany gone astray," he took responsibility for both—both mirrored in the good and bad sides of his doubles in the novel, where "narrator and the hero each embraced a part of me."[107] For Mann himself had sternly defended Nietzsche's aestheticism in the *Reflections of a Unpolitical Man* which he considered "virtually" as the "redemption" of the book by Bertram, whose enthusiasm for racial and nationalist ideology may well be mirrored in the literary historian Georg Vogler from the fascist Kridwiß-Circle.[108] "The genuine German Mephistopheles," Bertram had quoted Nietzsche, "climbs over the Alpine Mountains, and believes that everything there belongs to him"; and "a German Latinate," he then quoted Luther, "is a *diabolo incarnato*."[109] No wonder that Adrian Leverkühn meets the devil in the Italian town of Palestrina; no wonder that the devil assumes the voice of Theodor Wiesengrund-Adorno, who went by the name of his Italian mother; no wonder that Leverkühn's *Lamentations* recomposes Monteverdi's *Lamento d'Ariana*; and no wonder Mann preceded the intellectual inferno of *Doctor Faustus* with a motto from the second Canto of Dante's *Inferno*. In hindsight, Mann recognized the fatal consequences of his own cultural politics. If he had once hailed the opera *Palestrina* by the fascist Pfitzner, now the devil's gift of creative power to Adrian Leverkühn would parody how Pfitzner's angelic choir had triggered Palestrina's artistic breakthrough when composing the *Missa Papae Marcelli*.

Yet Mann's tortured dialectic of the divine and the diabolic seems to reach its utmost irony in distributing Faust's good and bad death over the angelic Echo and the demonic Leverkühn. For the novel's most unsettling causal nexus is not that the latter's evil gaze caused the former's death, but that Echo himself might be Leverkühn's own creation; that the heaven's blue of his eyes, like the blue of heaven, may indeed be an aesthetic illusion; that Echo might be the forbidden fruit of the composer's tryst with a succubus, the mermaid Hyphialta, alias Esmeralda, who is the devil's servant.[110] If nothing shatters human hope more than the death of a child, there can be no greater tragedy than this child being one's own; and no greater guilt than bearing the responsibility for its death. *Doctor Faustus* is nothing less than an attempt to expose that guilt and to assume that responsibility. It does so by redoing and undoing Nietzsche's twofold escape from history and religion through oblivion and through Dionysian drunkenness. Recognizing that Nietzsche's nihilistic concept of the aesthetic *Augenblick* was no longer the interface between historical time and eternity (as Kierkegaard had it), but had become the moment of eternal return in an aestheticized world without transcendence, Mann came to side with Adorno who would hold the darkness of the new music against the brightness of Zarathustra's "Mittags"; the *Urnacht* against the *Urlicht*; Mahler's Ninth against Mahler's Third.[111] Mann countered Nietzsche's hedonistic flight from history with Adorno's aesthetics of the historical apocalypse, where the breakdown is the condition for the breakthrough. In no other novel did Mann store so much German history to remind us where the German evil came from, and to explain how it led to the German catastrophe. In no other novel did he so thoroughly undermine any aesthetic illusion that could cover it up, showing instead that the illusion itself might lead to that catastrophe. Where Nietzsche's God was dead, Mann's God is absent. And where Nietzsche had no theology, Mann had negative theology. Even as the devil, Mann's Adorno was still speaking of God.[112]

This possibility of aesthetic redemption through negation—Adrian Leverkühn's redemption—brings us back to Benjamin's dialectics at a standstill, which Brinkmann has invoked as a "carefully designed position between the poles of political pessimism and spiritual optimism."[113] "In sharp contrast" to Benjamin's "melancholy" at the "crossroads of hope and despair," he sees the grandiose breakthrough of the "Sch'ma Yisroel" in Schoenberg's *A Survivor from Warsaw*—a breakthrough, as it were, from dystopia to utopia—as a "political eschatology" which is "almost another, a modern 'Ode to Joy,' borne out of the deepest desperation and terror of the twentieth century."[114] This raises the thorny questions of whether we should hear *A Survivor* primarily as a response to a Jewish tragedy and read *Doctor Faustus* primarily as a response to a German one. Or whether we may hear the ending of Schoenberg's work also as an uplifting statement about the persistence of the human spirit and the ending of Adrian Leverkühn's *Lamentations* as a sign of human hope.

Can we answer these questions in the same breath? Can we consider them in light of the experience of a Jewish woman from Hungary who recalls, in Steven Spielberg's Shoa project *The Last Days*, how she stopped speaking with God after seeing an SS soldier smash a child to death on a car and then throw it onto the back of a truck? Can the reality of the Holocaust be compared with the fictitious "twenty-two hours of crying, writhing torture, of a child, of this child, who folded his twitching little hands and stammered: 'Echo will be good, Echo will be good'"; and Adrian's denial "that it is not to be . . . the good and the noble"? Mann knew of the persecution of the Jews, of their mass murder, and of the goal, stated by Goebbels, of their complete annihilation. As part of his monthly radio broadcasts for the BBC, meant to mobilize German resistance against the Nazi regime, Mann had spoken out about *Der Judenterror* in the fall of 1942, giving details of widespread and systematic genocide: the "screams and prayers of the victims" and the "laughter of the SS savages."[115] Yet given that he "registered in his diaries shocking details concerning the massacre of Jews in Eastern Europe,"[116] why would he let Echo—so striking an emblem of German culture—be killed by the gaze of a German *Tonsetzer*, whose music employs the techniques of a Jewish composer from Vienna, whose compositions are described in the voice of a Jewish philosopher from Frankfurt, and whose works are wanted by the Jewish publisher Saul Fittelberg, who speaks of *une analogie frappante* between Germanness and Judaism, because "there are only two nationalisms, the German and the Jewish"?[117]

Blurring the line between victim and perpetrator, Mann struggled to negotiate a position between self-excuse and self-accusation—that "tendency toward self-criticism, often to the point of self-disgust and self-execration" which he had diagnosed as so "thoroughly German," and which made it for him "eternally incomprehensible how a people so inclined toward self-analysis could ever conceive the idea of world domination."[118] Yet having realized that Hitler could be the artist's "brother," it must have dawned on Mann that the Germans did not murder a Jewish other, but their own kin. When he divided Faust's death onto Echo and Leverkühn, yet had the latter kill the former with his evil gaze, both the division and its undoing are symptomatic of his tortured attempt to come to terms with the twofold trauma of the German crime and the Jewish catastrophe and to work through what Freud had identified as the "pathological disposition" of melancholia.[119]

When Freud defined, in his classic study, regular mourning as "the reaction to the loss of a loved person, or to the loss of some abstraction which has taken the place of one, such as one's country, liberty, and ideal and so on," he noted as distinguishing features of melancholia "a profoundly painful dejection, cessation of interest in the outside world, loss in the capacity to love, inhibition of all activity, and a lowering of the self-regarding feelings to a degree that finds utterance in self-reproaches and self-revilings, and culminates in a delusional expectation of punishment."[120] Much of this reads like a case history of the recluse Adrian Leverkühn, whose melancholic music ranges from the setting of Keat's *Ode on Melancholy* to the *Apocalypsis cum figuris* based on the magic square in Dürer's engraving *Melancholia,* and who trades his capacity to love for artistic perfection (and by implication, eternal punishment).[121] Moreover, for Freud the melancholic person does not suffer "from a loss in regard to an object," but projects "a loss in regard to his ego," so that "one part of the ego sets itself over against the other, judges it critically, and, as it were, takes it as its object." Melancholia, therefore, "borrows some of its features from mourning, and the others from the process of regression . . . to narcissism." Thus, "[i]f the love for the object—a love which cannot be given up though the object itself is given up—takes refuge in narcissistic identification, then the hate comes into operation on this substitute object, abusing it, debasing it, making it suffer and deriving sadistic satisfaction from its suffering."[122]

In *Doctor Faustus,* this internal division of the melancholic ego and the pathological abuse of the substitute object is most apparent in Mann's splitting of the authorial ego into protagonist (Leverkühn) and narrator (Zeitblom), who transfers his narcissistic identification with Germany (the lost object) onto his suffering friend (the substitute object). But the division is also replicated in the split between Adrian and Echo, both allegories of German culture and music. After losing his beloved nephew, the melancholic composer attempts to "take back" the Ninth, as a substitute object, canceling its *Freude* through lament. If melancholy is the condition of modern art, in *Doctor Faustus* it is the condition of modern music. It is the condition of what Max Pensky, referring to

Walter Benjamin, has called melancholy dialectics.[123] Its source is the profound alienation between sound and sense. And Echo is located at that source.

Recalling how Adorno had presented him with a copy of Benjamin's *On the Origin of German Tragic Drama* upon his return from medical treatment in Chicago in the spring of 1946, Mann noted that "when one is at work, pertinent and significant material is constantly appearing from all sides, thrown across one's path as if fate were acting as procurer."[124] The most suggestive trace that Benjamin's book may have left on *Doctor Faustus* is the discussion of the anonymous baroque play *Die glorreiche Marter Joannes von Nepomuck unter Wenzeslao dem Faulen, König der Böhmen.* Not only does the title resonate with Nepomuk Schneidewein's martyrdom, but Benjamin focused on a scene where one of the intriguers echoes the mythological speeches of his victim by changing the last word of each passage so that it would receive an ominous meaning.[125] For Benjamin, the echo effect illustrates how the separation of sound and meaning becomes a source of *Trauer:* "the spoken word is only afflicted by meaning, so to speak, as if by an inescapable disease; it breaks off in the middle of the process of resounding, and the damming up of the feeling, which was ready to pour forth, provokes mourning. Here meaning is encountered, and will continue to be encountered as the reason for mournfulness."[126] Given that sound is expressive and that meaning is constructed, however, Benjamin claimed "[t]he antithesis of sound and meaning would be at its most intense, where it were possible to combine both in *one*, without their actual coherence in the sense of forming an organic linguistic structure."[127] Benjamin's definition of allegory is a description of the total *Trauer* in Leverkühn's *Lamentations:* a composition of "utmost calculation" and "*at the same time* purely expressive"—both a word and a wail.[128] Deeper still, Benjamin's diagnosis applies directly to the musical dimension of Mann's montage technique, where names—Kretzschmar, Wiesengrund, Adrian, Nepomuk (and many more)—are echos of real names, so that "the echo, the true domain of the free play of sound, is now, so to speak, taken over by meaning."[129] Because of "the conversion of pure sound of creaturely language into richly significant irony," Mann's modernist musical montage is melancholic.[130] The novelist himself is the intriguer, who, as in a baroque play, masters "the harmless effusion of an onomatopoetic natural language" with meanings that become both "the obstacle, and so the origin of mourning."[131]

Thus what happens in Mann's novel is what Dominick LaCapra has argued about Freud's essay: melancholia is "both a precondition to (or even necessary aspect of) mourning and that which can block processes of mourning insofar as it becomes excessive or functions as an object of fixation."[132] That very excess is the strategy of Leverkühn's *Lamentations:* when its mournful tone has become excessive, blocking, and fixated; when the melancholic male gaze of the composer has completely usurped the mourning voice of woman; when the work "no longer knows anything unthematic" so that there is "no longer any free note"; and when the lament has become "non-dynamic, lacking in development, without drama, in the same way that concentric rings made by a stone thrown into water spread ever farther, without drama and always the same."[133] For Mann, the Nietzscheian *Augenblick* of a joyous eternal return had become synonymous with eternal misery. That total *Trauer* was the precondition for hope.

Although Adorno, as Mann reported, "took issue" with the end of the *Lamentations,* "in which after all the darkness, a ray of hope, the possibility of grace, appears"; although Mann admitted that he "had kindled too much light, had been too lavish with the consolation"—the revised ending, however scaled back, continued to invoke a "hope beyond hopelessness," a "transcendence of despair," and a "miracle that passes belief."[134] In abandoned pages for the *Story of the Novel,* Mann wrote that Adorno had "implored" the novelist "to mobilize all of his art" in order to speak of redemptive grace "in a more subtle, more vague, more soft, more doubtful way, indeed, to raise it to a paradox."[135] Hence Zeitblom came to speak of a double paradox: the "artistic paradox" that expression is "born out of the whole construction" which parallels the "religious paradox" that "out of the deepest irremediable despair hope might germinate."[136] Hence Zeitblom came to conclude the novel asking "when out of uttermost hopelessness—a miracle beyond the power of belief—will the light of hope dawn?" But his description of the cantata's ending had already given an answer:

> Only listen to the ending, listen with me: One instrumental group after the other steps back, and what remains as the work fades away is the high G of a Cello, the last word, the final sound dying away, slowly vanishing in a *pianissimo* fermata. Then nothing more—silence and night. But the tone which hangs there resounding in silence, which is no more, to which only the soul listens, and which was the dying note of sorrow—is no longer that; it changes its meaning, it abides in the night.[137]

Echoing the moment of Adrian's collapse, the novel's dialectical movement comes to a standstill in the twofold paradox of its double ending—the musical one in chapter 46 and the narrative one in the Epiloge, chapter 48. Lucifer is both the fallen angel and a source of light; both a fading morning star and the harbinger of a new day. That his "poetic final cadence" was, as Mann remarked already in 1949, "quoted in almost every discussion of the book"; that it has been quoted in almost every discussion of the book ever since; indeed, that it has been quoted here—all this testifies not only to the urgency of his need for transcendence, but also to his desire of satisfying this need through a poetry so powerful that it makes people cry.[138] If Mann's final poetic cadence continued to reverberate beyond the book itself, it has done so like an echo resounding beyond the *Echo des Verstummens.*

As the very *soul* of the cantata and the novel, Adorno would not have wanted to hear this echo as an "anthropological" but as an "historical" gesture; as the farewell to Germany and German culture, epitomized by a German music whose total modernism has reached the point of undoing itself. If the structural C♯ of the *Eroica* was, as Wagner claimed, the note that "represents *all* modern music," then the ornamental C♯ in the final statement of the Arietta theme would represent the particular moment that transcends all that music.[139] And its echo—the cello's high G ending the *Lamentations*—would need to be heard as an echo of Echo, who first comes alive in the variant with the added C♯, no longer scanning "heaven's blue" but "Oh *thou* heaven's blue." The minute alteration created Adorno's "humanizing variant." It is no longer merely a color, but the color of someone's eyes. Just as for Adorno "nature, having become the ego, opens its eyes *as* ego," Zeitblom hears the dying G as the "last word" of the *Lamentations* echoing the last words of the Arietta theme, which said "Oh thou heaven's blue" and took "a deep and silent farewell look."

The cello's high G, then, would be not only the last *modern* note, but also the last *German* note. Modern music, Adorno concluded in the first part of the *Philosophy of New Music* "sees absolute oblivion as its goal. It is the true message in the bottle."[140] Hence it is only as a *disappearing* tone that the high G could be, as the ending of *Negative Dialectics* asserts "of relevance to the absolute." Although Mann had followed Adorno's advice not to let Leverkühn leave the cantata unfinished, the concluding "symphonic Adagio" nevertheless ends like a fragment. While its open-endedness is reminiscent of "Der Abschied" from Mahler's *Das Lied von der Erde,* its gesture of falling silent recalls the "Adagissimo" concluding the last movement of Mahler's Ninth, often heard as a premonition of the end to the composer's life, or as a sign of the end of an era.[141] If Adorno's philosophy of the particular was to show "solidarity with metaphysics at the moment of its fall,"[142] then Zeitblom's invitation to listen beyond the ending of the *Lamentations* appears to be nothing less than Mann's gesture of solidarity with the metaphysics of German music at the very moment of *its* fall. Like Jean Paul, he heard its last note fade away into silence, yet continue to resound within. Just as the dying sound is a romantic trope of transcendence, the total negation at the end of the *Lamentations* is the very condition for overcoming that negation. If the "absolute oblivion" of modern music is the very condition for the "remembrance of otherness," such remembrance would require us to search for the message in the bottle.

The Message in the Bottle

From a philological perspective, that search is not difficult to initiate, if we follow up on the similarity (whether intended or not) between the endings of Mahler's Ninth and of Leverkühn's *Lamentations*. The detail to be pursued here is well-known, yet it takes on a particularly pertinent meaning in the present context. In the *Adagissimo,* Mahler quoted the final phrase from the fourth song of his *Kindertotenlieder* (ex. 6.2a).[143] It is the song where the parent imagines that the dead children only went out of the house for a long walk on a beautiful day, but eventually realizes that they have "gone ahead" and will have no desire to return. Since the concluding lines—"We will catch up with them on those heights in the sunshine! The day is beautiful on those heights"—are carried by a deep conviction of hope, they try to resolve the stark opposition of light and darkness haunting the first song of the cycle, where the tragedy of the night meets the glaring light of the rising sun. *Sonnenschein!* is the very word on whose melisma Mahler's self-quotation comes in.

Perhaps the most salient feature of Mahler's self-reference is how it expands the last six measures of the song's melody into a cantilena played by the first violins, spanning nearly all twenty-seven measures of the *Adagissimo,* with half of them just holding the final, fifth scale degree (ex. 6.2b). While the transposed melody is faithful to the original (except for the opening seventh A♭-G♭ and the b♭² in measure 166), Mahler's rhythmic alterations create a wholly new phrase, a composed-out expressive agogic to be played *mit inniger Empfindung.* The melody gradually speeds up, hesitates, and, while losing momentum, crests on a climactic e♭³ from where it descends stepwise to the final a♭² that lingers for six measures, before dying away from triple to quadruple *pianissimo* in three fading tones.

The seamlessness with which the segment of the song emerges from the motivic material of the last movement, stated in unison at the beginning like a motto, is reminiscent of the way Schumann handled the Beethoven quotation in the first movement of his Fantasy. At the beginning of the *Adagissimo,* the octave leap opening the movement from a♭ to a♭¹ is composed out as a gradual ascent from a♭¹ to a♭², while the other two characteristic components of Mahler's motto—the distinct turn figure and the stepwise descent—are the very gestures that mark the

Example 6.2. (a) Mahler's allusion to *Kindertotenlieder* in the "Adagissimo" from the last movement of the Ninth Symphony

beginning and the ending of the song segment. Mahler eases into the quotation with the turn figure in the viola that is the equivalent of the semitonal turn created by the Ab upbeat to *"im Sonnenschein"* (itself a segment from the instrumental introduction of the song). However conspicuous the turn figure as a common feature in Mahler's melodic style, one could hear it here, as Charles Rosen had argued for Schumann's Beethoven quotation in the Fantasy, "as much to derive from what has preceded as to be the source."[144] And yet, may we not ask, as with Schumann's use of Beethoven's song, whether the words behind the wordless melody tell us something? For they program perhaps the most absolute ending of absolute music, which Bruno Walter so aptly described as "a singular hovering between the sorrows of farewell and the presentiment of celestial light."[145] Despite the different musical styles, despite the different historical situations, and despite the different biographical significance, we can hear the *Adagissimo* of Mahler's Symphony end like the "Symphonic Adagio" of Leverkühn's *Lamentations*: as a "light" that "abides in the night," as a star, as an eye—Echo's eye.

And so the last interpretive move of this book comes perhaps closest to a hermeneutics of the moment as inspired by Benjamin's idea that critical constellations work like the tracings of celestial ones. If the perception of similarity "is in any case bound to a flash of light"; if "[i]t is presented to the eye as fleetingly and transiently as a constellation of stars," then that similarity among the light, the star, and the eye is the

Example 6.2. (b) The "Adagissimo" concluding Mahler's Ninth

Example 6.2. (b) (cont.)

very theme of the second song of *Kindertotenlieder*.[146] As the hermeneutic crux of the cycle, the song is not only an allegory of Benjamin's constellation, but also participates in my broader hermeneutic constellation tracing a link between the death of children and the moment of German music in Mahler, Mann, and Adorno.

Kindertotenlieder No. 2

Friedrich Rückert (Mahler's alterations from Rückert are underlined)

> Nun seh' ich wohl, warum so dunkle Flammen
> Ihr sprühtet mir in manchem Augenblicke,
> O Augen! O Augen! Gleichsam, um voll in einem Blicke
> Zu drängen eure ganze Macht zusammen.

Dort ahnt' ich nicht, weil Nebel mich umschwammen,
Gewoben vom verblendenden Geschicke,
Daß sich der Strahl bereits zur Heimkehr schicke
Dorthin, <u>dorthin,</u> von wannen alle Strahlen stammen.

Ihr wolltet mir mit eurem Leuchten sagen:
Wir möchten nah dir [immer] bleiben gerne,
Doch ist uns das vom Schicksal abgeschlagen.

Sieh' [recht] uns <u>nur</u> an,[!] denn bald sind wir dir ferne![.]
Was dir <u>nur</u> [noch] Augen sind in diesen Tagen:[,]
In künft'gen Nächten sind es dir nur Sterne.

Now I can see why you flashed
such dark flames at me in many moments.
O eyes, as if you compressed
all your powerinto a single glance.

Before, I had no presentiment,
enshrouded in mists woven from blinding fate,
that the ray was already preparing
to go back home to that realm whence all rays stem.

You wanted to tell me with your radiance:
we would like to stay always near you.
But fate has denied us this.

Only behold us, for soon we will be far from you.
What for you in these days are only eyes,
will for you, in future nights, be only stars.[147]

One of the salient musical features of the song is the pervasive occurrence of an appoggiatura motif from the brief introduction. Although
this motif is not "determined" (as Wagner would say) until line three by
the phrase, "O Augen"—an event clearly marked by a repetition not
existing in the poem—it is not certain whether this address to the eyes
triggered the melodic idea, or vice versa (ex. 6.3).[148] (The repetition is
similar to the one that Schenker heard in the repeated B♭'s at the opening
of Schubert's "Ihr Bild," suggesting that the repetition "amounts to
'staring' at it" just as the unhappy lover, "who stands 'in dark dreams'
[is] staring at the picture of his beloved."[149]) In his analysis of the song,
Kofi Agawu observed that "*Augen* in fact embodies the fundamental
symbolic element of the poem: direct and indirect references to light
including *Leuchten* (line 9), *Strahlen* (line 8), and *Ihr sprühtet mir* (line
2). The point, then, is that Mahler focuses on a single text-derived
element in the foreground texture. This element acts as a mediator

Example 6.3. Kindertotenlieder no. 2 mm. 10–14 ("O Augen")

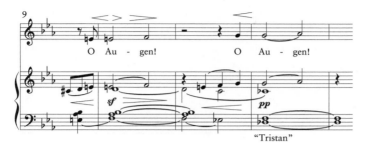

between the 'purely instrumental' and 'purely vocal' sections of the song, functioning ultimately as the essential unifying factor."[150] Agawu sees the entire melodic process to stem from the initial motivic germ, whose many occurrences develop into the song's totality.[151] If the motif signifies for Susanne Vill a single *Augenaufschlag* (an opening of the eye), the composer's addition of "voll" in line four strongly suggests how the motif encapsulates Adorno's Beethovenian totality: "The smallest detail can become the whole because it is already the whole."[152]

While the seeming pervasiveness of the *Augenaufschlag* clearly defines the song's *thematic* moment of the whole, the *harmonic* whole, which Agawu tries to capture with a Schenkerian diagram, is much more veiled on the musical surface, since the tonic emerges only very tentatively and does not receive a strong confirmation at the end (ex. 6.4). In fact, the sense of closure comes primarily when the last four measures bring back the opening motif an octave higher with a B♮ instead of B♭ and a final C-minor triad. That a Schenkerian background does not necessarily tell of striking foreground events is no news, but it invites us to reflect on the most important moment of the song: the sudden shift, via an augmented sixth chord to a D-major $^6_4$ chord above "Leuchten" in measure 41 (ex. 6.5). Here we might remind ourselves of Adorno's advice on how to listen to beautiful moments: "One only has to play the passage in the context of the whole movement and then alone in order to hear how much it owes its incommensurability, its radiance beyond the structure, to that structure."[153] The term radiance could not be more apropos. But if the harmonic progression is, taken by itself, a cliché, how can its "radiance" radiate beyond the structure of the entire song?

Two related shifts triggered by an augmented sixth chord occur besides the one on "Leuchten," both leading to the tonic, C major: one on "Strahlen" (line 8) and the other on "Sterne" (line 14). The first one may be described as what Robert Hatten has aptly termed an "arrival $^6_4$," while the second one in measure 66 (where the melody does not

Example 6.4. Background Graph of *Kindertotenlieder* no. 2 by Kofi Agawu

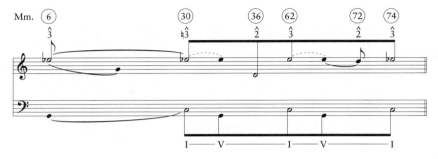

drop down to e^1 and thus effects a full "transformation to an 'elevated' major tonic triad") should be called what Hatten found in Liszt often to function as a "salvation $^6_4$."[154] The $^6_4$ at "Leuchten," by comparison, stands out at the mid-point of the song. It shifts to the supertonic; it is accompanied by the only appearance of the timpani, drawing attention to the bass motion from B♭ to A; and it is prepared by the song's longest uninterrupted melodic ascent for the voice alone, which is clearly an extension of the principal motive *without* its characteristic appoggiatura, arriving instead on the downbeat like the first sung variant of the motive in measure six. Thus highlighted in the foreground, the shift at "Leuchten" radiates beyond the background structure, becoming what might be called a *revelation* $^6_4$. Suddenly the eyes of the dying child reveal something: "You wanted to tell me with your radiance."

As a glance, therefore, that radiance is doubly telling. Besides answering to the parent's anguish, it also speaks—allegorically—to the hermeneutics of Schenker's mature harmonic theory (often seen as a paradigm of music theory), and to the general theory of hermeneutics. In *Der freie Satz* (1935), the third volume of his *Neue musikalische Theorien und Phantasien,* Schenker headed his first chapter on "The Background" with a passage from Goethe's *Farbenlehre* that contains the phrase "with every intent glance at the world we theorize."[155] Already in his analysis of Beethoven's piano sonata op. 110, Schenker had traced the German *theorizieren* to the Greek verb *theorein,* which means "to behold" or "to contemplate," and which he translated as *anschauen*— a verb that means both "to look at" and "to intuit."[156] Surely, Schenker was also aware that the Greek verb *phantazein* meant "to make visible." As William Pastille has shown, Schenker emulated Goethe's method of scientific interpretation—morphology—where the theoretical activity of "painstaking observation prepares the intuition for a spontaneous and sudden flash of insight called the *aperçu,* the apperception of the law

Example 6.5. Kindertotenlieder no. 2 mm. 38–47

underlying the varied appearances of similar phenomena."[157] Hence the "synoptic vision" of the *Ursatz* means "the resolution of all discrepancies in an ultimate unity."[158] Moreover, if "[t]he fundamental structure represents the totality," the totality of a piece enters into the totality of tonal music.[159]

Although Schenker conceived his theory in opposition to musical

Example 6.5. (cont.)

hermeneutics, he practiced a hermeneutics of the moment—that is, of the moment of the whole where the *aperçu* of intuition corresponds with the inspired *Augenblick* of creation. A central concept of the *Genieästhetik,* Schenker called it *das Wunder des Stegreifs,* best rendered as "the miracle of improvisation *on the spur of the moment,* which makes the whole into a single shape."[160] As early as the

Example 6.5. (cont.)

Harmonielehre, Schenker had suggested that "one should finally get used to looking the tones into the eyes like creatures"; and as late as in *Der freie Satz* he declared that in the "creating and re-creating" of the *Ursatz* one must "keep" the "triangle" of the I–V–I progression not only in one's "ear" but also one's "eye":

> The *Ursatz* is always creating, always present and active: this "simultane-ity" [*Gleichzeitigkeit*] in the vision of the composer is certainly not a greater miracle than that which issues from the true experiencing of a

moment of time [*Augenblick*]: in this most brief space we feel something very like the composer's perception, that is, the meeting of past, present, and future.[161]

In other words, if "the *Urlinie* is the composer's gift of sight," then we must look into the composer's eye. The more a Schenkerian analysis approaches the background as the moment of structure, the more its graphs approach the condition of pictures seen at a single glance and looking back at us.[162]

But thus beheld under the theoretical gaze, music no longer moves. In language, such pictorial arrest belongs to the tradition of ekphrasis, where, according to W.J.T. Mitchell, the ekphrastic hope to "give voice to a mute art object" also tends to conjure up what he called ekphrastic fear, which silences speech through the image.[163] In the analysis of music, ekphrastic fear is synonymous with the anxiety of losing what is specific to music: sound unfolding in time. As Rose Rosengard Subotnik has put it so aptly: "One is tempted to argue that structural listening makes more use of the eyes than of the ears."[164] Because *Augenmusik* is mute and motionless, it raises a deep suspicion against a music theory that Martin Jay would call "ocularcentric."[165] The constant fear that fluid music might be frozen into a formal, motivic, or harmonic diagram has fueled anxieties over the destruction of music's vital essence. The aesthetic premise of organicism in the early nineteenth century went hand in hand with the comparison of music analysis to the "dissection" of dead bodies, just as the medical gaze destroys life precisely when searching for its essence.[166] At worst, therefore, the absolute eye of Schenker's theoretical fantasies poses the greatest danger to absolute music. Just as Adrian Leverkühn denounced the deadening effect of his evil eye on Echo, he denounced the destructive power of his own "speculative" dodecaphony in which the compositional construction coincided with its theoretical systematization—*speculatio* being, along with *contemplatio,* the Latin translation of *theoria.*

Adorno was well aware of that danger. Hence the moment of the whole that the structural listener grasps like an image, had to be undone by the moment of the particular. For the very moment in which artworks become images, he wrote, "the instant in which what is interior becomes exterior, the outer husk is exploded; their *apparition,* which makes them an image, always at the same time destroys them as image."[167] Thus the theoretical gaze of the structural listener may seek to arrest the musical process, but at a particular *Augenblick* the work looks back—both exposing and exploding that gaze. Since for Benjamin "to experience the aura of an phenomenon means to invest it with the ability to look at us in return,"[168] the paradoxical dialectic between the

Augenblick of the whole and the *Augenblick* of the particular also lurks behind his distinction between trace and aura (discussed above in conjunction with Schumann's distinction between close reading and the poetics of distance): "The trace is the appearance of closeness, however distant what left the trace behind. The aura is the appearance of a distance, however close what created it. In the trace we get hold of a thing, in the aura the thing gets hold of us."[169]

Theory traces. Yet however close the theoretical gaze and however firm its speculative grasp on the whole, it remains as cold as the water of the Cow Trough. It makes us shiver. But the aura of the artwork, however distant, is its gaze which grasps *us*. It makes us shudder. It gives us the whole like a rainbow that recedes when one comes too close, still feeling its presence.[170] If "the instant of appearance in artworks is indeed the paradoxical unity or the balance between the vanishing and the preserved," the second song from *Kindertotenlieder* would be an allegory of that *Augenblick*: the suspension of the dialectic between the moment of the whole and the moment of the particular, or between shiver and shudder.[171] Although the fleeting appearance of the supertonic could never belong to the *Ursatz*, the d^2 at "Leuchten" may still connect to the melodic descent of the *Urlinie*. It is a structural moment and not. Mahler's shudder shatters Schenker's ekphrastic hope of fitting this crucial moment into the totality of the piece and that of tonal music. This is how, perhaps, the structural moment at "radiance" radiates beyond the moment of structure. If the musical "breakthrough" as a category of Adorno's material theory of form was meant "to endow music through theory with a voice"; if to understand Mahler "would be to endow the music's structure with speech, while technically locating the expressive intentions that appear like a flash of lightning"[172]—then the radiant breakthrough in "Nun seh ich wohl" coincides in the poem with the moment the eyes gain a voice and speak.

The line "You wanted to tell me with your radiance" marks the caesura between octave and sestet. Initially blind to the many former glances of the child's feverish eyes, suddenly the parent understands them. While the parent was tracing the eyes, they suddenly look back and speak: we will be stars. Stars stare. Although this is an old poetic trope, the parent discovers this similarity anew. That is why we can hear the song as an allegory of constellation, as expressed by Benjamin's sketch to his essay "On the Mimetic Faculty": "The perception of similarity is in any case bound to a flash of light. . . . It is presented to the eye as fleetingly and transiently as a constellation of stars."[173] The D-major $\frac{6}{4}$, then, transmits a simultaneous sense of arrival and transience: the music takes a deep breath and breathes out. It follows Adorno's "mimetic impulse," which is the moment of expression that breaks through rational construction to speak and to gesture. Where the moment of structure is immobile, the moment that radiates beyond it is moving. At the moment of death there is life beyond death. Suddenly, the child's dying eyes have a future as stars.

The progression with which Mahler expressed the parent's "longing for the children's radiant eyes" was instantly recognized as belonging to the family of Tristanesque "motives of longing."[174] As the late Christopher Lewis has pointed out, "the second 'O Augen,' the form of the motive towards which the music has been striving since its opening measures, is not merely reminiscent of *Tristan*: it quotes *Tristan*."[175] Surely Mahler knew that Wagner's perhaps most famous musical gesture received its dramatic determination at the very moment Tristan and Isolde consume the love potion (thinking it to be the death potion) at the end of act 1: "they both shudder and gaze into one another's eyes with the utmost emotion, but without changing their position, while their death-defiant expression changes to the glow of love." "Tristan" sings Isolde. "Isolde" sings Tristan. And the music shifts to the climatic deceptive cadence that will return in act 3 when he "raises his eyes to her, dying."

In Mahler's song the crucial chord of the Tristan quotation (Db-F-B-G/leading to Ab) occurs three times: first the second "O Augen" (m. 13), last in the postlude (m. 70), and in the middle right before "You wanted to tell me with your radiance" (m. 37). If we are meant to hear "O Augen" at these moments, the placement in the middle is the most telling one. Instead of blandly replicating Wagner's climatic deceptive cadence by resolving the dominant seventh on Db to D major at the moment of recognition, Mahler intervened, as it were, with the augmented sixth that added a sense of surprise to the feeling of arrival and transience. The D major at "Leuchten" thus functions more like the D major in the last movement of the First Symphony, which is the paradigmatic breakthrough in Mahler's oeuvre, sounding, in the composer's words, "as though it had fallen from heaven"—even though it is the tonic.[176] In the *Kindertotenlieder*, too, the modal mixture between D minor and D major frames the cycle with its characteristic chiaroscuro, which finally resolves in the D-major coda of the last song, where the children have "come to rest as if in the mother's house." *Schoß* ("womb") was the word that Mahler had in the manuscript of the song, changing the alteration back to "Haus" in the *Stichvorlage,* as if to erase a slip that could not be more Freudian. If this is Mahler's gesture of homecoming, the obsessive antagonism between D minor and D major in the first movement of the Ninth as well as the D-major breakthrough in the Burleske surely come to rest—like a distant echo—in the "Adagissimo"'s farewell. Twisted into the twilight of Db, the song's *Sonnenschein* has faded into an oscillation between F and F♭: like flickering starlight bending towards us; like Echo's eyes.

"Are there earthly beings as well as things that look back out of the stars that open their eyes only in the skies?" we should recall Benjamin one last time. "Are not the stars with their glance from afar the original phenomenon of aura?"[177] Nothing shatters human hope on the wholeness of life more than the death of a child. Yet the fact that this death is not only the source of greatest grief, but may also become a source of human hope is Adorno's "invariant" of an "anthropological gesture" that endures with the historical gesture of farewell in Mahler's Ninth and Mann's novel. As the anthropologist C. Nadia Seremetakis recorded from a Greek woman recalling from her youth: "When children died they told us they were up in the sky, and the stars of the sky [*asterákia touranoú*] were their eyes or the little candles they held to light up the earth."[178]

From the "Adagissimo" of Mahler's Ninth and the *Adagio* of Leverkühn's *Lamentations,* a glimpse of that light seems to look at us. "For sometimes it was white in the crack" of the dying Nepomuk's eyes. "The grace that Germany needs," Mann had concluded *Germany and the Germans,* "all of us need it."[179] Whether or not we want to echo that claim for the moment of German music depends on what we see in Echo's eyes; that is, whether the star whose light abides in the night is in modernist terms no less, or in postmodernist terms, no more than a moment.

NOTES TO INTRODUCTION

1. See *Neue Zeitschrift für Musik* 7 (1837), 35. Cf. Novalis, *Schriften,* ed. Richard Samuel and Paul Kluckhohn, (Stuttgart: W. Kohlhammer, 1960–88), 3:283–84. The passages in parentheses were part of the original entry, cut by Friedrich Schlegel and Ludwig Tieck in their edition of Novalis. Schumann possessed the fourth edition of *Novalis Schriften* (Berlin: G. Reimer, 1826), where the fragment appears in volume 2 on pages 130–31. See also pages 53 and 278 (note 8) below.

2. In a narrow sense, my title alludes to a series of articles initiated by Walter Wiora, "Zwischen absoluter und Programmusik," in *Festschrift Friedrich Blume zum 70. Geburtstag,* ed. Anna Amalie Abert and Wilhelm Pfannkuch (Kassel: Bärenreiter, 1963), 381–88; followed up first by Ludwig Finscher, "'Zwischen absoluter und Programmusik': Zur Interpretation der deutschen romantischen Symphonie," in *Über Symphonien: Beiträge zu einer musikalischen Gattung,* ed. Christoph-Hellmut Mahling (Tutzing: H. Schneider, 1979), 103–15, and later by Anthony Newcomb, "Once More Between Absolute and Program Music: Schumann's Second Symphony," *Nineteenth-Century Music* 7 (1984): 233–50. For diverse approaches to musical hermeneutics see Carl Dahlhaus, ed., *Beiträge zur musikalischen Hermeneutik* (Regensburg: G. Bosse, 1975); Gernot Gruber and Siegfried Mauser, eds., *Musikalische Hermeneutik im Entwurf: Thesen und Diskussionen* (Regensburg: Laaber, 1994); Wolfgang Gratzer and Siegfried Mauser, eds., *Hermeneutik in musikwissenschaftlichen Kontext: Internationales Symposion Salzburg 1992* (Laaber: Laaber, 1995).

3. David Blackbourn, *The Long Nineteenth Century: A History of Germany, 1780–1918* (New York: Oxford University Press, 1998), xiii.

4. David E. Wellbery, *The Specular Moment: Goethe's Early Lyric and the Beginnings of Romanticism* (Stanford: Stanford University Press, 1996), 3–26, especially 10–18.

5. Adorno's writings are generally cited throughout this book from the *Gesammelte Schriften,* ed. Rolf Tiedemann (Frankfurt am Main: Suhrkamp, 1971–86). Where translations for Adorno and other authors have been used or consulted, the page number of the translation will be given in parentheses, and, where applicable, a note that it has been modified. The current quote from *Philosophie der neuen Musik* is from volume 12 of the *Gesammelte Schriften,* 30; translation from Theodor W. Adorno, *Philosophy of Modern Music,* trans. Anne G. Mitchell and Wesley V. Blomster (New York: Seabury Press, 1973), 22.

6. Cosima Wagner, *Cosima Wagner's Diaries,* ed. Martin Gregor-Dellin and Dietrich Mack, trans. Geoffrey Skelton (New York: Harcourt Brace Jovanovich, 1978–1980), 1:378 (17 June 1871) (emphasis added); Scott Burnham, *Beethoven Hero* (Princeton: Princeton University Press, 1995), 3–28.

7. Carl Dahlhaus, *The Idea of Absolute Music*, trans. Roger Lustig (Chicago: University of Chicago Press, 1989) was the first to trace the idea of absolute music from its origins in early Romanticism through the fin-de-siècle, though others have more recently tried to limit or to expand its applicablity. While Mark Evan Bonds has argued that the idea of absolute music emerged only after 1850, as distinct from an idealist aesthetic of instrumental music, Daniel Chua has located the origin of opera as the starting point for a history of modern instrumental reason in Max Weber's sense. Of even broader historical scope, though with a more circumscribed thematic focus, is Gary Tomlinson's survey of the changing relations between the metaphysics of the operatic voice and modern subjectivy. See Mark Evan Bonds, "Idealism and the Aesthetics of Instrumental Music at the Turn of the Nineteenth Century," *Journal of the American Musicological Society* 50 (1997): 387–420; Daniel K.L. Chua, *Absolute Music and the Construction of Meaning* (Cambridge: Cambridge University Press, 1999); Gary Tomlinson, *Metaphysical Song: An Essay on Opera* (Princeton: Princeton University Press, 1999).

8. Carl Dahlhaus, "Das 'Verstehen' von Musik und die Sprache der musikalischen Analyse," in *Klassische und romantische Musikästhetik* (Laaber: Laaber, 1988), 318–29; and John Neubauer, *The Emancipation of Music from Language: Departure from Mimesis in Eighteenth-Century Aesthetics* (New Haven: Yale University Press, 1986).

9. Bonds, "Idealism and the Aesthetics of Instrumental Music at the Turn of the Nineteenth Century," 387.

10. Hermann Kretzschmar, "Anregungen zur Förderung musikalischer Hermeneutik," and "Neue Anregungen zur Förderung musikalischer Hermeneutik: Satzästhetik," in *Gesammelte Aufsätze über Musik und Anderes Vol. 2: Gesammelte Aufsätze aus den Jahrbüchern der Musikbibliothek Peters* (Leipzig: C.F. Peters, 1911), 168–92 and 280–93. Ian Bent, ed., *Music Analysis in the Nineteenth Century Volume 2: Hermeneutic Approaches* (Cambridge: Cambridge University Press, 1994), 1; Carl Dahlhaus, *Nineteenth-Century Music*, trans. J. Bradford Robinson (Berkeley: University of California Press, 1989), 11.

11. Wilhelm Heinrich Wackenroder, *Herzensergiessungen eines kunstliebenden Klosterbruders* (Stuttgart: P. Reclam, 1963), 109. Carl Dahlhaus, "Fragmente zur musikalischen Hermeneutik," in *Beiträge zur musikalischen Hermeneutik*, ed. Carl Dahlhaus, 159–72, at 159.

12. Friedrich Schlegel, *Kritische Friedrich-Schlegel-Ausgabe*, ed. Ernst Behler, Jean-Jacques Anstett, and Hans Eichner (Munich: F. Schöningh, 1958), 16:104 (fragment 245). Hans Georg Nägeli, "Versuch einer Norm für die Recensenten der musikalischen Zeitung," *Allgemeine musikalische Zeitung* 5 (1802/3): 225–37, 265–74, at 272. See also Heike Stumpf, " . . . *wollet mir jetzt durch die phantastisch verschlungenen Kreuzgänge folgen!": Metaphorisches Sprechen in der Musikkritik der ersten Hälfte des 19. Jahrhunderts* (Frankfurt am Main: P. Lang, 1996), 37–38.

13. Friedrich Schlegel, *Kritische Friedrich-Schlegel-Ausgabe*, 3:296.

14. Jean Paul, *Flegeljahre*, in *Sämtliche Werke* (Weimar: Hermann Böhlaus Nachfolger, 1927) ser. 1, vol. 10:181–82. See also Kretzschmar, "Anregungen zur Förderung musikalischer Hermeneutik," 169–70: "Denn diejenigen, die von

einer Instrumentalkomposition ein durchaus klares Bild mit hinwegnehmen, ihre Grundgedanken und *in jedem Augenblick auch deren Entwickelung verstanden haben,* bilden die Minderheit der Hörer." (emphasis added).

15. Theodor W. Adorno, "On the Fetish–Character in Music and the Regression of Listening," in *The Essential Frankfurt School Reader,* ed. Andrew Arato and Eike Gebhardt (New York: Urizen Books, 1978), 270–99, at 273, 286. In his provocative study *Music in the Moment* (Ithaca: Cornell University Press, 1997), Jerrold Levinson defines "concateationism" as the "idea that music essentially presents itself for understanding as a chain of overlapping and mutually involving parts of small extent, rather than either a seamless totality or an architectural arrangement" (p. 13).

16. Theodor W. Adorno, "Schöne Stellen," in *Gesammelte Schriften* 18:695–718, at 695 and 700.

17. *Kritische Friedrich-Schlegel-Ausgabe,* 16:163 (fragment 930): "Auch das größte System ist doch nur Fragment." For a variety of approaches to the problem of fragment and totality see, Lucien Dällenbach and Christiaan L. Hart Nibbrig, eds., *Fragment und Totalität* (Frankfurt: Suhrkamp, 1984).

18. Philippe Lacoue-Labarthe and Jean-Luc Nancy, *The Literary Absolute: The Theory of Literature in German Romanticism,* trans. Philip Barnard and Cheryl Lester (Albany: State University of New York Press, 1988), 11 and 43. See also Charles Rosen, *The Romantic Generation* (Cambridge: Harvard University Press, 1995), 48 and his extensive discussion of the fragment in romantic music.

19. *Kritische Friedrich-Schlegel-Ausgabe,* 16:67–68 (fragments 73 and 84). On the notion of "cyclical reading" see Willy Michel, *Ästhetische Hermeneutik und frühromantische Kritik: Friedrich Schlegels fragmentarische Entwürfe, Rezensionen, Charakteristiken und Kritiken* (1795–1801) (Göttingen: Vandenhoeck und Ruprecht, 1982), 56–83.

20. A late note to Hölderlin's draft of "Die Schlange" in Friedrich Hölderlin, *Sämtliche Werke,* ed. Friedrich Beissner (Stuttgart: W. Kohlhammer, 1946–1985), 2.1:339. Novalis, *Werke,* 3:256 (fragment 87).

21. Wilhelm Dilthey, "Die Enstehung der Hermeneutik," in *Gesammelte Schriften* (Stuttgart: B.G. Teubner, 1957), 5:317–31, at 330 (emphasis added). The Goethe quote stems from the letter to Lavater (20 September 1780), see *Goethes Briefe: Hamburger Ausgabe* (Hamburg: C. Wegner, 1962), 1:325. For Schleiermacher, the "difficult question" had been precisely "where the fore-knowledge of the whole should come from." Friedrich Schleiermacher, *Hermeneutik,* ed. Heinz Kimmerle (Heidelberg: C. Winter, 1959), 144.

22. Immanuel Kant, *Critique of Judgment,* trans. Werner S. Pluhar (Indianapolis: Hackett, 1987), 182.

23. Friedrich Schleiermacher, *Hermeneutics: The Handwritten Manuscripts,* ed. Heinz Kimmerle, trans. James Duke and Jack Forstman (Missoula: Scholars Press for The American Academy of Religion, 1977), 41 and 118.

24. See Mary Sue Morrow, *German Music Criticism in the Late Eighteenth Century: Aesthetic Issues in Instrumental Music* (Cambridge: Cambridge University Press, 1997) chapters 5 and 6; on the conjunction of inexhaustibility and genius (111); on indefiniteness and criticism (126); on unity and whole (143–44).

25. Peter Szondi, *Introduction to Literary Hermeneutics*, trans. Martha Woodmansee (Cambridge: Cambridge University Press, 1995), 108.

26. "Jedes Kunstwerk ist ein Augenblick; jedes gelungene ein Einstand, momentanes Innehalten des Prozesses, als der es dem beharrlichen Auge sich offenbart." Adorno, *Ästhetische Theorie, Gesammelte Schriften* 7:17. For a different translation see Theodor W. Adorno, *Aesthetic Theory*, ed. Gretel Adorno and Rolf Tiedemann, trans. Robert Hullot-Kentor (Minneapolis: University of Minnesota Press, 1997), 6.

27. Theodor W. Adorno, "Fragment über Musik und Sprache," in *Quasi una fantasia, Gesammelte Schriften*, 16:251–56, at 254; "Music and Language: A Fragment," in *Quasi una Fantasia: Essays on Modern Music*, trans. Rodney Livingstone (London: Verso, 1992), 1–6, at 4 (translation modified).

28. Karl Heinz Bohrer, *Suddenness: On the Moment of Aesthetic Appearance*, trans. Ruth Crowley (New York: Columbia University Press, 1994): 11, 39–69 (chapter 3), and 203–20.

29. Adorno, *Ästhetische Theorie*, 113 and 108, (72 and 69).

30. Arthur Schopenhauer, *Sämtliche Werke*, ed. Arthur Hübscher (Wiesbaden: E. Brockhaus, 1948), 3:415 (*Ergänzungen zum dritten Buch* of *Die Welt als Wille und Vorstellung*).

31. Theodor W. Adorno, "Über das gegenwärtige Verhältnis von Philosophie und Musik (1953)," in *Gesammelte Schriften* 18:154–55. Translation (amended) from Max Paddison, "The Language–Character of Music: Some Motifs in Adorno," in *Mit den Ohren denken: Adornos Philosophie der Musik*, ed. Richard Klein and Claus-Steffen Mahnkopf (Frankfurt am Main: Suhrkamp, 1998), 71–91, at 78.

32. Paul de Man, "The Rhetoric of Temporality," in *Blindness and Insight: Essays in the Rhetoric of Contemporary Criticism* (Minneapolis: University of Minnesota Press, 1983), 187–228, at 207.

33. Georg Friedrich Creuzer, *Symbolik und Mythologie der alten Völker, besonders der Griechen*, 2nd ed. (Leipzig: Heyer und Leske, 1819), 1:71 and 70. Cf. Walter Benjamin, *Ursprung des deutschen Trauerspiels* (Frankfurt am Main: Suhrkamp, 1963), 179–84; Walter Benjamin, *The Origin of German Tragic Drama*, trans. John Osborne (London: NLB, 1977), 163–67.

34. Benjamin, *Ursprung des deutschen Trauerspiels*, 182–83 (166, translation modified).

35. Alan Street, "Superior Myths, Dogmatic Allegories: The Resistance to Musical Unity," *Music Analysis* 8 (1989), 77–123, at 101–9.

36. Benjamin, *Ursprung des deutschen Trauerspiels*, 182 and 193–94 (165 and 174–75, translation modified).

37. Ibid., 221–22 (my translation; cf. 197).

38. Rolf Tiedemann, "Concept, Image, Name: On Adorno's Utopia of Knowledge," in *The Semblance of Subjectivity: Essays in Adorno's Aesthetic Theory*, ed. Tom Huhn and Lambert Zuidervaart (Cambridge: MIT Press, 1997), 123–45, at 126.

39. Ibid., 125.

40. Theodor W. Adorno, *Mahler: Eine musikalische Physiognomik*, in *Gesammelte Schriften*, 13:149–319, at 185; *Mahler: A Musical Physiognomy*,

trans. Edmund Jephcott (Chicago: The University of Chicago Press, 1992), 36 (translation modified).

41. Adorno, *Ästhetische Theorie,* 125 (80, translation modified); the second quote stems from Theodor W. Adorno, *Beethoven: Philosophie der Musik: Fragmente und Texte,* ed. Rolf Tiedemann (Frankfurt am Main: Suhrkamp, 1994), 344–45; *Beethoven: The Philosophy of Music,* trans. Edmund Jephcott (Stanford: Stanford University Press, 1998), 238.

42. Cited in Jacques Le Rider, *Modernity and Crises of Identity: Culture and Society in Fin-de-Siècle Vienna,* trans. Rosemary Morris (New York: Continuum, 1993), 50.

43. Walter Benjamin, *Gesammelte Schriften,* ed. Rolf Tiedemann and Hermann Schweppenhäuser (Frankfurt am Main: Suhrkamp, 1972–89), 5:578.

44. Adorno, *Beethoven,* 250–51 (174–75).

45. Theodor W. Adorno, *Negative Dialektik, Gesammelte Schriften* 6:400; *Negative Dialectics,* trans. E.B. Ashton (New York: Seabury Press, 1973), 408 (translation modified).

46. Theodor W. Adorno and Walter Benjamin, *The Complete Correspondence 1928–1940,* ed. Henri Lonitz, trans. Nicholas Walker (Cambridge: Harvard University Press, 1999), 283.

47. Christine Eichel, *Vom Ermatten der Avantgarde zur Vernetzung der Künste: Perspektiven einer interdisziplinären Ästhetik im Spätwerk Theodor W. Adornos* (Frankfurt am Main: Suhrkamp, 1993), 187–221.

48. Ernst Bloch, *Essays on the Philosophy of Music,* trans. Peter Palmer (Cambridge: Cambridge University Press, 1985), 98; Hans Heinrich Eggebrecht, *Die Musik Gustav Mahlers* (Wilhelmshaven: Florian Noetzel, 1999), 86–89; see also Eichel's discussion of Eggebrecht in, *Vom Ermatten der Avantgarde zur Vernetzung der Künste,* 197–221.

49. Andreas Huyssen, *After the Great Divide: Modernism, Mass Culture, Postmodernism* (Bloomington: Indiana University Press, 1986), 213. On the narrative and mimetic impulse in Adorno's philosophizing, see Fredric Jameson, *Late Marxism: Adorno, or, the Persistence of the Dialectic* (London: Verso, 1990), 68–69.

50. Ibid., 247.

51. Adorno, *Negative Dialectics,* 28–29. The claim is discussed by Lambert Zuidervaart, *Adorno's Aesthetic Theory: The Redemption of Illusion* (Cambridge: MIT Press, 1991), 304–7.

52. Adorno, *Philosophie der Neuen Musik,* 43 (37–8; translation modified).

53. Thomas Mann, *Doctor Faustus: The Life of the German Composer Adrian Leverkühn as Told by a Friend,* trans. Helen Tracy Lowe-Porter (New York: Modern Library, 1992), 658.

54. Max Pensky, *Melancholy Dialectics: Walter Benjamin and the Play of Mourning* (Amherst: University of Massachusetts Press, 1993). Eric L. Santner, *Stranded Objects: Mourning, Memory, and Film in Postwar Germany* (Ithaca: Cornell University Press, 1990).

55. Sigmund Freud, "Mourning and Melancholia," in *The Standard Edition of the Complete Psychological Works of Sigmund Freud* ed. and trans. James Strachey (London: Hogarth, 1953–74), 14:243–58, at 247.

56. See Dominick LaCapra, *History and Memory after Auschwitz* (Ithaca: Cornell University Press, 1998), 183.

57. Freud, "Mourning and Melancholia," 245.

NOTES TO CHAPTER 1—BEETHOVEN'S STAR

1. See Stephen Hinton, "Not *Which* Tones? The Crux of Beethoven's Ninth," *Nineteenth-Century Music* 22 (1998): 61–77, at 75–77; see also Richard Taruskin, "Resisting the Ninth," *Nineteenth-Century Music* 12 (1989): 241–56.

2. Rainer Maria Rilke, *Sämtliche Werke* (Frankfurt am Main: Insel, 1955–66), 1: 557.

3. Johann Joachim Winckelmann, "Beschreibung des Torso im Belvedere zu Rom," in *Kleine Schriften, Vorreden, Entwürfe*, ed. Walther Rehm (Berlin: De Gruyter, 1968), 169–73. Winckelmann's description of the Belveldere Apollo and Rilke's poem are compared in Wolfgang Schadewaldt, *Winckelmann und Rilke: Zwei Beschreibungen des Apollon* (Pfullingen: G. Neske, 1968), especially 24–28. See also Peter Horst Neumann, "Rilkes *Archaischer Torso Apollos* in der Geschichte des modernen Fragmentarismus," in *Fragment und Totalität*, eds. Lucien Dällenbach and Christiaan L. Hart Nibbrig (Frankfurt am Main: Suhrkamp, 1984), 257–74, especially 266–69.

4. Winckelmann, "Beschreibung," 170.

5. Georg Wilhelm Friedrich Hegel, *Aesthetics: Lectures on Fine Art*, trans. T.M. Knox (Oxford: Clarendon Press, 1975), 153–54 (translation modified).

6. Theodor W. Adorno, *Minima Moralia, Gesammelte Schriften* 4:55; Georg Wilhelm Friedrich Hegel, *Werke*, ed. Karl Markus Michel and Eva Moldenhauer (Frankfurt am Main: Suhrkamp, 1969–79), 3:24.

7. Adorno, *Ästhetische Theorie*, 17 (my translation; cf. 6).

8. Ibid., 104 (66).

9. Bohrer, *Suddenness: On the Moment of Aesthetic Appearance*, 11.

10. Theodor W. Adorno, *Notes to Literature*, ed. Rolf Tiedemann, trans. Shierry Weber Nicholsen (New York: Columbia University Press, 1991–92), 1:10 and 16.

11. Peter Uwe Hohendahl, *Prismatic Thought: Theodor W. Adorno* (Lincoln: University of Nebraska Press, 1995), 250–51.

12. Adorno, *Ästhetische Theorie*, 172 (112).

13. Ibid., 171 (112, translation slightly modified).

14. Georg Wilhelm Friedrich Hegel, *Enzyklopädie der philosophischen Wissenschaften im Grundrisse (1830): Erster Teil: Die Wissenschaft der Logik*, in *Werke*, 8:74. Translation modified from *Hegel's Logic: Being Part One of the Encyclopedia of the Philosophical Sciences (1830)*, trans. William Wallace (Oxford: Clarendon Press, 1975), 31.

15. *Ästhetische Theorie*, 137 (88; the translation of *Durchbruch*, a term central to Adorno's aesthetics, has been changed from "rupture" to the more appropriate "breakthrough").

16. Ibid., 125 (cf. 80). Again, "celestial phenomenon" is more appropriate than Hullot-Kentor's translation, "heavenly vision" (see note 26 of Introduction).

17. Günter Figal, "Aesthetic Experience of Time: Adorno's Avant-gardism and Benjamin's Correction," in *For a Philosophy of Freedom and Strife: Politics, Aesthetics, Metaphysics,* trans. Wayne Klein (Albany: State University of New York Press, 1998), 109–24, at 119. The most thorough study on Adorno and the *Augenblick* to date is Norbert Zimmermann, *Der ästhetische Augenblick: Theodor W. Adornos Theorie der Zeitstruktur von Kunst und ästhetischer Erfahrung* (Frankfurt am Main: P. Lang, 1989); the first approach in musicology is Wolf Frobenius, "Über das Zeitmaß Augenblick in Adornos Kunsttheorie," *Archiv für Musikwissenschaft* 36 (1979): 279–305. See also Frobenius's article "Momentum/Moment, instans/instant, Augenblick," in *Hanwörterbuch der musikalischen Terminologie,* ed. Hans Heinrich Eggebrecht (Wiesbaden: F. Steiner, 1972–).

18. See Rolf Tiedemann, "Dialektik im Stillstand: Annäherungen an das Passagen-Werk," in *Dialektik im Stillstand: Versuche zum Spätwerk Walter Benjamins* (Frankfurt am Main: Suhrkamp, 1983), 9–40; and Tiedemann, "Concept, Image, Name: On Adorno's Utopia of Knowledge."

19. *Ästhetische Theorie,* 130–31 (84, translation modified). See also Figal, "Aesthetic Experience of Time," 120.

20. Theodor W. Adorno, "On Some Relationships Between Music and Painting," trans. Susan Gillespie, *Musical Quarterly* 79 (1995): 66–79, at 67.

21. Benjamin, *Gesammelte Schriften,* 5.1:578; translation modified from Figal, "Aesthetic Experience of Time," 121.

22. Figal, "Aesthetic Experience of Time," 122.

23. Ibid., 124.

24. Benjamin, "Das Passagenwerk," *Gesammelte Schriften,* 5:1148; see Tiedemann, "Dialektik im Stillstand: Annäherungen an das Passagen-Werk," 31.

25. Theodor W. Adorno, "Die Aktualität der Philosophie," in *Gesammelte Schriften* 1:325–44, at 335. About the dedication see the same volume, 383. For more examples of the suddenness of the "erkennender Blick" in Adorno see Zimmermann, *Der ästhetische Augenblick,* 195–96.

26. Walter Benjamin, "Über einige Motive bei Baudelaire," *Illuminationen,* 185–229, at 223. Translation slightly modified from "On Some Motifs in Baudelaire," *Illuminations,* ed. Hannah Arendt, trans. Harry Zohn (New York: Schocken Books, 1969), 155–200, at 188.

27. Benjamin, *Gesammelte Schriften,* 2.3:958.

28. See W.J.T. Mitchell, "What Do Pictures *Really* Want?," *October* 77 (1996): 71–82.

29. Karl Marx, *Capital: Critique of Political Economy,* trans. Ben Fowkes (Harmondsworth: Penguin Books, 1976), 1:178; See the notorious sardine can anecdote in Jacques Lacan, *The Four Fundamental Concepts of Psycho-Analysis,* ed. Jacques-Alain Miller, trans. Alan Sheridan (New York: W.W. Norton, 1977), 93–97.

30. Benjamin, *Ursprung des deutschen Trauerspiels,* 16 (my translation; cf. 34).

31. Benjamin, "Lehre vom Ähnlichen," *Gesammelte Schriften* 2.1:204–10, at 206, and its revision "Über das mimetische Vermögen," ibid., 210–13; see Frobenius, "Über das Zeitmaß Augenblick," 285–86.

32. Adorno, *Ästhetische Theorie*, 280 (cf. 187–88, where the translation is unusually free). Adorno quotes from memory here. Goethe's original sentence goes: "Die Hoffnung fuhr wie ein Stern, der vom Himmel fällt, über ihre Häupter weg." Johann Wolfgang von Goethe, *Werke: Hamburger Ausgabe,* ed. Erich Trunz (Munich: C. H. Beck, 1981) 6:456.

33. Benjamin, "Goethes Wahlverwandtschaften," in *Illuminationen,* 63–135, at 116–17. "Goethe's Elective Affinities," trans. Stanley Corngold, in *Selected Writings,* ed. Michael W. Jennings (Cambridge, Mass.: Belknap Press, 1996, 1999), 1:297–360, at 340–41.

34. Ibid., 116–17 (340–41).

35. Ibid.

36. Ibid., 116 (340). See also Frobenius, "Über das Zeitmaß Augenblick in Adornos Kunsttheorie," 284–85; and Martin Zenck, *Kunst als begriffslose Erkenntnis: Zum Kunstbegriff der ästhetischen Theorie Theodor W. Adornos* (Munich: W. Fink, 1977), 149–53.

37. Benjamin, "Goethes Wahlverwandtschaften," 135 (355).

38. Benjamin, "Über einige Motive bei Baudelaire," 212 (179).

39. Benjamin, "Goethes Wahlverwandtschaften," 135 (355–56, translation slightly modified).

40. Rolf Tiedemann, "Gretel Adorno zum Abschied," *Frankfurter Adorno Blätter* 3 (1994): 148–51, at 151.

41. Adorno, *Beethoven,* 234 (162, translation modified). For a broader perspective on Adorno's unfinished book see Stephen Hinton, "Adorno's Unfinished *Beethoven,*" *Beethoven Forum* 5 (1996): 139–54.

42. This quote and the excerpts in the next four paragraphs are from Adorno, *Beethoven,* 34–37 (13–15).

43. Franz Brendel, "Robert Schumann with Reference to Mendelssohn-Bartholdy and the Development of Modern Music in General (1845)," trans. Jürgen Thym, in *Schumann and His World,* ed. R. Larry Todd (Princeton: Princeton University Press, 1994): 317–37, at 318–19.

44. Quoted in Kristin M. Knittel, "Wagner, Deafness, and the Reception of Beethoven's Late Style," *Journal of the American Musicological Society* 51 (1998): 49–82, at 72.

45. Adorno, "Über die musikalische Verwendung des Radios," *Gesammelte Schriften 15,* 369–401, 376.

46. Adorno, *Beethoven,* 46–47 and 288 (22 and 203).

47. Adorno, *Ästhetische Theorie,* 125 (cf. 80).

48. Adorno, *Beethoven,* 44 (21).

49. Ibid., 236 (164). As Goethe put it so inimitably: "Willst du dich am Ganzen erquicken,/ So mußt du das Ganze im Kleinsten erblicken." Cited in Andreas Anglet, *Der "ewige" Augenblick: Studien zur Struktur und Funktion eines Denkbildes bei Goethe* (Cologne: Böhlau, 1991), 280.

50. Adorno, "On Some Relationships Between Music and Painting," 66.

51. Franz Brendel, "Robert Schumann mit Rücksicht auf Mendelssohn-Barthholdy, und die Entwicklung der modernen Tonkunst überhaupt," *Neue Zeitschrift für Musik* 22 (1845): 63–67, 81–83, 89–92, 113–15, 121–23, 145–47, 149–50, at 67.

52. Adorno, "Spätstil Beethovens," in *Beethoven* 183 (cf. 125, my translation).

53. Rose Rosengard Subotnik, "Adorno's Diagnosis of Beethoven's Late Style: Early Symptom of a Fatal Condition," in *Developing Variations: Style and Ideology in Western Music* (Minneapolis: University of Minnesota Press, 1991), 15–41.

54. Adorno, "Spätstil Beethovens," in *Beethoven* 184 (cf.126).

55. Adorno, *Negative Dialektik,* 400 (408, translation modified).

56. Adorno, *Ästhetische Theorie,* 531 (358, translation modified); see also Adorno, *Beethoven,* 352–53 (243).

57. Ibid., 250 (174).

58. Benjamin, *Gesammelte Schriften,* 5:578.

59. Adorno, *Beethoven,* 250 (174).

60. Bloch, *Essays on the Philosophy of Music,* 243 (translation slightly modified).

61. Benjamin, "Theses on the Philosophy of History," 257–58.

62. Hans Mayer, "Beethoven und das Prinzip Hoffnung," in *Versuche über die Oper* (Frankfurt am Main: Suhrkamp, 1981), 71–89, at 71–72.

63. Ibid., 89.

64. I differ here from Andreas Eichhorn, *Beethovens Neunte Symphonie: Die Geschichte der Aufführung und Rezeption* (Kassel: Bärenreiter, 1993), 249, who places Bloch's reaction in the tradition of a melancholic Beethoven reception.

65. Tiedemann, "Concept, Image, Name," 126.

66. Helga Lühning, "Beethovens langer Weg zum 'Fidelio'," in *Opernkomposition als Prozeß: Referate des Symposiums Bochum 1995,* ed. Werner Breig (Kassel: Bärenreiter, 1996), 65–90, at 67–72.

67. Bloch, *Essays on the Philosophy of Music,* 242.

68. See for instance, Carl Dahlhaus, *Ludwig van Beethoven: Approaches to his Music,* trans. Mary Whittall (Oxford: Clarendon Press, 1991), 181–88; and more generally, Helga Lühning and Sieghard Brandenburg, eds., *Beethoven: Zwischen Revolution und Restauration* (Bonn: Beethoven-Haus, 1989).

69. Paul Robinson, ed., *Ludwig van Beethoven, Fidelio* (Cambridge: Cambridge University Press, 1996), 5–6, 68–101, and 145–65 for the history of the opera's reception.

70. Stefan Kunze, ed., *Ludwig van Beethoven: Die Werke im Spiegel seiner Zeit: Gesammelte Konzertberichte und Rezensionen bis 1830* (Laaber: Laaber, 1987), 156.

71. Ibid.

72. Adorno, *Beethoven,* 249 (173).

73. Ibid., 248–49 (172–73). The latter quote concludes fragment 358, which, though reversed by Tiedemann in his edition of *Beethoven,* appeared, in fact, later in Adorno's notebook 13 from the year 1948. See the concordance ibid., 372 (256).

74. Stéphane Mosès, "Ideen, Namen, Sterne: Zu Walter Benjamins Metaphorik des Ursprungs," trans. Andreas Kilcher, in *Für Walter Benjamin: Dokumente, Essays und ein Entwurf,* ed. Ingrid Scheurmann and Konrad Scheurmann (Frankfurt am Main: Suhrkamp, 1992), 183–92, at 184.

75. Benjamin, *Ursprung des deutschen Trauerspiels,* 19 (37). I have changed the translation of *Willkür* from "caprice" to "arbitrariness" to make the connection to Saussure's linguistics more explicit.

76. Ibid. (emphasis added).

77. Benjamin, *Ursprung des deutschen Trauerspiels,* 17 (36). See Susan Buck-Morss, *The Origin of Negative Dialectics: Theodor W. Adorno, Walter Benjamin, and the Frankfurt Institute* (Hassocks: Harvester Press, 1977), 77–81.

78. Adorno, "Music and Language: A Fragment," in *Quasi una Fantasia,* 1–6, at 2.

79. Adorno, *Beethoven,* 248 (172–73).

80. Ibid.

81. Ibid., 245 (170).

82. Ibid.

83. Hegel, *Aesthetics,* 2. See Zuidervaart, *Adorno's Aesthetic Theory,* 165.

84. Adorno, *Ästhetische Theorie,* 98 (62)

85. Ibid.

86. A more detailed account of the quartet takes up most of Joseph Kerman's vignette "*Augenblicke* in *Fidelio,*" in *Ludwig van Beethoven, Fidelio,* ed. Paul Robinson, 132–44, at 136–42.

87. Treitschke's "new" text for the recitative opened with Leonore's enraged reaction to Pizarro ("Abscheulicher"), which harked back both to Bouilly's "exécreable Pizare!" and Ferdinando Paer's "Esecrabil Pizzarro!" (a copy of Paer's 1804 *Elenore osia L'amore conjugale* was found in Beethoven's *Nachlass*). See Willy Hess, *Das Fidelio-Buch: Beethovens Oper Fidelio, ihre Geschichte und ihre drei Fassungen* (Winterthur: Amadeus, 1986), 327–63 (Bouilly/Gaveaux) and 365–92, at 345 (34/33 in the facsimile).

88. Lühning, "Beethovens langer Weg zum 'Fidelio'," 69–70.

89. Susan McClary, "Pitches, Expression, Ideology: An Exercise in Mediation," *Enclitic* 7 (1983): 76–86. The idea is further developed in Thomas Keith Nelson, "The Fantasy of Absolute Music" (Ph.D. diss., University of Minnesota, 1998), see especially chapters 3 and 4.

90. Friedrich Schiller, "On Naive and Sentimental Poetry," in *Essays,* ed. Walter Hinderer and Daniel O. Dahlstrom (New York: Continuum, 1993), 179–260, at 232.

91. Benjamin, "Zum Bilde Prousts," *Gesammelte Schriften,* 2.1: 310–24, at 313. See Stéphane Mosès, *Der Engel der Geschichte: Franz Rosenzweig, Walter Benjamin, Gershom Scholem* (Frankfurt am Main: Jüdischer, 1994), 103. On Benjamin's elegiac form of happiness see Karl Heinz Bohrer, *Der Abschied, Theorie der Trauer: Baudelaire, Goethe, Nietzsche, Benjamin* (Frankfurt am Main: Suhrkamp, 1996), 538–52.

92. Adorno, *Ästhetische Theorie,* 106 (68) and 100 (63, translation modified).

93. Carl Czerny, *On the Proper Performance of all Beethoven's Works for the Piano,* ed. Paul Badura-Skoda (Vienna: Universal Edition, 1970), 9.

94. For instance, in the reviews of the *Allgemeine Musikalische Zeitung* from 1806 and 1814, see Kunze, *Ludwig van Beethoven, die Werke im Spiegel seiner Zeit,* 151 and 153.

95. Reprinted ibid., 173–204, at 182.

96. Ibid., 198.

97. Ibid.

98. Winton Dean, "Beethoven and Opera," in *Ludwig van Beethoven, Fidelio,* ed. Paul Robinson, 22–50, at 46.

99. See Hector Berlioz, *A travers chants,* ed. Léon Guichard (Paris: Gründ, 1971), 87–103, at 96–97.

100. For Schenker's awareness of such "widely separated high points" see, for instance, Heinrich Schenker, *The Masterwork in Music: A Yearbook,* ed. William Drabkin, trans. Ian Bent et al. (Cambridge: Cambridge University Press, 1994–97), 2:28. On the dramatic connection between vocal high points see James Webster, "The Analysis of Mozart's Arias," in *Mozart Studies,* ed. Cliff Eisen (Oxford: Clarendon, 1991), 101–99, at 166–79.

101. See Edward Hanslick's discussion of that passage in *Vom Musikalisch-Schönen: Ein Beitrag zur Revision der Ästhetik in der Tonkunst,* ed. Dietmar Strauß,(Mainz: Schott, 1990), 1:57, as one that could both express joy and rage. In fact, however, it appears as if the music refers back (despite its later composition) to the opening of the E-major overture—a connection brought home when the horns join into the climactic concluding jubilation (mm. 92ff.).

102. In the original rondo-like version, Leonore already had hit it twice in the first statement, repeated the double gesture twice more when the section came back (mm. 151–57, and eventually surpassed it with a c^3—her highest note in *Leonore* (mm. 235 and 259).

103. Surprisingly, Michel Poizat, *The Angel's Cry: Beyond the Pleasure Principle in Opera,* trans. Arthur Denner (Ithaca: Cornell University Press, 1992), 133, mentions Leonore, but does not devote a discussion to her.

104. Originally, the trumpet's first note coincided with another bb^2 on "dead." But the f^1 in *Fidelio* cedes to the trumpet call and reinforces the echo effect.

105. For two opposite views on the divine intervention see Paul Robinson, "*Fidelio* and the French Revolution," in *Ludwig van Beethoven, Fidelio,* 68–100, at 96; and Rudolf Bockholdt, "Freiheit und Brüderlichkeit in der Musik Ludwig van Beethovens," in *Beethoven: Zwischen Revolution und Restauration,* 77–107, at 83. While Bockholdt holds that the god in "O Gott, welch ein Augenblick" (which celebrates liberation) is not the *Theatergott,* he asserts that Beethoven ultimately meant the "true" God.

106. Bloch, *Essays on the Philosophy of Music,* 242, see also 240.

107. Richard Wagner, "Über die Bestimmung der Oper," *Gesammelte Schriften und Dichtungen,* 2nd ed. (Leipzig: E. W. Fritzsch, 1887–88), 9:127–56, at 152. Translation (modified) from "The Destiny of Opera" *Prose Works,* trans. William Ashton Ellis (London: Routledge and Kegan Paul, 1892–99) 5:127–56, at 152.

108. See Alfred Heuß, "Die Humanitätsmelodien im 'Fidelio'," *Neue Zeitschrift für Musik* 91 (1924): 545–52; and Willy Hess, *Das Fidelio-Buch,* 242–47.

109. Adorno, *Beethoven,* 236 (164).

110. Ibid.

111. Ibid., 39 (16–17, translation modified).

112. Ibid., 251 (174).

113. On the question of B or B♭, see Helga Lühning, "*Fidelio* zwischen Oper und Opus: Über Beethovens Revisionen des Quartetts 'Er sterbe'," *Musiktheorie* 14 (1999): 121–41, especially 129–35.

114. The autograph page is reproduced ibid., 131.

115. See Wilhelm Seidel, "Die Peripetie: Über das Quartett des zweiten Aktes," in *Von der Leonore zum Fidelio: Vorträge und Referate des Bonner Symposions 1997,* ed. Helga Lühning and Wolfram Steinbeck (Frankfurt am Main: P. Lang, 2000), 277–92. For a thorough analysis of the text–music relations in the quartet, see Walther Dürr, *Analysen, Sprache und Music: Geschichten, Gattungen, Analysemodelle* (Kassel: Bärenreiter, 1994).

116. See Burnham, *Beethoven Hero,* 12.

117. In my analysis of the passage I have benefitted from suggestions by Yonathan Malin.

118. Georg Lukács, *Goethe and His Age,* trans. Robert Anchor (New York: Grosset and Dunlap, 1969), 109.

119. Theodor W. Adorno, "Huldigung an Zerlina," in *Moments musicaux, Gesammelte Schriften* 17:34–35. See also *Beethoven,* 60 and 97 (83 and 143).

120. Adorno, "Huldigung an Zerlina," 35 and *Ästhetische Theorie,* 111 (71).

121. Benjamin, "Theses on the Philosophy of History," in *Illuminations,* 255 (translation modified).

122. Rolf Tiedemann, "Historischer Materialismus oder politischer Messianismus? Zur Interpretation der Thesen 'Über den Begriff der Geschichte'," in *Dialektik im Stillstand,* 99–142, at 126.

123. Thomas Mann, *Letters of Thomas Mann 1889–1955,* ed. and trans. Richard Winston and Clara Winston (New York: A. A. Knopf, 1971), 482. And John Weiss, *Ideology of Death: Why the Holocaust Happened in Germany* (Chicago: Ivan R. Dee, 1996), 360.

124. Benjamin, "Theses on the Philosophy of History," 256.

125. Ibid., 256–57 (translation modified).

126. All quotations in what follows are taken (though sometimes rearranged) from Klemens von Klemperer, *German Resistance Against Hitler: The Search for Allies Abroad, 1938–1945* (Oxford: Clarendon Press, 1992), 35–37.

127. Albrecht Haushofer, *Moabiter Sonette* (Zurich: Artemis, 1948), 28; translation adapted with modifications from *Moabit Sonnets,* trans. M. D. Herter Norton (New York: W. W. Norton, 1978), 42.

NOTES TO CHAPTER 2—SCHUMANN'S DISTANCE

1. "Die Phil[osophie] ist die Prosa. Ihre Consonanten. *Ferne* Phil[osophie] klingt wie Poesie—weil jeder Ruf in die Ferne Vocal wird. Auf beyden Seiten oder um sie her liegt + und minus Poesie. So wird alles in der Entfernung *Poësie—Poëm. Actio in distans.* Ferne Berge, ferne Menschen, ferne Begebenheiten etc. alles wird romantisch, quod idem est—daher ergiebt sich unsre Urpoëtische Natur." Novalis, *Das allgemeine Brouillon,* in *Schriften,* 3:302.

2. In Walter Pater, "The School of Giorgione," in *The Renaissance: Studies in*

Art and Poetry (The 1893 Text), ed. Donald L. Hill (Berkeley: University of California Press, 1980), 102–22, at 106.

3. See Richard Kramer, "A Poetics of the Remote: Goethe's *Entfernte*," in *Distant Cycles: Schubert and the Conceiving of Song* (Chicago: University of Chicago Press, 1994), 85–101; Charles Rosen, "Mountains and Song Cycles," in *The Romantic Generation*, 116–236; Peter Franklin, "Distant Sounds—Fallen Music: *Der ferne Klang* as 'Woman's Opera'?" *Cambridge Opera Journal* 3 (1991): 159–72.

4. Carl Dahlhaus, "Absolute Music and *Poésie Absolue*," in *The Idea of Absolute Music*, 141–55.

5. See Novalis, *Werke, Tagebücher und Briefe Friedrich von Hardenbergs*, ed. Hans-Joachim Mähl and Richard Samuel (Munich: C. Hanser, 1978–87), 3:475.

6. Christian Gottlieb Schocher, *Soll die Rede auf immer ein dunkler Gesang bleiben, und können ihre Arten, Gänge und Beugungen nicht anschaulich gemacht, und nach Art der Tonkunst gezeichnet werden?* (Leipzig: A. L. Reinicke, 1791), esp. p. 8; see Novalis, Schriften 3:917.

7. See Friedrich A. Kittler, *Discourse Networks 1800/1900*, trans. Michael Metteer with Chris Cullens (Stanford: Stanford University Press, 1990), 27–53.

8. Novalis, *Schriften* 3:283–84; cf. Introduction p. 1. The critical distinction between *Ton* and *Schall* relates to the one by Schocher between *Lauten* and *Tönen* (see ibid., 3:917), which goes back to Herder's *Viertes kritisches Wäldchen*. Herder had suggested that the *Schall* had an effect on the ear as an external feeling, while the *Ton* affected the inner feeling of the soul. See Johann Gottfried Herder, *Herders sämmtliche Werke*, ed. Bernhard Ludwig Suphan (et al.) Berlin: Weidmann, 1877–1913), 4:110.

9. Immanuel Kant, "Metaphysical Foundations of Natural Science," in *Philosophy of Material Nature*, trans. James W. Ellington (Indianapolis: Hackett, 1985), 2:60–61 (emphasis added).

10. Friedrich Wilhelm Joseph von Schelling, *Ideas for a Philosophy of Nature*, trans. Errol E. Harris and Peter Heath (Cambridge: Cambridge University Press, 1988), 272.

11. Novalis, *Schriften* 3:300.

12. Ibid., 335.

13. Ibid., 472.

14. Jean Paul, *Vorschule der Ästhetik*, in *Sämtliche Werke*, ser. 1, vol. 11:77; translation (modified) from Margaret R. Hale, trans., *Horn of Oberon: Jean Paul Richter's School of Aesthetics* (Detroit: Wayne State University Press, 1973), 61.

15. Immanuel Kant, *Kritik der Urteilskraft*, ed. Gerhard Lehmann (Stuttgart: P. Reclam, 1963), 134 (para. 23).

16. Jean Paul, *Kleine Nachschule zur ästhetischen Vorschule*, in *Sämtliche Werke*, ser. 1, vol. 16:428.

17. Ibid.

18. Jean Paul, *Flegeljahre*, in *Sämtliche Werke*, ser. 1, vol. 10: 85.

19. Ibid., 272.

20. Ibid., 77.

21. *Neue Zeitschrift für Musik* 2 (1835): 25. The motto reappears six years later in volume 14 (1841): 199. Schumann somewhat tempered his provocative formulation "junge dichterische Zukunft" for the *Collected Writings*, to become the usually quoted "neue poetische Zeit." Compare *Neue Zeitschrift für Musik* 2 (1835): 3, with Robert Schumann, *Gesammelte Schriften über Musik und Musiker*, ed. Martin Kreisig, 5th ed. (Leipzig: Breitkopf und Härtel, 1914), 1:38.

22. Under the rubric *Miscellen;* see *Neue Zeitschrift für Musik* 1 (1834): 1.

23. D-Zsch 4871-VIII 2 A3. For a study of the mottobook see Leander Hotaki, *Robert Schumanns Mottosammlung: Übertragung, Kommentar, Einführung* (Freiburg: Rombach, 1998).

24. See ibid., 461, where Jean Paul's definition is excerpt number 29 on page 5 in the ninth of the eleven *Hefte* of the mottobook.

25. First mentioned in Wolfgang Boetticher, *Robert Schumann: Einführung in Persönlichkeit und Werk* (Berlin: B. Hahnefeld, 1941), 611–13. See also Edward A. Lippman, "Theory and Practice in Schumann's Aesthetics," *Journal of the American Musicological Society* 17 (1964): 310–45, esp. 315–20. Schumann's copy of Jean Paul, *Sämtliche Werke* (Berlin: G. Reimer, 1826–38) is in the possession of the Schumann Haus Zwickau.

26. For a cautious approach see Gerhard Dietel, "Die Papillons und ihr Programm," in *"Eine neue poetische Zeit": Musikanschauung und stilistische Tendenzen im Klavierwerk Robert Schumanns* (Kassel: Bärenreiter, 1989), 176–96.

27. A facsimile of this page is on plate 8 in Wolfgang Boetticher, *Robert Schumanns Klavierwerke: Neue biographische und textkritische Untersuchungen Teil I, Opus 1–6* (Wilhelmshaven: Heinrichshofen, 1976).

28. Letter of 19 April 1832, in Robert Schumann, *Jugendbriefe*, ed. Clara Schumann, 2nd ed. (Leipzig: Breitkopf und Härtel, 1886), 167–68. See also the letter to his family, written two days before, in ibid., 166–67.

29. Letter of 28 April 1832, in *Robert Schumanns Briefe: Neue Folge*, ed. F. Gustav Jansen (Leipzig: Breitkopf und Härtel, 1904), 36.

30. Letter of 22 August 1834, in *Robert Schumanns Briefe: Neue Folge*, 53–54. Translation (slightly modified) from Lippman, "Theory and Practice in Schumann's Aesthetics," 320.

31. *Robert Schumanns Briefe: Neue Folge*, 492 n. 22.

32. Jean Paul, *Flegeljahre*, 478–79.

33. Ibid., 270.

34. Cf. ibid., 201.

35. Jean Paul, *Flegeljahre*, 479.

36. Jean Paul, *Kleine Nachschule zur ästhetischen Vorschule*, 429.

37. See Robert Schumann, *Tagebücher*, eds. Georg Eismann and Gerd Nauhaus (Leipzig: VEB, 1971–87), 1:124.

38. See the letter to Henriette Voigt in *Robert Schumanns Briefe: Neue Folge*, 54.

39. Boetticher's transcription in *Robert Schumanns Klavierwerke* 1:74 is inaccurate on several counts. Note especially his unwarranted interruption of Schumann's chromatic line in the thirteenth measure from the end, where Schumann writes C♯ and not D. An edition of the Wiede Sketchbooks at the Universitätsbibliothek Bonn by Matthias Wendt is in preparation.

40. Hugo von Hofmannsthal, "Blick auf Jean Paul," in *Gesammelte Werke,* ed. Bernd Schoeller (Frankfurt am Main: S. Fischer, 1979), 8:434–37, at 437 (original emphasis).

41. Schumann, *Gesammelte Schriften* 1:462–63; translation (modified) from Lippman, "Theory and Practice in Schumann's Aesthetics," 325–26.

42. Schumann, *Gesammelte Schriften* 1:464.

43. Lippman, "Theory and Practice in Schumann's Aesthetics," 325–42.

44. As in this passage from one of the most frequently read novels of early Romanticism, Ludwig Tieck's 1798 *Franz Sternbalds Wanderungen,* ed. Alfred Anger (Stuttgart: P. Reclam, 1966), 221–22: "Suddenly they heard from the distance the touching play of intricate horns out of the forest; standing still they strained to hear whether it was imagination or reality; but a melodic singing flowed toward them through the trees like a rippling rill, and Franz thought that the spirit world had suddenly opened up, that perhaps, without knowing it, they had found the great magic word."

45. Paul Ricoeur, *Hermeneutics and the Human Sciences: Essays on Language, Action, and Interpretation,* ed. and trans. John B. Thompson (Cambridge: Cambridge University Press, 1981), 131–44 (chapter 4, "The Hermeneutical Function of Distanciation"). For a more recent discussion of Ricoeur's notion of distanciation in the wider context of music historiography, see Gary Tomlinson's *Music in Renaissance Magic: Toward a Historiography of Others* (Chicago: University of Chicago Press, 1993), 24–27.

46. Ricoeur, *Hermeneutics and the Human Sciences,* 139.

47. See ibid., 182–93.

48. Ibid., 141 and 143 (original emphasis).

49. Ibid., 113.

50. Ibid.

51. For a general survey of the opposing principles in music analysis, see the introduction to Ian Bent, ed., *Music Analysis in the Nineteenth Century,* 2:1–27.

52. For a brief introduction see ibid., 3–4 and 8–13. On the relationship between explanation and understanding, see Ricoeur, *Hermeneutics and the Human Sciences,* 145–64.

53. See Joseph Kerman, "How We Got into Analysis, and How to Get Out," *Critical Inquiry* 7 (1980): 311–31; Lawrence Kramer, "Haydn's Chaos, Schenker's Order; or, Hermeneutics and Musical Analysis: Can They Mix?" *Nineteenth-Century Music* 16 (1992): 3–17; and the ensuing "Counterpoint" between Scott Burnham ("The Criticism of Analysis and the Analysis of Criticism") and Lawrence Kramer ("Criticizing Criticism, Analyzing Analysis"), in *Nineteenth-Century Music* 16 (1992): 70–76 and 76–79 respectively.

54. *Neue Zeitschrift für Musik* 2 (1835): 42. Translation from Leon Plantinga, *Schumann as Critic* (New Haven: Yale University Press, 1967), 72.

55. As quoted in Plantinga, *Schumann as Critic,* 74.

56. Ibid., 72.

57. *Neue Zeitschrift für Musik* 3 (1835): 1–2. For a more recent translation of the complete review, see Bent, *Music Analysis in the Nineteenth Century,* 2:166–94.

58. Plantinga, *Schumann as Critic,* 78.

59. Sanna Pederson, "Enlightened and Romantic German Music Criticism, 1800–1850" (Ph.D. diss., University of Pennsylvania, 1995), 86.

60. Ibid., 81–86, at 85. See also the section "Declining Audience Sophistication" in Leonard B. Meyer, *Style and Music: Theory, History, and Ideology* (Philadelphia: University of Pennsylvania Press, 1989): 208–17.

61. See Schumann's comments after his general observations about the form of the work: "This will appear to everyone who will study the symphony more often." Schumann, *Gesammelte Schriften* 1: 463.

62. See Pederson, "Enlightened and Romantic German Music Criticism," 86 and 42–43.

63. Jean Paul, *Flegeljahre*, 181–82.

64. Adorno, "Schöne Stellen," 695.

65. Benjamin, *Gesammelte Schriften*, 5.1:560.

66. Walter Benjamin, "Das Kunstwerk im Zeitalter seiner technischen Reproduzierbarkeit," *Gesammelte Schriften*, 1.2:471–508, at 479; cf. 440.

67. Schumann, *Gesammelte Schriften* 1:464.

68. Ibid., 1:460.

69. On that point see David Lewin's "Music Theory, Phenomenology, and Modes of Perception," *Music Perception* 3 (1986): 327–92, esp. part 5, "Perception and the Productive Modes of Behavior."

70. Ricoeur, *Hermeneutics and the Human Sciences,* 185.

71. Ibid.

72. Schumann, *Tagebücher* 1:126–27. See also letter of 24 October 1828, in Schumann, *Jugendbriefe,* 38–40.

73. Letter of 31 August 1828, in Schumann, *Jugendbriefe,* 34.

74. Manfred Hermann Schmid, *Musik als Abbild: Studien zum Werk von Weber, Schumann und Wagner* (Tutzing: H. Schneider, 1981), 71–89.

75. Schumann, *Gesammelte Schriften,* 1:98. Schmid, *Musik als Abbild,* 84.

76. Schmid, *Musik als Abbild,* 84.

77. Ibid., 84 and 87: "Das Gehörte ist nur Erscheinung. Diesen 'metaphysischen' Zug der Aria spürt man, ohne den realen Gegenstand, das Lied, kennen zu müssen"; and 86: "Diese Erinnerung beschreibt Schumann hier noch, einige Jahre später komponiert er sie. Was im Tagebuch in Worte gefaßt ist, wird durch die Aria in Musik verwandelt. Die Aria ist musikalische Erinnerung—Musik über Musik."

78. Schumann, *Gesammelte Schriften* 1:98.

79. Justinus Kerner, *Ausgewählte poetische Werke,* vol. 1, *Die lyrischen Gedichte* (Stuttgart: Cotta, 1878–79), 24–29. "An Anna" is part of a cycle of six poems called "Episteln," letters exchanged between a soldier and his bride, Anna.

80. Quoted here from the letter, which has "the most distant echo" (emphasis mine) instead of the diary's "gentle echo."

81. The title of the slow movement (Andantino) of his G-Minor Sonata, op. 22, does not allude to its vocal origin.

82. See Schumann's letter to Clara Wieck from 11 February 1838: "I have done almost nothing but compose for four weeks, as I already wrote you; it just flowed; I always sang along while composing—and then I was most of the time successful." In Clara and Robert Schumann, *Briefwechsel,* ed. Eva Weissweiler,

(Frankfurt am Main: Stroemfeld/Roter Stern, 1984, 1987), 1:100; *The Complete Correspondence,* ed. Eva Weissweiler, trans. Hildegard Fritsch and Ronald L. Crawford (New York: P. Lang, 1994, 1996), 1:102 (translation modified).

83. Siegfried Kross, ed., *Briefe und Notizen Robert und Clara Schumanns* (Bonn: Bouvier, 1978), 23: "Cosí stando nella somma cima della montagna e niente conoscendo delle nuvole fredde e guardando in immensi oceani delle nebbie io senti una malinconia indicibile e mi credesti il solo della terra uomo." No attempt has been made to render Schumann's rather broken Italian in translation. Descriptions of this kind from journeys through southern Germany abound in Schumann's early diaries. To pick one example from his journey to Heidelberg: "Rüdesheim was mirrored in the waves, which the moon magically transfigured. On the other side, in the distance, was the St. Roch Chapel—my heart was completely filled." Schumann, *Tagebücher* 1:51.

84. Schumann, *Tagebücher* 1:99 (29 July 1828). For the text of the treatise see Frauke Otto, *Robert Schumann als Jean Paul-Leser* (Frankfurt am Main: Haag und Herchen, 1984), 67. See also the letter from 2 October 1828 to Wilhelm Götte, in Schumann, *Jugendbriefe,* 36; and the diary entry from Schumann's journey to Munich, in Schumann, *Tagebücher* 1:65: "Beautiful view—melancholy—and deep longing for a great Something."

85. "Mountains and Song Cycles," in Rosen, *The Romantic Generation,* 124–236.

86. Ibid., 135–42, at 139.

87. Schumann, *Tagebücher* 1:390. The *Kunstblatt* was the supplement to the *Morgenblatt für gebildete Stände.*

88. Rosen, *The Romantic Generation,* 151–52.

89. Quoted in Dahlhaus, *The Idea of Absolute Music,* 61.

90. See *Athenäumsfragment* no. 174, in *Kritische Friedrich-Schlegel-Ausgabe,* 193.

91. Carl Maria von Weber, *Sämtliche Schriften,* ed. Georg Kaiser (Berlin: Schuster und Loeffler, 1908), 452. For an alternative translation see Carl Maria von Weber, *Writings on Music,* ed. John Warrack, trans. Martin Cooper (Cambridge: Cambridge University Press, 1981), 324.

92. Brendel, "Robert Schumann mit Rücksicht auf Mendelssohn-Bartholdy," 89–90 (322–23, translation modified).

93. Gotthold Ephraim Lessing, *Laocoön: An Essay on the Limits of Painting and Poetry,* trans. Edward Allen McCormick (Baltimore: Johns Hopkins University Press, 1984). See especially sections 3 (pp. 19–22) and 12 to 16 (pp. 66–84). The currency of Lessing's view is evident from Johann Georg Sulzer's *Allgemeine Theorie der Schönen Künste in einzeln, nach alphabetischer Ordnung der Kunstwörter auf einander folgenden Artikeln abgehandelt,* 2nd ed. (Leipzig: In der Weidmannschen Buchhandlung, 1792): 224, which has under the entry *Augenblick:* "The moment of an event, which the history painter has chosen to represent. Because in a painting no sequence of events takes place, but everything stands still, only a single indivisible point in time from a story can be presented in a painting."

94. Schumann revised the work in 1850/51, in part by taking out the poetic

inscriptions and references to Florestan and Eusebius, his musical and literary double persona. The early version will be considered here.

95. See Peter Kaminsky, "Principles of Formal Structure in Schumann's Early Piano Cycles," *Music Theory Spectrum* 11 (1989): 222. See also Rosen, *The Romantic Generation,* 232.

96. Thus Otto Lorenz recalled: "Schumann's playing received its peculiar sound through his almost constant use of the pedal, though in such a carefully discrete way that no disturbing mixture of heterogeneous harmonies occurred." One evening, Alfred Dörffel heard Schumann improvising his *Nachtstücke* in an early stage: "It always sounded as if the pedal was half depressed; so the shapes became blurred. But the melody was distinct, as it is, for instance, appropriate for the second number." Quoted in F. Gustav Jansen, *Die Davidsbündler: Aus Robert Schumann's Sturm- und Drangperiode* (Leipzig: Breitkopf und Härtel, 1883), 72 and 74.

97. Robert P. Morgan, "Musical Time/Musical Space," *Critical Inquiry* 6 (1980): 527–38, at 528.

98. Adorno, "On Some Relationships Between Music and Painting," 67.

99. Ibid., 69 and 75.

100. Morgan, "Musical Time/Musical Space," 532, 529.

101. Ibid., 532.

102. Ibid., 529. For one alternative to a Schenkerian conception of musical space, see Fred Lehrdahl's "Tonal Pitch Space," *Music Perception* 5 (1988): 315–49.

103. Adorno, "Über die musikalische Verwendung des Radios," 376.

104. Brendel, "Robert Schumann with Reference to Mendelssohn-Bartholdy," 318–19.

105. Ibid., 319–20.

106. Richard Wagner, *Gesammelte Schriften und Dichtungen,* 1:147.

107. See ibid., 162–68, for Burnham's own ambivalence about the slippage between the two.

108. See Mark Evan Bonds, "*Sinfonia anti-eroica:* Berlioz's *Harold en Italie* and the Anxiety of Beethoven's Influence," *The Journal of Musicology* 10 (1992): 417–63; Sanna Pederson, "On the Task of the Music Historian: The Myth of the Symphony After Beethoven," *Repercussions* 2 (1993): 5–30; and Brendel, "Robert Schumann with Reference to Mendelssohn-Bartholdy," 334.

109. Burnham, *Beethoven Hero,* 121. Burnham here draws on Peter Thorslev, *The Byronic Hero: Types and Prototypes* (Minneapolis: University of Minnesota Press, 1982).

110. Kaminsky, "Principles of Formal Structure," 219 and 220.

111. John Daverio, *Robert Schumann: Herald of a "New Poetic Age"* (New York: Oxford University Press, 1997), 158.

112. Letters of 31 December 1837, 6 February 1838, and 19 March 1838, in Robert and Clara Schumann, *Complete Correspondence* 1:76, 94–95, and 130.

113. Nancy B. Reich, *Clara Schumann: The Artist and the Woman* (Ithaca: Cornell University Press, 1985), 231.

114. Surely the constellation of B and C and F♯ is central to *Davids-*

bündlertänze. Further investigation is needed to determine whether there are more connections. Some similarities between motivic gestures spring to the eye: for instance, the octaves in Schumann's Book 2, no. 4 relate to the section beginning in measure 57 of the *Valses.* And the dotted rhythms in Book 1, no. 9 are reminiscent of the grace notes in Clara's *scherzando* waltz in B♭ major (beginning in m. 89).

115. For other synthesizing uses of the motto see both Kaminsky, "Principles of Formal Structure," 217–24; and Rosen, *The Romantic Generation,* 223–24 and 229–32.

116. Cf. Adorno, "On Some Relations Between Music and Painting," 67: "In their contradiction, the arts merge into one another."

117. Personal communication from Linda Correll Roesner. See also her article "The Sources for Schumann's *Davidsbündlertänze,* Op. 6: Composition, Textual Problems, and the Role of the Composer as Editor," in *Mendelssohn and Schumann: Essays on Their Music and Its Context,* ed. Jon W. Finson and R. Larry Todd (Durham: Duke University Press, 1984): 53–70. See especially the structure of the manuscript on page 55.

118. Rosen, *The Romantic Generation,* 233.

119. Ibid., 235.

120. "Ganz zum Überfluß meinte Eusebius noch Folgendes; dabei sprach aber viel Seligkeit aus seinen Augen." Number 9 has a similar programmatic note, but one that accentuates the painful: Hierauf schloß Florestan und es zuckte ihm schmerzlich um die Lippen."

121. In the epilogue to *The Classical Style,* 2nd rev. ed. (New York: W.W. Norton, 1976), 451, Charles Rosen speaks of the *Fantasie* as "the monument that commemorates the death of the classical style." More recent articles on the *Fantasie* include John Daverio, "Schumann's 'Im Legendenton' and Friedrich Schlegel's *Arabeske,*" *Nineteenth-Century Music* 11 (1987): 150–63 (a revised version appears as "Schumann's Opus 17 Fantasie and the *Arabeske*" in his *Nineteenth-Century Music and the German Romantic Ideology* (New York: Schirmer, 1993), 19–47; Nicholas Marston, "'Im Legendenton': Schumann's 'Unsung Voice'," *Nineteenth-Century Music* 16 (1993): 227–41; and Linda Correll Roesner, "Schumann's 'Parallel' Forms," *Nineteenth-Century Music* 14 (1991): 265–78. Nicholas Marston, *Schumann: Fantasie, Op. 17* (Cambridge: Cambridge University Press, 1992), gives a useful overview of the work's genesis, analysis and criticism, and reception. See also Bodo Bischoff, *Monument für Beethoven: Die Entwicklung der Beethoven-Rezeption Robert Schumanns* (Cologne-Rheinkassel: C. Dohr, 1994), 194–238. The most recent interpretation is by Charles Rosen, *The Romantic Generation,* 100–112.

122. Letters of 19 March 1838, 25 January 1839, and 21 April 1839. Clara and Robert Schumann, *Briefwechsel* 1:126, 2:368, and 2:495 (cf. 1:129, 2:32, and 2:166). For reading the word in Schumann's difficult handwriting as "Passioniertestes," see Marston in "Comment and Chronicle," *Nineteenth-Century Music* 15 (1991): 166, which was confirmed by Gerd Nauhaus (personal communication with the author). Marston suggests that "it was Clara who inspired the first movement and Beethoven who inspired the other two" (*Schumann: Fantasie,* 8).

123. *Kritische Friedrich-Schlegel-Ausgabe* 5 (1962), 190–91.

124. Letters of 9 June 1838 and 16 June 1839, in Weisweiler, *Briefwechsel* 2:562 and 577, *Complete Correspondence* 2:237 and 253. The facsimile is reproduced from the *Briefwechsel*. Schumann's musical example is difficult to read because the ink spreads around the stems (suggesting eighth-note and sixteenth-note flags). Since a^1 appears to be crossed out, this seems to be a variant (parallel to mm. 45–46) of the later version.

125. Marston, *Schumann: Fantasie,* 38. On 11 June 1839, Clara wrote to Schumann: "Neulich hab ich Alkan Deine Fantasie vorgespielt, er war entzückt, doch so wie ich versteht Dich Keiner—kann auch nicht sein!" Clara and Robert Schumann, *Briefwechsel* 2:566 (cf. 2:241). The last remark is somewhat elliptical, but Clara seems to be saying, "Recently I played your *Fantasie* to Alkan. He was delighted, but nobody understands you like me—which can only be that way and no different." See also her enthusiastic response to the *Fantasie* in the letter from 23 May 1839 in *Briefwechsel* 2:532 (2:205).

126. In private conversation with the author and during public lectures.

127. Hermann Abert, *Robert Schumann,* 2nd rev. ed. (Berlin: Harmonie Verlagsgesellschaft für Literatur und Kunst, 1910), 64. See Anthony Newcomb, "Schumann and the Marketplace," in *Nineteenth-Century Piano Music,* ed. R. Larry Todd (New York: Schirmer, 1990), 258–315, at 295.

128. Ibid., 295. R. Larry Todd echoes the cautionary attitude in his "On Quotation in Schumann's Music," in *Schumann and His World,* 80–112, at 93.

129. Rosen, *The Romantic Generation,* 103. The thematic coherence of the first movement is affirmed by Daverio, "Schumann's 'Im Legendenton'," 161 and 157; Gernot Gruber, "Robert Schumann: Fantasie op. 17, 1. Satz—Versuch einer Interpretation," *Musicologica austriaca* 4 (1984): 101–30; Marston, *Schumann: Fantasie,* 61–67; and Bischoff, *Monument für Beethoven,* 208–9 and 227–30.

130. Schumann, *Gesammelte Schriften* 1:83–84.

131. Schumann, "Berlioz: *Fantastic Symphony,*" in Bent, *Music Analysis in the Nineteenth Century,* 2:192. For other references to Beethoven's cycle in Schumann, see Anthony Newcomb, "Once More Between Absolute and Program Music: Schumann's Second Symphony," *Nineteenth-Century Music* 7 (1984): 233–50. For Schubert see Kramer, *Distant Cycles,* 8–9 and 96; for Brahms see Kenneth Ross Hull, "Brahms the Allusive: Extra-Compositional Reference in the Instrumental Music of Johannes Brahms" (Ph.D. diss., Princeton University, 1989), 62–65. See also Christopher Reynolds, "An die ferne Geliebte," in *Beethoven: Interpretationen seiner Werke,* ed. Carl Dahlhaus, Albrecht Riethmüller, and Alexander L. Ringer (Laaber: Laaber, 1994), 2:99–108, esp. 105–8. Other aspects of the connection between Schumann's *Fantasie* and Sterndale Bennett's *Fantasie* op. 16 have been explored by Nicholas Temperley, "Schumann and Sterndale Bennett," *Nineteenth-Century Music* 12 (1989): 207–20. Bennett arrived in Leipzig for an eight-month stay in October 1836, during which he

became a close friend of Schumann's. He dedicated his *Fantasie* to Schumann and published it in 1837. Its main theme (esp. mm. 7–10) resonates strikingly with the passages in Schumann's *Fantasie* beginning at measures 41 and 65.

132. See Ludwig van Beethoven, *An die ferne Geliebte: Faksimile nach dem im Besitz des Bonner Beethovenhauses Befindlichen Original* (Munich: Henle, 1970); and Joseph Kerman, "*An die ferne Geliebte,*" in *Beethoven Studies,* ed. Alan Tyson (New York: W. W. Norton, 1973), 123–57, at 136–37.

133. For reasons that will become apparent later—the same key of E♭ being the most obvious—the theme will be discussed in the following as it appears in the recapitulation beginning in measure 253. The passage beginning at measure 41 is sometimes interpreted as the onset of the second group, with measures 33–40 being the transition (Daverio, *Nineteenth-Century Music and the German Romantic Ideology,* 25). When texture and gesture as parameters of form are taken into account, however, the sixteenth-note accompaniment places this section into a very long transitional process from the first to the second group. Only gradually does the opening accompaniment lose its momentum, ritarding via sextuplets (mm. 49–60) into the eighth-note rhythm of the second theme, beginning in measure 61. Roesner labels the section beginning in measure 41 the second theme, but gives what follows after measure 60 the status of a secondary, as opposed to a principal, key area (Roesner, "Schumann's 'Parallel' Forms," 274). Marston, *Schumann: Fantasie,* 54, considers measures 41–81 as simply the B section, since the relatively independent origin of the movement as a "Phantasie" obviated the need for a sonata form (see also his "'Im Legendenton'," 230).

134. See Rosen, *The Romantic Generation,* 103–4.

135. Ibid., 48–58; and Daverio, *Nineteenth-Century Music and German Romantic Ideology,* 49–86.

136. Schumann mentioned it in a letter of 19 December 1836 to his publisher Friedrich Kistner, to whom he also mentioned his use in the last movement of music from Beethoven's Seventh Symphony. See Hermann Erler, *Robert Schumanns Leben aus seinen Briefen geschildert* (Berlin: Ries and Erler, 1887), 1:102–3. Erler's added remark after the letter—"This intended allusion to Beethoven's 'Seventh' was later completely removed"—can be put to the test by comparing the passage beginning in Schumann's third movement at measure 30 with Beethoven's symphony as shown by Rosen, *The Romantic Generation,* 102–3. See also Marston, *Schumann: Fantasie,* 37.

137. Marston, *Schumann: Fantasie,* 23–33, discusses the different titles and their generic implications.

138. Jean Paul, *Vorschule der Ästhetik,* 155 (emphasis added). Cf. Hale, *Horn of Oberon,* 120. For a discussion of *Witz* in Schumann see Daverio, *Nineteenth-Century Music and the German Romantic Ideology,* 49–88, esp. 71–75.

139. See Jean Paul, *Vorschule der Ästhetik,* 157–58; cf. Hale, *Horn of Oberon,* 122.

140. For a discussion of the relation between wit and judgment in eighteenth-century aesthetics see W.J.T. Mitchell, *Iconology: Image, Text, Ideology* (Chicago: University of Chicago Press, 1986), 121–25.

141. Jean Paul, *Vorschule der Ästhetik,* 158; cf. Hale, *Horn of Oberon,* 122.

142. Schumann, *Tagebücher* 1:133.

143. Daverio, *Nineteenth-Century Music and the German Romantic Ideology*, 19–48.

144. Ibid., 28–34.

145. Heinrich Christoph Koch, *Musikalisches Lexikon* (1802), translated by Marston in "'Im Legendenton'," 230 and 236. The page of the autograph is reproduced as plate 2 in Marston, *Schumann: Fantasie* (before p. 33).

146. Marston, "'Im Legendenton'," 231.

147. The theme may have originated with Schumann, since it appears in his diary for 28/29 September 1830, Schumann, *Tagebücher* 1:321. See also Claudia Stevens Becker, "A New Look at Schumann's Impromptus," *The Musical Quarterly* 67 (1981): 568–86.

148. Example 2.10d shows the third appearance of the "Im Legendenton" theme, which inverts Clara's characteristic fourth, D–A.

149. Clara's "Romanza" seems to have held a special—amorous—connotation, resounding in Johannes Brahms's *Variationen über ein Thema von Robert Schumann*, op. 9, where the "Romanza" melody appears as an inner voice at the end of the tenth variation. As Bodo Bischoff has pointed out, Schumann also alludes to Clara's theme which he uses in the Impromptu in the third movement of the *Fantasie* (cf. *Impromtus über eine Thema von Clara Wieck*, op. 5 mm. 9–10 and the third movement of the *Fantasie*, mm. 123 et passim), see Bischoff, *Monument für Beethoven*, 219–20.

150. The page is reproduced in Marston, "'Im Legendenton'," 235.

151. Carolyn Abbate, *Unsung Voices: Opera and Musical Narrative in the Nineteenth Century* (Princeton: Princeton University Press, 1991), 26 and 29. See Marston, "Im Legendenton'," 237–38; and also Daverio, *Nineteenth-Century Music and the German Romantic Ideology*, 29 and 32.

152. See Marston, *Schumann: Fantasie*, 23 and 32–33.

153. Rosen, *The Romantic Generation*, 106. The E♭ frame begins with a second statement of the first theme in measure 28 and is recapitulated beginning in measure 225. On this point see Roesner, "Schumann's 'Parallel' Forms," 274.

154. Roesner, "Schumann's 'Parallel' Forms," 274.

155. The "S"/E♭ symbolism is corroborated by the "Sphinxes" and "A.S.C.H—S.C.H.A. Lettres dansantes" movements in Schumann's *Carnaval*, op. 9.

156. In the reprise of the coda for the original ending of the *Fantasie*, E♭ also appeared in the bass in the equivalent of measures 300 and 303. Marston, *Schumann: Fantasie*, 18–20; Rosen, *The Romantic Generation*, 110. Perhaps Schumann deleted the original ending because he might have felt that it would not reconnect with the poetic vision of the first movement.

157. Letter of 6 February 1838, in Clara and Robert Schumann, *Briefwechsel* 1:90–91 (cf. 1:91–92). On the relationship between Clara Wieck and "Wiecketten," and Clara Novello and "Novelletten," see Hans Joachim Köhler, "Die Stichvorlagen zum Erstdruck von Opus 21—Assoziationen zu Schumanns *Novelletten*," *Schumann Studien* 3/4 (1994): 75–94, esp. 92–93.

158. Letter of 11 February 1838, in Clara and Robert Schumann, *Briefwechsel* 1:100 (cf. 1:102).

159. ". . . wie im Himmel gelebt u. ein Seliger herumgewandelt—am 9ten en Brief v. m . Mädel—sonderbare Novelletten componirt in B Dur und in D Dur—

geschwärmt—warme Frühlingstage—ihr Bild." Schumann, *Tagebücher* 2:53.

160. See Köhler, "Die Stichvorlage zum Erstdruck von Opus 21," 76. The eighth Novellette appears here as the third, but is renumbered by Schumann as the fourth.

161. Jeffrey Kallberg, "The Harmony of the Tea Table: Gender and Ideology in the Piano Nocturne," in *Chopin at the Boundaries: Sex, History, and Musical Genre* (Cambridge: Harvard University Press, 1996), 54.

162. Ibid., 55–56. One might, therefore, distinguish between Schumann's creative appropriation of borrowed material for the sake of poetic allusion, and his corrections and improvements of works published under Clara's name, for instance her much-discussed *Trois Romances pour le piano*, op. 11.

163. Letter of 3 April 1838 to Joseph Fischof, in Erler, *Robert Schumanns Leben aus seinen Briefen geschildert* 1:151. Schumann himself used the term *cycle* in a letter to Clara on 1 December 1839, Clara and Robert Schumann, *Briefwechsel* 2:809 (2:495). For a discussion of the whole opus see Daverio, *Nineteenth-Century Music and the German Romantic Ideology*, 75–86.

164. In light of the early order of the cycle, the puzzling numbers for the *Fortsetzung* (5) and the *Fortsetzung und Schluß* (6) make perfect sense. Cf. Köhler, "Die Stichvorlage zum Erstdruck von Opus 21," 79–80.

165. Letter of 30 June 1839: "Von mir sind jetzt vier Hefte Novelletten erschienen, innig zusammenhängend und mit großer Lust geschrieben, im Durchschnitt heiter und obenhin, bis auf einzelnes, wo ich auf den Grund gekommen." Erler, *Robert Schumanns Leben aus seinen Briefen geschildert* 1:206.

166. Todd, "On Quotation in Schumann's Music," 102.

167. E.T.A. Hoffmann, *Sämtliche Werke: Historisch Kritische Ausgabe,* ed. Carl Georg von Maassen, 2nd ed. (Munich: G. Müller, 1909–25), 1:428–29; translation from *E.T.A. Hoffmann's Musical Writings: "Kreisleriana," "The Poet and the Composer," Music Criticism,* ed. David Charlton, trans. Martyn Clarke (Cambridge: Cambridge University Press, 1989), 160–61; emphasis added.

NOTES TO CHAPTER 3—ELSA'S SCREAM

1. Arthur Groos, "Back to the Future: Hermeneutic Fantasies in *Der fliegende Holländer*," *Nineteenth-Century Music*, 19 (1995): 191–211.

2. Wagner's writings are quoted from the second edition of his *Gesammelte Schriften und Dichtungen* (Leipzig: E. W. Fritzsch, 1887–88), cited in this chapter as *GS*. Translations are based, with some alterations, on Richard Wagner, *Prose Works*, trans. William Ashton Ellis (London: Routledge and Kegan Paul, 1892–99), henceforth cited as *PW*. The present quotations: *GS* 4:297; *PW* 1: 342. Wagner echoed this view in a letter to August Röckel, *Selected Letters of Richard Wagner*, ed. and trans. Stewart Spencer and Barry Millington (New York: W. W. Norton, 1988), 306.

3. Wagner, *GS* 4:301–2; *PW* 1:347.

4. Wagner, *GS* 4:296–7 and Richard Wagner, *My Life,* ed. Mary Whittall, trans. Andrew Gray (Cambridge: Cambridge University Press, 1983), 326.

5. *Selected Letters of Richard Wagner*, 130.

6. John Deathridge, "Through the Looking Glass: Some Remarks on the First

Complete Draft of *Lohengrin*," in *Analyzing Opera*, ed. Carolyn Abbate and Roger Parker (Berkeley: University of California Press, 1989), 56–91, esp. 71–80. Other studies of the opera include Ulrich Siegele, "Das Drama der Themen am Beispiel des *Lohengrin*," *Richard Wagner: Werk und Wirkung*, ed. Carl Dahlhaus (Regensburg: G. Bosse, 1971), 41–52; Michael von Soden, *Richard Wagner: Lohengrin* (Frankfurt am Main: Insel, 1980); Arnold Whittall, "Wagner's Great Transition? From *Lohengrin* to *Das Rheingold*," *Music Analysis* 2 (1983), 269–80. Most inspiring for the present chapter has been Reinhold Brinkmann, "Wunder, Realität und die Figur der Grenzüberschreitung," in *Lohengrin: Texte, Materialien, Kommentare*, ed. Attila Csampai and Dietmar Holland (Reinbek: Rowohlt, 1989), 255–74, which is an abbreviated version of an article with the same title published in *Programmhefte der Bayreuther Festspiele 1979: Programmheft I "Lohengrin*," ed. Wolfgang Wagner and Oswald Georg Bauer (Bayreuth: Verlag der Festspielleitung, 1979), 1–21, 94–106.

7. Hayden White, *Metahistory: The Historical Imagination in Nineteenth-Century Europe* (Baltimore: Johns Hopkins University Press, 1973), 8.

8. As discussed for instance in Hayden White, *The Content of the Form: Narrative Discourse and Historical Representation* (Baltimore: Johns Hopkins University Press, 1987).

9. On that point see Groos, "Back to the Future," 192–3, and James Treadwell, "The *Ring* and the Conditions of Interpretation: Wagner's Writing, 1848 to 1852," *Cambridge Opera Journal*, 7 (1995): 207–31.

10. Carl Dahlhaus, *Richard Wagner's Music Dramas*, trans. Mary Whittall (Cambridge: Cambridge University Press, 1979), 35.

11. Jean-Jacques Nattiez, *Wagner Androgyne: A Study in Interpretation*, trans. Stewart Spencer (Princeton: Princeton University Press, 1993), 8.

12. Julius Schaeffer, "Über 'Lohengrin' von Richard Wagner mit Bezug auf seine Schrift: 'Oper und Drama'," *Neue Berliner Musikzeitung* 6 (1852): 153–55, 161–63, 169–71, 193–96, 201–4. Joachim Raff, *Die Wagnerfrage*, (Braunschweig: F. Vieweg, 1854).

13. Thomas S. Grey, *Wagner's Musical Prose: Texts and Contexts* (Cambridge: Cambridge University Press, 1995), esp. chapter 3, "Engendering Music Drama: *Opera and Drama* and its Metaphors."

14. Additional perspectives are offered by Nattiez, *Wagner Androgyne*, 76–90, 139–55; and Grey, *Wagner's Musical Prose*, 151–80.

15. Wagner, *GS* 4:301; *PW* 1:346; translation (modified) partly from Nattiez, *Wagner Androgyne*, 94.

16. Wagner, *GS* 7:111–12; translation from "Music of the Future," *Three Wagner Essays*, trans. Robert Jacobs (London: Eulenburg Books, 1979), 28.

17. Nattiez, *Wagner Androgyne*, 94.

18. For an initial attempt at Wagnerian screams see Philip Friedheim, "Wagner and the Aesthetics of the Scream," *Nineteenth-Century Music* 7 (1983): 63–70. Much broader in scope is Michel Poizat's *The Angel's Cry*. Both pay little attention to *Lohengrin*.

19. "Über das Dichten und Komponieren" (Wagner, *GS* 10:137–51; *PW* 6:131–48); "Über das Opern-Dichten und Komponieren im Besonderen" (*GS* 10:152–75; *PW* 6:149–72); Über "Die Anwendung der Musik auf das Drama"

(*GS* 10:176–93; *PW* 6:173–92). See *Bayreuther Blätter* 2 (1879), 185–96, 249–66, and 313–25.

20. Wagner, *GS* 10:191–3; *PW* 6:189–91.

21. Some analyses of Wagner's music in neo-Riemannian terms have labeled this mode change with a "P" for "parallel" operation. See Brian Hyer, "Tonal Intuitions in *Tristan and Isolde*" (Ph.D. diss., Yale University, 1989), and David Lewin, "Some Notes on Analyzing Wagner: *The Ring* and *Parsifal*," *Nineteenth-Century Music* 16 (1992): 49–58.

22. Carolyn Abbate, "Wagner, 'On Modulation', and Tristan," *Cambridge Opera Journal* 1 (1989): 33–58. See also Grey, *Wagner's Musical Prose*, 182–211.

23. Raff, *Die Wagnerfrage*, 222: "The appearance of Lohengrin is introduced in an incomparably better way. Elsa's narration of the vision, whose content is the knight of the Grail, as well as the accompanying musical motivation, would be in themselves sufficient [to warrant such a judgement]. I would maintain that this preparation is a poetic masterpiece, with little that equals it. . . . I doubt that anyone would fail to recognize for a moment the perfection of what Wagner achieved [in this scene] and what will secure Wagner an honorary place among the poets of all times." ("Die Erscheinung des Lohengrin is ungleich besser eingeführt. Die Erzählung der Elsa von der Vision, deren Inhalt der Ritter des Grales ist, sowie die dabei auftretende musikalische Motivierung wären an sich schon völlig ausreichend. Ich möchte indeß behaupten, daß diese Vorbereitung ein poetisches Meisterstück ist, welchem nicht eben viel Ebenbürtiges zur Seite [steht]. . . . Ich bezweifle, daß Jemand das Vollendete, was Wagner hier geleistet hat und was ihm unter den Dichtern aller Zeiten einen Ehrenplatz sichert, je einen Augenblick verkennen werde.")

24. Ibid., 123–4.

25. See Dieter Borchmeyer, "Choral Tragedy and Symphonic Drama: Wagner's Contribution to Nietzsche's *Die Geburt der Tragödie*," in his *Richard Wagner: Theory and Theatre*, trans. Stewart Spencer (Oxford: Clarendon Press, 1991), 160–77.

26. Edward T. Cone first drew attention to this distinction in *The Composer's Voice* (Berkeley: University of California Press, 1974) and subsequently in "The World of Opera and Its Inhabitants," in *Music: A View from Delft*, ed. Robert P. Morgan (Chicago: University of Chicago Press, 1989), 125–38.

27. *Oper und Drama* is cited according to the edition by Klaus Kropfinger (Stuttgart: P. Reclam, 1984), 347; *PW* 2:333.

28. *Oper und Drama*, 336–7; *PW* 2:323. The eye/ear conjunction is also the central image that governs Wagner's theory of alliteration, in which consonants are perceived by the "eye" of hearing, and vowels by the "ear"; see *Oper und Drama*, 286.

29. *Oper und Drama*, 337; *PW* 2:323–4.

30. Through the famous letter to Mathilde Wesendonck, *Selected Letters of Richard Wagner*, 475.

31. See Friedrich Kittler, "World-Breadth: On Wagner's Media Technology," in *Opera Through Other Eyes*, ed. David J. Levin (Stanford: Stanford University Press, 1993), 215–35, at 222–4.

32. Richard Wagner, *Lohengrin: Edition und Untersuchungen*, ed. Thomas Cramer (Munich: W. Fink, 1971), 207.

33. San-Marte, ed., Lieder, *Wilhelm von Orange und Titurel von Wolfram von Eschenbach, und der jüngere Titurel von Albrecht in Uebersetzung und im Auszuge, nebst Abhandlungen über das Leben und Wirken Wolfram's von Eschenbach und die Sage vom Heiligen Gral* (Magdeburg: Creutz, 1841), 448. See *My Life*, 301. See also Franz Müller, *Lohengrin und die Gral- und Schwan-Sage: Ein Skizzenbild auf Grund der Wort- und Tondichtung Richard Wagner's* (Munich: C. Kaiser, 1867), 199ff.

34. *Oper und Drama*, 343; *PW* 2:329.

35. Theodor W. Adorno, "Versuch über Wagner," in *Gesammelte Schriften* 13:7–148, at 83; *In Search of Wagner*, trans. Rodney Livingstone (London: NLB, 1981), 87 (translation modified).

36. Adorno, "Versuch," 83: "Es ist Elsas Vision, in welcher sie als Träumende den Ritter und alle Handlung gleichsam herbeizieht."

37. For this distinction and the Wagnerian slippage between the two, see Abbate, *Unsung Voices*, 85–117 and Groos, "Back to the Future," 198–205.

38. *Oper und Drama*, 335–6; *PW* 2:322.

39. See the stage direction when Lohengrin approaches: "Elsa, die mit steigender Entzückung den Ausrufen der Männer gelauscht hat, verbleibt in ihrer Stellung in der Mitte der Bühne. Sie wagt gleichsam nicht, sich umzublicken." ("Elsa, who has been listening with increasing rapture to the shouting men, remains in her posture in the middle of the stage. She does not, as it were, dare to look.") Yet when Lohengrin arrives at the shore: "Elsa hat sich umgewandt und schreit bei Lohengrins Anblick laut auf" ("Elsa turns around and, seeing Lohengrin, cries out loudly").

40. Wagner, *GS* 2:3–4.

41. 11 February 1872. *Cosima Wagner's Diaries*, 1:457.

42. *Oper und Drama*, 108, and Wagner, *GS* 9:106. Nattiez, *Wagner Androgyne*, 99–101 and 173–8, for a summary of varying opinions and Nattiez's own position.

43. Nattiez, *Wagner Androgyne*, 176.

44. See Brinkmann, "Wunder, Realität und die Figur der Grenzüberschreitung," (Bayreuth Version), 18–19, citing Karl Philip Moritz: " . . . dies Vergessens unseres selbst, ist der höchste Grad des reinen uneigennützigen Vergnügens, welches uns das Schöne gewährt. Wir opfern in dem Augenblick unser individuelles eingeschränktes Dasein einer Art höherem Dasein auf. Das Vergnügen am Schönen muß sich daher immer mehr der uneigennützigen Liebe nähern, wenn es ächt sein soll."

45. *Oper und Drama*, 351; *PW* 2:337.

46. Dahlhaus quotes Kant in his *Esthetics of Music*, trans. William W. Austin (Cambridge: Cambridge University Press, 1982), 35: "The purposiveness in a product of fine art, therefore, although of course it is intentional, still must not seem intentional. In other words, fine art must look like nature, although we recognize it as art."

47. *Oper und Drama*, 222–3; *PW* 2:216.

48. Ibid., 219–30.

49. Ibid., 352; *PW* 2:338–9.

50. *Oper und Drama*, 220; *PW* 2:213. Schaeffer invokes this distinction, but does not explore its ramifications for the opera's plot ("Über 'Lohengrin' von Richard Wagner," 154).

51. *Oper und Drama*, 220; *PW* 2:213 (translation modified).

52. Ludwig Feuerbach, *Sämtliche Werke* (Leipzig: O. Wiegand, 1846–90), 7:331–2. For a general overview on Wagner's reception of Feuerbach, see chapter 5 of Rainer Franke, *Richard Wagners Züricher Kunstschriften: Politische und ästhetische Entwürfe auf seinem Weg zum "Ring des Nibelungen"* (Hamburg: K. D. Wagner, 1983).

53. Wagner, *GS* 4:295–96; *PW* 1:341.

54. *Oper und Drama*, 220; *PW* 1:213–14.

55. Wagner, *GS* 4:247; *PW* 1:287.

56. Wagner, *GS* 5:179; *PW* 3:231.

57. Wagner, *GS* 4:190; *PW* 1:335.

58. Feuerbach, *Sämtliche Werke* 7:16: "However, if religion, God's consciousness, is referred to as human self-consciousness, this does not mean that the religious person would immediately know that his consciousness of God is the self-consciousness of his life, since precisely the lack of this knowledge establishes the particular nature of religion."

59. Wagner, *GS* 4:290; *PW* 1:335.

60. *Oper und Drama*, 342–3; *PW* 2:329.

61. Wagner, *GS* 5:180; *PW* 3:233.

62. Manfred Hermann Schmid, "Metamorphose der Themen: Beobachtungen an den Skizzen zum 'Lohengrin'-Vorspiel," *Die Musikforschung* 41 (1988), 105–26, at 107–9 and 121.

63. Nattiez, *Wagner Androgyne*, 130, does not make that important distinction.

64. Wagner, *GS* 7:122; "Music of the Future," 35.

65. Remark by Heinrich Porges, quoted in Grey, *Wagner's Musical Prose*, 153, and the subsequent analysis of the music. See also Nattiez, *Wagner Androgyne*, 76–84.

66. For a broader approach to the question, see Grey, *Wagner's Musical Prose*, 306–11: "Warum? Motives to Musical Form."

67. Wagner, *GS* 7:111–12, 112, 121; "Music of the Future," 28, 29, 34.

68. *Oper und Drama*, 243; *PW* 2:235.

69. *Oper und Drama*, 243. Cited after Nattiez, *Wagner Androgyne*, 36. See also Grey's subchapter, "Melody, Origins, and Utopias of Regression (Melody as the Origin of Speech and Poetry in Opera and Drama)" in *Wagner's Musical Prose*, 257–69; and my "Musik, Text und 'Supplement': Skizze über Dekonstruktion und musikalische Hermeneutik," in *Musik als Text: Bericht über den Internationalen Kongreß der Gesellschaft für Musikforschung Freiburg im Breisgau 1993*. ed. Hermann Danuser and Tobias Plebuch (Kassel: Bärenreiter, 1998), 2:7–10.

70. *Oper und Drama*, 243; quoted from Nattiez, *Wagner Androgyne*, 92.

71. Letter of 8 September 1850. *Franz Liszt—Richard Wagner: Briefwechsel,* ed. Hanjo Kesting (Frankfurt am Main: Insel, 1988), 133–4.

72. Grey, *Wagner's Musical Prose,* 223–28.

73. Ibid., 227.

74. The terms "kinetic" and "static" are Philip Gossett's; see "The 'Candeur virginale' of 'Tancredi'," *The Musical Times* 112 (1971), 326–29, at 327. See also Harold Powers, "'La solita forma' and 'The Uses of Convention'," *Acta Musicologica* 59 (1987), 65–90.

75. Grey, *Wagner's Musical Prose,* 224.

76. *Oper und Drama,* 41; *PW* 2:39–40.

77. Wagner, *GS* 9:69–70; *PW* 5:69. For a discussion of Wagner's Schopenhauerian reception of the scream, see Poizat, *The Angel's Cry,* 69–74 and 77–78.

78. Wagner, *GS* 9:111; *PW* 5:111–12.

79. Raff, *Die Wagnerfrage,* 118: "Die Erzählung vom heil. Gral ist ein Mißgriff des Dichters, welcher sich stets durch das Gähnen eines großen Theiles des Publicums und durch die stillen Flüche des Darstellers rächen muß. . . . Der mystische Inhalt desselben ist im Vorspiel durch die Musik erschöpft. Der Sänger kann nun Nichts thun, als zu jenem Vorspiel zu declamieren."

NOTES TO CHAPTER 4—LISZT'S PRAYER

1. Franz Liszt, "Ueber Beethoven's Musik zu Egmont," in *Sämtliche Schriften,* ed. Detlef Altenburg (Wiesbaden: Breitkopf und Härtel, 1989—), 5:16–20, at 16.

2. Franz Pohl, *Neue Zeitschrift für Musik* 46 (1857), 42.

3. Translation (modified) from Keith Johns, "A Structural Analysis of the Relationship Between Programme, Harmony and Form in the Symphonic Poems of Franz Liszt" (Ph.D. diss., University of Wollongong (Australia), 1986), 311. The French version in the first edition (most likely by Liszt) notes that these words should "always" be added to the program and that nature's voice is "ineffable" and "singing of the beauty and the harmonies of creation" (*chantant la beauté et les harmoniies de la création*). Liszt also quotes more from Hugo's ode (lines 70, 67, and 69) and describes quite evocatively how the poet's contemplation "silently touches on the borders of the prayer" (*jusqu'à ce que la contemplation émue du poète touche silencieusement aux confins de la prière*).

4. Carl Dahlhaus, "Liszts 'Bergsymphonie' und die Idee der Symphonischen Dichtung," *Jahrbuch des Staatlichen Instituts für Musikforschung* (1975): 96–130, at 96–97 and 127.

5. August Göllerich, *Franz Liszt* (Berlin: Marquardt, 1908), 154–55.

6. Hans Joachim Moser, *Kleine deutsche Musikgeschichte* (Stuttgart: Cotta, 1949), 252.

7. Benjamin, "Theses on the Philosophy of History," in *Illuminations,* 253–64 (see also his appendix A).

8. Ibid., 262–63 (translation modified).

9. Ibid.

10. See Rolf Tiedemann, "Historischer Materialismus oder politischer Messianismus?," 126, and Benjamin, *Gesammelte Schriften* 1.3:1240–42.

11. Ibid., 129 and Benjamin, *Gesammelte Schriften* 2:79.

12. Benjamin, "Theses on the Philosophy of History," 258 (translation modified).

13. See Ralph P. Locke, *Music, Musicians, and the Saint-Simonians* (Chicago: University of Chicago Press, 1986), 101–106.

14. Tiedemann, "Historischer Materialismus oder politischer Messianismus?," 131.

15. Benjamin, *Gesammelte Schriften* 5.1:59; see Tiedemann, "Dialektik im Stillstand: Annäherungen an das Passagen-Werk," 29. For the idea of the monad, see Thesis 17, 262–63.

16. See Peter Ramroth, *Robert Schumann und Richard Wagner im geschichtsphilosophischen Urteil von Franz Brendel* (Frankfurt am Main: P. Lang, 1991) and Robert Determann, *Begriff und Ästhetik der "Neudeutschen Schule": Ein Beitrag zur Musikgeschichte des 19. Jahrhunderts* (Baden Baden: V. Koerner, 1989), and the review of the two books by James Deaville, *Notes* 52 (1996), 441.

17. Hegel, *Aesthetics,* 948. Also Carl Dahlhaus, "Die Kategorie des 'Charakteristischen in der Ästhetik des 19. Jahrhunderts," in *Klassische und romantische Musikästhetik* (Laaber: Laaber, 1988): 219–30, at 226–27. For a comprehensive study of the notion of the characteristic see part 3 of Jacob De Ruiter, *Der Charakterbegriff in der Musik : Studien zur deutschen Ästhetik der Instrumentalmusik 1740–1850* (Stuttgart: F. Steiner, 1989), especially the discussion on the "Verselbständigung des Einzelnen," at 243–48.

18. Franz Brendel, "F. Liszt's symphonische Dichtungen," *Neue Zeitschrift für Musik* 49 (1858): 73–76, 85–88, 97–100, 109–12, 121–23, 133–36, 141–43, at 122.

19. Franz Brendel, *Geschichte der Musik in Italien, Deutschland und Frankreich: Von den ersten christlichen Zeiten bis auf die Gegenwart,* 2nd ed. (Leipzig: H. Matthes (E. O. Schurmann), 1855), 2:182.

20. Ibid., 189 and 198.

21. Brendel, "F. Liszt's symphonische Dichtungen," 98–99.

22. Ibid., 99.

23. Letter to Johann Christian Lobe (1856) in Franz Liszt, *Briefe,* ed. La Mara (Leipzig: Breitkopf und Härtel, 1893–1905), 8:127 and Lobe's "Briefe über Liszt's symphonische Dichtungen," *Fliegende Blätter für Musik* 2 (1856): 385–416, at 403.

24. Richard Wagner, "Über Franz Liszt's Symphonische Dichtungen," in *GS* 5:195, *PW* 3:251.

25. Felix Draeseke, *Schriften 1855–1861,* ed. Martella Gutiérrez-Denhoff and Helmut Loos (Bad Honnef: G. Schröder, 1987), 164.

26. Victor Hugo, "Preface to Cromwell," in *Prefaces and Prologues to Famous Books,* ed. Charles W. Eliot (New York: Collier, 1910), 354–408, at 362–63, and Albert W. Halsall, *Victor Hugo and the Romantic Drama* (Toronto: University of Toronto Press, 1998), 66–67 (my emphasis).

27. See Suzanne Guerlac, *The Impersonal Sublime: Hugo, Baudelaire, Lautréament* (Stanford: Stanford University Press, 1990), 13–18.

28. Ibid., 17 and Franz Liszt, "Berlioz und seine Haroldsymphonie," *Neue Zeitschrift für Musik* 43 (1855): 25–32, 37–46, 49–55, 77–84, 89–97, at 43.

29. See, for instance, Manfred Kelkel, "Wege zur 'Bergsymphonie' Liszts," in *Referate des 3. Europäischen Liszt-Symposions, Eisenstadt 1983,* ed. Serge Gut

(Munich: E. Katzbichler, 1986), 71–89, at 75–77 and 79; Dahlhaus, "Liszts 'Bergsymphonie'," 104–107.

30. Alfred Heuß, "Eine motivisch-thematische Studie über Liszt's sinfonische Dichtung 'Ce qu'on entend sur la montagne'," *Zeitschrift der Internationalen Musikgesellschaft* 13 (1911/12): 10–21, at 20–21. Dahlhaus, "Liszts Bergsymphonie," 104 and 126.

31. Liszt, "Berlioz und seine Haroldsymphonie," 79. According to Ramann, Liszt wrote the article as early as 1850, although it was then rejected by a French journal as "trop élogieux"; see Lina Ramann, *Franz Liszt: Als Künstler und Mensch* (Leipzig: Breitkopf und Härtel, 1880–94), 2.2:77. The French original for the 1855 version was translated, not by Peter Cornelius, but by Richard Pohl; Liszt, *Briefe* 1:161.

32. A lucid account can be found in Grey, *Wagner's Musical Prose*, 18–41.

33. Eduard Krüger, "Hegel's Philosophie der Musik," *Neue Zeitschrift für Musik* 17 (1842), 25–28, 29–32, 35–37, 39–40, 43–45, 47–51, 53–56, 57–59, 63–64, 65–69, at 44. Hanslick, too, counted Hegel among the important voices who insisted that music was contentless. See *Vom Musikalisch-Schönen,* ed. Dietmar Strauß, 1:160. See also Hegel, *Aesthetics,* 939: "Music is spirit, or the soul which resounds directly on its own account and feels satisfaction in its perception of itself."

34. Liszt, "Berlioz und seine Haroldsymphonie," 51 (footnote). For the quotes see Hegel, *Ästhetik,* in *Werke* 15:154, 217, and 148–49.

35. Enrico Fubini, *History of Music Aesthetics,* trans. Michael Hatwell (London: Macmillan, 1990), 277, emphasizes the dual—*zweifach angelegte*—traditions in Hegel.

36. Liszt, "Berlioz und seine Haroldsymphonie," 40. See also Brendel, "F. Liszt's symphonische Dichtungen," 86: "Der Musik bleibt die Eigenthümlichkeit, das durch Worte unsagbare auszudrücken, ihre schönste, größte Seite." See also "Franz Liszt in Leipzig," *Neue Zeitschrift für Musik* 46 (1857): 101–5, at 103.

37. Liszt, "Berlioz und seine Haroldsymphonie," 50.

38. Ibid., 40 and 50, which appears like a direct rebuttal of Hanslick by asserting that this could only be if it would "express certain emotions and passions."

39. Dahlhaus, *Esthetics of Music,* 30.

40. See Christian Hermann Weisse, *System der Ästhetik als Wissenschaft von der Idee der Schönheit* (reprint Hildesheim: G. Olms, 1966), 49–50: "Die Instrumentalmusik ist demnach das *reine* und *unmittelbare* Dasein des von aller besonderen Gestaltung freien, absoluten oder *modernen Ideals.*" See Dahlhaus, *The Idea of Absolute Music,* 100.

41. Hegel, *Aesthetics,* 795.

42. Brendel, "Franz Liszt in Leipzig," 103.

43. Liszt, "Berlioz und seine Haroldsymphonie," 79.

44. Ibid., 39. See also Dahlhaus, "Liszts 'Bergsymphonie'," 100; and Grey, *Wagner's Musical Prose,* especially 42–50.

45. William Weber, *Music and the Middle Class: The Social Structure of Concert Life in London, Paris and Vienna* (London: Croom Helm, 1975), 58–61 and 75–84.

46. Liszt, "Berlioz und seine Haroldsymphonie," 50, quoting Hegel, *Ästhetik,* 154 and 216–17; *Aesthetics,* 906 and 954 (translation modified). The last quotation begins: "Therefore, it is in this region [of independent, i.e. purely instrumental, music] that an essential difference begins to arise between the dilettante and the expert."

47. Liszt, "Berlioz und seine Haroldsymphonie," 81.

48. Ibid., 50.

49. Alan Walker, *Franz Liszt: The Virtuoso Years 1811–1847,* rev. ed. (Ithaca: Cornell University Press, 1988), 296. Cf. Franz Brendel, *Geschichte der Musik,* 2:222.

50. Brendel, "Franz Liszt in Leipzig," 103.

51. Liszt, "Berlioz und seine Haroldsymphonie," 52.

52. Jürgen Habermas, *Der philosophische Diskurs der Moderne: Zwölf Vorlesungen* (Frankfurt am Main: Suhrkamp, 1985), 31.

53. Andrew Bowie, *Aesthetics and Subjectivity: From Kant to Nietzsche* (Manchester: Manchester University Press, 1990), 117.

54. James A. Hepokoski, however, maintains that the "essence of a *symphonische Dichtung* is situated in the listener's act (anticipated by the composer's) of connecting text and paratext, music and nonmusical image, and grappling with the implications of the connection. The genre exists, *qua* genre, solely within the receiver, who agrees to create it reciprocally by indicating his or her willingness to play the game proposed by the composer; it does not exist abstractly in the acoustical surface of the music." While Liszt would have agreed with the position, he would have felt stronger about his own role as a "proposing" composer. See Hepokoski, "Fiery-Pulsed Libertine or Domestic Hero? Strauss's *Don Juan* Reinvestigated," in *Richard Strauss: New Perspectives on the Composer and His Work,* ed. Bryan Gilliam (Durham: Duke University Press, 1992), 135–76, at 136.

55. Brendel, "F. Liszt's symphonische Dichtungen," 135.

56. Schumann, "Berlioz: *Fantastic Symphony,*" in Bent, *Music Analysis in the Nineteenth Century,* 2:192; and Brendel, *Geschichte der Musik,* 2:244–45.

57. Brendel, "F. Liszt's symphonische Dichtungen," 74–75.

58. Franz Brendel, *Die Musik der Gegenwart und die Gesammtkunst der Zukunft* (Leipzig: B. Hinze, 1854), 3.

59. Peter Raabe, *Franz Liszt* (Tutzing: H. Schneider, 1968), 2:94.

60. Ibid. The judgement was echoed by Otto Klauwell, who suggested that only those who don't take issue with the "utter formlessness" of the Mountain Symphony could understand the greatness of its ideas and that a *single* presentation of the opposition of nature and humanity would have sufficed. *Geschichte der Programmusik von Ihren Anfängen bis zur Gegenwart* (Leipzig: Breitkopf und Härtel, 1910), 147–48.

61. Raabe, *Franz Liszt,* 2:95.

62. Dahlhaus, "Liszts 'Bergsymphonie'," 96–97; Richard Kaplan, "Sonata Form in the Orchestral Works of Liszt: The Revolutionary Reconsidered," *Nineteenth-Century Music* 8 (1984): 142–52, at 152.

63. Hepokoski, "Fiery-Pulsed Libertine or Domestic Hero?" 135–76, especially 143; "Genre and Content in Mid-Century Verdi: 'Addio, del passato' (*La*

traviata, act 3)," *Cambridge Opera Journal* 1 (1989): 249–76. *Sibelius: Symphony No. 5* (Cambridge: Cambridge University Press, 1993), 4–9.

64. Liszt, "Berlioz und seine Haroldsymphonie," 81. For an extensive discussion of repetition in the programmatic symphony of the classical era, see Richard Will, "Programmatic Symphonies of the Classical Period" (Ph.D diss., Cornell University, 1994), 357ff.

65. Eduard Hanslick, *Aus dem Concert-Saal: Kritiken und Schilderungen aus 20 Jahren des Wiener Musiklebens 1848–1868* (Vienna: W. Braumüller, 1897), 127.

66. Raabe, *Franz Liszt,* 2:72.

67. Hepokoski, "Fiery-Pulsed Libertine or Domestic Hero?" 143.

68. Ibid.

69. For the distinction between explicit and implicit theory see Carl Dahlhaus, *Die Musiktheorie im 18. und 19. Jahrhundert: Grundzüge einer Systematik* (Darmstadt: Wissenschaftliche Buchgesellschaft, 1984), chapter 6.

70. Hepokoski, *Sibelius: Symphony No. 5,* 5–7.

71. Dahlhaus, "Liszts 'Bergsymphonie,'" 115. William S. Newman, *The Sonata Since Beethoven,* 3rd ed. (New York: W. W. Norton, 1983), 134 and 375. William Neumann, *Die Componisten der neueren Zeit: Adam, Auber, Beethoven, Bellini, Boieldieu, Cherubini . . . und Andere in Biographien geschildert* (Cassel: E. Balde, 1854–57). Cited in Detlef Altenburg, ed., *Liszt und die Weimarer Klassik* (Laaber: Laaber, 1997), 22.

72. Draeseke, *Schriften,* 245. For the following quotes see ibid., 243–44.

73. Ibid., 244.

74. In David Kopp's theory of mediant relations, the sharp mediant occupies a middle position: it is neither weak nor overstrong, but strong; and in Richard Cohn's hexatonic system, it is two (not one or three) semitonal steps away from the source triad. David Kopp, "A Comprehensive Theory of Chromatic Mediant Relations in Mid-Nineteenth-Century Music" (Ph.D. diss., Brandeis University, 1995), 12–13. Richard Cohn, "Maximally Smooth Cycles, Hexatonic Systems, and the Analysis of Late-Romantic Triadic Progressions," *Music Analysis* 15 (1996): 9–40, at 17 and 24.

75. Rimsky-Korsakov acknowledged its influence on his own tone-poem *Sadko,* where "the Introduction—picture of the calmly surging sea—contains the harmonic and modulatory basis of the beginning of Liszt's *Ce qu'on entend sur la montagne* (modulation by a minor third downward)"; quoted in Richard Taruskin, "Chernomar to Kashchei: Harmonic Sorcery; or, Stravinsky's 'Angle'," *Journal of the American Musicological Society* 38 (1985): 72–142, at 93.

76. See D-WRgs Z27. Liszt labeled the sequence harmonically *"in Septimen"* on account of the cyclical progression of dominant seventh chords.

77. See D-WRgs N1 sketchbook page 8. Liszt seems to have been particularly fond of the C-E♭-F♯-A tetrachord, which also appears in the Faust Symphony, at the beginning of *Orpheus,* and as early as the first version of *Harmonies poétiques et religieuses.*

78. Draeseke, *Schriften,* 236.

79. Ibid., 246.

80. Howard Cinnamon, "Tonic Arpeggiation and Successive Equal Third

Relations as Elements of Tonal Evolution in the Music of Franz Liszt," *Music Theory Spectrum* 8 (1986): 1–24, at 10–11.

81. Draeseke, *Schriften,* 247.

82. Brendel, "F. Liszt's Symphonische Dichtungen," 112.

83. Natalie Bauer-Lechner, *Recollections of Gustav Mahler,* ed. Peter Franklin, trans. Dika Newlin (London: Faber and Faber, 1980), 31.

84. Hepokoski, *Sibelius: Symphony No. 5,* 6.

85. Draeseke, *Schriften,* 248.

86. John Williamson, "Liszt, Mahler and the Chorale," *Proceedings of the Royal Musical Association* 108 (1981/82): 115–25, at 120.

87. Ibid.

88. Draeseke, *Schriften,* 248.

89. Ibid., 249.

90. Miller, "Elevation bei Victor Hugo und Franz Liszt," 154–59.

91. Ibid., 159. This bears out nicely Carolyn Abbate's point that music has no past tense, which makes the temporal distance that opens discursive space unavailable to a composer. Abbate, *Unsung Voices,* 52.

92. Miller, "Elevation bei Victor Hugo und Franz Liszt," 159 and Dahlhaus, "Liszts 'Bergsymphonie'," 127.

93. Hermann Danuser, *Musikalische Prosa* (Regensburg: G. Bosse, 1975), 105. Abbate, *Unsung Voices,* 55, dismisses Danuser's approach as an easy and unsatisfactory form of musical narration.

94. See Anthony Newcomb, "Narrative Archetypes and Mahler's Ninth Symphony," in *Music and Text: Critical Inquiries,* ed. Steven Paul Scher (Cambridge: Cambridge University Press, 1992), 118–36.

95. Abbate, *Unsung Voices,* 49 and 131–35.

96. James Buhler make a similar argument about Mahler's First Symphony in his "'Breakthrough' as Critique of Form: The Finale of Mahler's First Symphony," *Nineteenth-Century Music* 20 (1996): 125–43, at 133–34 and 137–43.

97. Peter Raabe, *Die Entstehungsgeschichte der ersten Orchesterwerke Franz Liszts* (Leipzig: Breitkopf und Härtel, 1916), 43.

98. The sources consulted here are (1) D-WRgs A1d ("Ouverture"), an incomplete set of parts formerly belonging to the Weimar Court Theater in an unknown hand (some extra parts in Conradi's hand) with woodwinds and brass (and harp?) missing ca. 1849; (2) D-WRgs A1b ("*Méditation Symphonie*"), a full score in Joachim Raff's hand with corrections by the composer from ca. 1850; (3) D-WRgs A1a ("Poème symphonique"), a full autograph score with numerous corrections from 1854; (4)D-WRgs A1e–g, a set of parts (violin 1 and 2 missing) based on A1a mostly in Raff's hand whose corrections correspond to A1c and additional revisions in the *Stichvorlage*; (5) D-WIbh [9382], the *Stichvorlage* based on A1a in Raff's hand with corrections by Raff and the composer showing at least two layers of corrections (those based on A1c are pasted in or are on newly written pages, as well as later corrections); (6) D-WRgs W1a, version for two pianos based on A1a incorporating corrections from A1c and the *Stichvorlage*; and (7) D-WRgs A1c, a collection of corrections for the *Stichvorlage* and the version for two pianos. The set of parts of the *Ouverture* from the Weimar Court Theater that Raabe listed in his *Entstehungs-*

geschichte (p. 44) may be the same as A1d, although they show no evidence of the corrections by the composer that Raabe saw in the copy for the section leaders. Most likely they were created together with a score now lost, which in turn was created from an autograph score, or short score, also lost.

99. See Pohl, note 2 above, p. 42. Erasures, cancellations, paste-overs, and rewritings in the *Stichvorlage* and the parts correspond to the collection of correction leaves (A1c), apparently intended for the *Stichvorlage*. They mostly affected the orchestration and the slow movements, which seem to have given Liszt the most trouble (among the corrections in A1c is a rejected version of the first slow movement).

100. The autograph of the two-piano arrangment shows some, but not all, revisions also appearing in the *Stichvorlage,* such as the division of a single whole note resulting in measures 9 and 10 (*et passim*).

101. After Liszt introduced triplets to Humanity 3 in the Gotha version, he matched these with triplets both in the New Theme and in the horn chords that punctuate the harmonic shifts in the introduction. Thus Liszt derived Nature 3 from the New Theme and not vice versa, even though it appears in the piece the other way around.

102. Liszt merely adds some corrections and separately written-out orchestral sections between pages 22–23 and 30–31, and after 39. Only the initial statement of Nature 3 in B major, for example, is written on the extra page, 10a, brass and timpani only.

103. Most insightful studies in the context of late 18th-century music are by Elaine R. Sisman, "Learned Style and the Rhetoric of the Sublime in the 'Jupiter' Symphony," in *Wolfgang Amadè Mozart: Essays on his Life and his Music* (Oxford: Clarendon Press, 1996), 213–38 and James Webster, "The *Creation,* Haydn's Late Vocal Music, and the Musical Sublime," in *Haydn and His World,* ed. Elaine R. Sisman (Princeton: Princeton University Press, 1997), 57–102.

104. Kant, *Critique of Judgment,* 103–106 and 119–23; lxx and 268. Edmund Burke, *A Philosophical Enquiry into the Origin of our Ideas of the Sublime and Beautitful,* ed. J. T. Boulton (New York: Columbia University Press, 1958), 36.

105. Kant, *Critique of Judgment,* 262, see also 264 (the peroration of § 28). See also Suzanne Guerlac, *The Impersonal Sublime,* 6.

106. Kant, *Critique of Pure Reason,* trans. Norman Kemp Smith, 2nd rev. ed. (London: Macmillan, 1933), 59.

107. Cited in Elaine R. Sisman, *Mozart: The 'Jupiter' Symphony* (Cambridge: Cambridge University Press, 1993), 19.

108. Kant, *Critique of Judgement,* 130.

109. Christian Friedrich Michaelis, "Einige Bemerkungen über das Erhabene in der Musik," *Berlinische musikalische Zeitung* 1 (1805): 179–81.

110. Translation quoted from Webster, "The *Creation,* Haydn's Late Vocal Music, and the Musical Sublime," 62.

111. See Nancy Kovaleff Baker and Thomas Christensen, eds., *Aesthetics and the Art of Musical Composition in the German Enlightenment: Selected Writings of Johann Georg Sulzer and Heinrich Christoph Koch* (Cambridge: Cambridge University Press, 1995), 106. See also Dahlhaus, *Klassische und romantische Musikästhetik,* 99–100.

112. Dahlhaus, *Klassische und romantische Musikästhetik,* 100.

113. Webster, "The *Creation,* Haydn's Late Vocal Music, and the Musical Sublime," 64.

114. Kant, *Critique of Judgment,* 116.

115. Ibid., 122–23.

116. Alan Walker, *Franz Liszt: The Weimar Years 1848–1861,* rev. ed. (Ithaca: Cornell University Press, 1989), 11.

117. Quoted from Paul Merrick, *Revolution and Religion in the Music of Franz Liszt* (Cambridge: Cambridge University Press, 1987), 19–20.

118. Ibid., 34.

119. Ibid., 111.

120. Ibid., 250.

121. Walker, *Franz Liszt: The Virtuoso Years,* 39–40 and 61–62.

122. Benjamin, "Theses on the Philosophy of History," 254.

123. Ibid.

124. Draeseke, *Schriften,* 249.

NOTES TO CHAPTER 5—SCHOENBERG'S GAZE

1. Cited by Reinhold Brinkmann, "Schoenberg the Contemporary: A View from Behind," in *Constructive Dissonance: Arnold Schoenberg and the Trans-formations of Twentieth-Century Culture,* ed. Juliane Brand and Christopher Hailey (Berkeley: University of California Press, 1997), 196–219, at 198.

2. The photograph is reproduced in Walter H. Rubsamen, "Schoenberg in America," *The Musical Quarterly* 37 (1951): 469–89, at 481. For a perhaps less arranged glimpse at Schoenberg's home, see the photograph that he sent to Kandinsky, reproduced as plate 1 in Jelena Hahl-Koch, ed., *Arnold Schoenberg, Wassily Kandinsky: Letters, Pictures, and Documents,* trans. John C. Crawford (London: Faber and Faber, 1984).

3. Brinkmann, "Schoenberg the Contemporary," 199.

4. See, for instance, Otto Breicha, *Gerstl und Schönberg: eine Beziehung* (Salzburg: Galerie Welz, 1993).

5. Benn is quoted in Thomas J. Harrison, *1910: The Emancipation of Disso-nance* (Berkeley: University of California Press, 1996), 1. "[O]n or about De-cember 1910 human character changed," noted Virginia Woolf in an essay on the end of the Edwardian, and by implication Victorian, era. The remark is routinely regarded as a comment on the first Post-Impressionist Exhibition, which opened at the Grafton Galleries on 8 November of that year and shocked the British public for the first time with the innovative works by Cézanne, Matisee, Van Gogh, and Gauguin. Edwin J. Kenney, Jr., "The Moment, 1910: Virginia Woolf, Arnold Bennett, and Turn of the Century Consciousness," *Colby Library Quarterly* 13 (1977): 42–66, at 45.

6. Halsey Stevens, "A Conversation with Schoenberg about Painting," *Journal of the Arnold Schoenberg Institute* 2 (1978): 178–80, at 179.

7. Courtney S. Adams, "Artistic Parallels between Arnold Schoenberg's Music and Painting (1908–1912)," *College Music Symposium* 35 (1995): 5–21; Brinkmann, "Schoenberg the Contemporary," 206.

8. Arnold Schönberg, "Mahler," in *Stil und Gedanke: Aufsätze zur Musik,* ed. Ivan Vojtech (Frankfurt am Main: S. Fischer, 1976), 7–24, at 24.

9. Arnold Schoenberg, "Painting Influences," *Journal of the Arnold Schoenberg Institute* 2 (1978): 237–39, at 237.

10. Benjamin, *Ursprung des deutschen Trauerspiels,* 206 (185, translation modified).

11. Alban Berg and [et al.], *Arnold Schönberg* (Munich: R. Piper, 1912), 13–21, at 18; translation in Walter Frisch, ed., *Schoenberg and His World* (Princeton: Princeton University Press, 1999), 199–260, at 207.

12. See Thomas Zaunschirm, ed., *Arnold Schönberg: Das bildnerische Werk* (Klagenfurt: Ritter, 1991), 371. Zaunschirm remarks that a similar aquarelle painting from 1919 is a variant of cat. no. 81 from 1910.

13. Martin Jay, *Downcast Eyes: The Denigration of Vision in Twentieth-Century French Thought* (Berkeley: University of California Press, 1993), 259.

14. Ibid.

15. Gerald Eager, "The Missing and the Mutilated Eye in Contemporary Art," *The Journal of Aesthetics and Art Criticism* 20 (1961): 49–59, at 59; cited in Jay, *Downcast Eyes,* 260.

16. Arnold Schoenberg, "Composition with Twelve Tones (1)," in *Style and Idea: Selected Writings of Arnold Schoenberg,* ed. Leonard Stein, trans. Leo Black (Berkeley: University of California Press, 1984), 214–45, at 240.

17. Schönberg, "Analyse der 4 Orchesterlieder op. 22," in: *Stil und Gedanke,* 286–300, at 293.

18. Quoted in Zaunschirm, ed., *Arnold Schönberg: Das bildnerische Werk,* 443.

19. Ibid.

20. Schoenberg, "Composition with Twelve Tones (1)," 223.

21. Adorno, *Philosophie der Neuen Musik,* 54 (51).

22. Ibid., 37 (30, translation modified). I will use the literal translation, *Philosophy of New Music,* throughout the text. For the Schoenberg quote, see "New Music: My Music," *Style and Idea,* 99–106, at 105–06.

23. Theodor W. Adorno, "Neunzehn Beiträge über neue Musik ('Musikalischer Expressionismus')," in *Gesammelte Schriften* 18:60–62, at 61; *Ästhetische Theorie,* 125 (cf. 80).

24. Adorno, "On Some Relationships Between Music and Painting," 66 (translation modified). On Schenker, see chapter 6 below.

25. See the preface to Anton Webern, *Sechs Bagatellen für Streichquartett op. 9* (Vienna: Universal Edition, 1924); translation from Robert P. Morgan, *Twentieth-Century Music: A History of Musical Style in Modern Europe and America* (New York: W.W. Norton, 1991), 80.

26. Ferruccio Busoni, *Selected Letters,* ed. and trans. Antony Beaumont (New York: Columbia University Press, 1987), 389.

27. Adorno, *Philosophie der Neuen Musik,* 43 (37, translation modified).

28. Ibid., 44 (39, translation modified).

29. Paul Bekker, "Schönberg: 'Erwartung'," in *Arnold Schönberg zum fünfzigsten Geburtstage, 13. September 1924* (Vienna: Universal Edition, 1924), 275–82, at 276–77.

30. Ibid., 280.
31. Ibid.
32. Ibid.
33. Ibid., 280–81.
34. Adorno, *Philosophie der Neuen Musik,* 47 (my translation; cf. 42).
35. Theodor W. Adorno, "Vers une musique informelle," in *Quasi una Fantasia,* 269–322, at 272.
36. Schoenberg, "Brahms the Progressive," in *Style and Idea,* 398– 441, at 414–15.
37. See Adorno, *Minima Moralia, Gesammelte Schriften* 4: 252–53 and Danuser, *Musikalische Prosa,* 143.
38. Adorno, "Vers une musique informelle," 272–73.
39. Karl Heinrich Wörner, "Schönberg's 'Erwartung' und das Ariadne-Thema," in *Die Musik in der Geistesgeschichte: Studien zur Situation der Jahre um 1910* (Bonn: Bouvier, 1970), 91–117, at 105.
40. Ibid., 111 and 103. For the early reception of Benda's piece see, Laurenz Lütteken, *Das Monologische als Denkform in der Musik zwischen 1760 und 1785* (Tübingen: M. Niemeyer, 1998), 472–80. Georg Anton Benda, *Ariadne auf Naxos,* ed. Thomas Bauman (New York: Garland, 1985). In her meritable and stimulating dissertation, "Revisioning Musical Modernism: Arnold Schoenberg, Marie Pappenheim, and *Erwartung*'s New Woman" (Ph.D., State University of New York at Stony Brook, 1999), Elizabeth Keathley offers extensive documentation about the collaboration between the librettist and the composer. Keathley also gives a provocative feminist reading of the work, suggesting that the (partly pseudo-) Freudian interpretation of the woman as hysterical and mad belongs to a different layer in the work's reception and does not do justice to Pappenheim's (and Schoenberg's) vision of an emancipating female subjectivity, which represents a distinct variant, and alternative to male modernism. Needless to say that Adorno is an accomplice in the Freudian reading (though he should certainly not be reduced to it). On the question of authorship, see also Bryan Simms, "Whose Idea was *Erwartung?*," in *Constructive Dissonance: Arnold Schoenberg and the Transformations of Twentieth-Century,* 100–111.
41. Tobias Plebuch, "Dark Fantasies and the Dawn of the Self: New Light on Gerstenberg's Lyrics to C.P.E. Bachs's C-minor Fantasy," unpublished paper given at the Annual Meeting of the American Musicological Society in Toronto, 2000.
42. Wörner, "Schönberg's 'Erwartung' und das Ariadne-Thema," 114.
43. Karlheinz Stockhausen, "Momentform: Neue Zusammenhänge zwischen Aufführungsdauer, Werkdauer, und Moment," in *Texte,* ed. Dieter Schnebel (Cologne: M. DuMont Schauberg, 1963–78), 1:189–210, at 190.
44. Anton Webern, "Schönbergs Musik," in *Arnold Schönberg: Mit Beiträgen von Alban Berg, [et al.],* 22–48, at 45 (cf. 227).
45. Wörner, "Schönberg's 'Erwartung' und das Ariadne-Thema," 100–101.
46. Benda, *Ariadne auf Naxos,* 96–98.
47. Wörner, "Schönberg's 'Erwartung',," 93–95.
48. "In here? One cannot see the way" (scene 1, mm. 3–6); "Is this still the

way?" (scene 2, m. 38); "He is not here either. Nothing living on the whole long road" (scene 4, m. 125).

49. Anglet, *Der "ewige" Augenblick: Studien zur Struktur und Funktion eines Denkbildes bei Goethe,* 136–61.

50. Adorno, *Philosophie der Neuen Musik,* 51 (46–47, translation modified).

51. Ibid.

52. Translation adapted from *Philosophy of Modern Music,* 47.

53. Herbert H. Buchanan, "A Key to Schoenberg's *Erwartung* (Op. 17)," *Journal of the American Musicological Society* 20 (1967): 434–49; Alan Philip Lessem, *Music and Text in the Works of Arnold Schoenberg: The Critical Years, 1908–1922* (Ann Arbor: UMI Research Press, 1979), 74–95.

54. Buchanan, "A Key to Schoenberg's *Erwartung,*" 436.

55. Lessem, *Music and Text in the Works of Arnold Schoenberg,* 95.

56. Arnold Schoenberg, *Theory of Harmony,* trans. Roy E. Carter (Berkeley: University of California Press, 1978), 394–95. To judge from Schoenberg's examples in the *Harmonielehre,* "suspended tonality" refers to the mutual suspension of clearly perceptible tonal centers, while a work like *Erwartung* is an exteme case of "extended tonality" whose chromaticism already obscures tonal language to the point that most commentators describe it, despite Schoenberg's disapproval of the term, as atonal. See the author's foonote ibid., 432; and Schoenberg, "My Evolution," in *Style and Idea,* 79–92, at 81–84.

57. Michael Cherlin, "Schoenberg and *Das Unheimliche*: Spectres of Tonality," *The Journal of Musicology* 11 (1993): 357–73, at 363.

58. Ibid., 361 and 364.

59. Susan McClary, *Feminine Endings: Music, Gender, and Sexuality* (Minneapolis: University of Minnesota Press, 1991), 104–109, at 107. See Keathley, "Revisioning Musical Modernism: Arnold Schoenberg, Marie Pappenheim, and *Erwartung*'s New Woman," 318–61, for a thorough discussion of Schoenberg's subtle connections between the music for "the way" with the *Am Wegrand* quotation.

60. Adorno, *Philosophie der neuen Musik,* 52 (48, translation modified).

61. Ibid.

62. Ibid., 52–53 (48–49, translation modified).

63. Cited from Adorno, "Vers une musique informelle," 274.

64. Ibid., 274–75.

65. Adorno, *Mahler: A Musical Physiognomy,* 139.

66. Adorno, *Beethoven,* 236 and 47 (164 and 22).

67. Schoenberg, "My Evolution," 88. To be sure, Schoenberg's self-construction (partly perpetuated by Adorno) needs to be discussed with a grain of salt. Joseph Auner has shown that Schoenberg had already been experimenting with the organization of all twelve pitches. See Joseph Auner, "In Schoenberg's Workshop: Aggregates and Referential Collections in the Composition of *Die glückliche Hand,*" *Music Theory Spectrum* 18 (1996): 77–105. For a detailed account of the whole period, see Ethan Haimo, *Schoenberg's Serial Odyssey: The Evoltuion of his Twelve-tone Method 1914–1928* (Oxford: Clarendon Press, 1990).

68. Jean Christensen, "Arnold Schoenberg's Oratorio *Die Jakobsleiter*" (Ph.D. diss., University of California, Los Angeles, 1979), 1:356.

69. Adorno, *Mahler: A Musical Physiognomy,* 139.

70. Adorno, "Music and Language: A Fragment," in *Quasi una Fantasia,* 2. See the discussion of the passage in chapter 1 above.

71. Schoenberg wrote this on the first of two added flyleaves at the back of the typescript of the libretto, whose corrections he marked as finished on 7 June 1917. See Christensen, "Arnold Schoenberg's Oratorio *Die Jakobsleiter*" 2:32.

72. Ibid., 2:30–32.

73. Ibid., 2:130 (Sketchbook 15–22, p. 30e).

74. Adorno, *Mahler: A Musical Physiognomy,* 139 and 140.

75. Ibid., 139.

76. Adorno, "Sacred Fragment," in *Quasi una Fantasia,* 225–48, at 227–28.

77. Ibid., 242. I translate *Ewigkeit* as eternity, not immortality; cf. "Sakrales Fragment," in *Gesammelte Schriften* 16:454–75, 469.

78. Ibid., 236.

79. Ibid., 229.

80. Ibid., 241 (translation modified, cf. "Sakrales Fragment," 468).

81. Ibid.

82. Gary Tomlinson, *Metaphysical Song,* 149 and 151 (original emphasis).

83. Philippe Lacoue-Labarthe, *Musica Ficta (Figures of Wagner)* (Stanford: Stanford University Press, 1994), 130–31.

84. Ibid., 145 and 131–32.

85. Adorno, "Sacred Fragment," 226 and 248.

86. Ibid., 226.

87. See Christensen, "Arnold Schoenberg's Oratorio *Die Jakobsleiter*" 1:100. In *Dichtung* 14, page 15 (next to "Grosses symphonisches Zwischenspiel") Schoenberg remarks: "Soll auch im Schlusschore, insbesonders der [sic] 'Amen' verwendet werden"; and on page 31 "aus dem grossen Zwischenspiel" he points with an arrow to "Amen."

88. Page 5 of the nine stapled pages making up the drafts for the libretto. Christensen, "Arnold Schoenberg's Oratorio *Die Jakobsleiter*" 1:76 and the transcription at 2:58.

89. Ibid., 2:60.

90. Ibid., 2:58.

91. As noted in the typewritten libretto (Dichtung 14: "*in schwebender Bewegung äusserst zart*"). Ibid., 1:98.

92. Adorno, "Sacred Fragment," 236.

93. Martina Sichardt, *Die Entstehung der Zwölftonmethode Arnold Schönbergs* (Mainz: Schott, 1990), 17; see also Lessem, *Music and Text in the Works of Arnold Schoenberg,* 195.

94. Schoenberg, *Die Jakobsleiter* (libretto), translation cited from Christensen, "Arnold Schoenberg's Oratorio *Die Jakobsleiter*" 2:47.

95. Ibid., 2:47.

96. Ibid., 2:28 and 2:47.

97. Honoré de Balzac, *La comédie humaine* (Paris: Gallimard, 1966), 1:12.

98. Jelena Hahl-Koch, ed., *Arnold Schoenberg, Wassily Kandinsky: Letters, Pictures, and Documents,* 54.

99. Ibid., 74.

100. Wassily Kandinsky, *Concerning the Spiritual in Art, and Painting in Particular 1912,* trans. Michael Sadleir, Francis Golffing, Michael Harrison, and Ferdinand Ostertag (New York: G. Wittenborn, 1947), 68.

101. Ibid., 24.

102. Gabriel's pressing to "go on" surely comes from Seraphita's speech before the assumption: "Do you not plainly hear the voice that cries to you, 'On! on!' Often in a celestial vision the angels descend and wrap you into song." Honoré de Balzac, *Séraphita,* trans. Clara Bell (Sawtry: Dedalus, 1989), 144.

103. Schoenberg, "Composition with Twelve Tones (1)," 223.

104. Morgan, "Musical Time/Musical Space," 529 and 532. John Covach, "The Sources of Schoenberg's 'Aesthetic Theology'," *Nineteenth-Century Music* 19 (1996): 252–62, at 261–62.

105. Balzac, *Séraphita,* 143.

106. Translation adapted from ibid., 146, using Schoenberg's copy of Honoré de Balzac, *Séraphita,* Auteurs célèbres, no. 456. (Paris: Ernest Flammarion, 19??), 237.

107. Schoenberg originally labeled the part *"Die* Sterbende" (my emphasis); see Christensen, "Arnold Schoenberg's Oratorio *Die Jakobsleiter"* 2:78. For an insightful treatment of the question of androgyny in op. 17, see Jennifer Shaw, "Androgyny and the Eternal Feminine in Schoenberg's Oratorio *Die Jakobsleiter,"* in *Political and Religious Ideas in the Works of Arnold Schoenberg,* ed. Charlotte M. Cross and Russell A. Berman (New York: Garland, 2000), 61–83.

108. Bloch, *Essays on the Philosophy of Music,* 124.

109. See above, chapter 1, note 72.

110. Kittler, *Discourse Networks 1800/1900,* 160. For a sensitive discussion of the dictum in the context of absolute music see Nelson, "The Fantasy of Absolute Music," 709.

111. Bloch, *Essays on the Philosophy of Music,* 98.

112. The unpublished paper by Yonathan Malin, "Prayer and the 'Unity of Musical Space' in Balzac's *Séraphita* and Schoenberg's *Die Jakobsleiter,"* grew out of the graduate seminar on Expressionism and *Doctor Faustus* in the winter quarter 1999 at the University of Chicago. Special thanks to Mr. Malin for allowing my use of his observation.

113. See Christensen, "Arnold Schoenberg's Oratorio *Die Jakobsleiter"* 2:136 (sketchbook 15–22, page 45).

114. Ibid., 2:129–30 (sketchbook 15–22, pages 30d and e).

115. Originally Schoenberg sketched a full-blown *Nebenstimme* for the solo viola starting in m. 617, eventually leaving merely the first two measures of the hexachord to the harmonium in mm. 617–18. See A-ASC sketchbook 15–22 page 105.

116. Lothar Brieger-Wasservogel, "Swedenborgs Weltanschauung: Ein Versuch," in *Emanuel Swedenborg: Theologische Schriften* (Jena: Eugen Diedrichs, 1904), 10–32, at 13.

117. See John Joseph Reible III, "Tristan-Romanticism and the Expressionism of the *Three Piano Pieces,* op. 11 of Arnold Schoenberg" (Ph.D. diss.,

Washington University, 1980); and Thomas Christensen, "Schoenberg's Opus 11, No. 1.: A Parody of Pitch Cells from *Tristan,*" *Journal of the Arnold Schoenberg Institute* 10 (1987): 38–44.

118. "A musical stimulus that comes from an altogether different sphere *chooses* the text of this song as a metaphorical expression of itself." Friedrich Nietzsche, *Sämtliche Werke: Kritische Studienausgabe,* eds. Giorgio Colli and Mazzino Montinari (Munich: Deutscher Taschenbuch Verlag, 1988), 7:366; "On Music and Words," trans. Walter Kaufman, in: Carl Dahlhaus, *Between Romanticism and Modernism: Four Studies in the Music of the Later Nineteenth Century,* trans. Mary Whittall (Berkeley: University of California Press, 1980), 112 (translation modified).

119. Adorno, *Philosophie der neuen Musik,* 122 (128).

120. Ibid., 122 (129).

121. Ibid.

122. Adorno, *Beethoven,* 25 (6).

123. The passage is discussed in Chua, *Absolute Music and the Construction of Meaning,* 49. See also Richard Cohn's "Uncanny Resemblances: The Hermeneutics of Hexatonic poles" (unpublished paper).

124. Adorno, "Sacred Fragment," 236 (emphasis added).

125. Adorno, *Ästhetische Theorie,* 201 (133).

126. Arnold Schönberg, "Gewissheit," *Musikblätter des Anbruch* 4 (1922): 2–3, at 2.

NOTES TO CHAPTER 6—ECHO'S EYES

1. Thomas Mann, *Doctor Faustus: The Life of the German Composer Adrian Leverkühn as Told by a Friend,* trans. Helen Tracy Lowe-Porter (New York: Modern Library, 1992), 625 (translation slightly modified); *Doktor Faustus: Das Leben des deutschen Tonsetzers Adrian Leverkühn erzählt von einem Freunde* (Frankfurt am Main: S. Fischer, 1967). In this chapter, I will quote primarily from the Lowe-Porter translation edition, but be mindful of the fine newer translation by John E. Woods (New York: A. A. Knopf, 1997), which, however, sometimes fails to grasp musical details correctly.

2. Ibid., 621 (translation slightly modified).

3. Such as Mann's daughter, Erika. See Thomas Mann, *The Story of a Novel: The Genesis of Doctor Faustus,* trans. Richard Winston and Clara Winston (New York: A.A. Knopf, 1961), 225–26.

4. Thomas Mann, *Tagebücher 28.5.1946–31.12.1948,* ed. Inge Jens (Frankfurt am Main: S. Fischer, 1989), 95 (6 February 1947). Surely, Echo is also a distant echo of Hanno Buddenbrooks.

5. Mann, *The Story of a Novel,* 219.

6. Ibid., 220–21.

7. Gerhard Herz, "The Music in Thomas Mann's *Doctor Faustus,*" *Orbis Musicae* 9 (1986/87): 205–23, at 206.

8. *Doctor Faustus,* 249.

9. See the letter to Adorno from 30 December 1945. Thomas Mann, *Briefe 1937–1947,* ed. Erika Mann (Frankfurt am Main: S. Fischer, 1963), 469–72. On

11 July 1950 Mann to Adorno: " . . . und daß der Teufel nach Ihrem Äußeren gezeichnet sein soll, ist nun schon ganz absurd. Tragen Sie überhaupt eine Hornbrille?" See Thomas Mann, *Briefe 1948–1955 und Nachlese* ed. Erika Mann (Frankfurt am Main: S. Fischer, 1965), 159. But the lack of outward similarity matters little. The excised passage from the *Story of the Novel* clearly emphasized the parallel between Adrian/Mann and the devil/Adorno and the *Philosophy of New Music*: " . . . vieles von dem, was Leverkühn später vom eiskalten Teufel über die bis zur Unmöglichkeit problematischen Rolle der Kunst—der Musik im Besonderen—in unserer Gesellschaft sich anhören muß ist nichts als diskursive Einschmelzung von Gedanken jener Schrift. *Adrian hört es, weil er es weiß, und ebenso ließ ich mir von außen sagen, was ich wußte, ließ mir helfen durch einen anderen—von mir selbst.* Der 'andere' hatte nicht wenig Spaß daran. 'Ich bin bekanntlich der Teufel', sagte er, als er mit dem Kapitel bekannt geworden war." *Tagebücher 28.5.1946–31.12.1948,* 949 (Anhang Text 58, my emphasis). See Tobias Plebuch, "Vom Musikalisch-Bösen. Eine musikgeschichtliche Annäherung an das Diabolische in Thomas Manns *Doktor Faustus,*" in *Thomas Mann: "Doktor Faustus" Zeitschrift für Germanistik, Neue Folge, Beiheft 3 (2000),* ed. Werner Röcke (1997), 207–62, at 255.

10. Pioneering was Gunilla Bergsten, *Thomas Mann's Doctor Faustus: The Sources and Structure of the Novel,* trans. Krishna Winston (Chicago: University of Chicago Press, 1969), 80–81; Hansjörg Dörr, "Thomas Mann und Adorno: Ein Beitrag zur Entstehung des *Doktor Faustus,*" *Literaturwissenschaftliches Jahrbuch im Auftrage der Görres-Gesellschaft Neue Folge* 11 (1970): 285–322; Rolf Tiedemann, "'Mitdichtende Einfühlung': Adornos Beiträge zum *Doktor Faustus*—noch einmal," *Frankfurter Adorno Blätter* 1 (1992): 9–33; Elvira Seiwert, *Beethoven-Szenarien: Thomas Manns "Doktor Faustus" und Adornos Beethoven-Projekt* (Stuttgart: J. B. Metzler, 1995); Volker Scherliess, "Zur Musik im *Doktor Faustus,*" in *"und was werden die Deutschen sagen?": Thomas Manns Roman Doktor Faustus,* ed. Hans Wißkirchen and Thomas Sprecher (Lübeck: Dräger, 1997), 113–52. About Mann's use of other sources in general see Jürgen Jung, *Altes und Neues zu Thomas Manns Roman Doktor Faustus: Quellen und Modelle: Mythos, Psychologie, Musik, Theo-Dämonologie, Faschismus* (Frankfurt am Main: P. Lang, 1985).

11. *Doctor Faustus,* 616. See also *Doktor Faustus,* 186: "Der Jüngste aber, Nepomuk, war ein Engel." On Mann's sources for the Echo figure, including its allusions to Luther, see Jung, *Altes und Neues zu Thomas Manns Roman Doktor Faustus,* 307–25.

12. *Doctor Faustus,* 606.

13. Ibid., 610.

14. Thomas Mann, *Tagebücher 1940–43,* ed. Peter de Mendelssohn (Frankfurt am Main: S. Fischer, 1982), 609–35. See the most thorough discussion of the interpretation's genesis and its aesthetic implications by Sabine Henze-Döhring, "'Abschied' oder 'Ende der Sonate'? Die Arietta aus Beethovens Klaviersonate op. 111: Möglichkeiten und Grenzen der Lesbarkeit von Musik," *Schweizer Jahrbuch für Musikwissenschaft/Annales Suisses de Musicologie* 15 (1995): 21–40, at 21–22 and 27.

15. Thomas Mann, *Tagebücher 1944–1.4.1946,* ed. Inge Jens (Frankfurt am Main: S. Fischer, 1986), 231; and Bruno Walter, *Briefe 1894–1962,* ed. Lotte

Walter Lindt (Frankfurt am Main: S. Fischer, 1969), 280. See Henze-Döhring, "'Abschied' oder 'Ende der Sonate'?" 23.

16. *Doctor Faustus,* 67. Compare with Adorno, "Spätstil Beethovens," in *Beethoven,* 183 (my translation; cf. 125).

17. *Doctor Faustus,* 68–71 (translation modified).

18. Mann owned a copy of Paul Bekker, *Beethoven* (Berlin: Schuster und Loeffler, 1912) in which he underlined the sentence (on page 192): "Mit dem Werk 111 nimmt Beethoven endgültig Abschied von der Form der Klaviersonate." See Henze-Döhring, "'Abschied' oder 'Ende der Sonate'?" 33.

19. Ibid., 25–26. Julius Bahle, *Eingebung und Tat im musikalischen Schaffen: Ein Beitrag zur Psychologie der Entwicklungs- und Schaffengesetze schöpferischer Menschen* (Leipzig: S. Hirzel, 1939), 182 Mann had received the book from Adorno on 6 July 1943. Bergsten, *Thomas Mann's Doctor Faustus,* 64–65 also mentions as a source Ernest Newman's *The Unconscious Beethoven: An Essay in Musical Psychology* rev. ed. (London: V. Gollancz, 1930), to which Mann refers in *The Story of a Novel,* 90.

20. Heinrich Schenker, *Die letzten fünf Sonaten von Beethoven: Kritische Ausgabe mit Einführung und Erläuterung [Sonate C moll Op. 111]* (Vienna: Universal Edition, 1916), 29. The introductory remarks are excised from Heinrich Schenker, *Beethoven: Die letzten Sonaten, Sonate C Moll Op. 111: Kritische Ausgabe mit Einführung und Erläuterung,* ed. Oswald Jonas, 2nd ed. (Vienna: Universal Edition, 1971).

21. Ibid.

22. *Die Musik* XVII/4 (1925), 246. Quoted in Robert Snarrenberg, *Schenker's Interpretive Practice* (Cambridge: Cambridge University Press, 1997), 1 (translation modified).

23. Schenker, *Die letzten fünf Sonaten von Beethoven [Sonate C moll Op. 111],* 69.

24. This and the following quotations from ibid., 69–70.

25. Ibid., 75.

26. William M. Drabkin, "The Sketches for Beethoven's Piano Sonata in C minor, op. 111" (Ph.D. diss., Princeton University, 1976), 1:158–59.

27. Ibid., 69.

28. Schenker, *Der Tonwille* 1 (1921), 22–26, at 23.

29. See the first chapter of Burnham, *Beethoven Hero,* especially 4–9 and 18–24.

30. Hans-Günter Klein, *Ludwig van Beethoven: Autographe und Abschriften, Katalog der Musikabteilung Staatsbibliothek Preussischer Kulturbesitz* (Berlin: Merseburger, 1975), 204. The C♯ is, in fact, notated in one of the melodic variants that appears on page 24; see Drabkin, "The Sketches for Beethoven's Piano Sonata in C minor, op. 111," 2:37.

31. Schenker, *Die letzten fünf Sonaten von Beethoven [Sonate C moll Op. 111],* 55. Jonas's 1971 edition, page 59, misreads nur as nun.

32. See above chapter 1. Adorno, *Ästhetische Theorie,* 531 (358, translation modified); *Beethoven,* 250 (174).

33. Benjamin, *Gesammelte Schriften,* 5:578.

34. Adorno, *Ästhetische Theorie,* 531 (358, translation modified).

35. Adorno, *Beethoven* 110–11 (70–71, translation modified).

36. Ibid., 252 (175–76, translation modified). Pertinent is the beginning of another related fragment: "The nullity of the particular; the fact that the whole means everything and—at the close of op. 111—that it retrospectively conjures up as something fulfilled details which were never actually there: this remains a central concern of any theory of Beethoven's music." Ibid., 47 (22–23).

37. See Zuidervaart, *Adorno's Aesthetic Theory*, 178–80.

38. Jameson, *Late Marxism*, 165 and 169.

39. Adorno, *Beethoven*, 244 (170).

40. Andreas Huyssen, "Memories of Utopia," in *Twilight Memories: Marking Time in a Culture of Amnesia* (New York: Routledge, 1995), 85–101, at 88.

41. Adorno, *Beethoven*, 237 (164, emphasis added).

42. Ibid., 244–45 (170). In Adorno's *Drei Gedichte von Theodor Däubler für vierstimmigen Frauenchor* op. 8 (1923–45), this "humanized star" also appears in the first poem ("Dämmerung") and most evocatively in the third poem ("Oft"), where it "looks down knowingly" and "begins to tremble":

Dämmerung

Am Himmel steht der erste Stern.
Die Wesen wähnen Gott den Herrn.
. . .

Oft

Warum erscheint mir immer wieder ein Abendtal,
sein Bach und Tannen?
Es blickt ein Stern verständlich nieder und sagt mir:
Wandle still von dannen.
Dann zieh ich fort von guten Leuten.
Was konnte mich nur so verbittern?
Die Glocken fangen an zu läuten,
und der Stern beginnt zu zittern.

43. Thus Adorno actually pointed out the connection between op. 111 and 31 no. 2 to Mann on the very evening when he played the Arietta Variations. See Mann, *Tagebücher 1940–43*, 634.

44. This is evident from the shortest of those seventeen early fragments from 1938—"Hope and star: Fidelio's aria and the second theme from the slow movement of the D-minor Piano Sonata, op. 31." Adorno, *Beethoven*, 245 (170). See also fragment 122, ibid. 86–87 (53) with another reference to Däubler's poem. Unfortunately the 1943 excerpts are not dated, although the *terminus post quem* is February 15. Special thanks to Dr. Henri Lonitz from the *Adorno Archiv Frankfurt* for checking these entries.

45. Cf. Schenker, *Der Tonwille* 1 (1921), 26: "Die Urlinie ist die Sehergabe des Komponisten."

46. Adorno, *Beethoven*, 252 (175). Schenker, *Die letzten fünf Sonaten von Beethoven [Sonate C moll Op. 111]*, 66.

47. Adorno, *Beethoven*, 249–50 (173, translation modified). This is the second fragment from 1943.

48. See Bergsten, *Thomas Mann's Doctor Faustus*, 182–84.

49. *Doctor Faustus,* 71 (emphasis added).

50. Ibid., 634.

51. Ernst Krenek, *Music Here and Now,* trans. Barthold Fles (New York: W.W. Norton, 1939), 119. See Bergsten, *Thomas Mann's Doctor Faustus,* 184. See also Ernst Krenek, "Musik und Humanität," in *Über neue Musik: Sechs Vorlesungen zur Einführung in die theoretischen Grundlagen* (Darmstadt: Wissenschaftliche Buchgesellschaft, 1977), 90–108, at 94: "Die Sprache der neuen Musik klingt voraus im Pathos von Fluch und Klage der Heiligen Schrift, ihre Farbe ist die der eschatologischen Trauer."

52. Arnold Schoenberg, "Aphorismen," *Die Musik* 9 (1909/1910), 159–163, at 159. Translation without emphases from Brinkmann, "Schoenberg the Contemporary," 197.

53. Rosemarie Puschmann, *Magisches Quadrat und Melancholie in Thomas Manns Doktor Faustus: Von der musikalischen Struktur zum semantischen Beziehungsnetz* (Bielefeld: Ampal, 1983), 90 (note 6).

54. *Doctor Faustus,* 635 (translation sightly modified).

55. Arnold Schmitz, *Beethovens "Zwei Prinzipe": Ihre Bedeutung für Themen- und Satzbau* (Berlin: Dümmlers Verlagsbuchhandlung, 1923); see Dahlhaus, *Ludwig van Beethoven: Approaches to his Music,* 38 and 246.

56. *Doctor Faustus,* 28.

57. Ibid., 547.

58. Ibid., 281.

59. Michael Beddow, *Thomas Mann: Doctor Faustus* (Cambridge: Cambridge University Press, 1994), 36–37.

60. *Doctor Faustus,* 231.

61. Ibid., 34.

62. On the relation between succession and simultaneity see Peter V. Brinkemper, *Spiegel & Echo: Intermedialität und Musikphilosophie im "Doktor Faustus"* (Würzburg: Königshausen und Neumann, 1997), 145–49.

63. *Doctor Faustus,* 232.

64. Ibid., 236.

65. Ibid., 239 (translation modified).

66. Ibid., 252–53.

67. Ibid.

68. Ibid. (translation slightly modified).

69. Ibid., 251 and 635; Adorno, *Philosophie der neuen Musik,* 63 (62).

70. *Doctor Faustus,* 637.

71. Ibid. (translation modified, emphasis added).

72. Ibid., 638. Cf. Adorno, *Philosophie der neuen Musik,* 100 (103).

73. Adorno, *Philosophie der neuen Musik,* 95–96 (98).

74. Ibid., 95 (98, translation modified) and *Doctor Faustus,* trans. Woods, 510 (translation slightly modified).

75. Ibid., 509–10 (translation slightly modified).

76. See, for instance, Harald Wehrmann, *Thomas Manns "Doktor Faustus": Von den fiktiven Werken Adrian Leverkühns zur musikalischen Struktur des Romans* (Frankfurt am Main: P. Lang, 1988), 120–129.

77. See *Doctor Faustus,* 143.

78. Ibid., 7.

79. Wehrmann, *Thomas Manns "Doktor Faustus,"* 126, quoting Mann, "Die Kunst des Romans," in *Werke: Das essayistische Werk,* ed. Hans Bürgin (Frankfurt am Main: Fischer Bücherei, 1968), 2:350–60, at 353.

80. Adapted from *Doctor Faustus,* 604 and Woods' translation, 485.

81. *Doctor Faustus,* 624 and 654.

82. Ibid., 655 and 666.

83. Cf. ibid., 316 (my translation).

84. *Doctor Faustus,* 309. Thomas Mann, "Bruder Hitler," in *Gesammelte Werke* (Frankfurt am Main: S. Fischer, 1960–79), 12:845–52. The essay appeared as "A Brother" in *Order of the Day: Political Essays and Speeches of Two Decades* (New York: A. A. Knopf, 1942), 153–61.

85. *Doctor Faustus,* 666–67.

86. Adorno, *Philosophie der Neuen Musik,* 99 (102).

87. *Doctor Faustus,* 637 (emphasis added).

88. Ibid., 635 (translation sightly modified).

89. Adorno, *Philosophie der Neuen Musik,* 43 (37, translation modified).

90. *Doctor Faustus* (Woods' translation), 256.

91. *Doctor Faustus,* 657–58 (emphasis added).

92. Ibid., 643 and 658.

93. Adorno, *Philosophie der neuen Musik,* 126 (133, translation modified).

94. *Doctor Faustus,* 7.

95. Translation from Morgan, *Twentieth-Century Music,* 80.

96. Adorno, *Philosophie der Neuen Music,* 108 (my translation; cf. 112). The other instance is Beckett's oeuvre where "aesthetic transcendence and disenchantment converge in the moment of falling silent." Adorno, *Ästhetische Theorie,* 123 (79, translation modified).

97. Theodor W. Adorno, "Toward a Portrait of Thomas Mann," in *Notes to Literature,* ed. Rolf Tiedemann (New York: Columbia University Press, 1991–92), 2:12–19, at 17–18 (translation slightly modified). See also Mann's account in *The Story of a Novel,* 222–23.

98. *Doctor Faustus,* 640.

99. Ibid.; cf. Adorno, "Toward a Portrait of Thomas Mann," 17.

100. *Doctor Faustus,* 641 (translation modified).

101. Thomas Mann, "Deutschland und die Deutschen," in *Essays,* ed. Hermann Kurzke and Stephan Stachorski (Frankfurt am Main: S. Fischer, 1993–97), 5:260–81, at 265 and 434. See also Thomas Mann, *Germany and the Germans* (Washington: Library of Congress, 1945), 5.

102. Mann, "Deutschland und die Deutschen," 269 and 275 (9 and 14).

103. Mann, *The Story of a Novel,* 32.

104. Ernst Bertram, *Nietzsche: Versuch einer Mythologie* (Berlin: G. Bondi, 1921), 102.

105. See Bernhard Böschenstein, "Ernst Bertrams Nietzsche: Eine Quelle für Thomas Manns *Doktor Faustus,*" *Euphorion: Zeitschrift für Literaturgeschichte* 72 (1978): 68–83, at 72, 82, and 79; citing Bertram, *Nietzsche: Versuch einer Mythologie,* 9, 347, and 152 (the last quote is from Nietzsche himself); and *Doctor Faustus,* 133.

106. Mann, "Deutschland und die Deutschen," 280.

107. Ibid., 279; and "Thomas Mann's Answer" in *Saturday Review of Literature* 32 (1 January 1949), 22–23, at 23. Cited in Bergsten, *Thomas Mann's Doctor Faustus*, 58.

108. Thomas Mann, *Thomas Mann an Ernst Bertram: Briefe aus den Jahren 1910–1955*, ed. Inge Jens (Pfullingen: G. Neske, 1960), 77.

109. Bertram, *Nietzsche: Versuch einer Mythologie*, 52. See Böschenstein, "Ernst Bertrams Nietzsche," 75.

110. See *Doctor Faustus*, 17 and 654.

111. See Thomas Mann, "Nietzsches Philosophie im Lichte unserer Erfahrung," in *Essays*, 6:56–92, at 70–71. About Nietzsche's conception of "eternal return" see Zimmermann, *Der ästhetische Augenblick*, 88–93 and 103–5.

112. Here I differ from Chua, *Absolute Music and the Construction of Meaning)*, 275, whose image of Adorno comes close to that of a Nietzschean atheist.

113. Brinkmann, "Schoenberg the Contemporary," 214.

114. Ibid., 214–15. For the conjunction of dystopia and utopia— the former being associated with the concentration camp, the latter with the shtetl as a figure of messianic redemption outside of history, see Philip Bohlman's "Jüdische Lebenswelten zwischen Utopie und Heterotopie, jüdische Musik zwischen Schtetl und Ghetto," in *Jahrbuch für Volksliedforschung* 47 (2002).

115. Mann, "Der Judenterror," in *Essays*, 5:201–3, at 203.

116. Mark H. Gelber, "Antisemitism, Indifferentism, the Holocaust, and Zionism: The Cases of Thomas Mann and Max Brod," in *Holocaust Studies Annual*, ed. Sanford Pinsker and Jack Fischel (New York: Garland, 1990), 53–62, at 60.

117. *Doctor Faustus*, 532. Gelber, "Antisemitism, Indifferentism, the Holocaust, and Zionism," 60, has noted that "the example of *Doctor Faustus* demonstrates Mann's lifelong incapability of being critical of Jews in fiction, while at the same time distancing himself sufficiently, dissociating himself as author, from antisemitic opinions common to European society, high and low."

118. Mann, "Deutschland und die Deutschen," 280 (19).

119. Freud, "Mourning and Melancholia," 243–58. The distiction plays a crucial role in Eric L. Santner, *Stranded Objects,* especially chapter 1; and Dominick LaCapra, *Representing the Holocaust: History, Theory, Trauma* (Ithaca: Cornell University Press, 1994), see especially 10–17 and 205–23; and Dominick LaCapra *History and Memory after Auschwitz*, chapter 2 and 181–85.

120. Freud, "Mourning and Melancholia," 243–44.

121. For a discussion of melancholy as a central theme in Mann's novel see Puschmann, *Magisches Quadrat und Melancholie in Thomas Manns Doktor Faustus*; the Freudian implications are also discussed from a different angle in Brinkemper, *Spiegel & Echo*, 314–45.

122. Freud, "Mourning and Melancholia," 247, 250, and 251.

123. On the relation between melancholy and modernity see: Max Pensky, *Melancholy Dialectics: Walter Benjamin and the Play of Mourning* (Amherst: University of Massachusetts Press, 1993); and Bohrer, *Der Abschied, Theorie der Trauer*, 538–52.

124. Mann, *The Story of a Novel*, 187–88.

125. See Martin Mueller, "Walter Benjamin und Thomas Manns Dr. *Faustus,*" *Archiv für das Studium der neueren Sprachen und Literaturen* 210 (Neue Folge 125) (1973), 327–30. See also Pushmann, *Magisches Quadrat und Melancholie in Thomas Manns Doktor Faustus,* 89–91. For the pertinent passage in Benjamin, see *Ursprung des deutschen Trauerspiels,* 236–37 (209–10).

126. Ibid., 236 (209).

127. Ibid. (translation modified).

128. *Doctor Faustus,* 637 (emphasis added).

129. See Benjamin, *Ursprung des deutschen Trauerspiels,* 236 (209–10).

130. Ibid., 236 (209).

131. Ibid., 236 (210).

132. LaCapra, *History and Memory after Auschwitz,* 183.

133. *Doctor Faustus,* 637 and 636.

134. Ibid., 641–42 and Mann, *The Story of the Novel,* 222–23.

135. See Lieselotte Voss, *Die Entstehung von Thomas Manns Roman "Doktor Faustus": Dargestellt anhand von unveröffentlichten Vorarbeiten* (Tübingen: M. Niemeyer, 1975), 197–98.

136. The translations are a mixture of both *Doctor Faustus,* 641 and *Doctor Faustus* (Woods) 515.

137. My translation draws on both Lowe-Porter and Woods, ibid.

138. Mann, *The Story of a Novel,* 223.

139. See Introduction, note 5.

140. Adorno, *Philosophie der neuen Musik,* 126 (133, translation modified). For a brief summary of how *Flaschenpost* became the shorthand for the *Dialectic of Enlightenment* see Gunzelin Schmid Noerr and Willem van Reijen, *Vierzig Jahre Flaschenpost: "Dialektik der Aufklärung," 1947–1987* (Frankfurt am Main: S. Fischer, 1987), 8–11. The distinct difference between Adorno's nineteenth-century commitment to metaphysics and Eisler's scathing twentieth-century critique of it could not be captured better than in the following anecdote. A melancholic Adorno had told Eisler about his wish, in the face of the unchanging (*das Immergleiche*), to condense his philosophical work into a single sentence, to write that sentence on a piece of paper, hide it in a bottle, and throw it into the ocean, where one day someone on the Fidschi Islands would find it. Eisler then asked what such a poor person would do with a piece of paper on which was written: "I am a metaphysical malcontent" (*Ich bin ein metaphysischer Miesmacher*). See Jürgen Schebera, *Hanns Eisler: Eine Biographie in Texten, Bildern und Dokumenten* (Mainz: Schott, 1998), 192.

141. See Vera Micznik, "The Farewell Story of Mahler's Ninth Symphony," *Nineteenth-Century Music* 20 (1996): 144–66, for a critique of the fictional account surrounding these "stories."

142. Adorno, *Negative Dialektik,* 400 (408).

143. Pointed out first on the occasion of the premiere by Julius Korngold in *Neue Freie Presse,* 27 June 1912: "vor allem der verklärte Ausklang—hier ein ausdrückliches Zitat aus den Kindertotenliedern—heben den Satz hervor"; see Manfred Wagner, *Geschichte der österreichischen Musikkritik in Beispielen* (Tutzing: H. Schneider, 1979), 390. For the most thorough discussion of the

relationship between the song and the symphony's ending, see Hans Heinrich Eggebrecht, *Die Musik Gustav Mahlers,* 227–53.

144. See chapter 2, note 129.

145. Quoted in Eggebrecht, *Die Musik Gustav Mahlers,* 250.

146. Benjamin, "Lehre vom Ähnlichen," *Gesammelte Schriften* 2.1:204–10, at 206 (and its revision "Über das mimetische Vermögen," ibid., 210–13); and Frobenius, "Über das Zeitmaß Augenblick," 285.

147. Translation (modified) from Edward Kravitt, "Mahler's Dirges for his Death: February 24, 1901," *The Musical Quarterly* 64 (1978): 329–53, at 340–41. Concise and thorough discusssions of the whole cycle can be found in Henry-Louis de La Grange, *Gustav Mahler, Vol. 2, Vienna: The Years of Challenge (1897–1904)* (Oxford: Oxford University Press, 1995), 825–46, at 835–37; and Peter Russell, *Light in Battle with Darkness: Mahler's Kindertotenlieder* (Frankfurt am Main: P. Lang, 1991).

148. See the contradictory ways in which Mahler described his approach to song composition to Natalie Bauer-Lechner, stating on the one hand, "[o]ne minute it is the poem that is the inspiration, the next it is the melody"; and asking on the other hand, "Have you noticed that, with me, the melody always grows out of the words? The words, so to speak, generate the melody—never vice versa. It is the same with Beethoven and Wagner." Bauer-Lechner, *Recollections of Gustav Mahler,* 33 and 50. See Russell, *Light in Battle with Darkness: Mahler's Kindertotenlieder,* 23; Kravitt, "Mahler's Dirges," 343–44; Susanne Vill, *Vermittlungsformen verbalisierter und musikalischer Inhalte in der Musik Gustav Mahlers* (Tutzing: H. Schneider, 1979), 113, speaks of an "upward glance" (*Augenaufschlag*).

149. Schenker, *Der Tonwille* 1 (1921), 46. The passage is cited in the beginning of Joseph Kerman's article, "A Romantic Detail in Schubert's *Schwanengesang,*" in *Schubert: Critical and Analytical Studies,* ed. Walter Frisch (Lincoln: University of Nebraska Press, 1986), 48–64, at 48–49. Special thanks to Yonathan Malin for pointing out Schenker's visual metaphor to me.

150. V. Kofi Agawu, "The Musical Language of *Kindertotenlieder* No. 2," *The Journal of Musicology* 2 (1983): 81–93, at 83.

151. See ibid., 85–88, especially example 3. For the "Entwicklungsprinzip" see Zimmermann, *Der ästhetische Augenblick,* 84–88.

152. Adorno, *Beethoven,* 236 (164).

153. Quoted above in chapter 1. Adorno, *Ästhetische Theorie,* 280 (cf. 188, where the translation is unusually free).

154. Robert S. Hatten, *Musical Meaning in Beethoven: Markedness, Correlation, and Interpretation* (Bloomington: Indiana University Press, 1994), 15.

155. Heinrich Schenker, *Free Composition: Volume III of New Musical Theories and Fantasies* ed. and trans. Ernst Oster (New York: Longman, 1979), 3.

156. Heinrich Schenker, *Die letzten fünf Sonaten von Beethoven: Kritische Ausgabe mit Einführung und Erläuterung [Sonate As dur Op. 110]* (Vienna: Universal Edition, 1914), 25. See William Pastille, "Ursatz: The Musical Philosophy of Heinrich Schenker" (Ph.D. diss., Cornell University, 1985), 125.

157. William Pastille, "Music and Morphology: Goethe's Influence on Schenker's Thought," in *Schenker Studies,* ed. Hedi Siegel (Cambridge: Cambridge University Press, 1990), 29–44, at 32. For a more detailed discussion of

the *Augenblick* of cognition in Goethe's conception of natural science see Andreas Anglet, *Der "ewige" Augenblick*, 252–97.

158. Heinrich Schenker, *Der freie Satz,* ed. Oswald Jonas, 2nd ed. (Vienna: Universal Edition, 1956), 28; translation from Pastille, "Ursatz: The Musical Philosophy of Heinrich Schenker" 32–33. See also Schenker, *Free Composition,* 5.

159. Schenker, *Free Composition,* 5.

160. Cf. Schenker, "Vom Organischen der Sonatenform," in *Das Meisterwerk in der Musik,* 2:41–54, at 50; *The Masterwork in Music,* 2:27 (to render the momentariness of improvisation, I translated "aus dem Stegreif" as "improviation on the spur of the moment").

161. Heinrich Schenker, *Harmonielehre* (Vienna: Universal Edition, 1978), 6; *Der Freie Satz,* 49 and 45 (15 and 18, translation modified).

162. Brian Hyer, "Picturing Music," unpublished paper, courtesy of the author. See also Adorno, "On Some Relationships Between Music and Painting," 67.

163. W.J.T. Mitchell, *Picture Theory: Essays on Verbal and Visual Representation* (Chicago: University of Chicago Press, 1994), 153–54.

164. Rose Rosengard Subotnik, "Toward a Deconstruction of Structural Listening: A Critique of Schoenberg, Adorno, and Stravinsky," in *Deconstructive Variations: Music and Reason in Western Society* (Minneapolis: University of Minnesota Press, 1996), 148–76, at 161.

165. Jay, *Downcast Eyes,* 3.

166. See Stumpf, ". . . *wollet mir jetzt durch die phantastisch verschlungenen Kreuzgänge Folgen!"* 32–33 and note 45 with further references to Ruckgaber, Schumann, and Fink.

167. Adorno, *Ästhetische Theorie,* 131–2 (85).

168. Benjamin, "Über einige Motive bei Baudelaire," 223 (188); see chapter 1, note 26.

169. Benjamin, *Gesammelte Schriften,* 5.1:560.

170. "Sucht einer dem Regenbogen ganz nahezukommen, so verschwindet dieser." Adorno, *Ästhetische Theorie,* 185 (122). See also *Negative Dialektik,* 366 (373).

171. Adorno, *Ästhetische Theorie,* 124 (80).

172. Adorno, *Mahler,* 44 (3–4, translation modified).

173. See note 146 this chapter.

174. Arnold Schering, "Gustav Mahler als Liederkomponist," *Neue Zeitschrift für Musik* 72 (1905): 672–73, 691–93, 753–55, at 753.

175. Christopher Lewis, "Zwischen Lied und Liebe: Mahler, 'Nun seh ich wohl,' and the Romantic Dilemma," unpublished paper, 14 and example 1. Special thanks to Patrick McCreeless for making a copy of the paper available to me.

176. Natalie Bauer-Lechner, *Recollections of Gustav Mahler,* 31.

177. Benjamin, *Gesammelte Schriften* 2.3:958.

178. C. Nadia Seremetakis, ed., *The Senses Still: Perception and Memory as Material Culture in Modernity* (Boulder: Westview Press, 1994), 25.

179. Mann, "Deutschland und die Deutschen," 281 (20).

Bibliography

Abbate, Carolyn. *Unsung Voices: Opera and Musical Narrative in the Nineteenth Century.* Princeton: Princeton University Press, 1991.

———. "Wagner, 'On Modulation', and Tristan." *Cambridge Opera Journal* 1 (1989): 33–58.

Abert, Hermann. *Robert Schumann.* 2nd rev. ed. Berlin: Harmonie Verlagsgesellschaft für Literatur und Kunst, 1910.

Adams, Courtney S. "Artistic Parallels between Arnold Schoenberg's Music and Painting (1908–1912)." *College Music Symposium* 35 (1995): 5–21.

Adorno, Theodor W. *Aesthetic Theory.* Translated by Robert Hullot-Kentor. Edited by Gretel Adorno and Rolf Tiedemann. Minneapolis: University of Minnesota Press, 1997.

———. *Beethoven: Philosophie der Musik: Fragmente und Texte.* Edited by Rolf Tiedemann. Frankfurt am Main: Suhrkamp, 1994.

———. *Beethoven: The Philosophy of Music.* Translated by Edmund Jephcott. Stanford: Stanford University Press, 1998.

———. *Gesammelte Schriften.* Edited by Rolf Tiedemann. 20 vols. Frankfurt am Main: Suhrkamp, 1971–86.

———. *In Search of Wagner.* Translated by Rodney Livingstone. London: NLB, 1981.

———. *Mahler: A Musical Physiognomy.* Translated by Edmund Jephcott. Chicago: University of Chicago Press, 1992.

———. *Negative Dialectics.* Translated by E. B. Ashton. New York: Seabury Press, 1973.

———. *Notes to Literature.* Translated by Shierry Weber Nicholsen. Edited by Rolf Tiedemann. 2 vols. New York: Columbia University Press, 1991–92.

———. "On Some Relationships Between Music and Painting." Translated by Susan Gillespie. *The Musical Quarterly* 79 (1995): 66–79.

———. "On the Fetish-Character in Music and the Regression of Listening." *In The Essential Frankfurt School Reader,* edited by Andrew Arato and Eike Gebhardt, 270–99. New York: Urizen Books, 1978.

———. *Philosophy of Modern Music.* Translated by Anne G. Mitchell and Wesley V. Blomster. New York: Seabury Press, 1973.

———. *Quasi una Fantasia: Essays on Modern Music.* Translated by Rodney Livingstone. London: Verso, 1992.

Adorno, Theodor W., and Walter Benjamin. *The Complete Correspondence 1928–1940.* Translated by Nicholas Walker. Edited by Henri Lonitz. Cambridge: Harvard University Press, 1999.

Agawu, V. Kofi. "The Musical Language of *Kindertotenlieder* No. 2." *The Journal of Musicology* 2 (1983): 81–93.

Altenburg, Detlef, ed. *Liszt und die Weimarer Klassik.* Laaber: Laaber, 1997.

Anglet, Andreas. *Der "ewige" Augenblick: Studien zur Struktur und Funktion eines Denkbildes bei Goethe.* Cologne: Böhlau, 1991.

Auner, Joseph. "In Schoenberg's Workshop: Aggregates and Referential Collections in the Composition of *Die glückliche Hand.*" *Music Theory Spectrum* 18 (1996): 77–105.

Bahle, Julius. *Eingebung und Tat im musikalischen Schaffen: Ein Beitrag zur Psychologie der Entwicklungs- und Schaffengesetze schöpferischer Menschen.* Leipzig: S. Hirzel, 1939.

Baker, Nancy Kovaleff, and Thomas Christensen, eds. *Aesthetics and the Art of Musical Composition in the German Enlightenment: Selected Writings of Johann Georg Sulzer and Heinrich Christoph Koch.* Cambridge: Cambridge University Press, 1995.

Balzac, Honoré de. *La comédie humaine.* Paris: Gallimard, 1966.

———. *Séraphita.* Auteurs célèbres, no. 456. Paris: Ernest Flammarion, 19??.

———. *Séraphita.* Translated by Clara Bell. Sawtry: Dedalus, 1989.

Bauer-Lechner, Natalie. *Recollections of Gustav Mahler.* Translated by Dika Newlin. Edited by Peter Franklin. London: Faber and Faber, 1980.

Becker, Claudia Stevens. "A New Look at Schumann's Impromptus." *The Musical Quarterly* 67 (1981): 568–86.

Beddow, Michael. *Thomas Mann: Doctor Faustus.* Cambridge: Cambridge University Press, 1994.

Beethoven, Ludwig van. *An die ferne Geliebte: Faksimile nach dem im Besitz des Bonner Beethovenhauses Befindlichen Original.* Munich: Henle, 1970.

Bekker, Paul. *Beethoven.* Berlin: Schuster und Loeffler, 1912.

———. "Schönberg: 'Erwartung'." In *Arnold Schönberg zum fünfzigsten Geburtstage, 13. September 1924,* 275–82. Vienna: Universal Edition, 1924.

Benda, Georg Anton. *Ariadne auf Naxos.* Edited by Thomas Bauman. New York: Garland, 1985.

Benjamin, Walter. *Gesammelte Schriften.* Edited by Rolf Tiedemann and Hermann Schweppenhäuser. 7 vols. Frankfurt am Main: Suhrkamp, 1972–89.

———. *Illuminationen.* Frankfurt am Main: Suhrkamp, 1977.

———. *Illuminations.* Translated by Harry Zohn. Edited by Hannah Arendt. New York: Schocken Books, 1969.

———. *The Origin of German Tragic Drama.* Translated by John Osborne. London: NLB, 1977.

———. *Selected Writings.* Edited by Michael W. Jennings. 2 vols. Cambridge, Mass.: Belknap Press, 1996, 1999.

———. *Ursprung des deutschen Trauerspiels.* Frankfurt am Main: Suhrkamp, 1963.

Bent, Ian, ed. *Music Analysis in the Nineteenth Century.* 2 vols. Cambridge: Cambridge University Press, 1994.

Berg, Alban, et al. *Arnold Schönberg.* Munich: R. Piper, 1912.

Bergsten, Gunilla. *Thomas Mann's Doctor Faustus: The Sources and Structure of the Novel.* Translated by Krishna Winston. Chicago: University of Chicago Press, 1969.

Berlioz, Hector. *A travers chants.* Edited by Léon Guichard. Paris: Gründ, 1971.

Bertagnolli, Paul Allen. "From Overture to Symphonic Poem, from Melodrama to Choral Cantata: Studies of the Sources for Franz Liszt's *Prometheus and his Chöre zu Herders 'Entfesseltem Prometheus'*." Ph.D. diss., Washington University, 1998.

Bertram, Ernst. *Nietzsche: Versuch einer Mythologie*. Berlin: G. Bondi, 1921.

Bischoff, Bodo. *Monument für Beethoven: Die Entwicklung der Beethoven-Rezeption Robert Schumanns*. Cologne-Rheinkassel: C. Dohr, 1994.

Blackbourn, David. *The Long Nineteenth Century: A History of Germany, 1780–1918*. New York: Oxford University Press, 1998.

Bloch, Ernst. *Essays on the Philosophy of Music*. Translated by Peter Palmer. Cambridge: Cambridge University Press, 1985.

Bockholdt, Rudolf. "Freiheit und Brüderlichkeit in der Musik Ludwig van Beethovens." In *Beethoven: Zwischen Revolution und Restauration*, edited by Helga Lühning and Sieghard Brandenburg, 77–107. Bonn: Beethoven-Haus, 1989.

Boetticher, Wolfgang. *Robert Schumann: Einführung in Persönlichkeit und Werk*. Berlin: B. Hahnefeld, 1941.

———. *Robert Schumanns Klavierwerke: Neue biographische und textkritische Untersuchungen Teil I, Opus 1–6*. Wilhelmshaven: Heinrichshofen, 1976.

Bohlman, Philip. "Jüdische Lebenswelten zwischen Utopie und Heterotopie, jüdische Musik zwischen Schtetl und Ghetto." *Jahrbuch für Volksliedforschung* 47 (2002).

Bohrer, Karl Heinz. *Der Abschied, Theorie der Trauer: Baudelaire, Goethe, Nietzsche, Benjamin*. Frankfurt am Main: Suhrkamp, 1996.

———. *Suddenness: On the Moment of Aesthetic Appearance*. Translated by Ruth Crowley. New York: Columbia University Press, 1994.

Bonds, Mark Evan. "Idealism and the Aesthetics of Instrumental Music at the Turn of the Nineteenth Century." *Journal of the American Musicological Society* 50 (1997): 387–420.

———. "*Sinfonia anti-eroica*: Berlioz's *Harold en Italie* and the Anxiety of Beethoven's Influence." *The Journal of Musicology* 10 (1992): 417–63.

Bonner, Andrew. "Liszt's *Les Préludes* and *Les Quatre Élémens*: A Reinvestigation." *Nineteenth-Century Music* 10 (1986): 95–107.

Borchmeyer, Dieter. *Richard Wagner: Theory and Theatre*. Translated by Stewart Spencer. Oxford: Clarendon Press, 1991.

Böschenstein, Bernhard. "Ernst Bertrams Nietzsche: Eine Quelle für Thomas Manns *Doktor Faustus*." *Euphorion: Zeitschrift für Literaturgeschichte* 72 (1978): 68–83.

Bowie, Andrew. *Aesthetics and Subjectivity: From Kant to Nietzsche*. Manchester: Manchester University Press, 1990.

Breicha, Otto. *Gerstl und Schönberg: eine Beziehung*. Salzburg: Galerie Welz, 1993.

Brendel, Franz. *Die Musik der Gegenwart und die Gesammtkunst der Zukunft*. Leipzig: B. Hinze, 1854.

———. "F. Liszt's symphonische Dichtungen." *Neue Zeitschrift für Musik* 49 (1858): 73–76, 85–88, 97–100, 109–12, 121–23, 133–36, 141–43.

———. "Franz Liszt in Leipzig." *Neue Zeitschrift für Musik* 46 (1857): 101–5.

———. *Geschichte der Musik in Italien, Deutschland und Frankreich: Von den ersten christlichen Zeiten bis auf die Gegenwart.* 2nd ed. 2 vols. Leipzig: H. Matthes (E. O. Schurmann), 1855.

———. "Robert Schumann mit Rücksicht auf Mendelssohn-Barthholdy, und die Entwicklung der modernen Tonkunst überhaupt." *Neue Zeitschrift für Musik* 22 (1845): 63–67, 81–83, 89–92, 113–15, 121–23, 145–47, 149–50.

———. "Robert Schumann with Reference to Mendelssohn-Bartholdy and the Development of Modern Music in General (1845)." Translated by Jürgen Thym. In *Schumann and His World,* edited by R. Larry Todd, 317–37. Princeton: Princeton University Press, 1994.

———. "Zur Anbahnung einer Verständigung." *Neue Zeitschrift für Musik* 50 (1859): 265–73.

Brieger-Wasservogel, Lothar. "Swedenborgs Weltanschaung: Ein Versuch." In *Emanuel Swedenborg: Theologische Schriften,* 10–32. Jena: Eugen Diedrichs, 1904.

Brinkemper, Peter V. *Spiegel & Echo: Intermedialität und Musikphilosophie im "Doktor Faustus."* Würzburg: Königshausen und Neumann, 1997.

Brinkmann, Reinhold. "Schoenberg the Contemporary: A View from Behind." In *Constructive Dissonance: Arnold Schoenberg and the Transformations of Twentieth-Century Culture,* edited by Juliane Brand and Christopher Hailey, 196–219. Berkeley: University of California Press, 1997.

———. "Wunder, Realität und die Figur der Grenzüberschreitung." In *Programmhefte der Bayreuther Festspiele 1979: Programmheft I "Lohengrin,"* edited by Wolfgang Wagner and Oswald Georg Bauer, 1–21, 94–106. Bayreuth: Verlag der Festspielleitung, 1979.

———. "Wunder, Realität und die Figur der Grenzüberschreitung." In *Lohengrin: Texte, Materialien, Kommentare,* edited by Attila Csampai and Dietmar Holland, 255–74. Reinbek: Rowohlt, 1989.

Buchanan, Herbert H. "A Key to Schoenberg's Erwartung (Op. 17)." *Journal of the American Musicological Society* 20 (1967): 434–49.

Buck-Morss, Susan. *The Origin of Negative Dialectics: Theodor W. Adorno, Walter Benjamin, and the Frankfurt Institute.* Hassocks: Harvester Press, 1977.

Buhler, James. "'Breakthrough' as Critique of Form: The Finale of Mahler's First Symphony." *Nineteenth-Century Music* 20 (1996): 125–43.

Burke, Edmund. *A Philosophical Enquiry into the Origin of our Ideas of the Sublime and Beautiful.* Edited by J. T. Boulton. New York: Columbia University Press, 1958.

Burnham, Scott. *Beethoven Hero.* Princeton: Princeton University Press, 1995.

———. "The Criticism of Analysis and the Analysis of Criticism." *Nineteenth-Century Music* 16 (1992): 70–76.

Busoni, Ferruccio. *Selected Letters.* Translated and edited by Antony Beaumont. New York: Columbia University Press, 1987.

Cherlin, Michael. "Schoenberg and *Das Unheimliche:* Spectres of Tonality." *The Journal of Musicology* 11 (1993): 357–73.

Christensen, Jean. "Arnold Schoenberg's Oratorio *Die Jakobsleiter*." Ph.D. diss., University of California, Los Angeles, 1979.

Christensen, Thomas. "Schoenberg's Opus 11, No. 1.: A Parody of Pitch Cells from *Tristan*." *Journal of the Arnold Schoenberg Institute* 10 (1987): 38–44.

Chua, Daniel K. L. *Absolute Music and the Construction of Meaning*. Cambridge: Cambridge University Press, 1999.

Cinnamon, Howard. "Tonic Arpeggiation and Successive Equal Third Relations as Elements of Tonal Evolution in the Music of Franz Liszt." *Music Theory Spectrum* 8 (1986): 1–24.

Cohn, Richard. "Maximally Smooth Cycles, Hexatonic Systems, and the Analysis of Late-Romantic Triadic Progressions." *Music Analysis* 15 (1996): 9–40.

Cone, Edward T. *The Composer's Voice*. Berkeley: University of California Press, 1974.

———. "The World of Opera and Its Inhabitants." In *Music: A View from Delft*, edited by Robert P. Morgan, 125–38. Chicago: University of Chicago Press, 1989.

Covach, John. "The Sources of Schoenberg's 'Aesthetic Theology'." *Nineteenth-Century Music* 19 (1996): 252–62.

Creuzer, Georg Friedrich. *Symbolik und Mythologie der alten Völker, besonders der Griechen*. 2nd ed. Leipzig: Heyer und Leske, 1819.

Czerny, Carl. *On the Proper Performance of all Beethoven's Works for the Piano*. Edited by Paul Badura-Skoda. Vienna: Universal Edition, 1970.

Dahlhaus, Carl. *Between Romanticism and Modernism: Four Studies in the Music of the Later Nineteenth Century*. Translated by Mary Whittall. Berkeley: University of California Press, 1980.

———. *Die Musiktheorie im 18. und 19. Jahrhundert: Grundzüge einer Systematik*. Darmstadt: Wissenschaftliche Buchgesellschaft, 1984.

———. *Esthetics of Music*. Translated by William W. Austin. English ed. Cambridge: Cambridge University Press, 1982.

———. *The Idea of Absolute Music*. Translated by Roger Lustig. Chicago: University of Chicago Press, 1989.

———. *Klassische und romantische Musikästhetik*. Laaber: Laaber, 1988.

———. "Liszts 'Bergsymphonie' und die Idee der Symphonischen Dichtung." *Jahrbuch des Staatlichen Instituts für Musikforschung* (1975): 96–130.

———. *Ludwig van Beethoven: Approaches to his Music*. Translated by Mary Whittall. Oxford: Clarendon Press, 1991.

———. *Nineteenth-Century Music*. Translated by J. Bradford Robinson. Berkeley: University of California Press, 1989.

———. *Richard Wagner's Music Dramas*. Translated by Mary Whittall. Cambridge: Cambridge University Press, 1979.

———, ed. *Beiträge zur musikalischen Hermeneutik*. Regensburg: G. Bosse, 1975.

Dällenbach, Lucien, and Christiaan L. Hart Nibbrig, eds. *Fragment und Totalität*. Frankfurt am Main: Suhrkamp, 1984.

Danuser, Hermann. *Musikalische Prosa*. Regensburg: G. Bosse, 1975.

Daverio, John. *Nineteenth-Century Music and the German Romantic Ideology*. New York: Schirmer, 1993.

Bibliography

———. *Robert Schumann: Herald of a "New Poetic Age."* New York: Oxford University Press, 1997.

———. "Schumann's 'Im Legendenton' and Friedrich Schlegel's *Arabeske.*" *Nineteenth-Century Music* 11 (1987): 150–63.

de Man, Paul. "The Rhetoric of Temporality." In *Blindness and Insight: Essays in the Rhetoric of Contemporary Criticism,* 187–228. Minneapolis: University of Minnesota Press, 1983.

De Ruiter, Jacob. *Der Charakterbegriff in der Musik: Studien zur deutschen Ästhetik der Instrumentalmusik 1740–1850.* Stuttgart: F. Steiner, 1989.

Dean, Winton. "Beethoven and Opera." In *Ludwig van Beethoven, Fidelio,* edited by Paul Robinson, 22–50. Cambridge: Cambridge University Press, 1996.

Deathridge, John. "Through the Looking Glass: Some Remarks on the First Complete Draft of *Lohengrin.*" In *Analyzing Opera,* edited by Carolyn Abbate and Roger Parker, 56–91. Berkeley: University of California Press, 1989.

Determann, Robert. *Begriff und Ästhetik der "Neudeutschen Schule": Ein Beitrag zur Musikgeschichte des 19. Jahrhunderts.* Baden Baden: V. Koerner, 1989.

Dietel, Gerhard. *"Eine neue poetische Zeit": Musikanschauung und stilistische Tendenzen im Klavierwerk Robert Schumanns.* Kassel: Bärenreiter, 1989.

Dilthey, Wilhelm. "Die Enstehung der Hermeneutik." In *Gesammelte Schriften,* 5: 317–31. Stuttgart: B. G. Teubner, 1957.

Dörr, Hansjörg. "Thomas Mann und Adorno: Ein Beitrag zur Entstehung des Doktor Faustus." *Literaturwissenschaftliches Jahrbuch im Auftrage der Görres-Gesellschaft Neue Folge* 11 (1970): 285–322.

Drabkin, William M. "The Sketches for Beethoven's Piano Sonata in C minor, op. 111." Ph.D. diss., Princeton University, 1976.

Draeseke, Felix. *Schriften 1855–1861.* Edited by Martella Gutiérrez-Denhoff and Helmut Loos. Bad Honnef: G. Schröder, 1987.

Dürr, Walther. *Analysen, Sprache und Musik: Geschichte, Gattungen, Analysemodelle.* Kassel: Bärenreiter, 1994.

Eager, Gerald. "The Missing and the Mutilated Eye in Contemporary Art." *The Journal of Aesthetics and Art Criticism* 20 (1961): 49–59.

Eggebrecht, Hans Heinrich. *Die Musik Gustav Mahlers.* Wilhelmshaven: Florian Noetzel, 1999.

Eichel, Christine. *Vom Ermatten der Avantgarde zur Vernetzung der Künste: Perspektiven einer interdisziplinären Ästhetik im Spätwerk Theodor W. Adornos.* Frankfurt am Main: Suhrkamp, 1993.

Eichhorn, Andreas. *Beethovens Neunte Symphonie: Die Geschichte der Aufführung und Rezeption.* Kassel: Bärenreiter, 1993.

Erler, Hermann. *Robert Schumanns Leben aus seinen Briefen geschildert.* 2 vols. Berlin: Ries and Erler, 1887.

Feuerbach, Ludwig. *Sämmtliche Werke.* 10 vols. Leipzig: O. Wigand, 1846–90.

Figal, Günter. "Aesthetic Experience of Time: Adorno's Avant-gardism and Benjamin's Correction." In *For a Philosophy of Freedom and Strife: Politics, Aesthetics, Metaphysics,* 109–24. Translated by Wayne Klein. Albany: State University of New York Press, 1998.

Finscher, Ludwig. "'Zwischen absoluter und Programmusik': Zur Interpretation der deutschen romantischen Symphonie." In *Über Symphonien: Beiträge zu einer musikalischen Gattung,* edited by Christoph-Hellmut Mahling, 103–15. Tutzing: H. Schneider, 1979.

Floros, Constantin. *Gustav Mahler: The Symphonies.* Translated by Vernon Wicker. Portland: Amadeus Press, 1993.

Franke, Rainer. *Richard Wagners Züricher Kunstschriften: Politische und ästhetische Entwürfe auf seinem Weg zum "Ring des Nibelungen."* Hamburg: K. D. Wagner, 1983.

Franklin, Peter. "Distant Sounds—Fallen Music: *Der ferne Klang* as 'Woman's Opera'?" *Cambridge Opera Journal* 3 (1991): 159–72.

Freud, Sigmund. *The Standard Edition of the Complete Psychological Works of Sigmund Freud.* Edited by James Strachey. 24 vols. London: Hogarth, 1953–74.

Friedheim, Philip. "Wagner and the Aesthetics of the Scream." *Nineteenth-Century Music* 7 (1983): 63–70.

Frisch, Walter, ed. *Schoenberg and His World.* Princeton: Princeton University Press, 1999.

Frobenius, Wolf. "Momentum/Moment, instans/instant, Augenblick." In *Handwörterbuch der musikalischen Terminologie,* edited by Hans Heinrich Eggebrecht. Wiesbaden: F. Steiner, 1972–.

———. "Über das Zeitmaß Augenblick in Adornos Kunsttheorie." *Archiv für Musikwissenschaft* 36 (1979): 279–305.

Fubini, Enrico. *History of Music Aesthetics.* Translated by Michael Hatwell. London: Macmillan, 1990.

Gelber, Mark H. "Antisemitism, Indifferentism, the Holocaust, and Zionism: The Cases of Thomas Mann and Max Brod." In *Holocaust Studies Annual,* edited by Sanford Pinsker and Jack Fischel, 53–62. New York: Garland, 1990.

Goethe, Johann Wolfgang von. *Goethes Briefe: Hamburger Ausgabe.* 4 vols. Hamburg: C. Wegner, 1962.

———. *Werke: Hamburger Ausgabe.* Edited by Erich Trunz. Munich: C. H. Beck, 1981.

Göllerich, August. *Franz Liszt.* Berlin: Marquardt, 1908.

Gossett, Philip. "The 'Candeur virginale' of 'Tancredi.'" *The Musical Times* 112 (1971): 326–29.

Gratzer, Wolfgang, and Siegfried Mauser, eds. *Hermeneutik im musikwissenschaftlichen Kontext: Internationales Symposion Salzburg 1992.* Laaber: Laaber, 1995.

Grey, Thomas S. *Wagner's Musical Prose: Texts and Contexts.* Cambridge: Cambridge University Press, 1995.

Groos, Arthur. "Back to the Future: Hermeneutic Fantasies in *Der fliegende Holländer.*" *Nineteenth-Century Music* 19 (1995): 191–211.

Gruber, Gernot. "Robert Schumann: Fantasie op. 17, 1. Satz—Versuch einer Interpretation." *Musicologica austriaca* 4 (1984): 101–30.

Gruber, Gernot, and Siegfried Mauser, eds. *Musikalische Hermeneutik im Entwurf: Thesen und Diskussionen.* Regensburg: Laaber, 1994.

Guerlac, Suzanne. *The Impersonal Sublime: Hugo, Baudelaire, Lautréament.* Stanford: Stanford University Press, 1990.

Habermas, Jürgen. *Der philosophische Diskurs der Moderne: Zwölf Vorlesungen.* Frankfurt am Main: Suhrkamp, 1985.

Hahl-Koch, Jelena, ed. *Arnold Schoenberg, Wassily Kandinsky: Letters, Pictures, and Documents.* London: Faber and Faber, 1984.

Haimo, Ethan. *Schoenberg's Serial Odyssey: The Evolution of his Twelve-tone Method 1914–1928.* Oxford: Clarendon Press, 1990.

Halsall, Albert W. *Victor Hugo and the Romantic Drama.* Toronto: University of Toronto Press, 1998.

Hansen, Miriam. "Benjamin, Cinema and Experience: 'The Blue Flower in the Land of Technology.'" In *Perspectives on German Cinema,* edited by Terri Ginsberg and Kirsten Moana Thompson, 558–95. New York: G. K. Hall, 1996.

Hanslick, Eduard. *Aus dem Concert-Saal: Kritiken und Schilderungen aus 20 Jahren des Wiener Musiklebens 1848–1868.* Vienna: W. Braumüller, 1897.

———. *Vom Musikalisch-Schönen: Ein Beitrag zur Revision der Ästhetik in der Tonkunst.* Edited by Dietmar Strauß. 2 vols. Mainz: Schott, 1990.

Harrison, Thomas J. *1910: The Emancipation of Dissonance.* Berkeley: University of California Press, 1996.

Harwood, Gregory W. "Robert Schumann's Sonata in F-Sharp Minor: A Study of Creative Process and Romantic Inspiration." *Current Musicology* 29 (1980): 17–30.

Hatten, Robert S. *Musical Meaning in Beethoven: Markedness, Correlation, and Interpretation.* Bloomington: Indiana University Press, 1994.

Haushofer, Albrecht. *Moabit Sonnets.* Translated by M. D. Herter Norton. New York: W.W. Norton, 1978.

———. *Moabiter Sonette.* Zurich: Artemis, 1948.

Hegel, Georg Wilhelm Friedrich. *Aesthetics: Lectures on Fine Art.* Translated by T. M. Knox. 2 vols. Oxford: Clarendon Press, 1975.

———. *Hegel's Logic: Being Part One of the Encyclopedia of the Philosophical Sciences (1830).* Translated by William Wallace. Oxford: Clarendon Press, 1975.

———. *Werke.* Edited by Karl Markus Michel and Eva Moldenhauer. Frankfurt am Main: Suhrkamp, 1969–79.

Henze-Döhring, Sabine. "'Abschied' oder 'Ende der Sonate'? Die Arietta aus Beethovens Klaviersonate op. 111: Möglichkeiten und Grenzen der Lesbarkeit von Musik." *Schweizer Jahrbuch für Musikwissenschaft/Annales Suisses de Musicologie* 15 (1995): 21–40.

Hepokoski, James A. "Fiery-Pulsed Libertine or Domestic Hero? Strauss's *Don Juan* Reinvestigated." In *Richard Strauss: New Perspectives on the Composer and His Work,* edited by Bryan Gilliam, 135–76. Durham: Duke University Press, 1992.

———. "Genre and Content in Mid-Century Verdi: 'Addio, del passato' (*La traviata,* Act III)." *Cambridge Opera Journal* 1 (1989): 249–76.

———. *Sibelius: Symphony No. 5.* Cambridge: Cambridge University Press, 1993.

Herder, Johann Gottfried. *Herders sämmtliche Werke*. Edited by Bernhard Ludwig Suphan (et al.). Berlin: Weidmann, 1877–1913.

Herz, Gerhard. "The Music in Thomas Mann's *Doctor Faustus*." *Orbis Musicae* 9 (1986/87): 205–23.

Hess, Willy. *Das Fidelio-Buch: Beethovens Oper Fidelio, ihre Geschichte und ihre drei Fassungen*. Winterthur: Amadeus, 1986.

Heuß, Alfred. "Die Humanitätsmelodien im 'Fidelio.'" *Neue Zeitschrift für Musik* 91 (1924): 545–52.

———. "Eine motivisch-thematische Studie über Liszt's sinfonische Dichtung 'Ce qu'on entend sur la montagne.'" *Zeitschrift der Internationalen Musikgesellschaft* 13 (1911/12): 10–21.

Hinton, Stephen. "Adorno's Unifinished *Beethoven*." *Beethoven Forum* 5 (1996): 139–54.

———. "Not *Which* Tones? The Crux of Beethoven's Ninth." *Nineteenth-Century Music* 22 (1998): 61–77.

Höckner, Berthold. "Musik, Text und 'Supplement': Skizze über Dekonstruktion und musikalische Hermeneutik." In *Musik als Text: Bericht über den Internationalen Kongreß der Gesellschaft für Musikforschung Freiburg im Breisgau 1993*, edited by Hermann Danuser and Tobias Plebuch, 7–10. Kassel: Bärenreiter, 1998.

Hoffmann, E.T.A. *E.T.A. Hoffmann's Musical Writings: "Kreisleriana," "The Poet and the Composer," Music Criticism*. Translated by Martyn Clarke. Edited by David Charlton. Cambridge: Cambridge University Press, 1989.

———. *Sämtliche Werke: Historisch Kritische Ausgabe*. Edited by Carl Georg von Maassen. 2nd ed. 10 vols. Munich: G. Müller, 1909–25.

Hofmannsthal, Hugo von. *Gesammelte Werke*. Edited by Bernd Schoeller. 10 vols. Frankfurt am Main: S. Fischer, 1979.

Hohendahl, Peter Uwe. *Prismatic Thought: Theodor W. Adorno*. Lincoln: University of Nebraska Press, 1995.

Hölderlin, Friedrich. *Sämtliche Werke*. Edited by Friedrich Beissner. 8 vols. Stuttgart: W. Kohlhammer, 1946–85.

Hotaki, Leander. *Robert Schumanns Mottosammlung: Übertragung, Kommentar, Einführung*. Freiburg: Rombach, 1998.

Hugo, Victor. "Preface to Cromwell." In *Prefaces and Prologues to Famous Books*, edited by Charles W. Eliot, 354–408. New York: Collier, 1910.

Hull, Kenneth Ross. "Brahms the Allusive: Extra-Compositional Reference in the Instrumental Music of Johannes Brahms." Ph.D. diss., Princeton University, 1989.

Huyssen, Andreas. *After the Great Divide: Modernism, Mass Culture, Postmodernism*. Bloomington: Indiana University Press, 1986.

———. *Twilight Memories: Marking Time in a Culture of Amnesia*. New York: Routledge, 1995.

Hyer, Brian. "Tonal Intuitions in *Tristan und Isolde*." Ph.D. diss., Yale University, 1989.

Jameson, Fredric. *Late Marxism: Adorno, or, the Persistence of the Dialectic*. London: Verso, 1990.

Jansen, F. Gustav. *Die Davidsbündler: Aus Robert Schumann's Sturm- und Drangperiode.* Leipzig: Breitkopf und Härtel, 1883.

Jay, Martin. *Downcast Eyes: The Denigration of Vision in Twentieth-Century French Thought.* Berkeley: University of California Press, 1993.

Jean Paul. *Horn of Oberon: Jean Paul Richter's School of Aesthetics.* Translated by Margaret R. Hale. Detroit: Wayne State University Press, 1973.

———. *Sämtliche Werke.* Weimar: Hermann Böhlaus Nachfolger, 1927–.

Johns, Keith. "A Structural Analysis of the Relationship Between Programme, Harmony and Form in the Symphonic Poems of Franz Liszt." Ph.D. diss., University of Wollongong (Australia), 1986.

Jung, Jürgen. *Altes und Neues zu Thomas Manns Roman Doktor Faustus: Quellen und Modelle: Mythos, Psychologie, Musik, Theo-Dämonologie, Faschismus.* Frankfurt am Main: P. Lang, 1985.

Kallberg, Jeffrey. *Chopin at the Boundaries: Sex, History, and Musical Genre.* Cambridge: Harvard University Press, 1996.

Kaminsky, Peter. "Principles of Formal Structure in Schumann's Early Piano Cycles." *Music Theory Spectrum* 11 (1989): 207–25.

Kandinsky, Wassily. *Concerning the Spiritual in Art, and Painting in Particular 1912.* Translated by Michael Sadleir, Francis Golffing, Michael Harrison, and Ferdinand Ostertag. New York: G. Wittenborn, 1947.

Kant, Immanuel. *Critique of Judgment.* Translated by Werner S. Pluhar. Indianapolis: Hackett, 1987.

———. *Critique of Pure Reason.* Translated by Norman Kemp Smith. 2nd rev. ed. London: Macmillan, 1933.

———. *Kritik der Urteilskraft.* Edited by Gerhard Lehmann. Stuttgart: P. Reclam, 1963.

———. *Philosophy of Material Nature.* Translated by James W. Ellington. Indianapolis: Hackett, 1985.

Kaplan, Richard. "Sonata Form in the Orchestral Works of Liszt: The Revolutionary Reconsidered." *Nineteenth-Century Music* 8 (1984): 142–52.

Keathley, Elizabeth Lorraine. "Revisioning Musical Modernism: Arnold Schoenberg, Marie Pappenheim, and *Erwartung*'s New Woman." Ph.D. diss., State University of New York at Stony Brook, 1999.

Kelkel, Manfred. "Wege zur 'Bergsymphonie' Liszts." In *Referate des 3. Europäischen Liszt-Symposions, Eisenstadt 1983,* edited by Serge Gut, 71–89. Munich: E. Katzbichler, 1986.

Kenney, Edwin J., Jr. "The Moment, 1910: Virginia Woolf, Arnold Bennett, and Turn of the Century Consciousness." *Colby Library Quarterly* 13 (1977): 42–66.

Kerman, Joseph. "*Augenblicke* in *Fidelio.*" In *Ludwig van Beethoven, Fidelio,* edited by Paul Robinson, 132–44. Cambridge: Cambridge University Press, 1996.

———. "*An die ferne Geliebte.*" In *Beethoven Studies,* edited by Alan Tyson, 123–57. New York: W. W. Norton, 1973.

———. "How We Got into Analysis, and How to Get Out." *Critical Inquiry* 7 (1980): 311–31.

———. "A Romantic Detail in Schubert's *Schwanengesang.*" In *Schubert: Critical and Analytical Studies,* edited by Walter Frisch, 48–64. Lincoln: University of Nebraska Press, 1986.

Kerner, Justinus. *Ausgewählte poetische Werke.* Stuttgart: Cotta, 1878–79.

Kittler, Friedrich A.. "World-Breadth: On Wagner's Media Technology." In *Opera Through Other Eyes,* edited by David J. Levin, 215–35. Stanford: Stanford University Press, 1993.

———. *Discourse Networks 1800/1900.* Translated by Michael Metteer with Chris Cullens. Stanford: Stanford University Press, 1990.

Klauwell, Otto. *Geschichte der Programmusik von Ihren Anfängen bis zur Gegenwart.* Leipzig: Breitkopf und Härtel, 1910.

Klein, Hans-Günter. *Ludwig van Beethoven: Autographe und Abschriften, Katalog der Musikabteilung Staatsbibliothek Preussischer Kulturbesitz.* Berlin: Merseburger, 1975.

Klemperer, Klemens von. *German Resistance Against Hitler: The Search for Allies Abroad, 1938–1945.* Oxford: Clarendon Press, 1992.

Knittel, Kristin M. "Wagner, Deafness, and the Reception of Beethoven's Late Style." *Journal of the American Musicological Society* 51 (1998): 49–82.

Köhler, Hans Joachim. "Die Stichvorlagen zum Erstdruck von Opus 21—Assoziationen zu Schumanns Novelletten." *Schumann Studien* 3/4 (1994): 75–94.

Kopp, David. "A Comprehensive Theory of Chromatic Mediant Relations in Mid-Nineteenth-Century Music." Ph.D. diss., Brandeis University, 1995.

Kramer, Lawrence. "Criticizing Criticism, Analyzing Analysis." *Nineteenth-Century Music* 16 (1992): 76–79.

———. "Haydn's Chaos, Schenker's Order; or, Hermeneutics and Musical Analysis: Can They Mix?" *Nineteenth-Century Music* 16 (1992): 3–17.

Kramer, Richard. *Distant Cycles: Schubert and the Conceiving of Song.* Chicago: University of Chicago Press, 1994.

Kravitt, Edward. "Mahler's Dirges for his Death: February 24, 1901." *The Musical Quarterly* 64 (1978): 329–53.

Krenek, Ernst. *Music Here and Now.* Translated by Barthold Fles. New York: W.W. Norton, 1939.

———. *Über neue Musik: Sechs Vorlesungen zur Einführung in die theoretischen Grundlagen.* Darmstadt: Wissenschaftliche Buchgesellschaft, 1977.

Kretzschmar, Hermann. *Gesammelte Aufsätze über Musik und Anderes Vol. 2: Gesammelte Aufsätze aus den Jahrbüchern der Musikbibliothek Peters.* Leipzig: C. F. Peters, 1911.

Kross, Siegfried, ed. *Briefe und Notizen Robert und Clara Schumanns.* Bonn: Bouvier, 1978.

Krüger, Eduard. "Hegel's Philosophie der Musik." *Neue Zeitschrift für Musik* 17 (1842): 25–28, 29–32, 35–37, 39–40, 43–45, 47–51, 53–56, 57–59, 63–64, 65–69.

Kunze, Stefan, ed. *Ludwig van Beethoven: Die Werke im Spiegel seiner Zeit: Gesammelte Konzertberichte und Rezensionen bis 1830.* Laaber: Laaber, 1987.

La Grange, Henry-Louis de. *Gustav Mahler, Vol. 2, Vienna: The Years of Chal-*

lenge (1897–1904). Oxford: Oxford University Press, 1995.

Lacan, Jacques. *The Four Fundamental Concepts of Psycho-Analysis*. Translated by Alan Sheridan. Edited by Jacques-Alain Miller. New York: W. W. Norton, 1977.

LaCapra, Dominick. *History and Memory after Auschwitz*. Ithaca: Cornell University Press, 1998.

———. *Representing the Holocaust: History, Theory, Trauma*. Ithaca: Cornell University Press, 1994.

Lacoue-Labarthe, Philippe. *Musica Ficta (Figures of Wagner)*. Stanford: Stanford University Press, 1994.

Lacoue-Labarthe, Philippe, and Jean-Luc Nancy. *The Literary Absolute: The Theory of Literature in German Romanticism*. Translated by Philip Barnard and Cheryl Lester. Albany: State University of New York Press, 1988.

Le Rider, Jacques. *Modernity and Crises of Identity: Culture and Society in Fin-de-Siècle Vienna*. Translated by Rosemary Morris. New York: Continuum, 1993.

Lehrdahl, Fred. "Tonal Pitch Space." *Music Perception* 5 (1988): 315–49.

Lessem, Alan Philip. *Music and Text in the Works of Arnold Schoenberg: The Critical Years, 1908–1922*. Ann Arbor: UMI Research Press, 1979.

Lessing, Gotthold Ephraim. *Laocoön: An Essay on the Limits of Painting and Poetry*. Translated by Edward Allen McCormick. Baltimore: Johns Hopkins University Press, 1984.

Levinson, Jerrold. *Music in the Moment*. Ithaca: Cornell University Press, 1997.

Lewin, David. "Music Theory, Phenomenology, and Modes of Perception." *Music Perception* 3 (1986): 327–92.

———. "Some Notes on Analyzing Wagner: *The Ring* and *Parsifal*." *Nineteenth-Century Music* 16 (1992): 49–58.

Lippman, Edward A. "Theory and Practice in Schumann's Aesthetics." *Journal of the American Musicological Society* 17 (1964): 310–45.

Liszt, Franz. "Berlioz und seine Haroldsymphonie." *Neue Zeitschrift für Musik* 43 (1855): 25–32, 37–46, 49–55, 77–84, 89–97.

———. *Briefe*. Edited by La Mara. Leipzig: Breitkopf und Härtel, 1893–1905.

———. *Franz Liszt—Richard Wagner: Briefwechsel*. Edited by Hanjo Kesting. Frankfurt am Main: Insel, 1988.

———. *Sämtliche Schriften*. Edited by Detlef Altenburg. Wiesbaden: Breitkopf und Härtel, 1989–.

Lobe, Johann Christian. "Briefe über Liszt's symphonische Dichtungen." *Fliegende Blätter für Musik* 2 (1856): 385–416.

Locke, Ralph P. *Music, Musicians, and the Saint-Simonians*. Chicago: University of Chicago Press, 1986.

Lühning, Helga. "Beethovens langer Weg zum 'Fidelio.'" In *Opernkomposition als Prozeß: Referate des Symposiums Bochum 1995*, edited by Werner Breig, 65–90. Kassel: Bärenreiter, 1996.

———. "*Fidelio* zwischen Oper und Opus: Über Beethovens Revisionen des Quartetts 'Er sterbe.'" *Musiktheorie* 14 (1999): 121–41.

Lühning, Helga, and Sieghard Brandenburg, eds. *Beethoven: Zwischen Revolution und Restauration*. Bonn: Beethoven-Haus, 1989.

Lukács, Georg. *Goethe and His Age*. Translated by Robert Anchor. New York: Grosset and Dunlap, 1969.

Lütteken, Laurenz. *Das Monologische als Denkform in der Musik zwischen 1760 und 1785*. Tübingen: M. Niemeyer, 1998.

Mann, Thomas. *Briefe 1937–1947*. Edited by Erika Mann. Frankfurt am Main: S. Fischer, 1963.

———. *Briefe 1948–1955 und Nachlese*. Edited by Erika Mann. Frankfurt am Main: S. Fischer, 1965.

———. "Die Kunst des Romans." In *Werke: Das essayistische Werk,* edited by Hans Bürgin, 350–60. Frankfurt am Main: Fischer Bücherei, 1968.

———. *Doctor Faustus: The Life of the German Composer Adrian Leverkühn as Told by a Friend*. Translated by John E. Woods. New York: A. A. Knopf, 1997.

———. *Doctor Faustus: The Life of the German Composer Adrian Leverkühn as Told by a Friend*. Translated by Helen Tracy Lowe-Porter. New York: Modern Library, 1992.

———. *Doktor Faustus: Das Leben des deutschen Tonsetzers Adrian Leverkühn erzählt von einem Freunde*. Frankfurt am Main: S. Fischer, 1967.

———. *Essays*. Edited by Hermann Kurzke and Stephan Stachorski. 6 vols. Frankfurt am Main: S. Fischer, 1993–97.

———. *Germany and the Germans*. Washington: Library of Congress, 1945.

———. *Gesammelte Werke*. 13 vols. Frankfurt am Main: S. Fischer, 1960–79.

———. *Letters of Thomas Mann 1889–1955*. Translated and edited by Richard Winston and Clara Winston. New York: A. A. Knopf, 1971.

———. *Order of the Day: Political Essays and Speeches of Two Decades*. New York: A. A. Knopf, 1942.

———. *The Story of a Novel: The Genesis of Doctor Faustus*. Translated by Richard Winston and Clara Winston. New York: A. A. Knopf, 1961.

———. *Tagebücher 28.5.1946–31.12.1948*. Edited by Inge Jens. Frankfurt am Main: S. Fischer, 1989.

———. *Tagebücher 1940–43*. Edited by Peter de Mendelssohn. Frankfurt am Main: S. Fischer, 1982.

———. *Tagebücher 1944–1.4.1946*. Edited by Inge Jens. Frankfurt am Main: S. Fischer, 1986.

———. *Thomas Mann an Ernst Bertram: Briefe aus den Jahren 1910–1955*. Edited by Inge Jens. Pfullingen: G. Neske, 1960.

Marston, Nicholas. "'Im Legendenton': Schumann's 'Unsung Voice.'" *Nineteenth-Century Music* 16 (1993): 227–41.

———. *Schumann: Fantasie, Op. 17*. Cambridge: Cambridge University Press, 1992.

Marx, Karl. *Capital: A Critique of Political Economy*. Translated by Ben Fowkes. Harmondsworth: Penguin Books, 1976.

Mayer, Hans. "Beethoven und das Prinzip Hoffnung." In *Versuche über die Oper*, 71–89. Frankfurt am Main: Suhrkamp, 1981.

McClary, Susan. *Feminine Endings: Music, Gender, and Sexuality*. Minneapolis: University of Minnesota Press, 1991.

―――. "Pitches, Expression, Ideology: An Exercise in Mediation." *Enclitic* 7 (1983): 76–86.

Merrick, Paul. *Revolution and Religion in the Music of Franz Liszt*. Cambridge: Cambridge University Press, 1987.

Meyer, Leonard B. *Style and Music: Theory, History, and Ideology*. Philadelphia: University of Pennsylvania Press, 1989.

Michaelis, Christian Friedrich. "Einige Bemerkungen über das Erhabene der Musik." *Berlinische Musikalische Zeitung* 1 (1805): 179–81.

Michel, Willy. *Ästhetische Hermeneutik und frühromantische Kritik: Friedrich Schlegels fragmentarische Entwürfe, Rezensionen, Charakteristiken und Kritiken (1795–1801)*. Göttingen: Vandenhoeck und Ruprecht, 1982.

Micznik, Vera. "The Farewell Story of Mahler's Ninth Symphony." *Nineteenth-Century Music* 20 (1996): 144–66.

Miller, Norbert. "Elevation bei Victor Hugo und Franz Liszt: Über die Schwierigkeiten einer Verwandlung von lyrischen in symphonische Dichtungen." *Jahrbuch des Staatlichen Instituts für Musikforschung* (1975): 131–59.

Mitchell, W.J.T. *Iconology: Image, Text, Ideology*. Chicago: University of Chicago Press, 1986.

―――. *Picture Theory: Essays on Verbal and Visual Representation*. Chicago: University of Chicago Press, 1994.

―――. "What Do Pictures *Really Want?*" *October* 77 (1996): 71–82.

Morgan, Robert P. "Musical Time/Musical Space." *Critical Inquiry* 6 (1980): 527–38.

―――. *Twentieth-Century Music: A History of Musical Style in Modern Europe and America*. New York: W.W. Norton, 1991.

Morrow, Mary Sue. *German Music Criticism in the Late Eighteenth Century: Aesthetic Issues in Instrumental Music*. Cambridge: Cambridge University Press, 1997.

Moser, Hans Joachim. *Kleine deutsche Musikgeschichte*. Stuttgart: Cotta, 1949.

Mosès, Stéphane. *Der Engel der Geschichte: Franz Rosenzweig, Walter Benjamin, Gershom Scholem*. Frankfurt am Main: Jüdischer, 1994.

―――. "Ideen, Namen, Sterne: Zu Walter Benjamins Metaphorik des Ursprungs." Translated by Andreas Kilcher. In *Für Walter Benjamin: Dokumente, Essays und ein Entwurf*, edited by Ingrid Scheurmann and Konrad Scheurmann, 183–92. Frankfurt am Main: Suhrkamp, 1992.

Mueller, Martin. "Walter Benjamin und Thomas Manns Dr. Faustus." *Archiv für das Studium der neueren Sprachen und Literaturen* 210 (Neue Folge 125) (1973): 327–30.

Mueller, Rena Charnin. "Liszt's Tasso Sketchbook: Studies in Sources and Revisions." Ph.D. diss., New York University, 1986.

Müller, Franz. *Lohengrin und die Gral- und Schwan-Sage: Ein Skizzenbild auf Grund der Wort- und Tondichtung Richard Wagner's*. Munich: C. Kaiser, 1867.

Nägeli, Hans Georg. "Versuch einer Norm für die Recensenten der musikalischen Zeitung." *Allgemeine musikalische Zeitung* 5 (1802/3): 225–37, 265–74.

Nattiez, Jean-Jacques. *Wagner Androgyne: A Study in Interpretation.* Translated by Stewart Spencer. Princeton: Princeton University Press, 1993.

Nelson, Thomas Keith. "The Fantasy of Absolute Music." Ph.D. diss., University of Minnesota, 1998.

Neubauer, John. *The Emancipation of Music from Language: Departure from Mimesis in Eighteenth-Century Aesthetics.* New Haven: Yale University Press, 1986.

Neumann, Peter Horst. "Rilkes *Archaischer Torso Apollos* in der Geschichte des modernen Fragmentarismus," In *Fragment und Totalität,* edited by Lucien Dällenbach and Christiaan L. Hart Nibbrig, 257–74. Frankfurt am Main: Suhrkamp, 1984.

Neumann, William. *Die Componisten der neueren Zeit: Adam, Auber, Beethoven, Bellini, Boieldieu, Cherubini . . . und Andere in Biographien geschildert.* Cassel: E. Balde, 1854–57.

Newcomb, Anthony. "Narrative Archetypes and Mahler's Ninth Symphony." In *Music and Text: Critical Inquiries,* edited by Steven Paul Scher, 118–36. Cambridge: Cambridge University Press, 1992.

———. "Once More Between Absolute and Program Music: Schumann's Second Symphony." *Nineteenth-Century Music* 7 (1984): 233–50.

———. "Schumann and the Marketplace." In *Nineteenth-Century Piano Music,* edited by R. Larry Todd, 258–315. New York: Schirmer, 1990.

Newman, William S. *The Sonata Since Beethoven.* 3rd ed. New York: W.W. Norton, 1983.

Nietzsche, Friedrich. *Sämtliche Werke: Kritische Studienausgabe.* Edited by Giorgio Colli and Mazzino Montinari. 15 vols. Munich: Deutscher Taschenbuch Verlag, 1988.

Noerr, Gunzelin Schmid, and Willem van Reijen, eds. *Vierzig Jahre Flaschenpost: "Dialektik der Aufklärung," 1947–1987.* Frankfurt am Main: S. Fischer, 1987.

Novalis. *Schriften.* Edited by Richard Samuel and Paul Kluckhohn. 5 vols. Stuttgart: W. Kohlhammer, 1960–88.

———. *Werke, Tagebücher und Briefe Friedrich von Hardenbergs.* Edited by Hans-Joachim Mähl and Richard Samuel. 3 vols. Munich: C. Hanser, 1978–87.

Otto, Frauke. *Robert Schumann als Jean Paul-Leser.* Frankfurt am Main: Haag und Herchen, 1984.

Paddison, Max. "The Language-Character of Music: Some Motifs in Adorno." In *Mit den Ohren denken: Adornos Philosophie der Musik,* edited by Richard Klein and Claus-Steffen Mahnkopf, 71–91. Frankfurt am Main: Suhrkamp, 1998.

Pastille, William. "Music and Morphology: Goethe's Influence on Schenker's Thought." In *Schenker Studies,* edited by Hedi Siegel, 29–44. Cambridge: Cambridge University Press, 1990.

———. "Ursatz: The Musical Philosophy of Heinrich Schenker." Ph.D. diss., Cornell University, 1985.

Pater, Walter. *The Renaissance: Studies in Art and Poetry (The 1893 Text).*

Edited by Donald L. Hill. Berkeley: University of California Press, 1980.

Pederson, Sanna. "Enlightened and Romantic German Music Criticism, 1800–1850." Ph.D. diss., University of Pennsylvania, 1995.

———. "On the Task of the Music Historian: The Myth of the Symphony After Beethoven." *Repercussions* 2 (1993): 5–30.

Pensky, Max. *Melancholy Dialectics: Walter Benjamin and the Play of Mourning.* Amherst: University of Massachusetts Press, 1993.

Plantinga, Leon. *Schumann as Critic.* New Haven: Yale University Press, 1967.

Plebuch, Tobias. "Vom Musikalisch-Bösen. Eine musikgeschichtliche Annährung an das Diabolische in Thomas Manns *Doktor Faustus.*" In *Thomas Mann: "Doktor Faustus" Zeitschrift für Germanistik, Neue Folge, Beiheft 3 (2000),* edited by Werner Röcke, 207–62, 1997.

Poizat, Michel. *The Angel's Cry: Beyond the Pleasure Principle in Opera.* Translated by Arthur Denner. Ithaca: Cornell University Press, 1992.

Powers, Harold. "'La solita forma' and 'The Uses of Convention.'" *Acta Musicologica* 59 (1987): 65–90.

Puschmann, Rosemarie. *Magisches Quadrat und Melancholie in Thomas Manns Doktor Faustus: Von der musikalischen Struktur zum semantischen Beziehungsnetz.* Bielefeld: Ampal, 1983.

Raabe, Peter. *Die Entstehungsgeschichte der ersten Orchesterwerke Franz Liszts.* Leipzig: Breitkopf und Härtel, 1916.

———. *Franz Liszt.* 2 vols. Tutzing: H. Schneider, 1968.

Raff, Joachim. *Die Wagnerfrage.* Braunschweig: F. Vieweg, 1854.

Ramann, Lina. *Franz Liszt: Als Künstler und Mensch.* 2 vols. Leipzig: Breitkopf und Härtel, 1880–94.

Ramroth, Peter. *Robert Schumann und Richard Wagner im geschichtsphilosophischen Urteil von Franz Brendel.* Frankfurt am Main: P. Lang, 1991.

Reible, John Joseph, III. "Tristan-Romanticism and the Expressionism of the *Three Piano Pieces*, op. 11 of Arnold Schoenberg." Ph.D. diss., Washington University, 1980.

Reich, Nancy B. *Clara Schumann: The Artist and the Woman.* Ithaca: Cornell University Press, 1985.

Reynolds, Christopher. "An die ferne Geliebte." In *Beethoven: Interpretationen seiner Werke,* edited by Carl Dahlhaus, Albrecht Riethmüller and Alexander L. Ringer, 99–108. Laaber: Laaber, 1994.

Ricoeur, Paul. *Hermeneutics and the Human Sciences: Essays on Language, Action, and Interpretation.* Translated and edited by John B. Thompson. Cambridge: Cambridge University Press, 1981.

Rilke, Rainer Maria. *Sämtliche Werke.* 6 vols. Frankfurt am Main: Insel, 1955–66.

Robinson, Paul. "*Fidelio* and the French Revolution." In *Ludwig van Beethoven, Fidelio,* edited by Paul Robinson, 68–100. Cambridge: Cambridge University Press, 1996.

———, ed. *Ludwig van Beethoven, Fidelio.* Cambridge: Cambridge University Press, 1996.

Roesner, Linda Correll. "Schumann's 'Parallel' Forms." *Nineteenth-Century Music* 14 (1991): 265–78.

———. "The Sources for Schumann's *Davidsbündlertänze*, Op. 6: Composition, Textual Problems, and the Role of the Composer as Editor." In *Mendelssohn and Schumann: Essays on Their Music and Its Context*, edited by Jon W. Finson and R. Larry Todd, 53–70. Durham: Duke University Press, 1984.

Rosen, Charles. *The Classical Style*. 2nd rev. ed. New York: W.W. Norton, 1976.

———. *The Romantic Generation*. Cambridge: Harvard University Press, 1995.

Rosenblatt, Jay Michael. "The Concerto as Crucible: Franz Liszt's Early Works for Piano and Orchestra." Ph.D. diss., University of Chicago, 1995.

Rubsamen, Walter H. "Schoenberg in America." *The Musical Quarterly* 37 (1951): 469–89.

Russell, Peter. *Light in Battle with Darkness: Mahler's Kindertotenlieder*. Frankfurt am Main: P. Lang, 1991.

San-Marte, ed. *Lieder, Wilhelm von Orange und Titurel von Wolfram von Eschenbach, und der jüngere Titurel von Albrecht in Uebersetzung und im Auszuge, nebst Abhandlungen über das Leben und Wirken Wolfram's von Eschenbach und die Sage vom Heiligen Gral*. Magdeburg: Creutz, 1841.

Santner, Eric L. *Stranded Objects: Mourning, Memory, and Film in Postwar Germany*. Ithaca: Cornell University Press, 1990.

Schadewaldt, Wolfgang. *Winckelmann und Rilke: Zwei Beschreibungen des Apollon*. Pfullingen: G. Neske, 1968.

Schaeffer, Julius. "Über 'Lohengrin' von Richard Wagner mit Bezug auf seine Schrift: 'Oper und Drama.'" *Neue Berliner Musikzeitung* 6 (1852): 153–55, 161–63, 169–71, 193–96, 201–4.

Schebera, Jürgen. *Hanns Eisler: Eine Biographie in Texten, Bildern und Dokumenten*. Mainz: Schott, 1998.

Schelling, Friedrich Wilhelm Joseph von. *Ideas for a Philosophy of Nature*. Translated by Errol E. Harris and Peter Heath. Cambridge: Cambridge University Press, 1988.

Schenker, Heinrich. *Beethoven: Die letzten Sonaten, Sonate C Moll Op. 111: Kritische Ausgabe mit Einführung und Erläuterung*. Edited by Oswald Jonas. 2nd ed. Vienna: Universal Edition, 1971.

———. *Der freie Satz*. Edited by Oswald Jonas. 2nd ed. Vienna: Universal Edition, 1956.

———. *Der Tonwille*. 1921–4. Reprint, Hildesheim: G. Olms, 1990.

———. *Die letzten fünf Sonaten von Beethoven: Kritische Ausgabe mit Einführung und Erläuterung [Sonate As dur Op. 110]*. Vienna: Universal Edition, 1914.

———. *Die letzten fünf Sonaten von Beethoven: Kritische Ausgabe mit Einführung und Erläuterung [Sonate C moll Op. 111]*. Vienna: Universal Edition, 1916.

———. *Free Composition: Volume III of New Musical Theories and Fantasies*. Translated by Ernst Oster. Edited by Ernst Oster. New York: Longman, 1979.

————. *Harmonielehre*. Vienna: Universal Edition, 1978.

————. *The Masterwork in Music: A Yearbook*. Translated by Ian Bent et al. Edited by William Drabkin. 3 vols. Cambridge: Cambridge University Press, 1994–97.

Schering, Arnold. "Gustav Mahler als Liederkomponist." *Neue Zeitschrift für Musik* 72 (1905): 672–73, 691–93, 753–55.

Scherliess, Volker. "Zur Musik im *Doktor Faustus*." In *"Und was werden die Deutschen sagen?": Thomas Manns Roman Doktor Faustus*, edited by Hans Wißkirchen and Thomas Sprecher, 113–51. Lübeck: Dräger, 1997.

Schiller, Friedrich. *Essays*. Edited by Walter Hinderer and Daniel O. Dahlstrom. New York: Continuum, 1993.

Schlegel, Friedrich. *Kritische Friedrich-Schlegel-Ausgabe*. Edited by Ernst Behler, Jean-Jacques Anstett and Hans Eichner. Munich: F. Schöningh, 1958.

Schleiermacher, Friedrich. *Hermeneutics: The Handwritten Manuscripts*. Translated by James Duke and Jack Forstman. Edited by Heinz Kimmerle. Missoula: Scholars Press for The American Academy of Religion, 1977.

————. *Hermeneutik*. Edited by Heinz Kimmerle. Heidelberg: C. Winter, 1959.

Schmid, Manfred Hermann. "Metamorphose der Themen: Beobachtungen an den Skizzen zum "Lohengrin"-Vorspiel." *Die Musikforschung* 41 (1988): 105–26.

————. *Musik als Abbild: Studien zum Werk von Weber, Schumann und Wagner*. Tutzing: H. Schneider, 1981.

Schmitz, Arnold. *Beethovens "Zwei Prinzipe": Ihre Bedeutung für Themen- und Satzbau*. Berlin: Dümmlers Verlagsbuchhandlung, 1923.

Schocher, Christian Gottlieb. *Soll die Rede auf immer ein dunkler Gesang bleiben, und können ihre Arten, Gänge und Beugungen nicht anschaulich gemacht, und nach Art der Tonkunst gezeichnet werden?* Leipzig: A. L. Reinicke, 1791.

Schoenberg, Arnold. "Aphorismen." *Die Musik* 9 (1909/1910): 159–63.

————. "Gewissheit." *Musikblätter des Anbruch* 4 (1922): 2–3.

————. "Painting Influences." *Journal of the Arnold Schoenberg Institute* 2 (1978): 237–39.

————. *Stil und Gedanke: Aufsätze zur Musik*. Edited by Ivan Vojtech. Frankfurt am Main: S. Fischer, 1976.

————. *Style and Idea: Selected Writings of Arnold Schoenberg*. Translated by Leo Black. Edited by Leonard Stein. Berkeley: University of California Press, 1984.

————. *Theory of Harmony*. Translated by Roy E. Carter. Berkeley: University of California Press, 1978.

Schopenhauer, Arthur. *Sämtliche Werke*. Edited by Arthur Hübscher. Wiesbaden: E. Brockhaus, 1948.

Schumann, Clara and Robert. *Briefwechsel*. Edited by Eva Weissweiler. 2 vols. Frankfurt am Main: Stroemfeld/Roter Stern, 1984, 1987.

————. *The Complete Correspondence*. Translated by Hildegard Fritsch and Ronald L. Crawford. Edited by Eva Weissweiler. 2 vols. New York: P. Lang, 1994, 1996.

Schumann, Robert. *Gesammelte Schriften über Musik und Musiker.* Edited by Martin Kreisig. 5th ed. Leipzig: Breitkopf und Härtel, 1914.

———. *Jugendbriefe.* Edited by Clara Schumann. 2nd ed. Leipzig: Breitkopf und Härtel, 1886.

———. *Robert Schumanns Briefe: Neue Folge.* Edited by F. Gustav Jansen. Leipzig: Breitkopf und Härtel, 1904.

———. *Tagebücher.* Edited by Georg Eismann and Gerd Nauhaus. 3 vols. Leipzig: VEB, 1971–87.

Seidel, Wilhelm. "Die Peripetie: Über das Quartett des zweiten Aktes." In *Von der Leonore zum Fidelio: Vorträge und Referate des Bonner Symposions 1997,* edited by Helga Lühning and Wolfram Steinbeck, 277–92. Frankfurt am Main: P. Lang, 2000.

Seiwert, Elvira. *Beethoven-Szenarien: Thomas Manns "Doktor Faustus" und Adornos Beethoven-Projekt.* Stuttgart: J. B. Metzler, 1995.

Seremetakis, C. Nadia, ed. *The Senses Still: Perception and Memory as Material Culture in Modernity.* Boulder: Westview Press, 1994.

Shaw, Jennifer. "Androgyny and the Eternal Feminine in Schoenberg's Oratorio *Die Jakobsleiter.*" In *Political and Religious Ideas in the Works of Arnold Schoenberg,* edited by Charlotte M. Cross and Russell A. Berman, 61–83. New York: Garland, 2000.

Sichardt, Martina. *Die Entstehung der Zwölftonmethode Arnold Schönbergs.* Mainz: Schott, 1990.

Siegele, Ulrich. "Das Drama der Themen am Beispiel des Lohengrin." In *Richard Wagner: Werk und Wirkung,* edited by Carl Dahlhaus, 41–52. Regensburg: G. Bosse, 1971.

Simms, Bryan. "Whose Idea was *Erwartung?*" In *Constructive Dissonance: Arnold Schoenberg and the Transformations of Twentieth-Century Culture,* edited by Juliane Brand and Christopher Hailey, 100–11. Berkeley: University of California Press, 1997.

Sisman, Elaine R. "Learned Style and the Rhetoric of the Sublime in the 'Jupiter' Symphony." In *Wolfgang Amadè Mozart: Essays on his Life and his Music,* 213–38. Oxford: Clarendon Press, 1996.

———. *Mozart: The 'Jupiter' Symphony.* Cambridge: Cambridge University Press, 1993.

Snarrenberg, Robert. *Schenker's Interpretive Practice.* Cambridge: Cambridge University Press, 1997.

Soden, Michael von. *Richard Wagner: Lohengrin.* Frankfurt am Main: Insel, 1980.

Stevens, Halsey. "A Conversation with Schoenberg about Painting." *Journal of the Arnold Schoenberg Institute* 2 (1978): 178–80.

Stockhausen, Karlheinz. *Texte.* Edited by Dieter Schnebel. Cologne: M. DuMont Schauberg, 1963–78.

Street, Alan. "Superior Myths, Dogmatic Allegories: The Resistance to Musical Unity." *Music Analysis* 8 (1989): 77–123.

Stumpf, Heike. " . . . *wollet mir jetzt durch die phantastisch verschlungenen Kreuzgänge folgen!*": Metaphorisches Sprechen in der Musikkritik der ersten

Hälfte des 19. Jahrhunderts. Frankfurt am Main: P. Lang, 1996.

Subotnik, Rose Rosengard. *Deconstructive Variations: Music and Reason in Western Society*. Minneapolis: University of Minnesota Press, 1996.

———. *Developing Variations: Style and Ideology in Western Music*. Minneapolis: University of Minnesota Press, 1991.

Sulzer, Johann Georg. *Allgemeine Theorie der Schönen Künste in einzeln, nach alphabetischer Ordnung der Kunstwörter auf einander folgenden Artikeln abgehandelt*. 2nd ed. Leipzig: In der Weidmannschen Buchhandlung, 1792.

Szondi, Peter. *Introduction to Literary Hermeneutics*. Translated by Martha Woodmansee. Cambridge: Cambridge University Press, 1995.

Taruskin, Richard. "Chernomar to Kashchei: Harmonic Sorcery; or, Stravinsky's 'Angle.'" *Journal of the American Musicological Society* 38 (1985): 72–142.

———. "Resisting the Ninth." *Nineteenth-Century Music* 12 (1989): 241–56.

Temperley, Nicholas. "Schumann and Sterndale Bennett." *Nineteenth-Century Music* 12 (1989): 207–20.

Thorslev, Peter. *The Byronic Hero: Types and Prototypes*. Minneapolis: University of Minnesota Press, 1982.

Tieck, Ludwig. *Franz Sternbalds Wanderungen*. Edited by Alfred Anger. Stuttgart: P. Reclam, 1966.

Tiedemann, Rolf. "Concept, Image, Name: On Adorno's Utopia of Knowledge." In *The Semblance of Subjectivity: Essays in Adorno's Aesthetic Theory*, edited by Tom Huhn and Lambert Zuidervaart, 123–45. Cambridge: MIT Press, 1997.

———. *Dialektik im Stillstand: Versuche zum Spätwerk Walter Benjamins*. Frankfurt am Main: Suhrkamp, 1983.

———. "Gretel Adorno zum Abschied." *Frankfurter Adorno Blätter* 3 (1994): 148–51.

———. "'Mitdichtende Einfühlung': Adornos Beiträge zum *Doktor Faustus*—noch einmal." *Frankfurter Adorno Blätter* 1 (1992): 9–33.

Todd, R. Larry. "On Quotation in Schumann's Music." In *Schumann and His World*, edited by R. Larry Todd, 80–112. Princeton: Princeton University Press, 1994.

Tomlinson, Gary. *Metaphysical Song: An Essay on Opera*. Princeton: Princeton University Press, 1999.

———. *Music in Renaissance Magic: Toward a Historiography of Others*. Chicago: University of Chicago Press, 1993.

Treadwell, James. "The *Ring* and the Conditions of Interpretation: Wagner's Writing, 1848 to 1852." *Cambridge Opera Journal* 7 (1995): 207–31.

Vill, Susanne. *Vermittlungsformen verbalisierter und musikalischer Inhalte in der Musik Gustav Mahlers*. Tutzing: H. Schneider, 1979.

Voss, Lieselotte. *Die Entstehung von Thomas Manns Roman "Doktor Faustus": Dargestellt anhand von unveröffentlichten Vorarbeiten*. Tübingen: M. Niemeyer, 1975.

Wackenroder, Wilhelm Heinrich. *Herzensergiessungen eines kunstliebenden Klosterbruders*. Stuttgart: P. Reclam, 1963.

Wagner, Cosima. *Cosima Wagner's Diaries*. Translated by Geoffrey Skelton.

Edited by Martin Gregor-Dellin and Dietrich Mack. 2 vols. New York: Harcourt Brace Jovanovich, 1978–80.

Wagner, Manfred. *Geschichte der österreichischen Musikkritik in Beispielen.* Tutzing: H. Schneider, 1979.

Wagner, Richard. *Gesammelte Schriften und Dichtungen.* 2nd ed. 10 vols. Leipzig: E.W. Fritzsch, 1887–88.

———. *Lohengrin: Edition and Untersuchungen.* Edited by Thomas Cramer. Munich: W. Fink, 1971.

———. *My Life.* Translated by Andrew Gray. Edited by Mary Whittall. Cambridge: Cambridge University Press, 1983.

———. *Oper und Drama.* Edited by Klaus Kropfinger. Stuttgart: P. Reclam, 1984.

———. *Prose Works.* Translated by William Ashton Ellis. 8 vols. London: Routledge and Kegan Paul, 1892–99.

———. *Selected Letters of Richard Wagner.* Translated and edited by Stewart Spencer and Barry Millington. New York: W. W. Norton, 1988.

———. *Three Wagner Essays.* Translated by Robert L. Jacobs. London: Eulenburg, 1979.

Walker, Alan. *Franz Liszt: The Virtuoso Years 1811–1847.* rev. ed. Ithaca: Cornell University Press, 1988.

———. *Franz Liszt: The Weimar Years 1848–1861.* rev. ed. Ithaca: Cornell University Press, 1989.

Walter, Bruno. *Briefe, 1894–1962.* Edited by Lotte Walter Lindt. Frankfurt am Main: S. Fischer, 1969.

Weber, Carl Maria von. *Sämtliche Schriften.* Edited by Georg Kaiser. Berlin: Schuster und Loeffler, 1908.

———. *Writings on Music.* Translated by Martin Cooper. Edited by John Warrack. Cambridge: Cambridge University Press, 1981.

Weber, William. *Music and the Middle Class: The Social Structure of Concert Life in London,* Paris and Vienna. London: Croom Helm, 1975.

Webern, Anton. "Schönbergs Musik." In *Arnold Schönberg: Mit Beiträgen von Alban Berg, [et al.],* 22–48. Munich: R. Piper, 1912.

Webster, James. "The Analysis of Mozart's Arias." In *Mozart Studies,* edited by Cliff Eisen, 101–99. Oxford: Clarendon, 1991.

———. "The Creation, Haydn's Late Vocal Music, and the Musical Sublime." In *Haydn and His World,* edited by Elaine R. Sisman, 57–102. Princeton: Princeton University Press, 1997.

Wehrmann, Harald. *Thomas Manns "Doktor Faustus": Von den fiktiven Werken Adrian Leverkühns zur musikalischen Struktur des Romans.* Frankfurt am Main: P. Lang, 1988.

Weiss, John. *Ideology of Death: Why the Holocaust Happened in Germany.* Chicago: Ivan R. Dee, 1996.

Weisse, Christian Hermann. *System der Ästhetik als Wissenschaft von der Idee der Schönheit.* Hildesheim: G. Olms, 1966 (1830).

Wellbery, David E. *The Specular Moment: Goethe's Early Lyric and the Beginnings of Romanticism.* Stanford: Stanford University Press, 1996.

White, Hayden. *The Content of the Form: Narrative Discourse and Historical Representation.* Baltimore: Johns Hopkins University Press, 1987.

———. *Metahistory: The Historical Imagination in Nineteenth-Century Europe.* Baltimore: Johns Hopkins University Press, 1973.

Whittall, Arnold. "Wagner's Great Transition? From *Lohengrin* to *Das Rheingold.*" *Music Analysis* 2 (1983): 269–80.

Will, Richard. "Programmatic Symphonies of the Classical Period." Ph.D. diss., Cornell University, 1994.

Williamson, John. "Liszt, Mahler and the Chorale." *Proceedings of the Royal Musical Association* 108 (1981/82): 115–25.

Winckelmann, Johann Joachim. *Kleine Schriften, Vorreden, Entwürfe.* Edited by Walther Rehm. Berlin: De Gruyter, 1968.

Wiora, Walter. "Zwischen absoluter und Programmusik." In *Festschrift Friedrich Blume zum 70. Geburtstag,* edited by Anna Amalie Abert and Wilhelm Pfannkuch, 381–88. Kassel: Bärenreiter, 1963.

Wörner, Karl Heinrich. "Schönberg's 'Erwartung' und das Ariadne-Thema." In *Die Musik in der Geistesgeschichte: Studien zur Situation der Jahre um 1910,* 91–117. Bonn: Bouvier, 1970.

Zaunschirm, Thomas, ed. *Arnold Schönberg: Das bildnerische Werk.* Klagenfurt: Ritter, 1991.

Zenck, Martin. *Kunst als begriffslose Erkenntnis: Zum Kunstbegriff der ästhetischen Theorie Theodor W. Adornos.* Munich: W. Fink, 1977.

Zimmermann, Norbert. *Der ästhetische Augenblick: Theodor W. Adornos Theorie der Zeitstruktur von Kunst und ästhetischer Erfahrung.* Frankfurt am Main: P. Lang, 1989.

Zuidervaart, Lambert. *Adorno's Aesthetic Theory: The Redemption of Illusion.* Cambridge: MIT Press, 1991.

Abbate, Carolyn, 106, 178
Abert, Hermann, 96
absolute, as detachment, 6; as fragment, 6,
  209, 214; in modernity, 15; in *Moses
  and Aron,* 213; music's grasp of, 7; and
  poésie absolue, 52; present and absent in
  art, 223; as preserved in particulars, 10,
  23; romantic view of, 6; as whole, 6,
  214
absolute music, 2, 11, 113–14, 165, 178,
  262; as allegorized in *Lohengrin,* 138–
  39, 143, 151; end of, 253; in *Die
  Jakobsleiter,* 219, 222; and meaning, 4;
  and opera, 118; versus program music,
  165–68, 222; role in Western art music,
  3; and song, 79; Wagner's view of, 138–
  39, 149
actio in distans, 51, 53–54, 97, 113
Adams, Courtney, 190
Adorno, Gretel, 20
Adorno, Theodor Wiesengrund, on
  aesthetics of the *Augenblick,* 7, 15;
  apparition, 16, 262; artwork as moment,
  7, 9, 197; atomistic listening, 5, 18–19;
  beautiful passages, 18, 257; on C♯ in
  "Arietta" from op. 111, 230, 234–37;
  critique of *Die Jakobsleiter,* 209–14; on
  hope, 19; immanent form, 178; kitsch,
  9; on *Lohengrin,* 132; material theory of
  form, 263; and notion of essay, 15;
  metaphysics of art, 223; on music's
  grasp of the absolute, 7, 28; on the
  power of the Name, 28; on structural
  listening, 5, 18–19, 21–22, 198–99; on
  truth, 10, 15–16; on vocal and instrumental music, 27–28, 40
—*Aesthetic Theory,* 7, 15;
—*Beethoven,* critique of *Fidelio,* 41;
  influence of Benjamin on, 12; Leonore's
  Adagio, 28; theory of, 20–21; relationship to Hegel, 21
—*Dialectic of Enlightenment,* 28, 209
—"Huldigung an Zerlina," (*Moments
  musicaux*), 46
—*Negative Dialectics*: ending of, 10–11,
  23, 251
—"On Some Relationships Between Music
  and Painting," 17, 85–86, 91–92
—*Philosophy of New Music,* 190, 222,
  244, 251; influence on *Doctor Faustus,*
  225–26, 240–41, 246; on *Erwartung,*
  196–99, 205–6; on Schoenberg as
  dialectical composer, 190, 241; on
  Webern, 244
—*Sacred Fragment*: dilemma of Moses and
  Aron, 213–14
—"Schöne Stellen," 5
—"Spätstil Beethovens," 22–23; influence
  on *Doctor Faustus,* 227, 240–41
—*Vers une musique informelle,* 199, 209–
  14
aesthetic appearance, 22, 235–36, 239,
  242
aesthetics of Argus-eyedness, 15, 189, 211,
  219, 223, 226, 231, 234
Agawu, Kofi, 256–57
allegory, temporality of, 7
analysis, distant, 71; fear of, 262;
  relationship of to criticism, 4–5, 65–71,
  113, 165–66, 229
apparition, 16; aesthetics of, 16, 18
arabesque, 103–4
Argus Panoptes, 14
art religion, 178, 187–88
Augenblick, aesthetics of, 15, 226. *See also*
  moment
aura, 18; end of, 208, 262, 265; versus
  trace, 68, 262. *See also* Benjamin, Walter
Auschwitz, 49

Babbitt, Milton, 66
Bach, Johann Sebastian, 2, 9, 165
Bahle, Julius, 229
Balzac, Honoré de, *Séraphita,* 211, 218–19
Barthes, Roland, 176
Bataille, Georges, 191

beauty, 5; as defined by Hegel, 14, 189; in *Elective Affinities*, 19, 226; natural, 28; relation to total vision, 15

Beddow, Michael, 239

Beethoven, Ludwig van, 2; hermeneutic criticism of, 165; late style, 21–23; musical heroism of, 86–87; unity of his music, 21; view of Kant, 183; Wagner's view of, 115, 143, 150–51

—*An die Ferne Geliebte*, op. 98: relationship to Schumann's *Fantasie*, op. 17, 96–109, 112–13

—*Egmont Overture*, 155; as seen by Liszt, 169, 173

—*Fidelio*, 12, 24–50; Leonore's recitative and aria No. 9, 25–26, 29–36; "Oh Gott welch ein Augenblick", 24, 41; Quartet No. 14 "Er sterbe," 36–46; role of instrumental music in, 26–27, 34–35, 38–40

—*Der glorreiche Augenblick*, op. 136, 45, 86

—Leonore Overture No. 3, 25

—Piano Sonata op. 31, no. 2 "The Tempest," 18, 236, 309n.43

—Piano Sonata op. 81a "Les Adieux," Adorno's view of, 10, 23, 235

—Piano Sonata op. 111, 3; "Arietta," 227–37; in *Doctor Faustus*, 3, 227–30, 234–35; as read by Adorno, 230, 234–37

—String Quartet op. 59, no. 1, 20

—String Quartet op. 59, no. 2, 34, 36

—Symphony no. 3 (*Eroica*), 3, 21, 86, 198; evil chord, 44; as moment, 198

—Symphony no. 5, 21, 71

—Symphony no. 7, 21

—Symphony no. 9, in *Doctor Faustus*, 224, 244; hermeneutic crux of, 12; "Ode of Joy," 187

Bekker, Paul, 197–99, 227, 229

Benda, Georg, *Ariadne auf Naxos*, 199–204

Benjamin, Walter, on allegory and symbol, 8; *Arcarde Project*, 10, 17; and Beethoven, 12; caesura, 19; concept of Name, 27–28; constellation, 7, 17, 240, 253, 263; dialectics at a standstill, 16–17, 159–61, 188, 246–47; distinction between trace and aura, 68; on the eternal, 10, 24; expressionless, 19, 214;
on Goethe's *Elective Affinities*, 19–20; hermeneutics of hope, 12, 19–20; hermeneutics of the moment, 235; notion of aura, 18, 68, 262; *Origin of German Tragic Drama*, 190, 249; physiognomic gaze, 9, 160; *Theses on the Philosophy of History*, 25, 46–47

Benn, Gottfried, 190

Bennett, Sterndale, 104

Bent, Ian, 4

Bergsten, Gunilla, 237

Berlioz, Hector, *Harold en Italie*, 177; *Symphonie fantastique*, 67, 96, 167; and review of *Fidelio*, 36

Bertram, Ernst, 245

Blackbourn, David, 2

Bloch, Ernst, 10, 220; on *Fidelio*, 24–26, 38, 41; *The Principle of Hope*, 9

Bockholdt, Rudolf, 276n.105

Bohrer, Karl-Heinz, 15

Bonds, Mark Evan, 4

Boretz, Benjamin, 66

Bouilly, Jean Nicholas, 26

Bowie, Andrew, 166

Brahms, Johannes, 3, 74

Brandes, Johann Christian, 200

breakthrough, in *Doctor Faustus*, 238, 241; as formal category, 169; as historical catetory, 197, 237; in Mahler, 173, 263–64; in Mountain Symphony, 173–79, 186; as star, 14

Brendel, Franz, 87; on Beethoven's heroic style, 21, 86; on Beethoven's late style, 22; *History of Music*, 173; on Liszt, 161, 165; on Schumann's piano music, 82, 85;

Brinkmann, Reinhold, 189–90, 246

Bruckner, Anton, 3

Buchanan, Herbert, 208

Buñuel, Luis, 191

Burke, Edmund, 55, 103, 182

Burnham, Scott, 3, 87

Busoni, Ferruccio, 197

Byron, Lord, 79

caesura, 14, 16; as defined by Benjamin, 19; in *Doctor Faustus*, 226; in *Fidelio*, 36–38, 49; in *Die Jakobsleiter*, 219–20; in *Moses and Aron*, 214

Carbonnières, Louis Ramond de, 81

Castelli, Ignaz, 57–58

Index

characteristic, aesthetic category of, 161–62

Cherlin, Michael, 208

Chirico, Giorgio de, 191

Christensen, Jean, 210

Chua, Daniel, 267n.7

Cinnamon, Howard, 172

Cohn, Richard, 222

constellation, 7, 17, 240, 253, 263; hermeneutics of, 18. *See also* Benjamin, Walter

Creuzer, Friedrich, 8

criticism, hermeneutic 4–5; versus musical analysis 4, 66–68, 113–14, 165–66, 229

Dahlhaus, Carl, 4; on absolute music, 52; on Hegel's musical aesthetics, 165; on *Lohengrin*, 117, 145; on Liszt's Mountain Symphony, 156, 163, 168–71, 177, 181, 188

Dali, Salvador, 191

Dannreuther, Edward, 21

Danuser, Hermann, 199

Däubler, Theodor, 236, 309n.42

Daverio, John, 103, 286n.133

Deathridge, John, 116

Debussy, Claude, 86

Dehmel, Richard, 209

De Man, Paul, 8

dialectics at a standstill, 16–17, 159–61, 188, 226, 246–47, 250

Dilthey, Wilhelm, 6, 66

distance, and aura, 68; in definitions of the Romantic, 51–62; effect on language, 52–54; in landscapes, 80–81; in Schumann's piano music, 60–62, 78–79, 87–93, 98–114

Drabkin, William, 234

Draeseke, Felix, review of Mountain Symphony, 162, 169–73, 176, 181, 188

Dürer, Albrecht, 248

dying sound, 51, 54–56, 60–62, 68, 71, 78, 92, 107, 250–51

Eggebrecht, Hans Heinrich, 10

Eichel, Christine, 10

Einstein, Alfred, 156

Eisler, Hanns, 313n.140

ekphrasis, 262

enucleation. *See* eye

Ernst, Max, 191

expression, 197; as gaze, 16; relationship of to construction, 10, 220, 222, 240–41, 250, 264

Expressionism, 206, 209, 213, 223; defined by Adorno, 197; moment of, 190, 210, 238; and painting, 189–96

expressionless, as defined by Benjamin, 19; in *Die Jakobsleiter*, 220, 223; in late Beethoven, 22; in *Moses and Aron*, 213–14

eye, 7; all-seeing, 236; in *Doctor Faustus*, 237–39, 242 enucleated, 190–96; in *Erwartung*, 204–9; evil, 242; in *Kindertotenlieder* no. 2, 256–57, 261; in music drama, 123–24, 133; as organ of the soul, 14–15, 190; in Schoenberg's paintings, 189–90; spiritual, 196; as star, 18, 253, 265; as tone, 261. *See also* gaze

Feuerbach, Ludwig, 136, 137

Fichte, Johann Gottlieb, 54

Figal, Günter, 16–17

Finscher, Ludwig, 266n.2

Forster, Edward Morgan, on Beethoven's Fifth Symphony, 227

fragment, 1, 6, 14–15, 102–3, 209, 214, 244

Frank, Hermann, 116

Freud, Siegmund, on melancholy, 11, 248–50; uncanny, 208

Friedrich, Caspar David, 79

Gadamer, Hans-Georg, 64

Gaveaux, Pierre, 26

gaze, of composer, 236; and expression, 16; hermeneutic, 191; physiognomic, 9–10, 160; in Schoenberg's paintings, 189–96; of stars, 18; theoretical, 10, 259–63; total, 14, 196, 236, 259. *See also* eye

George, Stefan, 20

German music, 156, 245; moment of, 2–3, 6, 190, 226, 251, 255, 265

Gerstenberg, Heinrich Wilhelm von, 200

Gerstl, Richard, 189

Goebbels, Joseph, 247

Göllerich, August, 159

Goethe, Johann Wolfgang von, 6, 22; and definition of novella, 200; *Elective Affinities*, 18–20; *Faust*, 2, 222; and notion of aperçu, 191, 260; *Theory of Colors*, 258

Grey, Thomas, 117, 145, 149

Habermas, Jürgen, 9, 64, 166
Halm, August, 229
Hanslick, Eduard, 66; *On the Musically Beautiful,* 163, 295n.33
Hatten, Robert, 257–58
Hausegger, Friedrich von, 66
Haushofer, Albrecht, 47–49; *Moabit Sonnets,* 48–49
Haushofer, Carl, 47
Haydn, Franz Joseph, 185
Hegel, Georg Wilhelm Friedrich, and aesthetics of music, 161, 165–66; and aesthetics of the whole, 15–16, 211; and definition of beauty, 14, 28, 189; and identity, 41
Hepokoski, James, 296n.54; and generic deformation, 168–70, 172
Herder, Johann Gottfried, 278n.8; and grasp of the whole, 5
hermeneutic circle, 6, 68
hermeneutics, and criticism, 4; critique of, 5; distanciation in, 64–65; historical, 3, 118; infinite understanding in, 6; limited role of author in, 6; musical, 4, 67, 118, 165, 229
hermeneutics of the moment, 2, 7, 12, 16–18, 68, 159, 235, 253 *See also* moment.
Herz, Gerhard, 225
Hess, Rudolf, 48
Heuß, Alfred, 163
Hinton, Stephen, 12
Hirschbach, Hermann, 112
historicism, 17, 159
Hitler, Adolf, 48, 242, 245
Hoffmann, E.T.A., *Johann Kreisler's Certificate of Apprenticeship,* 113–14; and review of Beethoven's Fifth Symphony, 26, 66
Hofmannsthal, Hugo von, 9, 62
Hohendahl, Peter Uwe, 15–16
Hölderlin, Friedrich, 1, 6, 19, 36
Holocaust, 11, 247
hope, 11, 19–20, 23–25, 28, 265; in *Doctor Faustus,* 226, 250; in *Fidelio,* 28–35, 50; hermeneutics of, 12
Hugo, Victor, *Les feuilles d'automne,* 155; *Preface to Cromwell,* 162–63
Husserl, Edmund, 27, 56
Huyssen, Andreas, 10, 236

ineffability, 16, 79–80
instant. *See* moment

Jameson, Fredric, 10, 236
Jansen, Gustav, 58
Jay, Martin, 191, 262
Jean Paul, definition by of the Romantic, 54–58, 112, 161–62, 251; *Flegeljahre,* 57–62; on musical listening, 5, 68; on romantic *Witz,* 103, 113; *Vorschule der Ästhetik,* 55–58
Joyce, James, 7

Kallberg, Jeffrey, 111
Kaminsky, Peter, 87, 93
Kandinsky, Wassily, 196; *On the Spiritual in Art,* 218
Kant, Immanuel, and aesthetic idea, 6; and art as second nature, 136; and definition of *actio in distans,* 53–54; and distinction between beautiful and sublime, 55; and notion of sublime, 181–87, 214; and *noumenon* and *phenomenon,* 178; and sublimity of the mind, 181–84
Kaplan, Richard, 168
Keathley, Elizabeth, 199, 302n.40
Keats, John, 248
Kerner, Justinus, 77
Kierkegaard, Søren, 7
Kittler, Friedrich, 220
Klauwell, Otto, 296n.60
Kleist, Heinrich von, 7
Kopp, David, 297n.74
Kramer, Richard, 52
Kraus, Karl, "Wiese im Park," 213
Krenek, Ernst, 238
Kretzschmar, Hermann, 4, 66, 227, 267n.14
Krüger, Eduard, 163
Kunstreligion. *See* art religion
Kurth, Ernst, 66

Lacan, Jacques, 18
LaCapra, Dominique, 11, 249
Lacoue-Labarthe, Philippe, 6, 214
language, and the absolute, 7, 28; effect of distance on, 51–54; about music, 4; and music, 1, 7, 77; of music, 2, 28
Lessing, Gotthold Ephraim, *Laocoön,* 17, 82, 86
Levinson, Jerrold, 268n.15

Lewis, Christopher, 264
Linke, Karl, 190
Lippman, Edward, 64
listening, associative, 165; atomistic
    (regressive), 5; programmatic, 165–66;
    social implications of, 5; structural, 5,
    21–22, 86, 91 197–99, 243, 262
Liszt, Adam, 187
Liszt, Franz, 96; religiosity of, 186–88;
    thematic work of, 162
—Berlioz and his Harold Symphony, 163,
    165–67
—Ce qu'on entend sur la montagne
    (Mountain Symphony), "Andante
    religioso," 156–61, 167–79, 186–88;
    form of, 167–79; genesis of, 179–84;
    and Méditation Symphonie, 160, 179–
    81; octatonic progression in, 172–73,
    176; program note for, 156; themes of,
    163–64, 177–78
—Dante Symphony, 155
—De Profundis, 187
—Faust Symphony, 155, 187
—Gran Mass, 186
—Die Ideale, 187
—Les Preludes, 155–56
—Tasso, 155–56
—Unstern, 187
—Via Crucis, 186
Lobe, Johann Christian, 162
Locke, John, 103
logos, 3, 79, 113, 151, 214
Lowe-Porter, Helen Tracy, 225
Lukács, Georg, 45
Luther, Martin, 245

Mackay, John Henry, "Am Wegrand," 206
Magritte, René, 191
Mahler, Gustav, 3, 9, 190
—Eighth Symphony, 210–11
—First Symphony, 173, 264
—Kindertotenlieder, no. 2, 252–65; as
    allegory of Augenblick, 256–57, 263–64;
    allusion to Tristan, 264
—Das Lied von der Erde, 251
—Ninth Symphony, 251; reference to
    Kindertotenlieder, 252–54
—Wunderhorn Songs, 240
Malin, Yonathan, 220
Mann, Thomas, 47; radio addresses of
    about the persecution of Jews, 247;

relationship of with Ernst Bertram, 245;
    247; and view of Pfitzner, 246
—"Bruder Hitler," 242
—Germany and the Germans, 245, 265
—Doctor Faustus, 1, 218, 224–53, 265;
    Adorno's influence on, 225–27, 229,
    246, 250; allusion to Adagissimo of
    Mahler's Ninth, 253; on Beethoven's op.
    111, 227–30, 234–35; breakthrough of,
    238, 241; dodecaphonic construction of,
    241; and eye symbolism, 237–39, 242;
    and figure of Echo, 224–25, 242–43,
    248–49, 265; historical dialectic in, 238–
    42; Lamentations of Doctor Faustus,
    218, 238, 251; and melancholy, 238,
    243, 248–50; as portrait of Nietzsche,
    245–46; and Philosophy of New Music,
    225–26, 240–41; in sonata form, 238
—Reflections of a Nonpolitical Man, 245
—Tonio Kröger, 239
Marston, Nicholas, 95, 104, 106
Marx, Adolf Bernhard, 161, 169
Marx, Karl, 18
Mayer, Hans, 25
McClary, Susan, 29
melancholy, in Doctor Faustus, 238, 243,
    247–50; Freud's view of, 11, 248–50;
    modern, 11
memory, 76–79, 92–93, 199; involuntary,
    81, 92
Mendelssohn, Felix, 3, 86, 161; Songs
    without Words, 76, 96
Michaelis, Friedrich Christian, 185
Michelangelo, Last Judgement, 242;
    Moses, 196
Milder, Anna, 35
Milhaud, Darius, 189
Miller, Norbert, 177
Mitchell, W.J.T., 262
modernity, 2–3, 7–9, 15, 86, 166, 178,
    197, 265; in art, 9; hermeneutics of, 16;
    and melancholy, 11; and music, 251–52
moment, as act of composition, 197, 260;
    as apparition, 16, 262; beautiful, 5, 18–
    19, 257; in Beethoven, 20–24, 161, 197–
    98; and brevity, 197; as central category
    of Adorno's aesthetics, 7, 15; as
    conceptual category, 4; in criticism, 67;
    in Erwartung, 196–98; of Expression-
    ism, 190, 197, 210, 238; in Fidelio, 24–
    25, 40–41, 49; German meanings of, 4;

moment, as act of composition (*cont.*)
in hermeneutic criticism, 5; historical, 3,
116, 200; in *Die Jakobsleiter,* 215–23; in
Kindertotenlieder No. 2, 256–61, 263–
64; and kitsch, 9; in *Lohengrin,* 118,
124, 133, 136, 154; lyric, 2; as material
category, 4; in Mountain Symphony,
159, 173–79; of music, 1–2; in painting,
282n.93; as part, 22, 221, 263; as
presence, 55; revolutionary, 116, 197; of
structure, 185–86, 197–98, 263; in
symbol and allegory, 8; as temporal
category 4; in traditional and modern
art, 9, 197; as whole, 22, 221, 226, 243,
257, 259–64. *See also* hermeneutics of
the moment; *Momentform*
Momentform, 199–200
Monteverdi, Claudio, 222–23, 238
Morgan, Robert, 85–86, 218
Moritz, Karl Philipp, 81
Morrow, Mary Sue, 5
Moser, Hans Joachim, 159
Mozart, Wolfgang Amadeus, 35, 185; *Don
Giovanni,* 45; *Le nozze di Figaro,* 30
musical prose, 199
musicology, 3–4, 53; essayistic, 11
Musil, Robert, 7

Nägeli, Hans Georg, 5
narration, epic, 241; historical, 117;
musical, 106, 177–79, 187
Nattiez, Jean-Jacques, 117–18, 136
Neumann, William, 170
Newcomb, Anthony, 96, 266n.2
New German School, 161
Newman, Ernest, 170
Newton, Isaac, 53
Nietzsche, Friedrich, 7, 15, 136, 222, 245–
46, 250
nonidentical, 8, 46
Novalis (Friedrich von Hardenberg):
definition of the Romantic, 6, 51, 53–54;
on music and language, 1

organicism, 22, 199, 262

painting, and music, 80–82, 85–86
Pappenheim, Marie, 199
particular. *See* moment
part-whole relationship, 5–7, 14–16, 20–
21, 49, 159–61, 196, 210, 221, 225–26,

256–57
Pastille, William, 258
Pater, Walter, 7, 51
Pederson, Sanna, 67
Pensky, Max, 11, 248
Pfitzner, Hans, 229; *Palestrina,* 210, 246
Plantinga, Leon, 67
Plato, 14–15, 27
Pohl, Richard, 155, 179, 181, 185
Poizat, Michel, 36, 40
postmodernism, 9–10, 156, 265
program music, 1, 96; formal problems of,
168–69; Liszt's view of, 161–67; versus
absolute music, 165–69
Proust, Marcel, 18

Raabe, Peter, 167–68, 179, 181
Raff, Joachim, 120, 122, 151, 169, 186,
290n.23
Ramann, Lina, 172–73
Ranke, Leopold von, 46
Ray, Man, 191
Redon, Odilon, 191
Reich, Nancy, 88
Reissiger, Carl Gottlieb, "Heimweh," 72–
78
Rellstab, Friedrich, 57
Ribbentrop, Joachim von, 48
Ricoeur, Paul, and hermeneutic
distanciation, 64–65, 87, 106
Riemann, Hugo, 22
Rilke, Rainer Maria, "Archaischer Torso
Apollos," 13–14, 16
Rimsky-Korsakov, Nikolay, 297n.75
Roesner, Linda Correll, 108, 286n.133
Romanticism, as defined by distance, 53–
63; as defined by Novalis, 1, 6, 51–54;
influence of on Adorno, 7; musical
aesthetics of, 4; and landscape painting,
79–82
Rosen, Charles, 80, 92, 96, 253
Rosenthal, Moritz, 96
Rousseau, Jean Jacques, 29

Santner, Eric, 11
Schein. See aesthetic appearance
Schelling, Friedrich Wilhelm, 54
Schenker, Heinrich, on Beethoven's op.
111, 229–37; and composer as seer, 234,
236; and composition on the spur of the
moment, 197, 260; *Fernhören,* 36, 234;

as hermeneut, 229–30; on theory as visual contemplation, 258–62; and tonal space, 86
Schiele, Egon, 189
Schiller, Friedrich, 26, 29, 220
Schindler, Anton, 227, 229
Schlegel, August Wilhelm, 1, 81, 92
Schlegel, Friedrich, 1, 7, 94; and arabesque, 103–4; on criticism, 5, 66; and definition of fragment, 6
Schleiermacher, Friedrich, 6, 66, 69
Schmid, Manfred Hermann, 72, 76–77, 140
Schocher, Christian Gottlieb, 53
Schoenberg, Arnold, 2; as dialectical composer, 190; as expressionist painter, 189–96; gazes of, 190–96; on Webern's *Bagatelles for String Quartet*, op. 9, 197, 244
—*Book of the Hanging Gardens*, op. 15, 240
—*Composition with Twelve Tones (1)*, 194, 218; conception of tonal space, 218
—*Erwartung*, op. 17, 196–209, 238; as momentary event, 198–200; "Am Wegrand" quotation in, 206–9; putative tonal center of, 208–9
—*Die glückliche Hand*, 199
—*Herzgewächse*, op. 20, 217
—*Hands*, 191, 194
—*Die Jakobsleiter*, 209–23; composed from hexachord, 210; allusion to *Tristan*, 220–23; literary sources of, 211, 218–19; role of The Soul in, 220–23; as turning point in Schoenberg's oeuvre, 210
—*Klavierstück*, op. 11, no. 1, 222
—*Moses and Aron*, 213–14
—*Red Gaze*, 189–90, 204
—*Selfportrait from Behind*, 190
—*Serenade*, op. 24, 217
—*A Survivor from Warsaw*, 247
—String Quartet, op. 10, 216
—*Tears*, 194–95
—*Verklärte Nacht*, 209, 222
—*Vision*, 194–95
Schopenhauer, Artur, 7, 136, 150
Schreker, Franz, *Der ferne Klang*, 52
Schubert, Franz, "Ihr Bild," 256; Symphony in C major D. 944, horncall in "Andante con moto," 64, 68–71, 170

Schumann, Clara. *See* Wieck, Clara.
Schumann, Robert, as critic, 63–71, 76–77, 165; influence of Clara on music of, 88–96, 104–5, 108–13; and reception of Novalis, 1; on romantic distance, 56–114; and view of landscape, 63, 68, 72, 79–81
—"An Anna," 72-79
—*Carnaval*, op. 9, 88–91
—*Davidsbündlertänze*, op. 6, 104; and Clara Wieck's *Valses romantiques*, 88–93; *Stichvorlage*, 92; "Wie aus der Ferne," 87–93
—*Fantasie*, op. 17, 93–109; and Beethoven's *An die ferne Geliebte*, 96–109, 113, 252–53; and Clara Wieck's *Romance variée*, op. 3, 104–6
—*Fantasiestücke*, op. 12, 82
—*Impromptu*, op. 5, 88, 104
—*Kinderszenen*, op. 15, 113–14
—*Novelletten*, op. 21, 108, 110–13; relationship to Clara Wieck's *Soirée musicales*, 108, 110–13; "Stimme aus der Ferne" in, 108, 110–13
—*Papillons*, 57–62, 88; as romantic definition, 62; relation to *Flegeljahre*, 57–62
—Piano Sonata, op. 11, 74–79, 88
—Piano Sonata, op. 22, 74
—review of Berlioz's *Symphonie fantastique*, 67, 96, 167
—review of Mendelssohn's *Lieder ohne Worte*, op. 19 and 30, 76–77, 79, 96
—review of Schubert's Symphony D. 944, 63–71
Schumann, Therese, 72
Schütz, Heinrich, 2
Seidel, Wilhelm, 41
Seremetakis, Nadia C., 265
Shakespeare, William, 115
Sichhart, Martina, 217
Sonnleitner, Joseph, 26
space, musical, 85–86, 91–92; spiritual, 218–19
Spielberg, Steven, *The Last Days*, 247
star, 13–14, 183, 235–36, 250, 257, 263–65; falling, 18–20, 23. *See also* constellation
Steuermann, Eduard, 3
Stockhausen, Karlheinz, 200
Strauss, Richard, 3, 169

Stravinsky, Igor, 86
Strindberg, August, 209
subjectivity, bourgeois, 3, 10; emancipated, 209; in Expressionism, 190; in late Beethoven, 22; and listening 165–66; modern, 2, 166, 178
sublime, 55, 181–87, 211; Kant's notion of, 181–87; and the mind, 181–84; musical, 185–86; and symphony, 185
Subotnik, Rose Rosengard, 22, 262
suddenness, 7–8, 15
Swedenborg, Emanuel, 211, 218, 222
symbol, temporality of, 7
Szondi, Peter, 7

Tiedemann, Rolf, 8, 20, 25, 160
Tomlinson, Gary, 213–14, 267n.7
totality. See whole
Tovey, Donald Francis, 230
Treitschke, Georg Friedrich, 29
truth, 10; for Adorno, 15–16; constructional and expressive, 220, 222; for Hegel, 14, 16

utopia, 3, 9–10, 24, 49, 114, 235, 247

Vill, Susanne, 257
vision. See gaze.
voice, composer's, 177–79; distant, 108, 110–13; exchange of, 108–9, 113; as given through theory, 263; versus instrumental music, 27–28; as vocalise, 217
Voigt, Henriette, 58, 77

Wackenroder, Wilhelm Heinrich, 5
Wagner, Cosima, 136
Wagner, Richard, on absolute music, 138–39; on Beethoven's Eroica, 3, 86; expressive tradition of, 197; on Fidelio, 40; on miracles, 137–38; on relationship between music and poetry, 117–18, 126–31, 143–45, 151; on modulation, 118, 161; on creation of motifs, 118–20, 126–31, 256; on organic form, 136, 154; art of transition, 124, 154
—Beethoven, 150–51
—Brief über Franz Liszt's Symphonische Dichtungen, 162
—Eine Mitteilung an meine Freunde, 115–17, 120

—Der fliegende Holländer, 115
—Lohengrin, 29, 115–54, 161; as allegory of absolute music, 138–39, 143, 151; as birth of music drama, 115–18, 151–54; bridal chamber scene in, 145–51; Elsa's dream in as model dramatic unit, 118–36; influence of Feuerbach on, 137–38; Wagner's view of, 115–18
—Mein Leben, 116
—Die Meistersinger, 210
—Oper und Drama, 115, 117, 119–20, 123–24, 133, 136–37, 144–45; Wagner's later view of, 136
—Parsifal, 222
—Der Ring des Nibelungen, 115–16, 120; prelude to Das Rheingold, 162
—Tannhäuser, 115
—Tristan, 120, 124, 220–23, 264
—"Über die Anwendung der Musik auf das Drama," 118–19
—Zukunftsmusik, 143–44
Walter, Bruno, 227, 253
Weber, Carl Maria von, Der Freischütz, 30; view on music and landscape, 82
Webern, Anton, Bagatelles for String Quartet, op. 9, 197, 244; condensed lyricism of, 2; view of Erwartung, 200; "Wiese im Park," op. 13, no. 1, 213
Webster, James, 185
Weisse, Christian Hermann, 165
Wellbery, David, 2
Wendt, Amadeus, 35
White, Hayden, 116
whole, 5–6, 14–16, 19, 133, 210–11, 214, 221, 225–26, 242, 259–60. See also part-whole relationship; moment
Wieck, Clara, influence on Schumann, 88–96, 104–5, 108–13; Quatre pièces caracteristiques, op. 5, 88; Romance variée, op. 3, 88; Soirées musicales, op. 6, 88, 108, 110–13; Valses romantiques, op. 4, 88–93
Williamson, John, 176
Winckelmann, Johann Joachim, 14
Wiora, Walter, 266n.2
Witz, 103, 113
Woolf, Virginia, 7, 300n.5
Wörner, Karl Heinrich, 199–200

Zuidervaart, Lambert, 10

DATE DUE

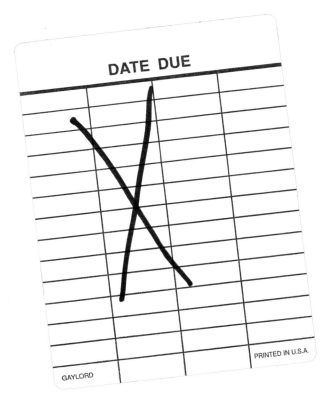

GAYLORD

PRINTED IN U.S.A.